DEMOCRACY'S RAILROADS

KENNIKAT PRESS

NATIONAL UNIVERSITY PUBLICATIONS

SERIES IN AMERICAN STUDIES

Under the General Editorial Supervision of

JAMES P. SHENTON

Professor of History, Columbia University

Robert J. Parks

DEMOCRACY'S RAILROADS

Public Enterprise in Jacksonian Michigan

National University Publications
Port Washington, N.Y./London
Kennikat Press 1972

DEMOCRACY'S RAILROADS

Library of Congress Catalog Card No: 79-189557

ISBN: 0-8046-9027-8

Manufactured in the United States of America

Published by

Kennikat Press, Inc.

Port Washington, N.Y./London

ACKNOWLEDGMENTS

Few studies result from the efforts of a single person, and this work is no exception. The energetic cooperation and services of Mr. Richard Hathaway and his staff in the State Library, and of Miss Geneva Kebler and the staff of the Michigan Historical Commission Archives reduced the problems of research immeasurably. Stuart Bruchey and W. Paul Strassman read the manuscript in full, and provided much helpful advice and criticism. Maps for the volume were prepared by Miss Jean A. Saffran and Mrs. Barbara Long, and my wife and my mother-in-law, Mrs. Ada Stelson, spent endless hours typing and proofreading several drafts. Finally, I wish to thank Mr. Harold Mead, who, in acting as a gracious host, asked a question that could not be answered, and triggered my interest in Michigan's state owned railroads and canals.

CONTENTS

MAPS

TABLES IN THE TEXT

TABLES IN THE APPENDIX

DEMOCRACY'S RAILROADS

INTRODUCTION

For nearly a century after the financially disastrous 1840s, the history of state internal improvements programs was the almost exclusive preserve of railroad buffs and tow-paths antiquarians. Conditioned by the dominant role assigned to private enterprise in the developing American economy, historians were content to treat public works programs as curious deviations in the story of American growth illustrating the inability of government to engage in business. Recent studies, however, have redefined the role of government in nineteenth-century American economic development and have created a need for reassessment of public programs.

No definitive statement of this modern interpretation has yet been formulated.[1] Reevaluation of the role of government in business began with the studies of Louis B. Hartz and Oscar Handlin, which revealed the absence of a strong laissez faire tradition in ante-bellum America, accompanied by frequent public support for government enterprise.[2] Unfortunately for economic historians, the Hartz and Handlin studies were designed to describe the development of an idea, and they avoided any discussion of the methods and results of government action. Supplemented by a series of monographs, subsequent studies by Carter Goodrich and Milton Heath have attempted to fill this void.[3] In general, these scholars have documented the existence of a strong tradition of public responsibility for economic growth in the nineteenth century, and have placed new emphasis on the role played by public treasuries and government officials. Central to these studies is the theme that government enterprise was designed to democratize the economy and expand the sphere of individual enterprise by providing essential facilities that private capital was unable to create. As Robert Lively has suggested:

> The need for capital was the factor that most frequently determined government entry into the field of enterprise; only public authorities could command sufficient credit at a reasonable interest rate for works of the size demanded. Subordinate considerations were usually present, of course: glib promoters reached eagerly for public funds; hopeful administrators sought state investments so profitable that taxes could be reduced; and in a day when works of public utility were by definition regarded as monopolistic, a people suspicious of power generally were sure to insist that their governments guide these developments with a firm regulatory hand. But underlying every justification for state endeavor was the hope that by public effort businessmen of a

3

locality would prosper, that land values would rise, and that the competitive position of the area would be improved. The whole business community was dependent on state execution of the general investment functions necessary to economic growth; it was by state endeavor that "idle resources could be brought into employment and the social income maximized."[4]

Detailed substantiation and modification of this hypothesis requires numerous studies of the special aspects of government promotion. Not only must the ambitions and expectations of nineteenth-century Americans be reexamined, but the means to these ends and the degree of their success must be carefully assessed. Such studies are particularly useful in the area of state enterprise, which has frequently been obscured by historical focus on national questions and constitutional struggles.

Although it has received widespread acceptance, the modern interpretation of the role of government has been subjected to serious criticism. Robert Lively has challenged the school to investigate the private aspects of quasi-public corporations and to produce careful estimates of private contributions to social overhead capital creation. Although there are some estimates, it is still difficult to accurately weigh the relative contributions of public and private capital. In addition, Lively has criticized scholars for their failure to investigate state banking activities, which are perhaps, as important as internal improvement itself. In a similar vein, Albert Fishlow has suggested that railroads constructed by states before the Civil War were usually ahead of demand and, therefore, a misallocation of resources.[5] If Fishlow's suspicions are correct, further evaluations of government contributions to economic growth, perhaps in a statistical vein, are in order.

No study of a single state over a limited period of time can hope to confirm or revise the hypotheses of a major school of historial interpretation. By the limits of its scope, such a study only strives to draw cautious, carefully qualified conclusions and must avoid bold generalizations. Its value, however, need not be as limited as such restrictions might suggest. Michigan's unusual choice of railroads in preference to the dominant canal technology offers unusual insights into the early stages of this rapidly expanding branch of the transportation industry. Indeed, the very status of Michigan's railroads as a public enterprise increases their historical value. Few of America's early railroads have left behind such rich accounts of their construction and operation as those found in the Annual Reports of the Board of Internal Improvements. Michigan's experience allows components of theories to be tested, and brings new evidence to bear on problems of current importance.

Past judgments on the success or failure of internal improvements programs were often based solely on the criteria of profit and loss. Advances in the tools of economic analysis, however, give the modern historian a distinct advantage in evaluating projects. Although project proposals in antebellum America sometimes recognized specific elements of what is now known as public utility theory, contemporaries and subsequent writers failed to cope with the special problems posed by social overhead capital. Indeed, the creation of a comprehensive body of knowledge to deal with social overhead capital is relatively recent and still in the process of refinement. In its broadest sense, social overhead capital embraces such diverse activities as law enforcement, education, sanitation, transportation, power, communication, and water supply. In short, it includes any basic service without which primary, secondary, and tertiary productive activities cannot survive. In practice, the concept is most frequently applied to power and transportation.

Criteria for inclusion in the category of social overhead capital are varied, but general agreement does exist within a broad range. Services provided should facilitate, or be basic to, a great variety of economic activities. In the twentieth century, these services are usually controlled or owned by public agencies, and are provided either free of charge or at a regulated rate. In most cases, the services cannot be imported. Finally, the investment required is characterized by technical indivisibility or "lumpiness," increasing returns to scale, and an unusually high capital-output ratio.[6]

Combined with the need for special pricing policies, these characteristics of social overhead capital have been used to justify government investment and control. Because final outputs are utilized by a broad range of industries and services as an input factor, more than a small portion of the benefits created by social overhead investment can seldom be realized by its owners; hence, the low rate of return. Without government financing, private enterprise would postpone investment in such large-scale, long-term projects until short-term alternatives with a higher rate of return were exhausted. This would delay growth in sectors or industries dependent on the project's external economies as input factors. In addition to the risk involved, technical indivisibilities tend to create monopolies calling for special pricing policies. If profits are maximized by limiting services to the point where marginal revenue equals marginal cost, full utilization of resources will be frustrated. Similarly, if facilities are operated at cost, so that total cost and total revenue are equal, maximization of external economies may still be restricted. Maximum returns to the economy from such investment can only be realized by operating at levels at which marginal use value equals marginal cost, even though such a policy involves running at a financial loss. A railroad, for example, involves heavy fixed capital investment with relatively small variable costs. Operation at maximum profits without price discrimination would mean excess capacity and wasted resources. Even operation at a price sufficient to cover interest and variable costs would prevent those goods produced efficiently enough to enter the market at cost plus the additional charges necessary to cover variable costs from being shipped. Maximum returns to the community would be realized only when the excess capacity was absorbed and goods could be shipped at prices sufficient to cover marginal or variable costs. Under these circumstances, community welfare would be increased by operating at variable cost, allowing society to absorb costs that would be more than paid for by the income realized from economies not absorbed in the road's revenues. Taxation to cover capital costs would be much less damaging than losses suffered by profit maximization or policies leading to financial solvency in the railroad.[7] Although the classical justification of investment, that profits equal the cost of capital, appeals to political and economic conservatives, the criterion of profits leads to misapplication of resources when applied to social overhead capital.

Developing citeria for evaluating public works and the allocation of capital has proven to be the most serious obstacle to objective application of social overhead theory. It is sufficient to note that all tests flounder when confronted with the necessity of assessing the absolute value of external economies. Perhaps the best summation is provided by Albert O. Hirschman:

> The trouble with investment in SOC [social overhead capital]—or is it its strength?—is that it is impervious to the investment criteria that have been devised to introduce some rationality into development plans. The computation of capital-output ratios often presents almost insuperable statistical difficulties (as in the case of highways) and is moreover considered to be misleading anyway because of the igniting effect SOC investment is expected to have on DPA [direct productive activity]—As a result, SOC investment is largely a matter of faith in the development potential of a country or region.
>
> The fact that there is so little possibility of evaluating objectively how much investment in SOC is really indicated in any given situation should give us pause. Such a situation implies at least the possibility of wasteful mistakes.[8]

Because of their unquantifiable returns, social overhead capital projects have often become a favorite tool of planners. Failure is difficult to prove statistically when external economies can be cited. At the same time, historians judging the success of internal improvements projects are required to take indirect returns into account.

Recent studies have cast some doubt on the wisdom of placing disproportionate emphasis on social overhead capital creation. Citing the asymmetric behavior of investment cycles in developed and underdeveloped economies, Paul Cootner suggests that investment may be pulled into underdeveloped nations through demand for raw materials by developed countries, and that most of the external economies may be realized by the investing areas. At the same time, he suggests that foresight, however imperfect, may induce private enterprise to invest in social overhead in the hope of realizing its economies if a sufficient pace of growth is sustained to produce faith in eventual returns. However, Cootner also warns that investment by private enterprise may tend to lag and bunch. Entrepreneurs may wait to invest until demand is more than sufficient to justify additional capital creation and then, because of the high level of demand and the need for lowering resource prices, overshoot requirements in their building program.[9] Another study, by Albert Hirschman, has gone so far as to suggest the possibilities of development through social overhead capital shortages.[10] Nevertheless, at this point of growth, the basic elements of the theory of social overhead are useful tools in evaluating past projects, and a useful backdrop in assessing the developmental expectations of early nineteenth-century Americans.

Notes to Introduction

1. The best summary of this literature is Robert Lively, "The American System: A Review Article," *Business History Review,* XXIX (March, 1955), 81-96.
2. *Ibid.,* p. 95.
3. Carter Goodrich, *Government Promotion of American Canals and Railroads, 1800-1900* (New York: Columbia University Press, 1960); Milton S. Heath, "Public Co-operation in Railroad Construction in the Southern United States" (Unpublished Ph. D. dissertation, Harvard University, 1937).
4. Lively, p. 85.
5. *Ibid.,* pp. 88-91; Albert Fishlow, *American Railroads and the Transformation of the Ante-bellum Economy,* Harvard Economic Studies, Vol. CXXVII (Cambridge: Harvard University Press, 1965).
6. Albert O. Hirschman, *Strategy of Economic Development* (New Haven: Yale University Press, 1958), p. 83.
7. Stephen Enke, *Economics for Development* (Englewood Cliffs, N.J.: Prentice-Hall, Inc., 1963), pp. 284-297.
8. Hirschman, p. 84.
9. Paul Cootner, "Social Overhead Capital and Economic Growth," *The Economics of Take-Off into Sustained Growth,* ed. W. W. Rostow (New York: St. Martin's Press, 1963), pp. 261-284.
10. Hirschman, p. 87.

1

THE MANIA FOR INTERNAL
IMPROVEMENTS

In 1837, Michigan launched a massive program of railroad and canal construction designed to promote its economic development. Nine years later, when enthusiasm had faded in the light of depression and financial disaster, the state sold its holdings and abandoned the policy of direct investment in its economic growth. In 1850, this decision was ratified in a new state constitution which prohibited participation in internal improvement. Observers have long regarded the program as a "white elephant." At best, the apologetic have excused it as the result of being "caught up in the mania for internal improvements" in a boom period in which it is difficult to understand "why the people of the time could have ignored clear indications that they were riding for a fall."[1] Even the most recent analysis of the developmental impact of American railroads has suggested that Michigan's program was ahead of demand.[2]

The result of Michigan's experiment in internal improvement is far from unique. Indiana and Illinois started programs at the same time with much the same result. All of the states of the Old Northwest had similar experiences. Even older, more populous and developed states found their programs in difficulty, and more than a few experienced bankruptcy and repudiation. This broad similarity in timing and experience has long suggested that complex external forces, distinct from local demands, influenced the decisions of most state governments during the 1830s and 1840s, and created common limits for the scope and effectiveness of state action. Most commonly cited are the "mania for internal improvements" and the Panic of 1837, but such a list is far from exhaustive. Equally important was the basic commercialism of American agriculture, together with the promise of federal subsidies and surplus payments, building cycles independent of the domestic business cycle, and structural changes in domestic and foreign banking.

Historians have labeled the apparent compulsion of states to engage in social overhead capital creation in the Jacksonian era, the "mania for internal improvements." It is not satisfactory, however, to dismiss the ardent desire of Americans to undertake transportation projects in the second quarter of the nineteenth century as a simple mania. More thorough investigation reveals that this desire was a manifestation of basic American intellectual dynamics, and more broadly, an outgrowth of the fundamental ideals

8

shaping modern Western civilization. Specifically, the "mania for internal improvements" stems from the American adaptation of the doctrine of progress.

In the history of ideas, the notion of progress is relatively new, but in terms of its impact, it is perhaps the most important factor shaping modern times. E. E. Hagen, an economist, considers it the most important factor in beginning economic development. According to Hagen, only when the rate of change becomes sufficient to bring the realization that pursuit of change might be rewarding can sustained economic growth begin. Until change or progress is consciously pursued, the sociological transformations necessary to economic growth will be suffocated by traditional authoritarianism.[3] Transposing this concept, it seems reasonable to accept a decline in traditional authoritarianism accompanied by sustained growth as evidence of a fundamental belief in progress.

By the end of the eighteenth century, a widely accepted framework of ideas had been erected among intellectuals. It was based on the idea that man was inherently good despite the erosion of his behavior by degenerated institutions, and it extended hope in his perfectibility, and suggested the alteration of civil and social institutions as a vehicle for human transformation.[4]

However, if the idea of progress was immediately evident to intellectuals taking the long view, the masses were slow to accept it. J. B. Bury dates its penetration to the common man in Europe between 1820 and 1850.[5] Arthur Ekirch traces the beginning of widespread mass appeal in America to the period after 1815.[6] Bury considers the rapid transformation of external conditions at this time to have been the impetus for mass acceptance of the idea of an indefinite increase in man's power over nature as his brain revealed its secrets. Continuing material progress sustained this belief.[7] Thus, in the first quarter of the nineteenth century, the words *progress* or *improvement* became examples of what Carl Becker characterized as "words with uncertain meanings that are permitted to slip off the tongue or the pen without fear and without research; words which having from constant repetition lost their metaphorical significance, are unconsciously mistaken for objective realities."[8]

Although America shared in the development of the doctrine of progress, various studies indicate that the American version was an adaptation of the European idea. Arthur Ekirch concludes that "in the United States... people felt that, although progress was indeed certain, it could nevertheless be impeded or accelerated by human will and effort."[9] It was not merely a prophecy or a theory, but a call to action that fell on fertile soil in a society rapidly carving a new land out of the wilderness.

Peace in 1815 brought more than an end to hostilities. "In 1815 for the first time Americans ceased to doubt the path they were to follow. Not only was the unity of their nation established, but its probable divergence from older societies was also well defined."[10] At a time when Europe was in the grip of political, social, and economic reaction, America seemed to be the last remaining stronghold of the democratic optimism that had swept the world at the close of the eighteenth century. This sense of uniqueness and mission was reinforced by the rapid material and political advances of subsequent decades. A rapidly expanding population was provided for by abundant resources and a growing frontier. New techniques of production were applied, and industrial growth began. With the exceptions of the serious panic of 1819-1820 and the depression of 1839-1844, it was an era of general prosperity. State constitutions were liberalized, and suffrage was broadly expanded:

> The reality provided by this material and cultural advance also served to strengthen the old idea that America enjoyed an especial and unique position in the world. The American people, imbued with a strong faith in the efficacy of their own physical and intellectual achievements, universalized their experience into a general theory of progress to which the rest of the world was expected to accede. In the eyes of the Americans the older civilization of Europe was already in a state of decay. Confident of their own future in the "era of good feeling" and of youthful nationalism prevailing after 1815, they emphasized the difference between the Old and New World with the proclamation of the Monroe Doctrine in 1823. Later, during the forties and fifties, the concept of a peculiar American mission, under the slogans of Manifest Destiny and of Young America, became transformed into a rationalization for territorial expansion in those regions considered necessary for the westward movement of the Republic.[11]

The doctrine of progress was an important component of the "mania for internal improvements." During this period, "improvement" seems to have been used interchangeably with "progress," and writers of the era often spoke of the "progress of improvement" and the "spirit of improvement" when discussing progress. Indeed, "improvement," and not "progress," seems to have been the more common term. The notion that man's progress depended on the fullest use of the material resources of his environment was central to the doctrine. In the 1820s and 1830s, this idea was frequently used to justify the application of federal funds to transportation projects, a use that is perhaps nowhere more eloquently revealed than in the writings of John Quincy Adams. Devoting a major portion of his Inaugural Address to listing the accomplishments of the nation since its foundation in 1789 "as an experiment upon the theory of human rights," he included the fact that "the dominion of man over physical nature has been extended by the invention of our artists."[12] But Adams was not content with the success of the past, and if his Inaugural was devoted to outlining past progress, his first State of the Union Message was a plan of action for its extension. In what might be considered a corollary to the theory of government outlined in the Declaration of Independence, Adams stated:

> The great object of the institution of civil government is the improvement of the condition of those who are parties to the social

compact, and no government, in whatever form constituted, can accomplish the lawful ends of its institution but in proportion as it improves the condition of those over whom it is established. Roads and canals, by multiplying and facilitating the communications and intercourse between distant regions and multitudes of men, are among the most important means of improvement. But moral, political, and intellectual improvement are duties assigned by the Author of Our Existence to social no less than to individual man. For the fulfillment of those duties governments are invested with power, and to the attainment of the end—the progressive improvement of the condition of the governed—the exercise of delegated powers is a duty as sacred and indispensable as the usurpation of powers not granted is criminal and odious.[13]

To fulfill this duty, Adams recommended a series of cultural and scientific programs, and federal involvement in transportation projects too great for the resources of a single state.[14]

Although Adams' specific plea is for federal participation in internal improvements, it characterizes the force with which the doctrine of progress served as a justification and general stimulus for government action. This partial correlation between the doctrine of progress and the "mania for internal improvements" does not necessarily mean that programs of internal improvement in ante-bellum America were solely the product of philosophic impulse. Both specific and general economic needs played an important causative role. But there was a justification transcending the purely economic that makes the "mania" an understandable phenomenon and explains the often apparently irrational compulsion to engage in such projects. The fact that Michigan was seduced by the spirit of internal improvement could almost have been predicted. Had the state stood aloof from the currents of the age and evaluated its needs and resources with perfect rationality, the reaction would have been far more worthy of note.

Widespread support for internal improvement projects was more than a simple philosophic impulse, however. There is ample evidence to support the belief that transportation problems were of major concern to the American people. Recent authors have emphasized the basic commercialism that made the American farmer fundamentally different from his European counterpart. The American farmer was never a peasant with a rural culture, tied to the soil by an emotional dedication to a traditional and precapitalistic outlook. He was an entrepreneur governed by market forces and the profit motive.[15] Even in the eighteenth century, complete self-sufficiency was rare, and farmers constantly sought a marketable product. Usually, the elements of self-sufficiency can be traced to the inadequacy of transportation at a particular time and place.[16] As settlement moved beyond the fall line and the mountains, the problem became more acute. Early in the nation's history, the Whiskey Rebellion made it clear that frontier farmers would react violently to measures isolating them from commerce.

At the same time, the example of Great Britain encouraged Americans to promote economic growth by improving internal transportation. Following construction of the Worsley Canal, which was begun in 1759, England underwent a "canal mania" similar to that later experienced in the United States. Within thirty years England was furrowed with canals built by private concerns bent on extracting profit from the new mode of transportation, and within a century the nation's system had been extended from 1000 miles of navigable rivers to about 4,250 miles of navigable waterways.[17] Although Paul Mantoux has dismissed the rash of construction as a transient phenomenon, another distinguished British historian, Witt Bowden, suggests that, in addition to the direct benefits of reduced transportation costs, canals had an indirect result of incalculable importance—the stimulation of interest in material improvement of all kinds.[18] Whatever the truth of this controversy, however, American attention was focused on the burst of canal construction and economic changes in England. Americans were impressed by the way canals stimulated trade, ports, and towns, as well as by the reduction in the cost of raw materials, canal profitability, and the small cost to the state. Success in England was repeatedly cited by Americans favoring canals.[19] Even though Americans strongly protested social and political practices with British or "monarchial" overtones, they had few scruples against adopting practices that were leading England to economic eminence. As Samuel Rezneck has pointed out: "Paradoxically, American industrial consciousness grew out of the broad wave of political and economic resentment, but was mainly directed almost from the start toward the transfer of English skill and technique to this country.[20]

Although the desire for transportation improvements is often associated with the drive for industrialism, the developmental expectations of early nineteenth-century Americans lead to the suspicion that a purely agrarian democracy could not have avoided building roads and canals. Even Jefferson, in his private desire for an agrarian utopia, only contemplated the reduction of commerce to the level necessary to carry off the agricultural surplus, and it is precisely on this ground that many contemporaries justified internal improvements. Adam Smith had given pivotal importance to canals because they widened the market for industrial products and increased the division of labor.[21] In another context, however, he had characterized good roads, canals, and navigable rivers as the "greatest of all improvements" because they equalized the rent of the land by allowing farmers in remote districts to market their crop surplus and break the monopoly of lands adjacent to towns. Most frequently, Americans relied on this justification. The possibility of raising the level of national income by providing markets for the commodity surplus was pointed out by Hamilton in 1792, in his *Report on Manufactures*, and in Gallatin's *Report on Roads and Canals* in 1808. The speeches of DeWitt Clinton and Governor John Schulze of Pennsylvania include these ideas in arguments for the programs of their respective states.[22]

Harvey Segal, in examining project proposals in the ante-bellum period, has commented that in view of the enormous risks borne in undertaking the early American canals he is struck by the lack of systematic analysis of long-range impacts. Nowhere does he find an exposition of Adam Smith's dictum that "the division of labour is limited by the extent of the market." Aside from Governor Schulze's statement that lower transport costs would lead to increased consumption and induce investment in "mills and manufactories," there is little suggestion that industrialization was seen by contemporaries as a consequence of internal improvements.[23] It is possible, however, that such effects were among the utilitarian aspects of internal improvement that Gallatin stated were "so universally admitted as to hardly require any additional proofs." In any event, disposal of the commodity surplus remained the most important economic expectation of advocates of internal improvements, a goal that reflects the fundamental commercialism of American agriculture.

By the beginning of the third decade of the nineteenth century, Americans had achieved an unparalleled degree of social and geographic mobility. As farmers moved west of the tidewater through the Appalachian barrier and into the Middle West the new mobility began to create problems incapable of individualistic solution. The American farmer was basically commercial, and even when he moved into isolated frontier regions where high transportation costs destroyed market incentives, it was in the hope of being able to market the abundant produce of his fertile and inexpensive land sometime in the immediate future. The American geographic environment, however, placed substantial obstacles in the path of an otherwise mobile population. Capital accumulations were small, large-scale entrepreneurial skills scarce, and distances were great. The absence of major population concentrations that could be connected by exploitative projects, when combined with the sheer physical size of obstacles and the necessity of depending on other works for feeder traffic, seemingly precluded dependence on uncoordinated private investment for the creation of transportation facilities. When physical obstacles threatened to block social and geographic mobility with barriers private capital could not overcome, Americans turned to government for help.

During the thiry years prior to Michigan's investment decision, the federal government vacillated in its response to popular demand for a comprehensive program of public works. Southern states, opposed to tax increases burdening the imports traded for their cotton, combined with representatives of states that had already financed their own programs to obstruct expenditures for public works. Although a series of executive reports gave broad interpretation to the government's ability to construct post roads and provide for the common defense, sincere constitutional scruples restricted the scope of federal action, and efforts to promote a constitutional amendment consistently met with failure.

Between 1816 and 1832, the limits of federal authority were spelled out in a series of executive vetoes. Although Madison's veto of the Bonus Bill in 1816 dashed hopes for a federal program, his successors found room for increased federal activity within the existing constitutional framework.

Through his veto of an act calling for toll gates on the National Road in 1822, and the constitutional essay attached, President Monroe redefined the scope of federal authority. Although Monroe clearly preferred a constitutional amendment defining the limits of federal power, his veto only prohibited federal jurisdiction: earning revenues from the public works, applying police power for protection, and exercising the right of eminent domain. Federal powers of appropriation were practically unlimited, as long as expenditures were confined to national projects.[24]

Michigan entered the final stage of territorial status during the Administration of John Quincy Adams, a new highpoint for internal improvements. Important bills were passed, and an annual average of $702,000 was expended by the government on internal improvements.[25] Several states received grants of public lands to aid specific projects: Ohio for the construction of a turnpike from Columbus to Sandusky; Illinois for a canal from the Illinois River to Lake Michigan; Indiana for a canal from the Wabash River to Lake Erie, and a road from Lake Michigan to the Ohio River. Three of these measures set the important precedent of granting alternate strips of land along the route of the improvement. As shall be seen later, the grants were important factors in raising the expectations of Michigan, and in the state's decision to undertake a program of internal improvements. At the close of the Adams Administration, the government had granted more than two million dollars for stock subscriptions and two and one-half million acres of public lands to projects.[26]

There is less agreement about the actions of Adams' successor, Andrew Jackson. Interpretations of the period, particularly state histories, have long pointed to Jackson's Maysville Road Veto as the terminal point for federal aid to state projects. At least two biographers have taken the position that Jackson was opposed to improvements, or at least opposed to them without a constitutional amendment.[27] More recently, cautious doubts have been expressed. George Rogers Taylor suggests that Jackson only momentarily opposed internal improvements, and points to a rise of average annual expenditures from $702,000 under Adams to $1,323,000 under Jackson, an evaluation in which Glyndon Van Deusen seems to concur.[28] But Carter Goodrich has pointed out that the increase in federal expenditures resulted from an increase in spending on old, rather than new, projects.[29]

Jackson's Veto Message seems to suggest that it was aimed at a purpose other than that of ending federal aid. In fact, the argument developed by Jackson was remarkably similar to that of Monroe. He assumed the government had no jurisdiction over internal improvements, but in reviewing positions taken by Madison, Monroe, and Adams, he found precedent for federal appropriations, and an escape clause that allowed him to avoid a general veto by ruling the Maysville Road a project of local, rather than national, importance. John Spencer Bassett, the distinguished biographer of Jackson, concurs in this interpretation and suggests that although Jackson had decided scruples about states' rights, "Jackson's views on the constitution were formed through feeling, rather than intellect," and as such could be mixed. His thinking generally lacked the cold intellectual consistency that characterized the arguments of Calhoun.[30] Marquis James, another biographer, agrees with Bassett on this point, and views Jackson's action as inspired by Van Buren, an ardent opponent of federal aid, whose intent was to strike at political logrolling in Congress.[31]

Evidence presented by Bassett tends to support the conclusion that the actions of Monroe, Adams, and Jackson departed from Madison's strict constructionist interpretation of federal authority. Van Buren, who drafted Jackson's Veto Message, later admitted that his interpretation of Madison's veto was of doubtful validity. His doubts were confirmed by Madison who, upon receiving a copy, wrote Jackson that he had vetoed both the jurisdictional and appropriative powers.[32]

If the Jackson Administration wrote an end to hopes for federal aid, contemporaries were not keenly aware of it. Historians have often attributed the surge of state programs after the veto to the realization by the states that they would have to undertake improvement projects themselves, and to the confidence, created by New York's success, that they could do it. It seems more probable, however, that the statements and actions of the administration may have fostered these programs and that the rash of investment decisions that created the "second canal cycle" was the result of heightened expectations of a new form of federal aid.

Carter Goodrich believes that the election of Andrew Jackson marked the beginning of the end of the national projects era. Yet, he has also pointed out that the vetoes of Madison, Monroe, and Jackson did not put an end to federal aid, but only confined it to more closely defined limitations. The government could aid transportation projects as long as it did not receive a direct revenue, because collection of tolls would require use of federal police power and thus violate state sovereignty. The government could not subscribe to the stock of improvement companies, and finally, it could not undertake a planned system of internal improvements.[33] However, federal aid was not prohibited. Jackson's veto had not altered Monroe's interpretation, which allowed direct federal construction if works were turned over to the states after completion. The fact that Jackson allowed appropriations to continue on projects authorized by previous administrations is in itself an indication that he had no strong constitutional objections to federal aid that did not create federal jurisdiction. The man who vetoed the new charter of the Second Bank of the United States did not hesitate where his personal conception of right and wrong was concerned. On several occasions Jackson raised the possibility of a new form of aid: direct grants of federal money to the states on a prorated schedule on an implied permanent basis. In both his First Annual Message and his veto of the Maysville Road, however, Jackson established a distinct set of priorities for the use of federal funds. First and above all else, he wanted to extinguish the national debt. Since a protective tariff was desirable and not likely to be reduced, he thought revenues would remain high, and that the continuing surplus should be distributed to the states. An amendment authorizing distribution would be preferable, but he thought it would not be too difficult to obtain. To avoid a sectional battle over distribution formulas, he stated a preference for distribution based on the ratio of representation.[34]

Studies of the surplus revenue distribution have pointed to the sustained level of expectation of the states in sharing the surplus from the time of the Jefferson Administration. The application of an annual surplus of from two to six million dollars from 1816 to 1826, not only reduced the public debt to a point where extinction could be foreseen within a dozen years; it also heightened expectations.[35] Jackson's suggestions, however, set off a prolonged debate. Congressional quarreling centered on the problem of equity in distribution, and plans were advanced favoring the use of land area, population, and the use of imports as a basis for division, but no equitable solution could be reached. By the early 1830s, Jackson became so irritated that he declared he would sanction no scheme, and instead recommended tariff reduction. Pressure for distribution continued in Congress, however.[36]

Despite Jackson's new stand, the possibility of sustained distribution of excess revenues heightened the expectations of the states and fed the desire for further improvements. In his opening address to the Legislative Council in January of 1834, Governor Porter of Michigan exemplified this attitude when he recommended application to Congress for aid to build a railroad across the peninsula. "It is believed," he told the Council, "that no more propitious period has occurred in the history of our country for presenting these subjects to the consideration of Congress. By wise and prudent administration of the general government, the national debt is nearly extinguished...." The nullification crisis had passed.[37] As an intimate friend of Andrew Jackson and an appointee of his after the Maysville Road Veto, Porter must have seemed to speak with authority.[38]

At long last, in January of 1836, the hope of harnessing federal resources to the projects of the states seemed about to be fulfilled. With the debt extinguished and the surplus rapidly mounting, a bill was introduced for the distribution of federal surplus land revenues. Jackson's constitutional scruples stood in the way, however, and it was only in June, after receiving an amended version providing for deposit of the funds with the states, that he signed the bill into law. The states must have regarded January 1, 1837, when the first installment was due, as the beginning of the millennium. Since the act provided only for surpluses as of January 1837, Congress quickly turned to the problem of future surpluses before any appeared.[39] During the panic, the surplus vanished and failed to reappear for more than half a century. In several states, however, the payments provided vital support just as the strain of heavy state financing was beginning to be felt, and in Michigan it proved a stimulus to state enterprise and provided support for initial construction.[40]

Although hopes of a comprehensive program of national planning were dashed by the vetoes of Madison and Monroe, federal aid continued in various forms through 1837. The constitutional authority to provide military and post roads was broadly construed to include any facility that might in some way contribute to national defense, add indirectly to federal revenues, or strengthen the national economy. In addition, the federal government was allowed to build projects under its authority to appropriate funds, as long as it did not assume jurisdiction, levy taxes, or charge tolls for maintenance. In general, special interest opposition proved to be a more serious obstacle to broader application of federal authority than constitutional objections. In the end, states were aided directly in the guise of deposits that apparently would not be called in. The new form of aid was actually broader than before, for it overcame special interest opposition and allowed the application of federal funds to local, as well as national, projects. Regular aid was delayed by Jackson's preference for payment of the public debt, and the depression caused a sharp reduction in federal funds. In the last years of the Jackson Administration, however, the promise of renewed federal aid encouraged the states to undertake internal improvements programs through the use of their own resources.

Notes, Chapter 1.

1. Willis Dunbar, *Michigan: A History of the Wolverine State* (Grand Rapids, Michigan: Eerdmans Publishing Company, 1965), pp. 330, 335.
2. Fishlow, p. 190.
3. Everett E. Hagen, *On the Theory of Social Change: How Economic Growth Begins* (Homewood, Illinois: Dorsey Press, Inc., 1962), pp. 12-13, 26, 35, 52.
4. J. B. Bury, *The Idea of Progress: An Inquiry into its Origin and Growth* (New York: Dover Publications, 1955), pp. 128, 136, 142-143, 220.
5. *Ibid.*, p. 324.
6. Arthur A. Ekirch, *The Idea of Progress in America, 1815-1860* (New York: Peter Smith, 1951), pp. 32-33.
7. Bury, p. 324.
8. Carl L. Becker, *The Heavenly City of the Eighteenth Century Philosophers* (New Haven: Yale University Press, 1932), p. 47.
9. Ekirch, p. 11.
10. Henry Adams, *History of the United States*, IX, 220, as quoted in Ekirch, pp. 32-33.
11. Ekirch, p. 36.
12. *Ibid.*, p. 73.
13. *A Compilation of the Messages and Papers of the Presidents, 1789-1897*, ed. James D. Richardson, 10 vols. (Washington: Government Printing Office, 1896-1899), II, 295. Cited hereafter as *Messages of the Presidents*.
14. *Ibid.*, pp. 299-317.
15. Fishlow, pp. 165-166.
16. Stuart W. Bruchey, *The Roots of American Economic Growth, 1607-1861* (New York: Harper & Row, 1964), pp. 26-27.
17. Charles Hadafield, "Canals: Inland Waterways of the British Isles," *A History of Technology*, ed. Charles Singer, E. J. Holmyard, A. R. Hall, and Trevor I. Williams (Oxford: Clarendon Press, 1958), IV, 563.

18. Witt Bowden, *Industrial Society in England towards the end of the Eighteenth Century,* second ed. (New York: Barnes & Noble, Inc., 1965), p. 63.
19. Carter Goodrich, *Canals in American Economic Development* (New York: Columbia University Press, 1961), pp. 1-2.
20. Samuel Rezneck, "The Rise and Early Development of Industrial Consciousness in the United States, 1760-1830," *Journal of Economic and Business History,* IV (1932), 778.
21. Adam Smith, *Wealth of Nations* (New York: Modern Library, 1937), p. 3.
22. Goodrich, *Canals and American Economic Development,* p. 217.
23. *Ibid.*
24. For a more detailed development of this problem and interpretation, see my arguments in *The Democracy's Railroads: Internal Improvements in Michigan, 1820-1845* (Unpublished Ph. D. dissertation, Michigan State University, 1967).
25. George Rogers Taylor, *The Transportation Revolution, 1815-1860,* Vol. IV of *The Economic History of the United States,* ed. Henry David and others, 9 vols. (New York: Rinehart & Co., Inc., 1951), p. 21.
26. Goodrich, *Government Promotion,* pp. 39-43.
27. James Parton, *Life of Andrew Jackson,* 3 vols. (Boston: James R. Osgood and Company, 1876), III, 285; Harold C. Syrette, *Andrew Jackson and his Contribution to the American Tradition* (New York: Bobbs-Merrill Company, Inc., 1953), p. 135.
28. Taylor, p. 21; Glyndon Van Deusen, *The Jacksonian Era* (New York: Harper & Brothers, 1959), p. 51.
29. Goodrich, *Government Promotion,* p. 42.
30. John Spencer Bassett, *The Life of Andrew Jackson* (New York: Macmillan Co., 1925), pp. 483-484.
31. Marquis James, *The Life of Andrew Jackson* (New York: Bobbs-Merrill Company, 1938), pp. 524-525.
32. Bassett, p. 495.
33. Goodrich, *Government Promotion,* pp. 41-43.
34. *Messages of the Presidents,* II, 451,484.
35. Edward G. Bourne, *The History of the Surplus Revenue of 1837* (New York: G. P. Putnam's Sons, 1885), pp. 5-6.
36. *Ibid.,* pp. 7-9.
37. *Messages of the Governors of Michigan,* ed. George N. Fuller, 4 vols. (Lansing: Michigan Historical Commission, 1925), I, 103-108. Cited hereafter as *Messages of the Governors of Michigan.*
38. *Ibid.,* pp. 77-85.
39. Bourne, pp. 18-19, 29.
40. Taylor, p. 50.

2

CYCLICAL INTERFERENCE

Between 1834 and 1837, a number of states responded to pressure for programs of internal improvement. In addition to popular approval and the possibility of federal subsidies, state action was encouraged by temporary reversals of the balance of payments and terms of trade, which added depth to the capital market and allowed the sale of securities abroad. Success or failure of state programs, however, hinged on more than intelligent planning and faithful application of funds. Sudden changes in world market conditions created forces beyond state control that destroyed many programs before they were completed and severely restricted others.

Recent studies of the ante-bellum canal movement by H. Jerome Cranmer and Harvey Segal have shown that the period witnessed not one, but three distinct movements.[1] Building on data presented by Cranmer, Segal has presented the picture of ante-bellum canal development summarized in Table I. These movements are longer than, and generally independent of, concurrent business cycles in the forty-five-year period covered in the study. Since their shape and duration do not seem dictated by the business cycle, explanations must be sought elsewhere. The technology of canal construction, commercial and political rivalry, and the availability of funds for construction, all seem to be responsible factors. The principal reason for long cycles is the clustering and short gaps in the spacing of new construction starts. In a model, if starts are staggered at dates longer than a year, short cycles result.[2]

The first cycle was primarily the result of attempts by the seaboard states to breach the Appalachian barrier and capture the trade of the West. Dominated by uninterrupted completion of projects in New York, Pennsylvania, and Ohio, the cycle not only produced the most enduring and successful state enterprises of the period, but changed the direction and channels of American inter-regional trade.

The second cycle can be accounted for by the unfulfilled demand for laterals in New York, Pennsylvania, and Ohio, as well as a desire for routes to supplement the Mississippi-Erie transportation network.[3] This cycle, which included Michigan's internal improvements program, exhibited a higher peak and was of shorter duration. The contraction phase, occurring over a four-year period, was more precipitous than that of either the preceding or following cycle. It was accompanied by a sharp inflation of land and commodity prices, a large expansion of the money supply, increased uncer-

TABLE I

Cycles of Canal Construction, 1815-1860[a]

Cycle	Duration (Years)	Peak Year	Completed Mileage	Investment Over Cycle (Millions of Dollars)	% of total
1st Cycle, 1815-1834	19.5	1828	2,188	58.6	31.1
2d Cycle, 1834-1844	10	1840	1,172	72.2	38.4
3d Cycle, 1844-1860	16.5	1855	894	57.4	30.5
Total for all Cycles	46.0		4,254	188.2	100.0

[a]Harvey H. Segal, "Cycles of Canal Construction," *Canals and American Economic Development,* ed. Carter Goodrich (New York: Columbia University Press, 1961), p. 172.

tainty in banking, and a massive influx of foreign capital.[4] In the Old Northwest, the land boom and improvements program coincided with accelerated immigration and settlement induced by the opening of markets to these formerly isolated territories. The cycle was also marked by a greater proportion of public investment and construction in the West than there had been during other periods. Public investment rose from less than sixty to almost seventy percent of expenditures, while Western investment rose from ten to thirty percent of the total.[5] Finally, the second cycle is the only one whose shape is heavily influenced by concurrent business cycles.

The third cycle, from 1844 to 1860, has been characterized as an "echo effect," during which funds and initiative were devoted to salvaging and completing projects stalled by the depression. This characterization, however, gives a distorted picture of American social overhead capital creation because of its focus on canal technology, which was rapidly approaching obsolescence. Inclusion of railroad data, although of negligible importance in the second cycle, would undoubtedly alter the shape and magnitude of the third. It is also important to note that the investment of the late 1830s and early 1840s was part of a continuing, and not a declining, trend.

The second cycle, and Michigan's internal improvements program, was brought to a precipitous conclusion by the depression of 1839-1843. This simultaneous downward trend was more than the simple coincidence of phase by cycles of differing periodicity. The relationship was one of cause and effect. The depression not only lowered the general level of economic activity and profitability of public works, but it destroyed the supply of capital essential to the successful completion of the construction cycle.

The role of foreign capital in American development has been the subject of frequent and lively debate. Its role, as the counterpart of capital scarcity, has often been cited as central to economic planning by the states.[6] More recently, its importance has been questioned. Nathan Miller, in his study of the Erie canal, points to the critical role of small domestic investors, and concludes that foreign capital never did play a dominant role. The bulk of New York's canal stock was still in domestic hands in 1825, and large foreign and domestic purchases occurred only after the canal was an obviously safe investment.[7] The fact that foreign capital in America before the Civil War accounted for less than one-third of total investment adds to the suspicion that its role was less than crucial. These factors are offset, however, by the disproportionate concentration of foreign investment between 1825 and 1840. From the latter half of the first through the whole of the second cycle, foreign capital played a dominant role, linking investment to international commodity movements and prices, foreign banking and speculation, and the international balance of payments. Even the final collapse of American investment credit ultimately stemmed from foreign political and economic changes. A partial explanation of the conditions governing Michigan's investment program can be found in foreign finances, particularly those of Great Britain.[8]

American stocks and bonds were nothing new to Englishmen in the

1820s. A large portion of the Revolutionary War debt and Louisiana purchase bonds had been transferred from Amsterdam to London during the Napoleonic wars, and investment in the Bank of the United States was popular. In addition, British merchants extended large amounts of credit in attempts to control the American market.[9] Around 1825, however, the structure of British investment began to shift. Previously, the bulk of England's overseas capital had been channeled into securities of the restored Bourbon Monarchy and South American Republics, but between 1825 and 1830, not a single foreign government was able to float a loan in London, despite a persistent demand for political funds. At the same time, heavy losses suffered in 1825 by British merchants extending credit to Americans put an end to that system of finance. Subsequently, exchange and shipment was concentrated in the Bank of the United States in America and eight "American houses" led by Brown Brothers and Baring Brothers in England.[10] The British investor shifted his preferences from financing foreign trade through political loans to productive loans creating their own means of repayment. A new flow of funds opened from country investors who had made their fortunes in British industrialization, and now sought safe ways to tap the increment of progress elsewhere. To these investors, American state and municipal securities for promotional activities seemed highly desirable. Such bonds were seldom sold in the London market, but in blocks to bankers and brokers in America, and then transferred to one of the "American houses" in London. Next, they were passed on to country bankers and favored clients who usually bought the stock, not on its merits, but on the recommendation of a banker.[11] Estimates of the total quantity of foreign investment in the United States between 1825 and 1840 show little basic agreement, except that the quantity was large. It is significant, however, that all of them reveal the same basic trend, in which foreign investment grew by more than fifty percent between 1825 and 1835, and doubled or tripled in the next three years.[12]

Capital transfers of this magnitude depend not only on the availability of willing investors, but on the smooth functioning of financial machinery. In the period before 1845, when states relied heavily on loans to finance internal improvements, their ability to raise funds was determined by the ratio of specie held in banks to their note and deposit liabilities.[13] During periods of optimism, banks in the United States and Britain were able to purchase readily and shift the stocks to individuals, but at the same time, they were extremely sensitive to internal and external disturbances. Any shift in the public desire to hold specie, crop failure, or change in the relationship of foreign and domestic prices could quickly dry up the supply of foreign funds. While the demand for loans was fairly constant, the supply of funds was highly unstable.

During this time, structural changes in the loan and discount policy of the Bank of England played a crucial role in determining the volume of available funds. Because the discount rate was consistently above the market rate of brokerage on bills after 1825, London banks stopped channeling surplus funds into government securities that were discountable at the Bank, and placed their funds with bill brokers. As a result, the Bank could control the flow of funds only in difficult times when the market rate rose above the discount rate, and British banks enjoyed unusual freedom.[14] As discounting fell off, the Bank was forced to rely heavily on "moral suasion" to shape economic events. In succeeding years, the Bank adopted new currency control policies. On December 6, 1827, the Board of Governors decided to combat unfavorable gold exchanges by contracting the currency, selling exchequer bills to dry up the market, and selling silver for gold in Paris. In 1830, country bankers were notified to curtail loans in times of foreign gold demand, or face the possibility of having discounting services withdrawn. Finally, in 1831, it was decided that a decline in the Bank's reserves below seven million pounds would be the signal to begin contraction.[15] During the next decade, these policies and practices exercised important effects on the flow of funds.

Through 1835, economic conditions in Britain favored capital export. Good harvests from 1831 to 1835 allowed wheat prices to fall to a fifty-year low, and an accompanying decline in food imports allowed gold exchanges to remain steady.[16] Available funds were increased after 1832 when the British East India Company began to liquidate its assets. The company pressured the Bank to pay interest on its deposits, and these funds, previously neutralized, went out into the market as loans to bill brokers. By February of 1836, nearly four million pounds of these funds were out with five brokers.[17] Such conditions facilitated easy credit in London and the flow of capital to America.

Massive capital transfers, such as those sustained by the United States and Great Britain, require a delicate balance of factors that become more complex as the level of interdependency increases. Not difficult in itself, the transfer process calls for the importation of gold or goods in excess of exports. Problems develop in the primary and secondary effects of maintaining a level of dynamic equilibrium in both the lending and borrowing countries without serious inflation or misallocation of resources. In its simplest form, America had to maintain the balance of payments and exchanges under the pressure of an imbalance of merchandise shipments without heavy inflows or outflows of specie or serious inflation. An important component of this stability was maintenance of the world market price of cotton because between 1836 and 1840 cotton constituted sixty-three percent of the value of American exports and was the major source of funds for repayment of foreign claims.[18] Maintenance of the balance of specie flow was important not only because it could effect the domestic price level, but because any heavy outflow of specie from Great Britain would force the Bank of England into contraction and dry up America's sources of foreign credit. Inflation in America would not only raise the cost of investment, but would ultimately lead to deterioration of exchanges and a general recession in the economy.

The first crisis of the Anglo-American credit system was precipitated by the economic and political policies of the Jackson Administration. Too rapid repayment of the national debt and surplus revenues from the tariff and land sales brought funds that should have been neutralized into the market, increasing inflationary pressure. At the same time, the government lost all control of the currency by withdrawing its funds from the Bank of the United States, and aggravated the situation by depositing in banks of issue where the funds served as reserves for unlimited currency expansion. Between 1834 and 1839, the money supply expanded fifty-five percent, and the number of banks increased from five hundred to nine hundred.[19] The credit system was further endangered when attempts to establish a specie currency caused a heavy short-term gold drainage into the United States. In 1834, Congress had changed the mint ratio from 15:1 to 16:1, thus changing the sterling-dollar mint-par ratio from 4.44:1 to 4.87:1, a ratio favorable to gold imports. Many of America's creditors left their funds in the United States in order to collect higher rates of interest and avoid losses through conversion. This pressure increased when Jackson insisted on collecting the indemnities due from France and Naples in gold. The result of these policies was an average net gold import of ten million dollars a year from 1833 to 1836, at a time when capital importation was increasing rapidly.[20] As a result, America became Europe's short-term creditor.

The first substantial break in the credit system came with the Panic of 1837. Like the system itself, the Panic is an involved story, displaying such a high level of action and reaction among a multitude of interlocking forces that any complete explanation or assessment is impossible. Salient characteristics, however, are evident. Both America and Britain were caught up in an obvious speculative bubble, and early in 1836, actions designed to slow down the rate of expansion began on both sides of the Atlantic. British speculation in American bonds and import commodities was so great it forced exchanges below the gold points and made it profitable to export gold.[21] In late March of 1836, an outflow began which lasted for eleven months and became a source of concern to the Bank of England. Convinced that loose practices by the "American houses," which were using discounted bills based on uncovered credits and remitted securities as collateral for loans from the Bank, were the cause of the problem, the Bank began to contract and raised its discount rate.[22]

Contraction had scarcely begun in England when Jackson applied drastic surgical techniques to the American boom, followed by fiscal bungling that aggravated the crisis. The Specie Circular of July 1836, designed to slow the speculative boom in Western lands by curbing the dangerous note-issue-land-purchase spiral created by deposit of federal revenues in state banks, locked up specie in Western land speculation at a time when it was badly needed in the Northeast. By November, commerce was paralyzed. The crisis was seriously prolonged by Secretary Woodbury's decision to distribute federal funds by an actual transfer of money, instead of simply granting drafts on deposit banks. These two measures virtually exhausted the exchange of the seaboard banks, while locking specie up in land sales and the transfer of federal deposits.[23]

Afraid the Specie Circular would lead to an even heavier gold drain, the Bank of England increased its contraction. Discount rates were raised again and loans were refused. In October 1836, the Governor of the Bank of England interviewed representatives of six of the "American houses" and "explained to them that excessive facilities given to foreign bankers, 'either as open Credits or in anticipation of the sale of State Securities in this country,' were objectionable to him and the Company as note issuers." [24] Through the winter, this pressure began to take effect, and overextended banks began to go to the wall. The following spring, British curtailment brought a heavy return of protested bills to America at a time when specie was being tied up and driven out of circulation by Jacksonian fiscal policies.[25] On May 10, 1837, American banks suspended specie payments.

Although the Panic of 1837 severely shook the credit system, it did not make great changes in the flow of long-term credit. In fact, the volume of capital imports increased every year through 1839. As long as interest payments were maintained, the Panic had relatively little effect on the willingness of the British public to lend. American credit was still good, and even as panic began to sweep American financial centers, recovery had begun in England.[26] As Douglas North has suggested: "The Panic of 1837 was an interruption and not an end to the underlying expansive forces in the economy."[27] The bottom was reached in the summer of 1837; by the spring of 1838, the economy was experiencing full-scale recovery.[28] This temporary recovery helps to explain why Michigan persisted in its efforts to finance a program approved on the brink of a panic. Serious depression was still many months away.

The suspension of American banks did not reflect a heavy specie drainage abroad, but rather, an internal drainage into public and private hoards.[29] Even before suspension, forces to revitalize the economy had been set in motion. The central figure in these efforts, and in decisions having important repercussions on Michigan's internal improvements program, was Nicholas Biddle and the Bank of the United States of Pennsylvania. Believing in individual action when government abdicated its responsibility, Biddle set out to restore the Bank to its previous functions of regulating the currency, checking other banks, and dominating the foreign exchange market until this bank could be reestablished under national charter.[30]

When initial efforts to restore stability were frustrated by suspension, Biddle began a program to restore credit and gain control of exchange in the London market.[31] The operation depended on the marketing of cotton and securities. Agencies, drawing on the dummy firm of Bevan and Humphries for United States Bank notes, were set up throughout the South to buy cotton and ship it to London, where it would be received by the firm of Humphries and Biddle and held against price advances. At the same time, Samuel Jaudon, cashier of the parent bank in Philadelphia, was sent to London to market American securities that the Bank of England would not permit the "American houses" to handle. Funds from the sale of these securities were used to honor drafts on Humphries and Biddle for cotton shipped by Bevan and Humphries, and post-notes of the Bank as they fell due. Through this complex arrangement, Biddle was able to harness capital available to state enterprise, stabilize the cotton and exchange markets, provide funds for the states, liquidate outstanding mercantile indebtedness, and end the dumping of cotton on arrival by British consignment merchants. Due mainly to the willingness of Englishmen to invest in state securities, operations were an immediate success. By April 1838, full-scale recovery was underway, and on August 13, specie payments were resumed on the East Coast. Biddle's brilliant operations had not only outwitted the Bank of England and earned its hostility, but had restored the balance of payments and the flow of capital.[32] The renewed flow of foreign capital allowed the second cycle to continue through 1839.

American difficulties in the Panic of 1837 had been easily surmounted because of the continued willingness of foreigners to invest in American economic development, and the continued stability of basic relationships within the Atlantic economy. The Depression of 1839 was another story. It began abroad, and was transmitted to the American economy through the flow of investment capital and the primary product export sector. Unlike the Panic of 1837, recovery depended not only on a basic readjustment of economic forces, but on an alteration of international and domestic political conditions.

Pressure on the reserves of the Bank of England resumed in December 1838, following the collapse of commercial credit on the Continent. Armed only with tools to curb note redemption, the Bank was almost powerless against heavy runs by its depositors. Despite desperate attempts to stem the tide by raising the discount rate to an unprecedented six percent, the Bank lost specie at a rate of over one million pounds a month from December through August. By August 1839, reserves had fallen to £1,174,000 "and that was not the bottom." The Bank of England narrowly missed suspension, and then only because of specie borrowed in Paris.[33]

Although the Bank of England managed to stave off disaster by desperate expedients, basic disruptions in the Atlantic economy postponed recovery for several years. In Britain, harvests lost their brilliance, and specie had to be exported to pay for food. Yarn exports to Germany and Belgium fell heavily as crisis struck their young textile industries, further damaging the nation's exchange position. At the same time, political tensions brought economic repercussions that were reversed only after years of effort. At one point, England and France came to the brink of war in the Middle East, and trouble with Russia flared up on the border of Afghanistan. American and British commerce in the Far East was disrupted by disputes with China over the opium trade, and a French blockade at Buenos Aires destroyed trade in that sector. Finally, the Maine boundary incidents increased tension between the United States and Great Britain. In sum, political problems destroyed the markets through which the finished products of American cotton were distributed, and unfortunately, political problems could not be solved by financial manipulation.[34]

In America, pressure transmitted from England turned to panic in June 1839. Biddle was gone from the Bank of the United States, and lesser men were in control. By July, a million dollars in specie had been lost, and the Bank began to draw heavily on Jaudin against cotton held by Humphries and Biddle.[35] For the second time, America's credit and exchange position hinged on the price of cotton and sale of securities. In 1839, however, the price of cotton could not be raised by cornering the market. British spinners had agreed to combine against cost cutting and price increases by American monopolies. For emphasis, they restricted purchases and went on short time, while the contracted textile market made violation of the agreement unprofitable.[36]

As time passed, Jaudin's position in London became progressively worse. A million pounds in debts were maturing in the autumn, and American stocks were unsalable. Then, in August, the United States Bank made his position untenable by selling a mass of drafts on him to organize a run on the New York banks. Jaudin and the Bank would have been ruined, if friends of the Bank in Europe whose fortunes were staked on American prosperity had not combined to support American credit. Rothschild and Hope advanced eight hundred thousand pounds secured by American state bonds to liquidate outstanding debts, and cotton held in London was sold at a loss. Although the Bank was solvent, failure in this venture had stripped it, the credit system, and American securities of respectability.[37] The bonds used to secure the loan of exchange, and other bonds sent abroad to secure the Bank's debts in later years, would have important and unfortunat effects on Michigan.

The Depression was long and continuous. Recovery was not experienced until 1844. Douglas North, among others, has compared it to the Great Depression of 1929 in length and severity.[38] Work on internal improvements did not stop immediately, but proceeded slowly until borrowed funds ran out. Several projects were financed by state notes and post-dated checks through 1840, but after that, work was slow and sporadic. Eventually, most states were unable to meet interest payments on their debts.[39]

As the Depression deepened, a wave of hostility toward borrowing, credit, the credit system, and financial institutions swept the United States. As people saw homes, farms, and businesses swept under by forces they did not understand, they reacted against the institutions apparently at fault. Worst of all, the feeling that credit was a fraud led politicians to call for repudiation. Between June 1840 and August 1842, the market for American securities fell off. When the failure of the Bank of the United States was added to the default or repudiation of the states in 1841, the market was badly damaged. Even solvent states and institutions were refused credit and forced to suspend operations. America was pictured abroad as a "nation of swindlers," because Europeans regarded the failure of one state as the responsibility of all.[40]

By 1844, an era had ended. The surplus was gone and the people were disillusioned. State enterprise was in disrepute, and railroads were beginning to challenge canals for transportation supremacy. State credit was gone, at least as far as foreign capital was concerned. Many of the states adopted constitutional restrictions against state support for internal improvements.

Michigan's experience was far from unique. The optimism and sense of mission that aroused ambitions was universal to Americans of the era, and the need for improved transportation was widespread. Even Michigan's timing coincided with other states' decisions to the point that a cycle was generated. Finally, the forces outside Michigan's control that led to financial failure were experienced in most other states of the Union. Michigan's program was far from a self-contained phenomenon. Events occurred in Philadelphia, Washington, London, Paris, and Amsterdam. The creative forces reached back half a century in political and economic development, through a complex network of economic variables. None of this, of course, completely explains or justifies the decisions made by Michigan's leaders between 1830 and 1850.

Notes, Chapter 2

1. Segal, in *Canals and American Economic Development*, p. 170; H. Jerome Cranmer, "Canal Investment, 1815-1860," *Trends in the American Economy in the Nineteenth Century*, ed. William N. Parker and others "National Bureau of Economic Research: Studies in Income and Wealth," XXIV (Princeton, N. J.: Princeton University Press, 1960), 554. Hereafter cited as *Trends in the American Economy*.
2. Segal, in *Canals and American Economic Development*, p. 173.
3. *Ibid.*, pp. 178-179.
4. *Ibid.*, p. 189.
5. Cranmer, *Trends in the American Economy*, p. 554.
6. Goodrich, *Government Promotion*, p. 9.
7. Nathan Miller, *The Enterprise of a Free People: Aspects of Economic Development in New York State During the Canal Period, 1792-1828* (Ithaca: Cornell University Press, 1962), p. 85.
8. Segal, in *Canals and American Economic Development*, p. 180.
9. Leland H. Jenks, *The Migration of British Capital to 1875* (New York: Knopf, 1927), p. 65.
10. John Harold Clapham, *The Bank of England: A History*, 2 vols. (New York: Macmillan Co., 1945), II, 136, 142.
11. Jenks, pp. 71-78.
12. *Historical Statistics of the United States*, p. 556; Jenks, p. 85; Bray Hammond, *Banks and Politics in America from the Revolution to the Civil War* (Princeton, N. J.: Princeton University Press, 1957), p. 450; Segal, in *Canals and American Economic Development*, p. 191.
13. *Ibid.*, p. 180.
14. Clapham, II, 136, 142.
15. *Ibid.*, 116-119.
16. *Ibid.*, 146.
17. *Ibid.*, 147; Jenks, pp. 69-70; Ralph W. Hidy, *The House of Baring in American Trade and Finance* (Cambridge: Harvard University Press, 1949), pp. 183-184.
18. Douglas C. North, *The Economic Growth of the United States, 1790-1860* (Englewood Cliffs, N. J.: Prentice-Hall, Inc., 1961), p. 75.

19. Thomas P. Govan, *Nicholas Biddle: Nationalist and Public Banker, 1786-1844* (Chicago: University of Chicago Press, 1959), p. 297; Segal, in *Canals and American Economic Development,* p. 190; Hammond, pp. 453-454; Clapham, II, 150. In his recent study, *The Jacksonian Economy* (New York: Norton, 1969) Peter Temin has taken sharp exception to this interpretation, and in effect, denies that Jacksonian policies contributed to the Panic. I find his arguments, however, unconvincing. The complete absolution of Jackson is simplistic, and, his statistical base is too narrow and unreliable to support the conclusions drawn.
20. Clapham, II, 151; Jenks, p. 85; Reginald C. McGrane, *Foreign Bondholders and American Debts* (New York: Macmillan Co., 1935), p. 14.
21. Govan, p. 305.
22. Hidy, p. 205; Clapham, II, 151.
23. Govan, pp. 298, 302.
24. Clapham, II, 154.
25. McGrane, pp. 14-15, Hidy, p. 210.
26. Hidy, p. 237.
27. North, p. 200.
28. *Ibid.,* p. 201.
29. Hammond, p. 461.
30. Govan, pp. 294-295.
31. *Ibid.,* pp. 308-316.
32. Jenks, pp. 88-92; Hammond, pp. 467-470; Hidy, pp. 185-186; Govan, pp. 295, 300, 327, 339.
33. Clapham, II, 161-170.
34. Jenks, p. 95.
35. Govan, pp. 360-361.
36. Jenks, pp. 92-93.
37. Hidy, pp. 275-276; Clapham, II, 168-169; Jenks, pp. 95-98; Govan, p. 363.
38. North, p. 202.
39. Segal, in *Canals and American Economic Development,* pp. 198-201.
40. Hidy, pp. 289, 309; Jenks, pp. 99-101; Govan, p. 376.

3

THE TERRITORIAL IMPETUS

Michigan, although west of the Appalachians, was really the western-most extension of the Atlantic seaboard. Draining its waters through the St. Lawrence Valley, but politically annexed to the United States, the peninsula was out of context with its geographic environment. Cut off to the east by Niagara Falls and the mountain barrier, and to the west and south by ridges separating the Ohio and Mississippi basins from the Great Lakes, water travel was frustrated in all directions. By land, the obstacles were almost insur-mountable.

The land itself was not new. Europeans had begun to explore the Upper Lakes before Boston was founded, and by 1701, settlements had been located at Detroit and Sault Ste. Marie. Still, for more than two centuries after Etienne Brulé entered the St. Mary's River, Michigan remained the domain of the *voyageur* and the *coureur de bois*. National ownership made little difference; even after the United States gained control in 1795, the land was valued more for furs than wheat and corn. As late as the War of 1812, there was neither a mile of improved road in the Territory, nor a mile of road linking it to the rest of the United States. In 1810, the population numbered 4,762 and, by 1820, it had increased to only 8,896, with both figures including territory west to the Mississippi. Yet, the tide of settlement rolling down the Ohio Valley had already bypassed the region. In 1820, Ohio, Indiana, and Illinois had achieved statehood, and Missouri was knocking on the door. In Michigan, the federal government had not even bothered to open a land office until 1818.

A few feeble attempts were made to connect Michigan with the rest of the Union. In 1806, the Territorial Government authorized a lottery to raise six thousand dollars for a road from Detroit to the present site of Toledo, but apparently nothing came of it.[1] During the War of 1812, Detroit was still cut off from the rest of the country whenever the Lakes were closed. In the course of the war and its aftermath, three passable routes were constructed from the Ohio Valley to the rapids of the Miami (later known as the Maumee), but the route from there to Detroit remained unimproved.[2] In May of 1816, the Secretary of War finally ordered troops, under the command of Alexander Macomb at Fort Meigs, to construct a road from the rapids to Detroit. By the fall of 1818, Macomb was able to report that seventy miles of the road were finished, and the balance would probably be completed by the next meeting of Congress.[3] Official reports stated that the

30

Detroit-Miami road was constructed in a "masterly manner," but the bridging was apparently inadequate for civilian transportation. In four acts between 1818 and 1819, the Territory granted corporate charters to companies planning to bridge the Rouge, Ecorces, Huron, and Raisin Rivers. The bridges were not considered part of the public road, but were granted monopolies for a mile on either side of the bridge, with a life of twenty to twenty-five years, as long as they remained toll-free to troops and the mail.[4] Even then, the roads remained little more than military trails, fit only for the transportation of troops and supplies. The bridges, however, played a role in creating popular support for free public transportation.[5]

Until 1824, settlement and road building proceeded slowly. Several towns were founded in a circle within thirty miles of Detroit: Utica in 1816; Rochester in 1818; Pontiac in 1819; Ypsilanti in 1823; and Ann Arbor in 1824. The new settlements were confined to the valleys of the Clinton and Huron Rivers, and there is little evidence of road building activity by the Territorial Government.[6] In 1818, the sum of five hundred dollars was appropriated to extend Detroit's Congress Avenue forty miles, and in 1822, one hundred dollars was appropriated for a road from the Huron River to Swan Creek. The same year, two hundred dollars went for a road from Pontiac to Saginaw.[7] But these sums were scarcely adequate to improve transportation in the Territory. Although some form of overland communication must have been maintained, the routes could have been little more than trails.

Michigan's development reached a watershed in 1824. In that year, the Territory was organized under a popular government, with a Territorial Legislative Council replacing the older governor and judges. New promise was given by the pending completion of the Erie Canal, the effects of which were already being felt in the Old Northwest. Land sales in 1824 more than doubled the previous record, and the first of the "Territorial Roads" was authorized.[8] Contemporaries were keenly aware that a massive transformation was taking place in Michigan. Lewis Cass, the Territorial Governor, revealed this awareness in his opening address to the new Legislative Council when he said:

> An auspicious change has taken place in our situation and prospects....
> That great artificial river, which is about to unite the Lakes with the
> Ocean, one of the proudest monuments of human genius and industry,
> has brought us almost in contact with the Atlantic border, and fur-
> nished a communication with the commercial metropolis of the nation,
> with an economy, safety, and facility, which have almost annihilated
> the intervening distance.[9]

Completion of the Erie Canal had an important impact on the growth of the Old Northwest. Within twenty-five years, the population of Ohio, Indiana, Illinois, and Michigan grew from 792,000 to over 4,200,000. Equally important was the shift in geographic origins of immigrants after a convenient route was opened to residents of New York and New England. At the same time, the canal effected important changes in the trade patterns of the nation. In the decades between the opening of the Canal and the Civil War, a northern trade route through the Great Lakes, along with the railroad in the 1850s, channeled goods north and east through New York. Previously, the Old Northwest had been dominated by the Ohio-Mississippi Valley route. Trade on the northeastern route not only increased, but moved a greater portion of western shipments each year—from 23.7 percent of Northwestern trade in 1835, to 62.2 percent in 1853. During a period when national commodity output increased 145.5 percent, freight from the West on the Erie Canal grew 718.1 percent.[10] Although substantial portions of this increasing trade originated in western New York, its effect on Michigan should not be minimized. The Erie Canal created an easy route for shipping farm produce from the Great Lakes region and spurred agricultural development. The route also provided an opportunity for people in the region to benefit by the shifting pattern of national traffic and to earn an income from the transportation of goods.

Great Lakes trade had long-standing access to the Mississippi along three major routes—by way of Chicago and the Illinois River, through Green Bay over the Fox and Wisconsin Rivers, and through Lake Superior over a chain of lakes and rivers to the Mississippi.[11] Although trade was subsequently channeled through the canals of Ohio to the Ohio River Valley, it was hoped that the Upper Lakes would provide a more economical route between New York and the Mississippi Valley. In 1829, and again in 1834 and 1835, the Legislative Council granted charters to corporations to build either canals, rail, or macadamized roads between the Fox and Wisconsin Rivers.[12] Apparently, none of these companies fulfilled its charter obligations, and by the time Michigan started a program of internal improvements, the area had been removed from their jurisdiction. But by their failure, the companies demonstrated to the public the inadequacy of private enterprise for improving the transportation of frontier regions.

Failure of the Fox-Wisconsin companies, however, was not a bitter disappointment; other routes promised increased traffic through the Peninsula. During the Adams Administration, federal land grants were awarded to three important projects. The first two, the Maumee and Erie Canal in Ohio, and the Wabash and Erie in Indiana, had their eastern terminals at Toledo, then within the boundaries of Michigan. A third, the Illinois and Michigan Canal connecting the navigable waters of Lake Michigan with the Mississippi, gave rise to even greater hopes. In 1831, the Detroit *Democratic Free Press* reported that E. C. March, a merchant, had sent goods from New York through the Great Lakes to Chicago, transported them by wagon around the rapids of the Illinois River, and placed them on a steamboat bound for the South. Merchandise, they reported, could be shipped at two-thirds of the cost of the New Orleans-ocean route, and in less than half the time. The article expressed hope that a profitable trade could be built with Illinois and Missouri, and perhaps even with Tennessee and Arkansas.[13]

To the burgeoning cities of Toledo, Monroe, and Detroit, the Erie Canal and its feeders offered more than a chance to become merchandising centers for a fertile hinterland; they contained the promise of commercial empire. There sprang up in the Twenties and Thirties, an illusive vision of a great commercial metropolis on the Upper Lakes that would funnel the trade of the West and the Mississippi over the new northern route through Buffalo and Albany to New York and Boston. This dream, from which Chicago materialized, proved as powerful as that held on the Atlantic seaboard by cities attempting to penetrate the Appalachian barrier, and sparked the agitation for internal improvement in the decades that followed. Rivalry among lake port states and cities for control of the western route, and the accompanying rewards of success, further increased the urgency of demands. It was against this backdrop that road-building began in earnest.

The heart of Michigan's transportation problem lay in a belt of land varying from twenty to forty miles in width, that cut the eastern coast line of the state off from the interior—a belt of clay soil from Ohio to Saginaw Bay that was wet, wooded, and practically impassable.[14] As one early resident later described it: "For forty miles in every direction around Detroit lies one heavy timbered, level, muddy plain, where the soil is alluvial on the surface and a cold, squeasy, heavy clay beneath, through and over which, even now, transit is almost impossible."[15] Penetration of this barrier, and maintaining facilities in a condition to transport goods from the interior, remained major problems throughout the nineteenth century.

In the decade following 1824, two types of roads were built in the Territory. The first, a series of wagon roads built by the federal government, became popularly known as "Territorial Roads." The second, little more than trails, were built under the authority and control of the Territorial Government.

Between 1824 and 1835, Congress authorized and built five major wagon roads and several lesser roads in the Territory. Typical of these roads and of construction methods was the Fort Gratiot Turnpike, running from Detroit to Fort Gratiot, near the present site of Port Huron. Persistent efforts by Michigan's delegates, together with numerous popular petitions, resulted in Congressional approval of the project in March 1827. Surveying began in June of the same year, and contracts were let to local builders in half-mile sections for several years before the road was finally completed in September 1832. Total cost for fifty-six and one-half miles of highway and five bridges was $44,575.31. After 1833, Congress made no further appropriations for maintenance until 1911, when its national origin was used as a justification for federal highway expenditures. The road was supposed to be two rods wide, with a crown two and one-half feet above the surface level. Although it was a free public road, it became popularly known as the Fort Gratiot Turnpike because of its raised crown. In spite of the stress given to the road's importance to national defense, it was used only once for the transportation of military supplies. During the Land Rush of 1835, however, it served as an important artery carrying settlers into the interior.[16]

Similar stories exist concerning the other "Territorial Roads" built by federal authority. Construction on the road between Detroit and Saginaw began in 1829, and continued to a point five miles beyond the Flint River, where it was abandoned by the government in 1835. The Detroit-Fort Meigs road, authorized in 1824, was opened to Toledo in 1829 at a cost of about thirty-eight thousand dollars. Efforts to build a road between Detroit and the rapids of the Grand River began in 1832, but as late as 1837 it had been cleared and grubbed only as far as Howell, leaving the third tier of counties without a major wagon road.[17] The Chicago road, through the southern tier of counties on the Old Sauk Trail from Detroit to Chicago, was the result of determined lobbying by the Territorial Delegate, Father Gabriel Richard. At Father Richard's request, the Secretary of the Treasury authorized witholding sections for a mile on either side of the route in anticipation of a federal land grant, but Father Richard's successor, Austin Wing, was either unwilling or unable to have the subsidy approved. On June 23, 1826, the reserved sections were returned to the market, and construction was financed by direct appropriation.[18] The road was completed to the Indiana line in December 1835, at a cost of about eighty-seven thousand dollars. A connector from Monroe, known as the La Plaisance bay road was completed from Monroe to Tecumseh between 1833 and 1837.[19]

In addition to road construction, the federal government also undertook a canal linking Monroe, on the River Raisin, with the navigable waters of La Plaisance Bay. Between 1827 and 1836, forty-nine thousand dollars was appropriated, but the canal remained uncompleted for two decades after federal abandonment in 1836. Although Monroe's charter authorized the village to build the canal by voluntary subscription, there is no record of locally financed construction. In 1833, Army surveyors recommended construction of a ship canal and organized pressure from the village was placed on Congress through the Territorial Delegate. Although the project was not successful, the promise of becoming a lake port spurred Monroe's ambitions to become the commercial metropolis of Michigan and the West, and contributed to the village's demand for a state-sponsored program.[20]

The last of the major traffic arteries of Territorial Michigan was established by the Legislative Council. Territorial Road, as it was known, was authorized by the Council under an act of November 4, 1829, to run west from the Chicago road at Plymouth, down the St. Joseph Trail to the mouth of the St. Joseph River at Lake Michigan. Although not officially surveyed and opened until 1836, it was passable and in use five or six years earlier.[21] Writers have often appeared puzzled at the lack of energy displayed by the Legislative Council in prosecuting the work; their confusion stems from a failure to realize that the road was never intended as a wagon road. To the contrary, it was one of hundreds of roads authorized by the Council during the decade preceding statehood under the stipulation that "the expenses or damages of laying out and establishing said road shall not be charged upon, or paid out of the territorial treasury."[22] Unlike the other roads established by the Legislative Council, its strategic position through the center of the

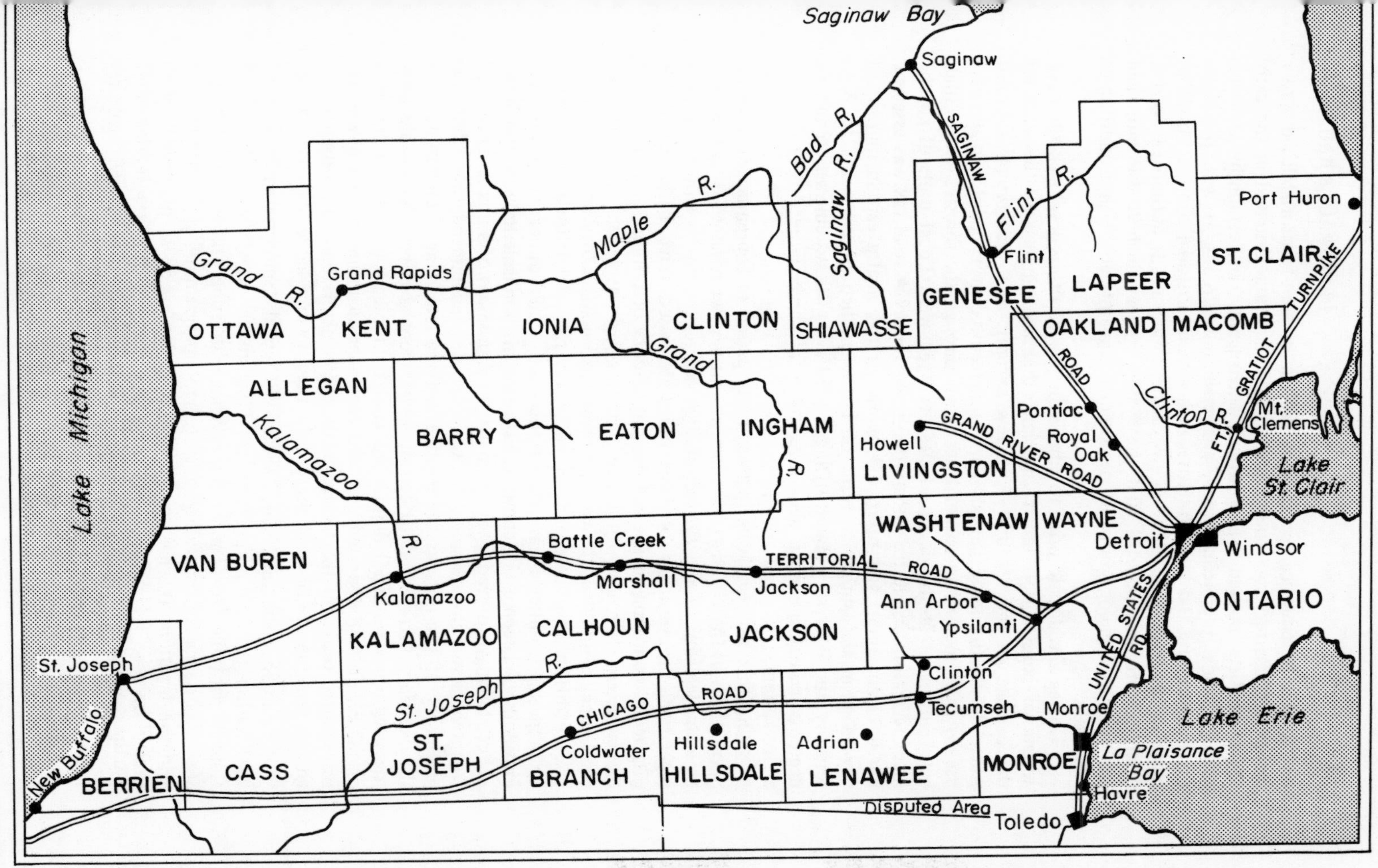

THE TERRITORIAL ROADS

MAP 1

second tier of counties spurred the growth of the Territorial Road into a major traffic artery. As the pressure of immigration mounted in the early 1830s, settlers poured west through the second tier, establishing towns, opening lands, producing crops, and maintaining roads. It was, therefore, external pressure and local initiative, rather than territorial construction, that made it an important route. Few of the other roads authorized by the Council were as successful, and the system under which it was built and serviced was a major source of persistent complaints about the condition of the roads.

During the decade prior to admission, the Territory developed the basic system of construction and maintenance that was retained by the state for the balance of the century. With few exceptions, it was typical of most states during the same period. Early nineteenth-century public roads were usually little more than rutted lanes hewn through the forests, with stumps cut below axle height or sometimes even removed. Local units of government were responsible for construction and repair. A road tax was assessed, but a "man could, and often did, work on the road a certain number of days a year and supply a team of horses in lieu of payment."[23] As a territory and later as a state, Michigan used a similar system, with a varying degree of compulsion that made it resemble the *corvee* more closely than the above system.

The first act regulating highways was passed in September of 1805.[24] Seven times in the next twenty years, similar acts were passed, suggesting the basic inadequacy of the system of highway regulation.[25] With remarkable regularity, the speeches of Governor Cass raised three basic issues: the disgraceful condition of the militia; the wisdom of refraining from changing the laws; and the need for revising existing highway legislation. Each time the Council responded, the new act proved as unsatisfactory as the old.

Historians have long commented on the role of territorial governments in preparing frontier areas for statehood. It would appear, however, that under the leadership of Lewis Cass and his fundamentally Jeffersonian policy, Michigan moved away from the establishment of an experienced and comprehensive government. It was at his recommendation that the machinery of taxation was dismantled and the remaining fiscal resources of the Territory surrendered to county government—a policy that would leave the newborn state saddled with the endless problems of constructing fiscal machinery from the ground up.[26] It was under his influence that power was increasingly vested in the township, on the principle that "In proportion as all governments recede from the people, they become liable to abuse."[27]

From the beginning, the Legislative Council demonstrated an aversion to taxation for the purpose of providing roads. At its first session, the Council petitioned the United States Senate, stressing, among other subjects, the importance of providing a systematic program of road construction without taxation. It characterized taxation for roads as poor and unjust policy because it fell upon the migrating farmer who was buying land, erecting shelter, and preparing the soil. "Before he can fit his newly acquired land for cultivation, a year must elapse, during which he and his family must subsist upon what may remain of means...." On the basis of this need, the Council asked that five percent of the receipts of federal land sales be reserved for construction of roads.[28]

In addressing the opening of the Legislative Council in November 1826, Governor Cass restated the need for stronger township government and road improvement. Good roads, he told them, were everywhere essential, but in a new country with a thin population and scattered settlement, such roads were basic to supplying the most common needs. He warned the members, however, that present taxes, both in labor and money, were as much as the people ought to bear, and left the Council to find a solution to the problem.[29] They responded by producing the Highways Act of 1827, which appears to have been the basis for the state's road policy almost to the close of the internal improvements era.[30]

The Act of 1827 placed responsibility for the roads squarely on the township authorities. Commissioners elected on the township level were authorized and compelled to lay out and alter roads and to assess labor to be used on the highways within their borders. Townships were further divided into road districts with elected overseers who were responsible for supervising work, notifying persons of labor assessed, and collecting commutation money. All free males over twenty-one years of age were liable for two to thirty days labor on the roads, with three days per poll being the minimum average assessment. The rate of commutation was raised to seventy-five cents per day, and failure to appear for labor was subject to a fine of one dollar. Provision was made for laying out private roads and public roads at popular request.

Subsequent acts added to rather than revised the structure of the Act of 1827. An Act of July 30, 1830, placed all roads constructed by the United States government under township jurisdiction, to be cared for in the same manner as existing highways.[31] In June 1832, the Act was amended to raise the limit for labor assessments from thirty to fifty days of labor.[32] Finally, an Act of the newly created state legislature in March 1836, placed all state roads under the jurisdiction of township commissioners.[33]

Evidence suggests that the system more closely resembled forced labor than taxes payable in labor. The Act itself spoke of assessments in terms of labor convertible into money, rather than the reverse. Affidavits and remonstrances submitted during the disputed election of 1825, one of them signed by Henry Schoolcraft, testified that payment in labor was accepted as a tax receipt for purposes of voting, and that fully twenty-five percent of the voters of the Territory would be disenfranchised by the decision of the board of canvassers to accept only monetary tax payments as a basis for suffrage.[34] In 1833, Governor Porter vetoed a highway bill that he felt set commutation prices out of proportion, stating that the accepted hire of a horse, cart, and man was $1.25 per day.[35] Since the acts of the period accepted the three components at an equal value, it suggests that the average farmer was forced to work instead of paying commutation because both the earlier rate of sixty-five cents and the later rate of seventy-five cents were substantially above the common wage rate, particularly for the eight-hour day specified by the Act. When prices and wages rose during the inflationary year of 1837, the government quickly raised the rate of commutation to one dollar.[36] A study of state taxation, ordered by Governor Woodbridge in 1840, revealed assessments as high as five dollars on an eighty-acre lot, and several counties with an average rate of four dollars for the same size plot. Since payment was often evaded by nonresidents and unequally distributed within the counties, taxation on many farms must have been substantial. At the reduced rates of the Depression, between one week and two weeks labor would have been forced on the owner of an eighty-acre farm.[37]

The Legislative Council also provided guidelines for private road construction with the passage of "An Act relative to turnpike companies," on August 5, 1824. The Act allowed corporations to be formed to build turnpikes under government supervision of routes and rates. On the same day, the Pontiac and Paint Creek turnpike company was incorporated.[38] Little apparently came of it because capital was scarce and the crushed stone used for macadamization was practically unavailable in the southeastern portion of the state. While private enterprise failed to respond, public hostility toward toll facilities increased.

Between 1827 and 1833, a wave of popular indignation rose against the toll bridges erected on the Detroit-Miami road under acts passed between 1816 and 1819. In March 1827, a select committee of the Legislative Council recommended repeal of all toll bridge authorization, charging that the bridge acts were illegal and the bridges in poor repair. When the report was tabled, the committee chairman sent a copy to the Secretary of War. In November, a petition complaining of the "heavy and enormous toll" was forwarded to Congress with two hundred and fifteen signatures, including those of the bridge proprietors. The following year, a similar petition with over one hundred and forty signatures was sent to Congress.[39] Finally, in 1829, the Legislative Council authorized a lottery to raise ten thousand dollars to buy bridges or build turnpikes around them, proclaiming: "Free roads and a free communication to and through all parts of this territory are highly necessary to the growth and prosperity thereof...."[40] The Act never went into effect.

At the same time the Highways Act of 1827 was passed, the Council passed an act defining the method of laying out and establishing roads under its authority. The Act provided that all road bills should appoint commissioners to hire surveyors. The surveyors' charges and all damage claims submitted within six months were to be paid from the county treasury, which would be reimbursed from Territorial funds.[41] In practice, however, the provision was nullified as early as 1828, by the insertion in road bills of clauses stipulating payment of expenses by county commissioners. By 1830, the clause stating that "the expense of laying out and establishing said roads, and any damages to individuals...shall not be charged to, or paid from the treasury of the Territory..." had become the standard final clause of bills passed by the Legislative Council.[42] The same practice was subsequently followed by the state. Between 1832 and 1835, the total spent by the Territorial Government for transportation improvement amounted to $3,700 for roads, and $1,030 for a railroad survey, although hundreds of roads were authorized. During the same period, the Council expended $3,857 for fuel and stationery.[43] For nearly fifty years after statehood, the same basic system was followed. County administration was not provided until 1893, and the last county administration was not formed until after 1920.[44]

Considering the system of construction and maintenance, it is not difficult to understand the complaints that a generation hardened to bad roads voiced in the mid-1830s concerning conditions in Michigan. Toqueville, traveling the uncompleted Saginaw road in the early 1830s, described it as "a narrow path, scarcely recognizeable to the eye."[45] Thomas Cather, traveling the Chicago road in 1836, described his experience more vividly:

> This has been a very tedious and toilsome journey. Where there were roads, they were execrable, such as a European could have no conception of. If a man were to set about describing bad roads and were to draw on the powers of the liveliest imagination, he would fall far short of the realities which I have experienced. Sometimes the horses were swimming in the water, sometimes floundering through quagmires. At times the wagon was all but upset over the stumps of trees. At some places where attempt had been made to form corduroy roads, it went bumping and crashing along in such an awful manner that I did not know whether to wonder more at its timbers not being shaken to pieces, or at *our* bones escaping dislocation.[46]

Testimony by other contemporaries indicates that Cather was understating the case. Even Charles Lanman, whose state-subsidized history was written to lure settlers by singing the state's praises, commented that:

> During the spring and fall, the roads across the state are such as to try the patience of the traveler. Those on the level and heavily timbered land are almost impassable....Composed, as the soil is, of new rich loam and clay, which retains and mixes with the water, it forms a deep mud, except during the summer and winter, when it is dried up or frozen.[47]

With all that can be said against them, however, the roads made the land accessible to settlers. As R. C. Buley has pointed out: "While soil, timber, availability of damsites, the nature of the scenery even, were all important factors in determining settlers' locations, most important was the lack of roads."[48] Henry Utley, in his history of the state, has cited the Erie Canal and Territorial Roads as the two most important factors in the settlement of the state between 1824 and 1834.[49] As the tide of settlement swelled, the influence of roads was apparent. Chips from the surveyor's axe had scarcely fallen when a town site was plotted adjacent to the road, and men took up farms along the trail of blazes because a road would be built there. Bad as they were, the roads brought population and bare necessities. Still, more was needed.

The settler could bring his family, tools, and possessions into the interior by cart or wagon. He could clear brush and girdle the widely spaced burr oaks of the oak openings. He could even plant his first crop of wheat, avoiding the progression from corn to pork to wheat that was necessary in the heavy forests of Ohio and Indiana. But then he had to market his crop. This could not be done economically over roads on which ten miles a day was difficult for a loaded wagon, and on which wagons were smashed and livestock drowned. A second alternative was travel on the rivers, but these, too, had their limitations. The state was well supplied with waters capable of floating flatboats and barges to the lakes, but first, the rivers required extensive clearing and improvement. An additional handicap was the peninsular watershed in the southern half of the state, which is located only a third of the distance west of Lakes Erie and St. Clair. West of Jackson, goods shipped by water had to be carried a hundred miles west, and hundreds of miles north and south through the stormy Straits of Mackinac on lakes closed by wind and ice six months of the year, to reach a point less than a hundred miles east of their origin. Wheat milled into flour in the summer and fall might not reach market before the following June. It is not difficult to understand why the farmer was as eager as the merchants in coastal cities to find an economical means of transportation through the interior.

As the volume of immigration rose and a marketable crop was produced, the need became increasingly urgent. From a population of 8,896 in 1820, the total rose to 31,369 by 1830, only five years after the Erie Canal was opened. Within two more years, talk began of the population having reached the 60,000 required for statehood. A special census, authorized in 1834, revealed the population had actually increased to 87,273; by the time of the state census in 1837, it had grown to 175,000. Three years later, when depression had appreciably slowed the rate of settlement, the federal census showed a population of 212,267.[50] During the same period, sales of public lands increased rapidly. Nearly half a million acres were purchased in 1834, and during the next two years, sales reached epic proportions as the "Michigan Fever" struck in full force. In 1835, 1,817,000 acres of the public domain were purchased, and the following year, 4,189,000 acres, more than a quarter of the lands sold by the government in a record-breaking year of speculation, were bought in Michigan alone.[51] Many of the purchases were undoubtedly speculative, but the substantial increase of population during the same period indicates that many buyers actually settled. In the area west of the peninsular divide, where a cash crop could be produced almost immediately, the heavy volume of pent-up productivity must have added to the urgency for improved transportation.

Incoming settlers did not populate the state in uniform density. Population concentrated in the three southern tiers of counties, decreasing in numbers from east to west. New arrivals were forced to take up lands further west, increasing the difficulty of transportation. Settlement in the first tier of counties, from Monroe through the valley of the St. Joseph River, lagged behind that of the second or central tier that stretched west from Detroit to Lake Michigan. The third tier, west of Mount Clemens and Pontiac, was only thinly populated, and the fourth tier, between Port Huron and Grand Rapids, along the valley of the Grand River, was the least populated area in the southern half of the state. To the north and in the Upper Peninsula, there was little settlement outside isolated pockets at Saginaw and the Soo.[52]

During the decade of the Territorial Government, Michigan had witnessed far-reaching changes, but limited accomplishments. The opening of the Erie Canal promised to place the peninsulas in the main current of American economic life and astride a major transportation route. The Territorial Roads opened lands and facilitated the settlement of increasing numbers of immigrants. A system of road-building and maintenance was developed that served the state, however poorly, for the rest of the century. Finally, a sufficient population was developed to create demands for statehood. Under these conditions, the demand for internal improvement grew into a significant movement culminating in the adoption of a formal program in 1837.

Notes, Chapter 3

1. Michigan, *Laws of the Territory of Michigan,* IV, 35 ff. Cited hereafter as *Territorial Laws.*
2. Caroline E. MacGill and Others, *History of Transportation in the United States before 1860,* ed. Balthasar Henry Meyer (Washington, D. C.; Carnegie Institution of Washington, 1917), p. 27.
3. United States, Department of State, *The Territorial Papers of the United States,* ed. Clarence Edwin Carter (Washington: U.S. Government Printing Office, 1942), X, 639-40, 670, 782, 280, 859, 691. Cited hereafter as *Territorial Papers.*
4. Michigan, *Territorial Laws,* I, 290, 295, 306; II, 144.
5. George B. Catlin, *The Story of Detroit* (Detroit: Detroit News, 1923), p. 259.
6. *Ibid.,* p. 281.
7. Michigan, *Territorial Laws,* I, 290, 295, 306.
8. See Appendix I.
9. Michigan, *Journal of the Legislative Council of the Territory of Michigan,* 1st Council, 1st Session, 1824, p. 6. Cited hereafter as *Journal of the Legislative Council.*
10. Segal, *Canals and Economic Development,* 229-230.
11. *Territorial Papers,* X, 574-575.
12. Michigan, *Territorial Laws,* II, 720; III, 1296; IV, 138.
13. *Democratic Free Press* (Detroit), December 1, 1831.
14. John M. Gordon, "Michigan Journal, 1836," ed. Douglas H. Gordon and George S. May, *Michigan History,* XLIII (1959), 258.
15. George C. Bates, "By-gones of Detroit," *Michigan Pioneer and Historical Collections,* XXII (1893), 348.
16. William L. Jenks, "Fort Gratiot Turnpike," *Michigan History,* IX (1927), 150-161.
17. R. Carlyle Buley, *The Old Northwest,* 3 vols. (Bloomington: Indiana University

Press, 1951) II, 83; Roger L. Morrison, *The History and Development of Michigan Highways*, (reprinted from the *Michigan Alumnus Quarterly Review* [Autumn, 1937], pp. 59-73), p. 4; Henry M. Utley and Byron M. Cutcheon, *Michigan as a Province, Territory and State, the Twenty-sixth Member of the Federal Union*, 4 vols. (New York: Americana Press, 1906), II, 273-283.
18. *Territorial Papers*, XI, 691-693, 623, 976, 980.
19. Morrison, p. 4; Utley and Cutcheon, II, 282.
20. Michigan, *Territorial Laws*, IV, 141; Utley and Cutcheon, I, 283; *Territorial Papers*, XII, 592, 594-595, 633, 635, 639, 640.
21. Buley, II, 83.
22. Michigan, *Territorial Laws*, I, 744.
23. Charles R. Adrian, *State and Local Governments* (New York: McGraw-Hill, 1960), p. 472.
24. Michigan, *Territorial Laws*, I, 177.
25. *Ibid.*, I, 449-461, 661; II, 93-102, 118-125, 132, 289; IV, 43 ff.
26. Michigan, *Journal of the Legislative Council*, 1st Council, 1st Session, 1824, p. 7.
27. *Ibid.*, 2d Council, 2d Session, 1826, p. 9.
28. *Territorial Papers*, XI, 604 ff.
29. Michigan, *Journal of the Legislative Council*, 2d Council, 1st Session, 1826, p. 7.
30. Michigan, *Territorial Laws*, II, 495-508.
31. *Ibid.*, III, 820-821.
32. *Ibid.*, 947-1049.
33. Michigan, *Acts of the Legislature of the State of Michigan*, 1835 and 1836, pp. 102-103. Cited hereafter as *Legislative Acts*.
34. *Territorial Papers*, XI, 711-781, 843-844, 862.
35. *Messages of the Governors of Michigan*, I, 98.
36. Michigan, *Legislative Acts*, 1837, no. LII.
37. *Ibid.*, 1841, p. 262, Appendix No. 9.
38. Michigan, *Territorial Laws*, II, 202, 212-214.
39. *Territorial Papers*, XI, 1123 ff, 1127, 1129, 1224.
40. Michigan, *Territorial Laws*, II, 731.
41. *Ibid.*, 593.
42. For example, see Michigan, *Territorial Laws*, II, 744, 746. Phraseology changes slightly from act to act.
43. E. Grosvenor, "Financial History of Michigan," *The Semi-centennial of the Admission of the State of Michigan into the Union* (Detroit: Michigan Commission for the Semi-centennial Celebration, 1886), p. 41. Cited hereafter as *Semi-Centennial Addresses*.
44. Morrison, pp. 9, 10.
45. Alexis de Toqueville, "Fortnight in the Wilderness," *Toqueville and Beaumont in America* ed. George W. Pierson (New York: Oxford University Press, 1938), p. 250.
46. Thomas Cather, *Voyage to America: The Journals of Thomas Cather* (New York: 1961), pp. 128-129.
47. James Henry Lanman, *History of Michigan* (New York: E. French, 1839), p. 254.
48. Buley, II, 83.
49. Utley and Cutcheon, II, 337.
50. See Appendix I.
51. See Appendix I.
52. See Appendix II.

4

THE CAMPAIGN FOR INTERNAL
IMPROVEMENTS

Although traditional accounts of Michigan's public works begin with Governor Mason's Annual Message in January 1837, events leading to the Legislature's adoption of a program of internal improvements began long before statehood was envisioned. Rooted in the national movement for internal improvement, the campaign in Michigan produced a long history of popular agitation, political factionalism, sectional rivalry, and local speculation. Historians describing investment decisions in the first canal cycle, particularly in the East, have the advantage of dealing with established societies and established social orders. Comparatively speaking, the societies are well ordered; pressure groups and social demarcations are both stable and established; and political factions and leaderships are readily identifiable. Frontier Michigan presents a startling contrast. In addition to the excited flux characterizing Jacksonian America, with its burgeoning industrial capitalism, social mobility, newly discovered political techniques, and budding political parties, the frontier environment offers complicating factors. In the midst of a population that doubled and tripled every two or three years, and, in which centers of political power shifted with the progress of settlement, the ordinary pace of time was compressed in forming a government that met basic needs.

Agitation for a program of internal improvements appeared simultaneously with demands for increased federal road construction. The vast number of petitions for roads, canals, and railroads, preserved in the *Territorial Papers*, indicates that frontier farmers had few qualms about appealing to the federal government for aid. Indeed, if the number and bulk of petitions sent to Washington is any indication, the demand for improved roads far outweighed the demand for canals and railroads. Petitions for railroads and canals, however, were significant because of the influential signatures appended to them. Often, they were submitted by the Legislative Council itself, or by large municipal committees. And regardless of their origin, they were usually headed by men of regional and national importance. Concurrent with increased demands for a federal program, the sectional rivalry that was to play a decisive role throughout the period began to develop.

The first petition to Congress, submitted by citizens of Detroit in November 1827, asked for a canal linking Lake Erie with Lake Michigan through Detroit. The petitioners argued that such a canal would make navigation of the lakes perfectly safe even in the storm season, and form an important link in the national line of communication between New York and the Mississippi by cutting the distance between terminal points from eight hundred to two hundred miles. By opening large tracts of land and facilitating westward travel, the canal was expected to increase the population of the Territory. Seeking to impress Congress with the practicability of such a project, the petition cited the absence of rock, easy grades, and sufficient water levels at the summit. Total lift was expected to be only one hundred and fifty feet, at a point sixty miles west of Detroit. Finally, the petitioners argued that the present was the best time to begin because ownership of most of the right-of-way land by the government would be an important cost-saving factor. The petition asked Congress to authorize federal construction, award a land grant to the Territory, or charter a corporation for that purpose. For emphasis, they added: "that this canal should commence at Detroit, is beyond question; it has never been doubtful that Nature has marked out that city for the emporium of Michigan."[1]

Counter-petitions were not long following. In February 1828, the southern section submitted its petition, asking for a canal from La Plaisance Bay, at the mouth of the River Raisin, through the first tier of counties, to the mouth of the St. Joseph. In addition to the arguments in the Detroit petition, they claimed that their route would serve both the Kalamazoo and St. Joseph Valleys. It would also end the threat of western shipping in the British-dominated straits between Port Huron and Lake Erie being cut off in time of war.[2]

Partisans of the southern route were not content, however, with merely petitioning Congress. In June of the same year, they took the matter to the Legislative Council. Henry R. Schoolcraft, Representative from the Soo, put a resolution before the Council, reporting its awareness of the first tier's economic potential and recommending the project to Congress. The resolution was assigned to a committee of five, including four men from areas that would eventually belong to the southern-northern coalition, and it was promptly recommended for passage. The committee was also assigned the task of determining what means, if any, should be employed to undertake a survey, but the records do not contain any further reports, and no action seems to have been taken.[3]

In 1829, both interests again petitioned Congress. Partisans of the central route, west from Detroit through the second tier, asked Congress for an unspecified number of sections of land or dollars for surveying a canal from the Detroit River to Lake Michigan, and an unspecified number of sections for construction of its eastern portion. Among the signatures were those of C. C. Trowbridge, Conrad Ten Eyck, and John Biddle.[4] In December, southern interests submitted another petition asking for land or money and citing the practicability of a canal. "A connection between the waters flowing into the head of Lake Erie with some of the streams falling into the Southern Part of Lake Michigan," said the petition, "is obviously a necessary part of the great scheme of internal navigation uniting the Missippi [sic] with the city of New York."[5]

The following year, a new dimension was added to the movement for a federally sponsored program when Governor Cass brought the whole matter to the Council's attention in his Annual Message. The Territory, he told them, had facilities and advantages rarely equaled by any region in the nation:

> But there is one obvious and signal improvement, which could be made, which no doubt eventually will be made. And that is, to unite the mouth of the St. Joseph with our eastern coast, by a canal or rail-road, as experience may establish the superiority of either, across the base of the Peninsula. The country presents no formidable obstacle to the execution of these works. It is generally level and well watered. And the summit on each side, with the exception of one small tract, is attained by a gradual and imperceptible elevation. There is probably no similar extent of country in the Union, where less labor or expense would be required, to produce so important a result."[6]

Citing its importance to national defense and trade, he suggested the President be encouraged to authorize a survey that would make the route more definite and known to the public. It is an interesting comment on his political sagacity that Cass, the man who favored local government, did not hesitate to call on the resources of the federal government when the opportunity presented itself. Both positions undoubtedly enjoyed widespread support within the Territory by maximizing returns and minimizing taxes.

Two features of the Governor's message are characteristic of the balance of the territorial internal improvements movement: advocacy of railroads and the assumption of latent profitability. Suggested at a period when there were less than seventy miles of operating railroad in the United States, the promise of railroads in Michigan nevertheless took quick hold of public attention. All the advantages cited for canals, particularly the freedom from mountains, low summits, and light grades, were repeatedly enlisted to support the contention that Michigan had a "peculiar suitability" for railroads. For a time, petitions continued to ask for either a canal or railroad, but by 1834, railroads had gained ascendancy in the public mind. Gerald Reagan, who has studied public opinion as expressed in newspapers during the era of internal improvements, reports failure to uncover a single expression of doubt in the feasibility of a railroad across the peninsula.[7] There seems to have been no doubt concerning profitability either. Indeed, prior to the Depression, the thought that such a work might lose money apparently never crossed the public mind.

The Council responded to the Governor's suggestion at the end of July, by adopting a memorial to the President, pointing out the advantages of a railroad across the peninsula. It also expressed the opinion, however, that terrain and location favored a canal because when the federally aided canal through Chicago was completed, a canal across Michigan would form a water connection between the Gulf of St. Lawrence and the Gulf of Mexico. For this reason, they also asked for a canal survey across the peninsula.[8]

The following year, the Legislative Council petitioned Congress for a topographical survey to determine the practicability of a canal connecting Lake Huron and Lake Michigan through the Saginaw and Grand Rivers. Such a canal, said the Council, would connect two of the largest rivers in Michigan, freeing the Grand River Valley and the whole West from the storms and ice that closed the Straits of Mackinac six months of the year. Although the summit level was unknown, the rivers were known to run through a belt of the richest soil in the Territory, and the area was expected to produce coal, gypsum, and saline waters.[9] Four years later, a second petition was sent by territorial residents promising construction of a canal within two years if obstructions were removed from the Flint, Shiawassee, and Maple Rivers, and lighthouses built at the entrance to the lakes.[10]

In the fall of 1831, a public internal improvements meeting, described by the petition it produced as "large and respectable," was held in the Council Room in Detroit. The Mayor of Detroit was elected President, and a memorial drafted by General John R. Williams was read and endorsed. It argued that the people of Michigan were migrants from other states who should not be deprived of the privileges of citizenship by moving to an area which had not achieved statehood. The memorial called on Congress to honor the precedent set in granting internal improvement lands to Ohio, Indiana, and Illinois by extending "the same favor and measure of justice...to Michigan. No district of the country seems to be more favorably adopted [sic] either to railroads or canals." A flourishing treasury and the general prosperity of the nation were expected to furnish "ample means for the improvement of every portion of the Union." In consequence, government promotion of several projects was requested. A ship canal to Lake Superior would allow exploitation of the region's vast copper deposits and fisheries, and could be built at a "trifling" expense. In addition, the memorial asked for completion of the Chicago road and all others started by the federal government, for bridges over the rivers, and improvement of the St. Joseph River. The petitioners also suggested the region was well suited to canals and railroads. A committee of the most important residents of the Territory was appointed to circulate petitions in Michigan and neighboring states to add strength to these demands.[11]

According to surviving documents, 1832 was a quiet year, but agitation was renewed in the winter of 1833. In November, a petition containing over three hundred signatures was sent to Congress by residents of St. Joseph County, requesting a railroad to connect Lakes Michigan and Erie. Along with the usual arguments and appeals, petitioners complained of an inability to market their crops and asked that a corporation be chartered with a grant of lands along the proposed route. Finally, they requested that commissioners be appointed by the national government to determine the route and thus "prevent the baneful influence of conflicting private interest."[12] A similar petition containing one hundred and forty signatures was sent from the residents of Calhoun County, in the second tier.[13]

At the same time, Detroit interests culminated a massive petition drive by sending a series of duplicate petitions to Congress. The original was headed by the name of John R. Biddle, and over four hundred signatures were attached to the copies. Requesting a land grant for a trans-peninsular railroad similar to that given to Illinois and Indiana, they pointed out:

> Your petitioners believe that the opinion is now nearly universal in the territory that a rail-road would be the preferable mode of connecting Lake Michigan with the waters of the Eastern side of the Peninsula.
>
> And further, that there is a well founded belief that a rail-road on the route would in connexion with a similar work uniting Chicago with the Illinois river become one of the great lines of travel between the Atlantic and the West.[14]

As 1833 rounded into 1834, excitement rose to a fever pitch. Notice was given in the Ann Arbor *Michigan Emigrant* of a forthcoming meeting concerning a railroad across the peninsula.[15] On January 13, Congress received the first of seven petitions, with duplicate headings, bearing over five hundred signatures of residents along the proposed route of the Detroit and St. Joseph railroad. Signatures on the several copies represented Comstock, Spring Arbor, Washtenaw, Grass Lake, Sandstone, and other towns in the out-state counties along the route. Since the petitioners requested a grant of land for the Detroit and St. Joseph, the drive was probably instigated by the Detroit and central tier interests.[16]

Late in 1833, a citizens committee asked Lewis Cass, who had recently been promoted from Governor to Secretary of War, if the federal government would make a railroad survey across the peninsula. Cass replied that government policy was to furnish an engineer and assistants, if those who had made the request would pay their services. Detroit newspapers applauded the committee's decision to accept the proposal.[17]

On January 8, 1834, Governor Porter sent his Annual Message to the Legislative Council, advising that the time was right to appeal for federal aid. Urging application for aid to improve the St. Joseph, Kalamazoo, Grand, and St. Clair Rivers, and the Fox-Green Bay route, he told the Council:

> A liberal provision has heretofore been made for works connected with the internal improvement of this territory. Is there any subject more worthy of their fostering care than the construction of this Rail Road? A large revenue is derived from the sale of public lands within this peninsula. Nature has prepared the ground, and the small expense which would be incurred in constructing a Rail Road, would soon be reimbursed by the increased amount of sales, and the numerous advantages that would result as well to the government as to individuals.
>
> May we not, therefore, reasonably ask the Federal government to construct this road;—forming as it does, so important a link in the chain of communication between the Atlantic and the Mississippi;—in which all the North, Northeast, and Western sections of the Union are so deeply interested?[18]

Porter was convinced, as were others of his day, that railroads could be inexpensively built and operated, as well as rapidly constructed. It appears that part of the enthusiasm for railroads was not only the speed of transportation and ability to harness motive power, but their apparent inexpensiveness in comparison to canals, whose costs could be approximated from the Erie Canal and others.

On the same day the Governor's message was delivered, southern interests met at Jonesville, in Hillsdale County, for the purpose of petitioning Congress for a trans-peninsular railroad through their section. Although the Convention claimed to be an impartial body "unshackled by local or sectional interests," only two of the thirty-four delegates were from the central tier. Sixteen were from Monroe, and the balance represented other southern tier counties. The Convention, presided over by Austin E. Wing, petitioned Congress to continue the chain of communication from New York to Lake Erie across the state, and to send a Corps of Engineers surveying team to examine the potential route. Since Detroit was at the northern end of the Detroit River at the foot of Lake St. Clair, the Convention was presumably endorsing a road from Monroe or Toledo when it specified a Lake Erie route.[19]

Following the Jonesville Convention, promotional efforts temporarily subsided. During the summer, the army engineering team requested by Detroit interests the previous summer arrived with instructions from the Secretary of War to survey a railroad route from Detroit to St. Joseph. In September, attempts by partisans of the central route to convince the Council of their responsibility to pay for the survey erupted into the first of many bitter sectional struggles within Michigan's legislative body.

Trouble developed when the young Acting Governor, Stevens T. Mason, asked the Council to appropriate territorial funds to finance the survey.[20] His suggestion precipitated a major legislative crisis, as representatives of the northern and southern sections vied for extension of the survey to their own districts. Although no single section was able to gain sufficient strength to pass the bill, voting revealed the existence, at this early date, of a northern-southern coalition to frustrate attempts by the Detroit-central tier interests to use their numerical superiority to advantage. Attempts to gain passage of a second survey from Monroe to Lake Michigan failed by a vote of five to five in the Council. In subsequent voting, members of the coalition failed to support each other in bids to endorse projects through other sections, but apparently retained sufficient strength to block passage of appropriations for the Detroit-St. Joseph route alone. Finally, the bill was referred to a select committee for further consideration.

The Legislative Council adjourned the same day the bill was assigned to committee, and although an adjourned session sat through November and December, the bill was not reported back.[21] Meanwhile, private forces were at work on a compromise to end the deadlock. A meeting was called in Detroit for December 24, to support efforts for a land grant railroad across the peninsula by petitioning throughout the Territory. In Ann Arbor and elsewhere, meetings were called to elect delegates to the Convention. The Ann Arbor *Whig* reported such a meeting, and passage of the following resolution:

Resolved, that we respectfully request the people of Monroe to send delegates to said meeting at Detroit on the 24th instant with a view to reconcile the conflicting interests of the different sections of the country in relation to the contemplated Rail Road, and thereby the better to ensure the success of our applications to Congress.

In return, they promised to work for passage of a Territorial Road from the bend of the River Raisin to Ann Arbor.[22]

On December 18, 1834, the federal surveyor John MacPherson Berrien, Jr., submitted his report. The route he had surveyed from Detroit to St. Joseph was reported favorable, with few obstacles. The surveyed line ran along the Chicago road to the forks of the River Rouge, where it turned to Dearborn and Ypsilanti. From there, it followed the valley of the Huron River to Ann Arbor, and the Territorial Road to Jackson. West of Jackson, the highest point of elevation was crossed four hundred and thirty-eight feet above the reference point at Detroit. Berrien was afraid of following either the valley of the Kalamazoo River or the ridge between it and the St. Joseph Valley, so he projected a line from Jackson to Prairie Ronde along the south slope of the ridge. The route had the advantage of crossing streams at their sources, thus avoiding costly bridging. The only steep grade was at the headwaters of the Paw Paw River, where Berrien recommended the use of an inclined plane. The total length of the surveyed route was one hundred and ninety-two miles, with no heavy embankments or cuts necessary. Most of the soil was solid enough to build on, but since there was no source of stone along the line, local timber would have to be used for the bed. Oak was abundant and available locally.[23]

On December 24, the Convention met in Detroit and elected John R. Biddle President. The Berrien report was endorsed and forwarded to Congress with a memorial asking for a grant of land to finance construction of the Detroit and St. Joseph, including a branch to Monroe and such other places as might be directed. Although the memorial argued that the route was central to the state and that Detroit offered more facilities to the traveler and businessman than any other place, the forces of reconciliation had won an apparent victory.[24]

On March 18, 1835, the select committee of the Legislative Council assigned to consider paying for the survey reported with a bill. Under the leadership of Daniel S. Bacon of Monroe, the committee expressed its concurrence with the suggestions of the Detroit Convention. A copy of Berrien's survey was placed in the library, "politely furnished" by John Biddle, and a statement from Biddle was attached and presented. The appropriations bill passed its first and second readings, and there the record ceases. There are other indications, however, that the bill passed and the Territory paid for the survey.[25]

The survey bill was the Legislative Council's final step toward a program of public works. Within six months of the bill's passage, the Council

Key to Map II

1. Detroit and Pontiac
2. Detroit and St. Joseph
3. Romeo and Mt. Clemens
4. Erie and Kalamazoo
5. Gibralter and Clinton
6. Detroit and Shelby
7. River Raisin and Grand River
8. Macomb and Saginaw
9. Detroit and Lake Erie
10. Maumee Branch
11. Shelby and Belle River
12. Monroe and Ypsilanti
13. Allegan and Marshall
14. Clinton and Adrian
15. St. Clair and Romeo
16. Palmyra and Jacksonburgh
17. Kalamazoo and Lake Michigan
18. Havre Branch
19. Monroe and Ann Arbor
20. River Raisin and Lake Erie
21. Constantine and Niles
22. Detroit and Shiawassee
23. Saginaw and Genesee
24. Port Sheldon and Grand Rapids

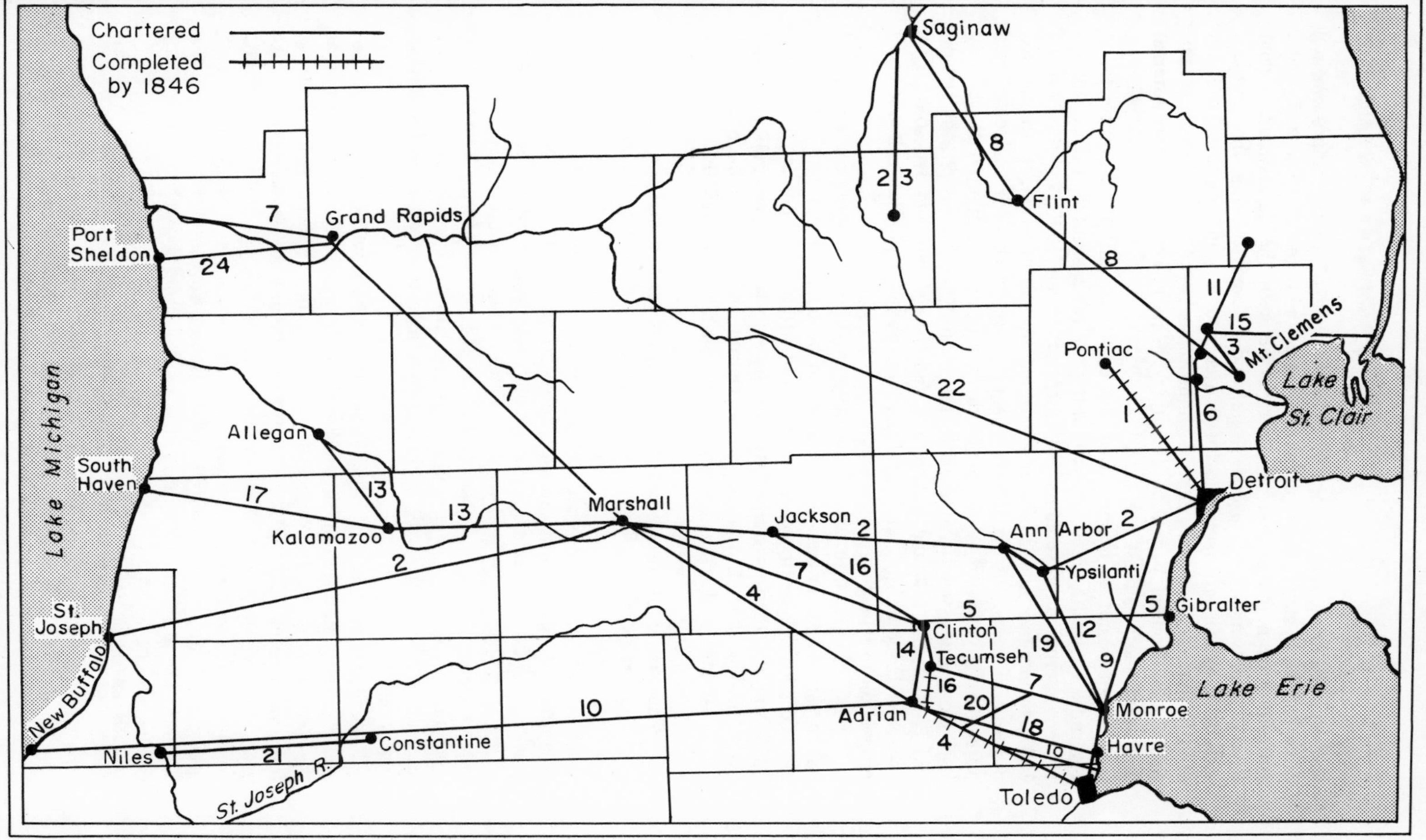

PRIVATE RAILROAD CHARTERS

MAP 2

was replaced by a state government. In the field of internal improvements, there had been many accomplishments under the Council. It had endorsed a railroad through the central tier, a canal between the Saginaw and Grand Rivers, improvement of several rivers, and a canal through the southern section. It appears to have paid for Berrien's survey, and approved the idea of government-sponsored internal improvements under a federal grant. Indeed, the Council had done everything in its power to promote internal improvements for almost a decade.

Although not as important as the efforts of citizens committees and government encouragement, private enterprise made significant contributions to the internal improvements movement. Between 1830 and the end of 1837, twenty-five railroads were chartered by the government. In the vast majority of cases, the records of the roads end with their charters. Seven were definitely started, and two more were possibly begun. Of these, only four showed any significant growth: the Detroit and St. Joseph; the Detroit and Pontiac; the Erie and Kalamazoo; and the Palmyra and Jacksonburg. A fifth, the River Raisin and Lake Erie, later played a political role out of all proportion to its actual achievements.

Early charters offered an interesting mixture of corporate privilege and public safeguards, several of which would become important in subsequent railroad policy. The first charter, given to the Detroit and Pontiac on July 31, 1830, was also the first granted west of the Appalachians, and was somewhat irregular. The second, granted to the Detroit and St. Joseph on June 29, 1832, assumed a standard form that was generally followed throughout the period.[26]

The charter of the Macomb and Saginaw, granted in the middle of the period, provides a typical example of charters issued before 1837.[27] The act appointed commissioners to open books for capital subscriptions, and specified the limits of capitalization and minimum subscription for beginning operations. A few charters allowed books to be opened "at such times and places as they shall direct," but usually, sale points were specified. Most often, stock had to be sold locally, at the terminal points and in important villages along the route. Acts allowing sale at Detroit or in the East were the exception. Apparently, promoters and legislators were neither willing nor anxious to allow "foreign" capital to dominate or profit from local transportation projects.

Deadlines were set for completion of sections as well as the entire road, under penalty of forfeiture. In addition, a provision, increasingly common as the period progressed, compelled any road that received net profits of fourteen percent to begin construction of subsequent sections within five years, or lose all profits above fourteen percent to the state. To facilitate construction, companies were given the right of eminent domain not only over right-of-way, but also over materials used for construction and maintenance. Local rights were protected by requiring a twelve-man jury for condemnation.

In all cases before 1837, the territory or state retained the right of purchase after a period of time, usually twenty years, for original cost plus fourteen percent. In 1836, a clause was added allowing state purchase at seven percent if the company had realized twelve percent profits on its investment. At a time when state enterprise was impossible because of territorial status, such provisions were probably regarded as public safeguards against abuses by a natural monopoly, while at the same time, granting monopoly privileges sufficient to attract private investment. This was the justification given by the Legislature for inserting a similar provision in the charter of the Michigan Central in 1846.[28] In the case of railroad-banks, where, under specified conditions reversion to the state became automatic, roads were to be operated by the state free of charge except for a toll sufficient to cover costs.[29]

In March 1835, the Legislative Council chartered two railroad-banks, and during the closing days of its last session, three existing charters were amended to include banking privileges. The group of five railroad-banks included the Detroit and Pontiac, the Erie and Kalamazoo, the Detroit and St. Joseph, the Macomb and Saginaw, and the River Raisin and Grand River.[30] The charters were a simple combination of standard banking and railroad charters, with a few special exceptions. Debts, excluding specie on deposit, were limited to three times the amount of paid-in capital. Notes were payable on demand or at sixty day's sight, on penalty of forfeiture of charter. In order to obtain a charter, the company was required to raise ten thousand dollars within two years, and to construct ten miles of road within six years. Until ten miles of road were constructed, fifty thousand dollars collateral was required on deposit with the State Treasurer to secure notes issued. In addition, the stock of the railroad was to be delivered to the bank as security for all notes and debts. When the roads were completed and had returned proceeds equal to costs, operating expenses, repairs, and a profit ranging from seven to fourteen percent, the road would revert to the state to be operated on tolls covering costs, and the bank would become a separate institution. The state also had the right of purchase included in almost all other railroad charters.

Railroad-banks, the final policy developed by the Legislative Council, were adopted in an attempt to induce investment through exploitation of the banking mania that followed in the wake of the Bank War. When the state failed to follow in step, it became a temporary departure, rather than a trend in railroad policy. There are no extant records of companies chartered by the state, if they ever existed at all. The only collection that survives consists of right-of-way quitclaims and a few business papers of little significance. Thus, it is impossible to evaluate the actual importance of banking privileges to these joint corporations. It is worth noting, however, that of the four roads with significant construction before 1846, three were chartered as railroad-banks: the Detroit and Pontiac; the Detroit and St. Joseph; and the Erie and Kalamazoo.

These three roads experienced their most signficant growth between assumption of statehood and formal admission into the Union. The Detroit and Pontiac was chartered in 1830 to "boom" Pontiac, and books were opened in February 1832, in the terminal cities.[31] Apparently, no significant capital subscriptions were raised. The charter had to be renewed in 1834, and banking privileges were added in 1835. Unable to raise capital in Michigan, the local promoters ventured to Buffalo, where they contacted Sherman Stevens, a former Michigan fur trader who had gone into business as a bill broker. The prospect of becoming a banker proved attractive to Stevens, who, although only able to raise five thousand dollars, managed to form a partnership with Alfred Williams and gain control of another similar amount. Arriving in Pontiac in May 1835, with ten thousand dollars in coin, Stevens began banking operations and realized a profit of thirty thousand dollars the first year.[32] At the same time, work began between Detroit and Royal Oak. Unlike the roads northeast of Detroit, the railroad bed was kept dry by elevation and ditching. Two horses hauled three tons or twenty-four passengers over oak rails for a dollar per passenger or fifty cents per hundred weight of freight. At these rates, earnings were sufficient to finance construction as far as Birmingham, where the soil proved too soft for solid footing, and right-of-way difficulties developed. Stevens later claimed that farmers refused to sell necessary land through fear that local markets would be damaged by imported grain, and that each farm that was crossed required a separate condemnation suit. Stevens was defensive about the charges, claiming that under his management the cost of transporting a barrel of flour from Pontiac to Detroit dropped from one dollar to eighteen cents, doubling the value of local farm lands. By 1838, business had increased to the point that rails were being crushed, and money good in the East was necessary for strap iron and a locomotive. A loan of one hundred thousand dollars was secured from the Legislature, and combined with a similar amount from the State of Indiana. With this money, iron and a locomotive were procured, and the road was completed to Pontiac in 1843. The railroad itself was a financial success until 1839, when failure of its bank drove it into insolvency.[33]

The Erie and Kalamazoo was chartered in 1833, to run from Toledo to the navigable waters of the Kalamazoo River. Construction was undertaken by a group of investors from Lenawee County, Toldeo, and New York, and the road was completed to Adrian in 1836.[34] For the first year it operated as a horse-drawn road on oak rails, but in 1837, strap iron rails and a locomotive were added. Total costs were reported to the state as $300,000, with net earnings of $15,804, or, slightly over five percent.[35] The Erie and Kalamazoo never attempted to build beyond Adrian, but contributed to the construction of the Palmyra and Jacksonburg as far as Tecumseh, for use as a branch.[36] It was content to drain traffic from Lenawee and Jackson Counties, and the milling centers around Clinton and Manchester. When Toledo was officially transferred to Ohio, the road changed from the pride of the southern tier into a "foreign corporation." It was a constant source of irritation to the state, draining trade from Michigan merchants to those in the "foreign port" of Toledo, and substantial revenues from the Southern. In

1849, the track was leased to the Michigan Southern in perpetuity, for an annual rental of thirty thousand dollars, and became a major component linking the Lake Shore and Michigan Southern and, later, the New York Central.[37]

The Detroit and St. Joseph, chartered in 1832 to cross the peninsula, received little financial support despite a central position in the campaign for internal improvements. Advocates of the route were content to petition the federal government privately and through the Legislative Council. Construction began only when state aid or purchase seemed· imminent. There are at least three plausible and conflicting accounts of its beginning, but none is documented.[38]

The project had been supported since 1833 by a group of Detroit businessmen, apparently led by John R. Biddle, clerk of the Detroit land office, who was elected President when the charter was finally taken up after the federal survey.[39] Actual construction was delayed until sectional rivalry and the certainty of state aid or purchase spurred supporters to commit themselves financially. The Ann Arbor *Michigan Whig* ran two articles in 1835, encouraging its readers to subscribe to the road. The second, reviewing progress on the Erie and Kalamazoo, complained that: "The people of Monroe and Lenawee have gone before us in enterprise. The work in progress there will draw the trade of the Western counties to Toledo unless communication with Detroit is made equally easy."[40] Estimating the cost of the road to Ann Arbor at one hundred thousand dollars, they speculated that completion would add seventy-five percent to the value of property along the route. Similar statements appeared in the Detroit papers.[41] A more powerful stimulus was provided by a joint resolution of the State Legislature in July 1836, authorizing the Governor to receive proposals from the Detroit and St. Joseph and other railroads to surrender their charters. Biddle replied to Mason's inquiry in August, reporting that he could not give a definite answer without a stockholders meeting, but that he was sure they would agree because their purpose was to secure the work's completion.[42] By May 1837, when the state assumed control of the road, the company had cleared and grubbed a hundred foot right-of-way from Detroit to Ypsilanti, graded thirteen miles, laid mud sills for ten miles, and placed iron on the first two miles. Total cost was reported at over one hundred and sixteen thousand dollars.[43] Through its efforts, and the cession of Toledo to Ohio, Detroit had gained two years in its battle with the southern section.

Public demand for improved transportation was also reflected in the rash of railroad charters granted during the speculative bubble that enveloped Michigan between 1835 and 1837. Growing in part from national fiscal and banking policies, and from conditions in the international capital market, the bubble was magnified in Michigan by an influx of settlers and speculators eager to buy up public lands in the rapidly developing area. During its peak in 1836, when over four million acres of public lands were sold, speculative frenzy reached a pitch that came to be described as the "Michigan Fever." One speculator, John M. Gordon, was attracted to the state in the summer of 1836, by reports in the East. Even before he left Baltimore, Gordon had heard that lands taken at a dollar and a quarter doubled in price as soon as they were purchased from the government. Land patents, he understood, were three years in arrears, and offices so crowded that people would buy land second hand outside the office for fear of not getting in to file. He had even heard of an eighty-acre plot at the rapids of the Grand River that had been purchased for one hundred dollars and sold for forty-thousand dollars, and was afraid that by the end of the year, all of the good lands would be gone.[44]

Turnerian historians have taken great pains to describe the stages of the western movement. After the hunter and trapper came the squatter-speculator, living on lands he did not own in hope of selling his improvements. He was followed by the speculator who bought up quantities of desirable land to sell at a profit, and the farm maker who, with his small capital, carved a homestead on his own land in the wilderness. Finally, the big farmer bought out the farm makers and established large-scale, commercial agriculture. In Michigan, the stages were compressed between 1830 and 1837 into a single, fevered movement, as the farmer accompanied the speculator and the squatter into the forest to replace played-out or marginal lands in the East. The individual who purchased a parcel of land for himself, and another for speculation or his sons, participated with zeal in the growing land bubble. As Lanman phrased it, "The habitudes of thought connected with the constantly advancing value of real property; the custom of *'dickering'* makes almost every individual a speculator."[45] According to Gordon, every farmer he met along the Territorial Road knew the current market value of his land and could quote the price that would induce him to sell and move on. Speculators on all levels staked their fortunes against advancing land prices, a movement that could be continued only with the development of local markets, or transportation to distant markets, for the products of commercial agriculture.

Equally as important as the farm maker and the speculator in creating demand for improved transportation, was the town site and its promoter, the town "boomer." Reflecting on the living patterns of New Englanders and New Yorkers, Gordon was temporarily infected with enthusiasm for the potential of town sites, and observed that:

> If one considers that Michg. has now none or few towns, that its population is pouring in at the rate of 50 thousand a year, that they have been accustomed to and must have their villages, that the soil is of excellent quality generally, it will be perceived that these town speculations have a real basis of intrinsic value & are not like investment in town plats in old states, where the wants of the people have been supplied in this particular gradually with their slow growth. Suppose New York without towns & villages tomorrow, that all are sunk by an earth quake. The wants of the people would soon build them up again with great rapidity—such on much smaller scale is the process of town manufacture now going on in Michg.[46]

Although Gordon's southern agrarian prejudices kept him from engaging in town lot speculation, there were others who were willing. Speculators and surveyors "cruising" the Territory looked not only for fertile soil and location, but for sites with water power where towns could be platted. After filing on the land, a grist mill and a saw mill would be erected, a general store built, and a bank chartered, promising settlers a continuation of services customary in the East. Every addition enhanced the value of the platted towns and adjacent farms. Ambitious promoters added a railroad charter to their list of inducements. At Port Sheldon, the grandiose speculation of Alexander Jaudon and a group of eastern capitalists on Lake Michigan, at the mouth of the Pigeon River, a fortune was invested in the projected commercial metropolis. In addition to the usual inducements, the promoters added a hotel and chartered a railroad to Grand Rapids. Two miles of the road were cleared and grubbed, ties laid, and a depot with Greek columns was built to service future traffic.[47] Another speculation, Biddle City, was laid out between the junction of the Grand and Red Cedar Rivers. After the promoters had cruised and platted the city (there is some question whether they bothered to purchase the land), they returned to New York and sold a substantial number of lots.[48] Before they left, however, they stopped at Detroit to amend the charter of the Detroit and Shiawassee Railroad, and extend it to Biddle City.[49]

In many people's minds, the acquisition of a railroad charter added real value to property, even without actual construction. Lucius Lyon, Michigan's congressional delegate and one of the state's richest land speculators, advised a friend not to sell his land at Mount Clemens at the price offered because the Legislative Council had granted a railroad charter through it to some point west, and the charter increased the value of the property. In his own promotions, Lyon, who seems to have owned most of the strategic land in the Grand River Valley, engaged in transportation projects to enhance the value of his property. It was Lyon's land that Gordon had been discussing at the rapids of the Grand River, where he and Isaac Crary sold one hundred and forty-five town lots between 1836 and 1839, for $106,156. Lyon also held the town site, modestly named after him, at the junction of the Maple and Grand Rivers.[50] Because his land was on navigable water, Lyon tried to increase its value by underwriting half the expense of a canal around the rapids, and by building a steamboat to navigate the Grand River.[51] When his fortunes collapsed during the Depression, he lobbied in the Legislature for completion of the Northern Railroad to restore the value of his holdings.[52]

Speculation was also rampant in established commercial centers, when it became apparent that transportation projects would be undertaken and trade would course through the ports. Early in 1836, a speculative mania reportedly swept Monroe, with town lots changing hands rapidly, and corner lots selling for two or three thousand dollars. In Detroit, part of the Cass farm adjacent to the city was sold for one hundred and seventy-five thousand dollars, and most of the money was invested in banks and railroads in the state.[53]

It can be misleading to draw general principles from a few specific examples, but events in Michigan during this period tend to support the conclusions of Paul Gates concerning the basic nature of American farmers.[54] The settlers who went west in the 1830's were not frontiersmen in a classic sense, but commercial farmers attempting to salvage economic positions threatened by the opening of more efficient lands in the West by the Erie Canal. In locating their farms in the wilderness, adequate facilities linking them with the market, or the promise of such facilities in the immediate future, was a consideration as important as the fertility of the soil itself. This importance is reflected in the inclusion of railroad charters in the list of social services provided by town promoters.

In a recent study, *American Railroads and the Transformation of the Ante-Bellum Economy,* Albert Fishlow points to the central role played by "anticipatory settlement" in the growth of railroads.[55] Fishlow suggests transportation improvements that breached the Appalachian barrier westward, created settlement in the path of potential routes. Anticipation of improvements, projected along either a specific route or through a general region, actually laid the foundation for the construction of profitable transportation projects. He maintains, however, that the pattern was more prevalent in the 1850s than in the 1830s. Michigan's experience seems to deny this.

When the Erie Canal was opened, it became obvious to residents of the Territory that some form of cross-peninsular project would probably be undertaken to shorten the distance of the northern transportation route and eliminate the hazards of the Mackinac passage. This supposition underlies petitions submitted to Congress for railroad and canal projects between 1825 and 1834, and is usually given as a basic argument in favor of government support. However, anticipatory settlement failed to develop during those years. To a limited extent, the motive was probably operative in the concentration of settlement in the seaboard counties of Wayne and Monroe, and the immediately adjacent counties of Lenawee, Washtenaw, and Oakland, in preference to the equally fertile Saginaw Valley. However, settlement to the northwest of Detroit and in the St. Joseph Valley seems to support the argument that anticipatory settlement was not the dominant motive as late as 1834.

Appendices II and III indicate a transformation of settlement patterns between 1834 and 1837. In 1834, settlement in both the central and southern tiers declined toward the interior counties, and increased again in the west as the distance to Lake Michigan diminished. The low level of settlement in the extreme western counties bordering Lake Michigan can be attributed to poor soil quality. In 1837, however, while the southern tier continued to follow earlier patterns, population in the interior counties of the second tier increased substantially. Settlement in the third and fourth tiers continued to follow the pattern of the southern, declining toward the center of the state and increasing again as the counties approached Lake Michigan. In the central tier, along the surveyed route of the Detroit and St. Joseph, population growth was so heavy in the interior counties that population density waɔ greater than in western counties closer to Lake Michigan.

The changing pattern of settlement in the central tier is significant because settlers had easier access to the southern tier along the federally constructed Chicago Road, a major traffic artery, than along Territorial Road, which had been haphazardly constructed by local governments. The construction of the Detroit and Pontiac, and the Erie and Kalamazoo Railroads accounts for the heavy settlement in the first and third tiers in Oakland and Lenawee Counties during the same period. After the announcement of a federal survey through the central tier, the rate of settlement grew substantially. At least part of this pattern may be attributable to the clerk of the Detroit Land Office, John R. Biddle, who was also the head of the Detroit railroad interests, and in a position with potential for creating "anticipatory settlement." Such evidence suggests, but cannot confirm, a process of anticipatory settlement. The period is too short, and other factors influenced the pattern of settlement. In terms of fertility, however, the land in the southern tier was as highly regarded as any in the state, particularly the land of the St. Joseph Valley. The statistical evidence would be more credible if the time span were longer and events had moved at a slower pace.

Impressionistic evidence, with all its limitations, seems to substantiate the conclusions indicated by Appendix II. John M. Gordon, the land speculator, was acutely aware of the railroad's potential in developing land value, and observed the effects of efforts to build west from Detroit in 1836. Gordon thought the peninsula would become one of the granaries of the country. "When the railroad to St. Joseph from Detroit is finished, immigrants will pour in, and the improvement of the former advance with rapid strides thence forward. The first 30 miles of this road will be completed next spring, if work goes as fast as is expected."[56] Gordon's cruising took him down Territorial Road, through the central tier, and along the route of the Detroit and St. Joseph. At every town he was told the railroad would soon be coming through. He was impressed with the slow graduation of the land, and the small cost at which railroads could be built. In Jackson County, he found all the good lands taken up, and to the west, around Marshall, most of the land was already located, even though settlement was thin. Town lots were selling for one to five hundred dollars because both the Detroit and St. Joseph, and the Maumee Railroads were to pass through the town. Even at the western end of the central tier, in Van Buren county, he found the railroad increasing land values, along with the facilities of the Paw Paw River. He regarded the land in the interior of the central tier as having been "settled *thickly* 4 or 5 years."[57] Gordon's observations as a land speculator indicate residents were keenly aware of the potential effects of the railroad on property values. Anticipatory settlement can explain the surge of population into the interior of the central tier when other factors, such as soil fertility and the presence of roads and rivers, cannot. There can be little doubt that settlement was strongly influenced by the probability of a railroad from Detroit to St. Joseph. This does not contradict Fishlow's general hypothesis, but it does suggest that the commercial nature of the American farmer was as strong a factor in location in the 1830s as it was in the 1850s, and that anticipatory settlement could develop at this early date.

It is doubtful, in fact, whether the designation "frontier railroad" strictly applied to the Detroit and St. Joseph, even at its beginning in 1836. Half a century later, investors who took the roads over from the state remembered breathing new life into a broken-down strap iron track through virgin wilderness, and bringing population and civilization to the frontier. State historians have been too quick to accept these generalizations. The census of 1837 suggests that the frontier, in the officially designated sense of an area with a population of two per square mile, had long disappeared, and that the concentration was approaching ten per square mile in the western central tier. The same census reveals that all the counties of the central tier, except Wayne, which did not report, and the sand hills of Van Buren County, produced over a hundred thousand bushels of wheat that year.[58] Instead of "frontier," a more adequate description would be "moderately developed."

Between 1825 and 1837, a strong public demand for transportation improvement developed in Michigan. The Legislative Council had done everything within its limited power to persuade Congress to subsidize programs, and to secure transportation facilities from private enterprise. Private capital, however, proved incapable of sustaining projects on anything but a limited basis. Meanwhile, the efforts of public and private groups created an illusion of imminent construction that led to heavy settlement along the path of the Detroit and St. Joseph, and financial commitment to farms and villages on other chartered routes. As the crisis over statehood developed during the land bubble of 1835-1836, the fortunes of most of Michigan's farmers, villagers, and merchants were staked on a continuing increase in property values. This movement could only be sustained through the immediate construction of canals and railroads.

Notes, Chapter 4

1. *Territorial Papers*, XL, 131 ff.
2. *Ibid.*, 1163-1164.
3. *Ibid.*, 1190.
4. *Ibid.*, XII, 12.
5. *Ibid.*, 102 ff.
6. *Messages of the Governors of Michigan*, I, 48.
7. Gerald M. Reagan, "The State Railroad Program in Michigan as a Public Issue, 1834-1846," (Unpublished master's thesis, Department of History, Western Michigan University), p. 6.
8. Michigan, *Journal of the Legislative Council*, 4th Council, 1st Sess., 1830, 127-128.
9. *Territorial Papers*, XII, 254.
10. *Ibid.*, 1031-1032.

11. *Ibid.,* 365 ff. The committee included John R. Williams, Andrew Mack, Charles Larned, A. D. Frasier, John Biddle, Oliver Newberry, Marshall Chapin, E. P. Hastings, T. H. Rowland, D. G. Jones, James Abbott, Reynolds Gilett, Ralph Wadhams, Henry V. Disbrow, and Levi Cook.
12. *Territorial Papers,* XII, 621-625.
13. *Ibid.,* 626.
14. *Ibid.,* 656.
15. *Michigan Emigrant* (Ann Arbor), December 12, 1833.
16. *Territorial Papers,* XII, 688-690.
17. Reagan, p. 8.
18. *Messages of the Governors of Michigan,* I, 104.
19. *Territorial Papers,* XII, 688-690.
20. *Messages of the Governors of Michigan,* I, 123.
21. Michigan, *Journal of the Legislative Council,* 6th Council, Extra Session, 1834, pp. 14-16, 132.
22. *Michigan Whig* (Ann Arbor), December 11, 1834.
23. *Territorial Papers,* XII, 825 ff. A negative photocopy of the survey map is available in the special collections of the University of Michigan Transportation Library.
24. *Territorial Papers,* XII, 850 ff.
25. Michigan, *Journal of the Legislative Council,* 6th Council, Extra Session, 1835, p. 132.
26. See Appendix IV. With a few significant exceptions, charters were similar to those granted by other states in the pioneer railroad era. Taylor, pp. 86-94.
27. Michigan, *Territorial Laws,* IV, 124-134.
28. Michigan, Legislature, "Report of the Select Committee on the Sale of Works of Internal Improvement upon Introducing a Bill for the Sale of the Central Railroad" (*House Documents,* 1846, H. D. No. 2), pp. 1-6. Cited hereafter as *House Document No. 2, 1846.*
29. Michigan, *Territorial Laws,* III, 1387 ff, sec. 18.
30. *Ibid.,* III, 1392 ff, 1387 ff; IV, 112 ff, 124 ff, 142 ff.
31. *Democratic Free Press,* (Detroit), February 10, 1832; Catlin, p. 364.
32. Sherman Stevens, "Continuation of Early Days in Genesee County," *Michigan Pioneer and Historical Collections,* VIII (1884), 394 ff.
33. Buley, II, 313.
34. Letter of A. J. Comstock to J. A. Barker, April 18, 1836, in Jacob A. Barker Papers (Michigan Historical Collections, Ann Arbor).
35. Michigan, Legislature, "Report of the Erie & Kalamazoo Railroad" (*House Documents,* 1841, II, H. D. No. 40) pp. 149-150.
36. Clarence Frost, "The Early Railroads of Southern Michigan," *Michigan Pioneer and Historical Collections,* XXXVII (1913), 498-501.
37. Buley, II, 313; W. C. Ransom, "Address in the Senate Chamber," *Semi-Centennial Addresses,* p. 187.
38. There are at least three conflicting accounts of the sources of investment in the Detroit and St. Joseph Railroad, none of which have any evidence to support them. According to Arthur S. Hill, "The Romance of a Railway," *Michigan History,* XXIII (1939), 58-59, $50,000 was contributed by the city of Detroit, in essence making it a quasi-municipal railroad. Alvin F. Harlow, *The Road of the Century: The Story of the New York Central* (New York: Creative Press, 1947), pp. 213-214, in what is apparently a company history says that the money was raised by stock subscription, $9000 in Ann Arbor, $70,000 in Detroit, and $100,000 in Ypsilanti. Finally, according to George Bates, "By-gones of Detroit," *Michigan Pioneer and Historical Collections,* XXII (1893), 248, Lewis Cass, John Biddle, and two others each subscribed $25,000, and large subscriptions were made by Trowbridge, Newberry, Jones, Shubael Conant, and Major Whiting. None of these accounts has any documentation, and the Burton Historical Collections has lost documents in their custody relating to the Detroit and St. Joseph. I favor the

Bates version because it is supported by more facts than any of the others.

39. Nicholas Biddle's brother.

40. *Michigan Whig and Washtenaw Democrat* (Ann Arbor), July 2, 1835; July 15, 1835.

41. *Detroit Journal and Courier,* July 8, 1835; July 15, 1835; and the *Detroit Daily Advertiser,* July 6, 1835; August 5, 1835; December 28, 1835; as cited in Reagan, pp. 14-16.

42. Michigan, *Legislative Acts,* 1836, p. 150; Michigan, Legislature, "John Biddle to Stevens T. Mason, August 8, 1836" (*Senate Documents,* 1837, S. D. No. 1), p. 1.

43. Michigan, Legislature, "Annual Report of the Board of Internal Improvements, 1838" (*Senate Documents,* 1838, S. D. No. 11), p. 161.

44. Gordon, *Michigan History,* XLIII (1959), 4-12.

45. Lanman, p. 299.

46. Gordon, *Michigan History,* XLIII (1959), 448-449.

47. Catlin, p. 349; Buley, II, 89; Ralph Meima, "A Forgotten City," *Michigan History,* V, (1921), 296 ff. None of these sources are highly accurate, although the vague outlines of the speculation at Port Sheldon are apparent. The speculation and the involvement of eastern capital, particularly the role of the BUS, deserves further investigation.

48. Samuel W. Durrant, *History of Ingham and Eaton Counties, Michigan* (Philadelphia: D. W. Ensign and Company, 1880), p. 122.

49. Michigan, *Legislative Acts, 1837-1838,* No. 106.

50. Gordon, *Michigan History,* XLIII (1959), 12, n. 21; Letter from Lucius Lyon to Edward Lyon, Feb. 24, 1836; Letter from Lucius Lyon to Arthur Bronson, Jan. 8, 1836, in "Letters of Lucius Lyon," *Michigan Pioneer and Historical Collections,* XXVII (1896), 471, 481. Cited hereafter as Lyon Papers, *MP&HC,* XXVII.

51. Letter from Lucius Lyon to Lucretia Lyon, Oct. 9, 1835, *Ibid.,* 449-450.

52. Letter from Lucius Lyon to Gen. Burdick, Feb. 2, 1838, *Ibid.,* 502.

53. Frank Woodford, *Lewis Cass: The Last Jeffersonian* (New Brunswick, N. J.: Rutgers University Press, 1950) p. 191; Letter from J. Q. Adams to Alpheus Felch, Jan. 10, 1836, in the Alpheus Felch Papers (Michigan Historical Collections, Ann Arbor, Mich.). Cited hereafter as Felch Papers (MHC).

54. Paul Gates, *The Farmer's Age: Agriculture, 1815-1860,* Vol. III of the *Economic History of the United States,* ed. Henry David and Others, 9 vols. (New York: Rinehart & Company, Inc., 1960), p. 400.

55. Fishlow, pp. 165-166.

56. Gordon, *Michigan History,* XLIII (1959), 435.

57. *Ibid.,* 143, 260, 262, 269-273.

58. *Michigan Census of 1837,* in Lanman, pp, 301 ff.

5

THE DECISION TO BUILD

By the time Michigan was admitted into the Union, the demand for internal improvement had developed into a strong movement. The Erie Canal had opened the way to market, and the Territorial Roads had opened the land. As settlement increased and a marketable surplus developed, pressure for improved transportation increased. Under the leadership of commercial groups in coastal cities eager to develop an interior market and tap the growing trade between New York and the Mississippi Valley, Congress was repeatedly petitioned by the people and the Legislative Council. In the decade preceding statehood, the Council put its stamp of approval on nearly all of the major projects embodied in the Omnibus Bill of 1837. Official sanction and private attempts to begin construction led to anticipatory settlement, which, in turn, increased public expectations and reinforced demands. At the same time, the sectional rivalry plaguing the state throughout its program became a major political force. Even before 1835, when it was checked by a temporary truce, the rivalry between commercial centers was so strong that Detroit's opponent was referred to as the "independent state of Monroe."[1]

Despite the intensity of petitioning and lobbying, federal aid was neither fast enough nor in sufficient volume to satisfy local ambitions. Road-building was slow, no money was appropriated for repairs, and the canal at Monroe was far from completion. Under these conditions, and a more abstract desire for political equality, pressure mounted for statehood and the exploitation of a developing region it would provide. A systematic program of internal improvements was the most important objective of Michigan's citizens in their seizure of statehood. The Omnibus Bill of 1837 was the culmination of a single movement in which other events played a secondary and subordinate role.

The Northwest Ordinance provided that:

> There shall be formed in the said territory, not less than three nor more than five states....And, whenever any of the said states shall have sixty thousand free inhabitants therein, *such State shall be admitted, by its delegates, into the Congress of the United States, on an equal footing with the original States in all respects whatever,* and shall be at liberty to form a permanent constitution and state government; *Provided...*so far as it can be consistent with the general interest of the confederacy, such admission shall be allowed at an earlier period, and when there may be a less number of free inhabitants in the State than sixty thousand.[2]

Residents of the Territory took the provisions of the Ordinance literally, thinking statehood was a right when population reached the requisite sixty thousand. The equality clause was construed to mean that, in addition to political parity, federal aid for internal improvements and other projects would be awarded in quantities sufficient to create retroactive equality.

The results of the 1830 Census were disappointing; only thirty-one thousand inhabitants were reported. The influx of population in the next two years, however, convinced the Council the time had come to petition Congress for a constitutional enabling act. Unfortunately, the request was shelved in Washington because of congressional reluctance to become involved in the volatile Ohio boundary dispute.[3] For the next two years, while strong political organizations were forming in Michigan, Congress turned a deaf ear to pleas from the Territory, and weakened the control of moderates in the developing Democratic Party.

A recent study of party formation in Jacksonian America by Richard P. McCormick, provides a more meaningful analytical vehicle than the obsolete debtor-farmer analysis of Michigan by Floyd Streeter.[4] Instead of concentrating on the stated issues and differences of parties and their leaders, McCormick focuses on the emergence of organizational techniques and procedures. After studying the development of political parties in every state admitted into the Union before 1824, he concludes that party structure grew neither from a polarization of attitudes on specific issues, nor from congressional cleavages, and that it did not represent a revival of party alignments preceding the era of good feeling. The party system emerged from successive presidential contests between 1824 and 1840, and was governed primarily by regional identification with the candidates. McCormick believes the two-party system was unique in American experience because of its "balanced" and "artificial" nature. It produced parties of nearly equal strength in every region, and could survive only by avoiding regionally devisive issues.[5] What the study implicitly suggests is that party struggle in the Jacksonian era was essentially a contest between similar groups divided by the possession and lack of power. More succinctly, it was a struggle between the "ins" and "outs" in a patronage-oriented party system.

Between 1833 and 1835, Michigan was essentially what McCormick has characterized as a "no-party system," with parties beginning to develop. Federal elections and issues were of little importance when only non-voting delegates could be sent to the national capital. Political contests within the Territory were usually personal and factional and lacked party overtones, although the territory was governed by appointees of the Democracy and was generally Democratic. Two letters from Stevens T. Mason (then Territorial Secretary) to his father give brief insight into the developing party system and factions within the party. An apparent rift of indeterminate nature had developed between the Secretary and the Governor. Mason reported that neither he nor the Governor had yielded an inch and, apparently, were not on speaking terms. The Governor, he told his father, had alienated everyone in the Territory by refusing to either sign or veto some favored measure. At the same time, attempts were in the making to tighten the organization of the party:

> The approaching contest for the election of Delegate bids fair to be warm and bitter, but not closely contested. "The Democratic Republican Convention" as they style themselves, which met at Ann Arbour, as was anticipated nominated Lucius Lyon as their candidate, and intended making the support of him the test of every mans faith and principles. The presumption of this little faction would almost provoke one, if it were not that their assumption of consequence has made them rediculous [sic]. The unfortunate people of Michigan have set over them a Regency more formidable than the famous Albany Regency itself, and have only to bow their necks and be trampled on by Andrew Mack, David C. McKinstry, John P. Sheldon and Elliott Gray.
>
> The Ann Arbour convention has constituded [sic] those gentlemen a committee to regulate all appointments, whether comming [sic] from the Executive of the United States or the Territory, and have proclaimed to the world that no man can receive an office in this Territory, without first receiving the Sanction of this Committee, and procuring from them an endorsement that he is a "true Democrat dyed in the Wool."

Mason reported that Wing, who had served six terms as delegate, was making a strong bid, but that the Ann Arbor convention had been so cut and dried, that he was defeated with only two votes in his favor. The Secretary was confident, however, that nomination of a candidate by the Anti-masons on March 10, would split the factions and insure Wing's election.[6]

On April 16, Mason reported that the Anti-masons had nominated William Woodbridge, a move that hurt Wing by attracting the opposition. Woodbridge, later the Whig Governor, was not running as an Anti-mason, but as an independent. From this, Mason decided that Woodbridge wanted to represent someone besides the people who had elected him. Wing's friends, unable to hold a convention, were trying to nominate him through county meetings.[7]

The significance of Mason's observations lay in the revelation of a tightening party organization in the Territory. Factional splits were nothing new. Austin Wing, the sheriff of Monroe County, was a perennial candidate and leader of a personal faction. Elections of delegates had often meant bitter struggles between opposing candidates. For the first time, however, the Democracy was attempting to build a party structure that controlled not only elections, but federal and local appointments. Of equal significance is the fact that the convention, held in the central tier, nominated a candidate from the western part of the state, signifying the growing political power of the region. Mason, who seems to have favored Wing, was apparently outside the confines of the newly organized party at this point. Whig organizational efforts began about the same time, for, early in January 1835, George Corselius reported to Woodbridge that Washtenaw County was in the party fold and subordinate to the central committee, and that efforts would be concentrated on building political machinery in Oakland County.[8]

Despite efforts to unify the parties, the struggle for statehood caused internal dissension within the Democracy and brought it to the brink of dissolution. Liberal Democrats, led by Mason, John Norvell, James Doty, John R. Williams, and Ross Wilkins, were anxious for admission and strongly in favor of democratic reform. A second faction, led by Robert McClelland, Lucius Lyon, Edward Ellis, Elijah Cook, Ralph Wadhams, and John Clark, opposed any course of action leading to a break with the Jackson Administration. In the ensuing struggle, Lyon's absence in Washington and his failure to pass an enabling act, combined with the death of Governor Porter and the succession of Stevens T. Mason, weakened conservative control of the party.[9]

During the crisis over statehood, internal improvements never became a devisive issue either between or within parties. The truce negotiated early in 1835 quieted sectional rivalries until 1837, and the basic consensus that a program should be undertaken was reflected by the absence of controversy. Issues dividing the parties and factions centered on the method of acquiring statehood and the extension of suffrage. The same unanimity was displayed in Michigan's opposition to Ohio's claim on Toledo, an important part of internal improvement plans. As William Woodbridge, leader of the Whigs, stated on two separate occasions: "No complex proposition was ever perhaps presented for the consideration of a *whole people*, in respect to which there was so little Diversity of Opinion, as, that, as regarded the obnoxious claim of Ohio to the disputed Country...."[10] The reason, he told Daniel Webster, was: "The comprehension is the Miami Bay is considered indispensable to our future importance & prosperity—It constituted *our Only* harbor on Lake Erie—The statute books and acts of congressional appropriation may indeed show some colors for the pretext that La Plaisance Bay & the Mouth of the River Raisin May furnish a harbor there—but that is only on paper—Nothing can compensate us for the loss of Miami Bay."[11] Throughout the struggle for statehood, internal improvement was never lost from sight, even when factions differed over the means of policy implementation.

When the Legislative Council met in special session in September 1834, they took the first steps toward statehood. The new Acting Governor's address to the Council was forceful. He told them statehood was a right, not a privilege, and that if Congress would not extend the right, they must seize it. He recommended a census, followed by a constitutional convention. The Council authorized the census and adjourned.[12] At the same session, the question of paying for the survey of the Detroit and St. Joseph was introduced. When the Legislative Council met again in January 1835, they came to grips with the problem of statehood. In his message to the session, Mason repeated his arguments supporting Michigan's right to statehood and warned them not to "barter away their sovereignty by accepting five per cent of federal land revenues and a land grant in exchange for the Toledo strip." The grant and the five percent funds were the state's by right, supposedly awarded by the provision of the Northwest Ordinance granting

equality to newly admitted states.[13] On January 26, 1835, the Council
passed its own constitutional enabling act.[14]

Between passage of the enabling act and the constitutional convention,
the "Toledo War," as it came to be known, reached a climax. The location
of the port, with its access to the Maumee and the canals being planned by
Ohio and Indiana, as well as the railroad serving the southern tier, made it
central to the state's economic future, and its loss was a severe blow. The
marching of militia and hurling of insults kept the Territory in a state of
excitement that was high even for Jacksonian America in the midst of a
speculative bubble. Frightened by the turbulence among the people, Woodbridge's Whig lieutenants predicted that the will of the people would lead to
mob rule, and that events would seize control of the movement's leaders.[15]
Ultimately, however, the young Acting Governor's resolute actions in dealing
with the national government raised him to new peaks of popularity and
strengthened the liberals' control of the government. As Woodbridge phrased
it: "The puerile extravagancies of our Young Secretary, (then acting Govr)
were proofs of patriotism & high honor!—& he, & his Magnus Apollo, were
wafted together into high favour, by the storm of passion that swept over
the country!"[16]

On April 4, 1835, eighty-nine delegates were elected to the constitutional convention. Under the provisions of the enabling act, aliens, as well as
citizens, were permitted to vote, and Woodbridge suggests that many people
were so disgusted that they boycotted the polls.[17] Only ten or twelve Whigs
were elected. The remaining delegates were equally divided between the
liberal and conservative wings of the Democracy. At a convention held in
January, the Democrats had laid down the lines of the upcoming struggle,
focusing attention on the problems of immediate statehood and free white
male suffrage.[18] When the constitutional convention met, it appears that the
two wings of the Democracy were as divided as the two parties on the
question of alien suffrage.[19] Unable to cooperate within the party, the
convention was forced to elect a Whig, John Biddle, as president. The rift
was so deep that the leader of the conservatives, Lucius Lyon, doubted it
could ever be healed.[20]

Once assembled, the convention became a revolutionary body. Since the
Legislative Council had only the authority to recommend, the convention
regarded itself as the representative of the people, directly elected and free
to define its own jurisdiction. Seizing authority, it appropriated money,
remodeled the capital, and authorized elections for ratification. The convention even went so far as to attempt a compact with the federal government
on the disposal of public lands within the Territory.[21]

The convention that met in May proved too bulky to proceed with the
business of drafting a constitution, and a committee was appointed to write
the rough draft. The committee, in turn, proved unwieldy, and the first draft
was finally drawn up in secret session by five men headed by Edward Ellis
of Monroe. Their draft was unanimously accepted by the committee and
submitted to the convention on May 19.[22] Between then and adjournment

on June 24, debate over the draft centered on the issues of suffrage and education. On June 18, when the basic issues had been settled, the internal improvements clause was submitted and passed with only one minor grammatical alteration. In its final form, the constitution required that:

> Internal improvements shall be encouraged by the government of this state; and it shall be the duty of the legislature, as soon as may be, to make provisions by law for ascertaining the proper objects of improvement, in relation to [roads], Canals, and navigable waters; and it shall also be their duty to provide by law for an equal, systematic, and economical application of the funds which may be appropriated to these objects.[23]

As adopted, the constitution did more than authorize internal improvements; it required them. It also required that application of funds be *equal, systematic, and economical,* terms that later proved contradictory.

When the convention adjourned, copies of the constitution were sent to Washington, accompanied by the Census of 1834, and an ordinance adopted by the convention, requesting certain acts by Congress that would be binding on the state as a condition of admission. The ordinance petitioned Congress for a grant of section sixteen for public schools, four sections of land for a seat of government, and a transfer to the state of the seventy-two sections of land granted for the University of Michigan in 1826. In addition, it requested the appropriation of seven hundred sections of land for state construction of one or more railroads across the peninsula, and improvement of such other roads, rivers, or canals as the state should stipulate. The convention also asked for five percent of the net proceeds of land sales after January 1, 1836; three-fifths for schools and two-fifths for internal improvements. And, finally, they asked for possession of all the salt springs in the state, with one section of land for each, and completion and repair of all roads authorized by the national government. In submitting these requests the convention pointed out that the United States Constitution was a compact between the federal government and the state, and that they regarded these grants as basic to being admitted on an equal footing.[24] In short, the convention was offering prior terms for proceeding with negotiations. Before Congress could reply, however, the first steps were taken toward adoption of an internal improvements program.

When the convention adjourned, a new political balance had been struck in the state. Suffrage had been extended to all white males, including aliens, after six months of residence. Elections for ratification of the constitution were scheduled for October 5, and the convention was so confident of its approval that voting for state officials was set for the following day. Terms under which the state would consider admission had been submitted to Congress, and an internal improvements program was required by the constitution. The conservatives had clearly been defeated in their struggle to continue a moderate course of action.

The excitement created by the Toledo War was sustained through the summer by Jackson's dismissal of Stevens T. Mason, and the appointment of

John Horner to replace him. After having his life threatened by the citizens of Monroe and his lodging pelted with stones and horse dung in Ypsilanti, Horner quietly isolated himself in Detroit and ruled over a Territorial Government that had meanwhile voted itself out of existence.[25] The voters knew what kind of man they wanted in office, and the *Michigan Whig* listed qualifications. In addition to a long list of admirable qualities, they demanded that "he be a man of good sense, competent information, experience, business habits; attached to the true interests of Michigan, his head full of plans of internal improvement—rail-road cars, schools, and colleges:—a correct judge of men to fill the Judiciary...."[26] In October, Mason was overwhelmingly elected Governor, and the Democrats established a comfortable majority in both houses of the Legislature.

The new Legislature met briefly in November, but accomplished little. In February 1836, the program began to take shape. After discussing the statehood-boundary problem at length in his opening address, the Governor turned to the subject of internal improvements. Pointing to the constitutional imperative, he urged the legislators to make it one of the first objects of their attention, and warned that too much attention could not be devoted to it:

> The spirit and enterprise which has arisen among our citizens, if fostered and encouraged by the State, cannot fail to lead to lasting prosperity. Your liberal legislation should embrace within its range every section of the state. No local prejudice or attachments should misdirect the equal liberality with which you should guard the interests of your constituents. The wealth of the state must be composed of the individual wealth of its citizens, and in this respect no portion of them are independent of the other.

Mason called for the appointment of an engineer, commissioner, or board of commissioners, regulated by law, to provide for the equal, systematic, and economical application of funds, and required by law to report at each session of the Legislature. Such a system, he argued, would prevent waste due to misinformation given to the Legislature, and channel funds into projects doing the "greatest good for the greatest number of our fellow citizens." The lands requested in section four of the ordinance attached to the constitution, which he felt Congress would surely grant, "will afford a fund ample to give effect to our plans of internal improvement." He asked that the attention of Congress be called to this application before all the valuable lands in Michigan were exhausted.

Projects undertaken by private citizens presented another problem. While it was the duty of the Legislature to afford them every aid, he said: "It is also desirable, that they should never be beyond at least, the partial control of the state." He recommended state subscription to large amounts of their stock, paid for by a loan contracted at eastern banking houses for a "trifling" commission.[27] "The land which must be obtained by Michigan from congress [sic] for purposes of internal improvement, if guarded with prudent husbandry, would enable us to extinguish the debt contracted, and ultimately become a source of additional revenue to the state." At the same time, he urged strict economy to conserve the state's resources and reliance on loans to pay the expenses of government, postponing taxes until the people were better able to pay.[28]

The Governor's message reveals several important factors in the plans for internal improvement. Writers, skeptical of the program's wisdom, have missed the point in criticizing the state for undertaking massive programs on the slender financial resources then available. Aware of its limitations, the state was counting on federal aid to finance programs, and, if the aid had materialized, it would have been adequate. Land granted by the government for the University of Michigan had been chosen from the best virgin soil in the Territory, and was selling for over ten dollars an acre. Five hundred thousand acres, similarly handled, would have netted between five and ten million dollars for internal improvements, if prices had held. The absence of financial resources added to the need for a program instead of acting as a limitation. Faced with the problem of taxing a population in the process of farm-making, with inadequate facilities for marketing their products, the liberals turned to the alternative of improving transportation and then using the proceeds to diminish, or abolish, the burden of taxation.

Within a week after the Governor's address, petitions for improvements projects began flooding the House. Between February 4 and 9, petitions from drives led by John Biddle and O. Wilder, promoters of the Detroit and St. Joseph, were presented to the Legislature to support construction of a railroad from Kalamazoo to Allegan through the Kalamazoo Valley, which had been bypassed by Berrien's survey of 1834. Similar petitions were sent by residents of Calhoun, Allegan, and Kalamazoo Counties.[29] The same week, Henry Lothrop brought in a petition from Kalamazoo County, asking the state to appoint a committee to recommend internal improvements projects and report on their expediency. The committee was authorized, and seven members were appointed by the chair.[30] Two weeks later, the Legislature passed resolutions asking for federal appropriations for river improvement.[31]

On March 1, Elisha Ely, Chairman of the House Internal Improvements Committee, reported on the section of the Governor's message relating to the intended program. The report was accompanied by a bill that was subsequently referred back to committee with instructions to include provisions authorizing the Governor to borrow three million dollars to finance public works. Two days later a resolution was passed instructing the committee to inquire into the expediency of constructing a railroad from Monroe to the Detroit and St. Joseph at Ypsilanti, either under state ownership or corporate charter. On March 8, Ely reported bills authorizing the appointment of a board of commissioners of internal improvement, and a three-million-dollar loan. On the twenty-fifth, the bill was recommitted on Ely's motion, and remained in committee for the rest of the session.[32]

A week after the Legislature reconvened in July, the three-million-dollar loan bill was reported and, on July 19, the House accepted a substitute with similar provisions which was subsequently passed and sent to the Senate. On a motion by John Barry, conservative senator from the southwest district, the bill was tabled and not revived during the remainder of the session.[33] In failing to pass, the bill suffered the fate of most major legislation approved by the House in 1836; the Senate refused to act because of doubts raised by conservatives about the legality of proceedings under assumed statehood. In consequence, all definite action was avoided.[34]

On July 12, Mason returned a bill chartering the St. Clair and Grand River Railroad to the Legislature with a veto message. He objected to provisions allowing the company to buy lands along the route because the speculation would be harmful to settlement. It would be better, he argued, if the state built the road by taxing settlers because it would be less of an absolute burden, particularly since the state was contemplating such a road anyway. Lack of a provision allowing the state to regulate tolls, limiting profits to a reasonable return on investment, was characterized as "extortion from the public." Finally, he objected to a provision that had been standard in previous charters, allowing the company to increase its stock if the state took its allotted number of shares because the provision would neutralize state control.[35]

On July 22, a resolution was introduced into the Senate by Conrad Ten Eyck, authorizing the Governor to purchase the "Detroit and Grand River [sic]" (Detroit and St. Joseph) railroad. Three days later, the resolution was amended to include the Detroit and Maumee, and on the third reading, Comstock added: "all other railroads of the state." The resolution passed the Senate and was returned from the House the same day without amendment.[36] During the same session, acts were passed authorizing the State Treasurer to receive deposits from the federal surplus and the five percent funds.[37]

During 1836, the outlines of a program of internal improvements emerged in sessions of the Legislature, with passage halted only by senatorial doubts about legality. A three-million-dollar loan was authorized by the House, and the Governor was authorized to inquire into the purchase of the Detroit and St. Joseph and other railroads. A select committee was appointed to investigate the feasibility of projects and was required to report their findings. By the end of the session, most of the projects undertaken by the Legislature during 1837 had assumed a general form. It was understood that a trans-peninsular railroad would be built with a branch to Monroe and that river clearance would be undertaken. A canal from Detroit to the rapids of the Grand River was even projected.[38] Had it not been for the doubtful legality of acts passed under assumed statehood, it seems likely that the internal improvements program would have been authorized in 1836 instead of in 1837.

During the transition to statehood, hostility to private control of major transportation routes mounted in both parties. In the fall of 1834, the Ann Arbor *Michigan Emigrant,* a Whig paper, reprinted an article from the *National Intelligencer,* advocating the use of steam engines on turnpike-type roads instead of railroads. Not only would they be more efficient, but "railroads have a tendency to monopolize the travel, whereas the common road, improved, would be of use to all."[39] As spokesman for the liberal Democrats, Mason warned the Legislative Council early in 1835 against the issue of too many corporate charters because they were aristocratic and stifled individual enterprise. On February 11, 1835, he vetoed the issue of charters to two steamboat companies, repeating his warnings and cautioning the Legislature not to interfere with a branch of business unless it was important to the public and could not be undertaken by individual citizens.[40] In late 1836 and early 1837, Whig journals expressed agreement. When it was reported that the Legislature was likely to purchase the Detroit and St. Joseph in 1837, the editor of the Detroit *Daily Advertiser* commented:

> Objections have been made to this policy, but we see no evil likely to arise from it, but greater benefit rather; after the completion of the work, the state may reduce the tolls to the lowest rate sufficient to pay the expenses of its construction and keep it in repair. When Ohio commenced her great work, the Cincinnati and Cleveland Canal, the state followed the earnest recommendation of Dewitt Clinton, and built the canal with the funds of the state. What would be thought of the policy of surrendering that great work to the control of a private corporation.[41]

Hostility to private control of major transportation routes was shared by leaders of both parties in the closing months of 1836, and during debates preceding adoption of the program, the propriety of public enterprise was never an important issue.

During the summer and fall of 1836, the admissions issue reached a climax. Outlines of the settlement offered by Congress were known as early as March, and the liberals used the terms as grounds for further attacks on conservative Democrats. Mason used a letter from Senator-elect Lucius Lyon to discredit the conservatives, but Lyon, who blamed the attack on John Biddle, thought Mason's cooperation with the Whigs would do him more harm than good.[42] On June 15, Congress passed the well-known boundary compromise and a week later passed a supplementary act dealing with the financial terms submitted with the constitution. In addition to exchanging the western Upper Peninsula for the Toledo strip, Congress awarded the section sixteen lands, the capital and University lands, and five percent of the net proceeds of all land sales. The state was also given six salt springs with a section of land attached to each.[43] Neither the seven-hundred-section grant for internal improvements, nor federal completion and maintenance of roads was awarded.

Smarting under the terms of the compromise, a convention assembled under legislative authorization in September and rejected admission under the conditions put forward by Congress. Almost before the convention was over, there were expressions of regret but with the Legislature adjourned, no authority existed to call another convention. By the time the Legislature could have been recalled, it would have been too late for the state to gain admission and benefit from the federal surplus distribution. As an alternative, the Governor suggested that the people act in their original capacity and call a spontaneous convention. The convention, duly called through the Democratic party machinery, met in Ann Arbor on December 14, 1836. With the Whigs refusing to participate in a convention of such dubious legality, the outcome was never in doubt. In two days, the "Frostbitten Convention," little more than a caucus of the Democratic party, decided to accept the government's terms. A special messenger was dispatched to Washington, and on January 26, 1837, President Jackson signed the act granting Michigan statehood. Many reasons have been offered by state historians for what was, in effect, a *coup d'état* by the Democracy.[44] A letter from Mason to his sister expresses it best: "I must not omit to tell you, that our recent convention has saved us our share of the surplus revenue; that a bill has passed the Senate of the U. S. for our admission, and that in a few days our troubles will be ended by the State of Michigan becoming a member of the Confederacy"[45]

On January 2, 1837, the Governor delivered his annual message, which dealt at length with the problem of internal improvements. "The period has arrived," he said, "when Michigan can no longer, without detriment to her standing and importance as a state, delay the action necessary for the development of her vast resources and wealth." After asking the Legislature to make a disposition of federal surplus payments, he reported the results of inquiries made about the purchase of railroads under the joint resolution of the previous session. Only the Detroit and St. Joseph, and the St. Clair and Romeo had answered. The first would surrender its charter if the state would cover its advances, but the St. Clair and Romeo was willing to give up its charter only if the state guaranteed completion to Lake Michigan within six years. Mason suggested that if the state did not wish to become engaged in construction of these roads, it could take enough stock on the major routes to "secure the people a controlling influence over them." He was clearly against the major routes falling into private hands.

The Governor repeated his recommendation of the previous year—that a board of internal improvements be created during the session to employ engineers to investigate routes and other problems. No project, he said, should be undertaken without their approval. He was hopeful that this would help the state avoid "extravagant, unprofitable and useless expenditures." The state was quite capable of constructing its own internal improvements and, if careful, could "supercede the necessity of placing all those resources of wealth in the hands of private companies."

Mason's project recommendations sounded a strange note by giving canals preference over railroads. He suggested several surveys be undertaken to connect rivers within the state: the Grand River to the Black River of St. Clair County, the Looking Glass and the Shiawassee, continuation of the Looking Glass—Shiawassee to the Detroit River or to Saginaw, the Huron to the Red Cedar, and the River Raisin to the headwaters of the St. Joseph or Kalamazoo Rivers. When the rivers were surveyed, he wanted the Legislature to select one or more routes. "In the event, however, that sufficient water for canal purposes cannot be obtained at the summit level between Lake Michigan and Lake Erie, the state will be compelled to direct all her energies and resources to the construction of rail or Macadamized roads, or roads laid with wood, and to the improvement of the navigation of her inland streams."

In view of the acquisition of the western Upper Peninsula, he recommended that a ship canal be opened around the falls of the St. Mary's River to exploit the fisheries and commerce of the region, predicting that its resources might be beyond one's wildest expectations. Since the distance would not exceed one mile, Mason felt that a hundred thousand dollars would cover construction, and at such a minute cost, the project should be undertaken even if the federal government refused to help.

The Governor warned the Legislature against excessive issue of corporate charters to railroads, stating that it was his duty to approve such charters only when he was satisfied that public and not private interests were the object of the charter:

> In assuming this rule of conduct, I shall not fail at the same time to keep before me the fact that railroads are only of advantage to the great body of the people where they tend to increase the value of the products of agriculture and the demand for labor. These results are only to be expected from such railroads as open a market for produce, by supplying better and cheaper facilities of transportation to such parts of the state as were in a measure before deprived of them. I am led to these suggestions from the circumstance that all applications for railroad charters are apt to be too readily granted whether running from one section to another, from village to village, or from neighborhood to neighborhood. The result of this course of legislation, if persevered in, must be that the common roads of the country will become neglected and forgotten, will be rendered unfit for ordinary purposes of travel, and the farmer must ultimately be dependent on private companies for the transportation of his produce, upon such terms and at such prices as individual interests may dictate.

Mason's fears indicate the early stage at which the danger of the natural monopoly of railroads was realized. Such fears were instrumental in the state's adoption of its own program of construction. In view of the general hostility to private ownership of major transportation facilities, it seems possible that state enterprise might have played an important role in the development of American railroads if Michigan's program had been more successful.

Finally, the Governor asked for authorization to borrow the necessary funds to carry out the program. He recommended a loan of five million dollars, which would be sufficient to cover all the important improvements demanded by the public. "That economy may be considered as misjudged," he told them, "which, for the sake of avoiding an immediate advance of money would subject the community to inconveniences and evils a hundred fold greater than the benefits to be derived from procrastination."[46]

It has been traditional in discussions of Michigan's internal improvements program to give causal significance to the Governor's messages, either in 1836 or 1837. In part, this stems from the assumption that demand for the program sprang full blown from the soil in 1837 and was adopted by promiscuous whim of the Legislature. It is also due to the conclusion that the plan adopted by the Legislature was identical to Mason's recommendations. Mason's scheme called for a board of internal improvement to investigate the feasibility of projects. The Legislature would then adopt those found to be practicable. Giving primary emphasis to canals, he recommended the construction of railroads only in the event that canals proved physically impossible. Even then, he recommended stock subscription over state involvement in actual construction, and emphasized control rather than ownership. Only his suggestions about the size of the loan and about the Soo canal were finally adopted by the Legislature.

Mason's address dealt with other problems that would in time bear on the program undertaken in 1837. He cautioned the Legislature against excessive issue of bank paper as an answer to pressures on the money market. Banks, he said, were not the foundation of public wealth, but only facilitated trade. Wealth could be found only in the labor of the people. Pressure on the money market stemmed from the diversion of capital into speculation, and excessive note issues only increased the evil. While asking the Legislature to build all possible safeguards into bank charters, the Governor warned: "It is impossible, and perhaps not to be desired, that a metallic circulating medium should be altogether substituted for bank paper." Instead, enough should be kept in circulation that bank notes would pass at par. He asked that notes be limited to denominations of five dollars or more, and that the usury laws be repealed. The latter, he complained, only aggravated capital shortages in periods of high demand, and were an abridgement of individual freedom of contract.[47] Finally, he called for an investigation of the River Raisin and Lake Erie Railroad charter. By an oversight in granting the charter, the Legislature had failed to insert a clause prohibiting banking, and the company was issuing notes it could not be forced to redeem in specie. Even though it was not chartered as a bank, the company had banking privileges. Mason wanted the Legislature to correct the error.

In his first speech touching on the subject, Mason showed an unusual grasp of the problems of currency and banking that were to plague his Administration. Later speeches revealed a growing knowledge of the subject, and as time passed it became more important in the Governor's messages. The source of his knowledge is obscure. His father had been a director of the Lexington branch of the Bank of the United States, and the younger Mason was an interested student who often reflected his studies. But whatever the source, his grasp of the subject was equaled by only a few contemporaries and very few Democrats. Unlike the leaders of his party, he understood the impossibility of an entirely metallic currency and assigned banks and banking a useful role in the community, preferring control to elimination. In time, an intricate linkage would develop between banking and internal improvements that would eventually lead to the downfall of Mason and Michigan's system of public works.

Four days after the Governor's message, a special committee was appointed by the House to investigate canal possibilities around the St. Mary's rapids, and the Ways and Means Committee was required to report on the means for redemption of principal and interest on a foreign loan.[48] On January 24, the Committee on Internal Improvements reported with a plan that gave basic shape to the program adopted by the Legislature.[49]

In opening, the Committee submitted a classic statement of the spirit of internal improvement that summarized their motives and goals and overcame the confusion of terms and ideological ambivalence that Marvin Meyers finds characteristic of Jacksonian rhetoric:

> The Progress of Centuries in other lands, is here realized in as many years. The sound of the falling forest is everywhere heard—abundant harvests usurp the rank luxuriance of her prairies—farms, villages and cities spring up on every side under the magical hand of intelligent labor—the wide embracing arms of her surrounding seas bear to her indented shores a thousand keels, freighted with tribute to the enterprise and industry of her numerous and enlightened population. Peopled as Michigan is, in great measure, from the most intelligent and enterprising of her sister states, she justly looks forward to stand beside them on an equal footing in the great family of states.
>
> This can alone be accomplished, in the opinion of your committee, by advancing with them *pari passu* in the high road of national prosperity—internal improvement.
>
> The subject of internal improvement is one occupying the intelligence of the age....It is no longer an experiment. It has ceased to be a question, whether the calm and peaceable occupations of a pastoral and agricultural life, are more conclusive [sic] to human happiness than the excitement and activity of commerce and manufactures. Every portion of our community, whether near the seaboard or remote, is struggling to obtain its due share of the general wealth. Internal improvement is the great lever which is opening the sealed up fountains of natural wealth and civilization.[50]

Only a few years earlier, the Committee said, experiments in England established the superiority of railroads for internal communication. And, if Michigan were not held back by timidity, it could become the focal point of East-West transportation, the junction where the roads of the seaboard would meet the roads tapping the Mississippi Valley. The roads were not envisioned as feeders to the Great Lakes, as critics have charged, but as part of a "great northern chain of communication," completing railroads already chartered through the center of New York and Massachusetts, and linking with roads chartered in Rhode Island, Connecticut, New Hampshire, Vermont, and Pennsylvania. Michigan's railroads were to be joined with the New York system by the "Detroit and Niagara." It was Michigan's duty, the Committee stated, to complete the system to Lake Michigan by way of the Detroit and

St. Joseph, where fifty miles of steam navigation would connect the route with Chicago and its canal to the Mississippi. The road was expected to give the state not only markets and sources of raw materials, but revenues from through traffic. A short line from the main route to the Maumee would complete the linkage to the Mississippi Valley and tap the whole trade of that region by freeing it from the hazards of lake and river navigation. According to the Committee, works in progress to the south threatened to sweep trade from the state unless the crisis was met by energetic action. "The present is in the opinion of your committee the proper period to carry through at least *one* perfect line of communication across the state."

The Committee urged that private enterprise be harnessed to aid the completion of a statewide transportation network. Under its program, the state would concentrate its efforts on cross-peninsular routes and leave the building of short connectors to private capital. "The end in view being the prompt effectuation of a full development of our internal resources, the attempt by the state to grasp the entire control of all such works, will of necessity, impede the progress of the whole." On the other hand, a few leading routes in successful operation would attract capital for successful completion of others, and thereby avoid the waste and delay of too many projects at once, as well as local and sectional struggles. The Committee urged the state to strive for completion of a single route before concentration of wealth and population at particular points led to heavy and insurmountable sectional rivalry. They also recommended a southern railroad to connect with the works of other states.

In addition to immediate construction of the Detroit and St. Joseph to complete the line of communication from the Atlantic to the Mississippi, the Committee considered a series of projects designed to supplement other national routes. A northern route, from Fort Gratiot to the mouth of the Grand River, would unite the sections of a contemplated railroad through the Canadas to the foot of Lake Huron, with a railroad being considered in Wisconsin from Milwaukee to Cassville by sixty miles of navigation. This combination of railroad and steamships would constitute the shortest direct route to the Mississippi. A canal from the headwaters of the Saginaw to the Grand would advance the interests of the northern section of the state. Finally, the Committee thought it might be desirable to build a railroad through the center of the peninsula to Mackinac at some time in the future, to complete a line of North-South communication.

It is clear the committee had a larger picture in mind than outlets for local markets. The recommended roads were all presented in terms of the works with which they would connect in the development of railroad systems linking Michigan with the Atlantic Coast. The assessment of potential routes was sound. With some alteration, all the suggested roads and networks would eventually be built. The error lay in confusing the plans and charters of other states with actual construction and the reality of completion. Most of the lines discussed would not be completed for at least two decades, but the sense of urgency in the Committee's recommendations gave the impression they were practically on Michigan's doorstep.

In addition to the trans-peninsular projects, two other projects were approved. A canal around the Sault de Ste. Marie was suggested because it would open the trade of the Northwest, as well as fisheries and mines in the Superior country. Finally, because the Erie and Kalamazoo Railroad made the southern portion of the state tributary to Ohio, they approved construction of a railroad from Havre to Adrian. With the aid of the port of Monroe, it was hoped that the road would "afford us the ability to compete with our grasping neighbor" for the trade of the southern tier and the commerce of Lake Erie.

The Committee justified its recommendations by citing both the economic development and financial returns the program would bring. "Whatever will tend to multiply our population and increase the amount of industry, which is the prime and only source of wealth, and whatever may allure the investment of capital and skill to sustain and direct that industry is manifestly the true policy of the State." Such projects were expected to benefit the whole spectrum of economic activity. By reducing transportation costs, they expected to raise the real income of the entire population. Since transportation costs were a part of the price of every article, public works were expected to increase real income by reducing the price paid for imports, while allowing farmers to compete on the Eastern market and bring marginal lands into production. Finally, withdrawal of horses from the transportation of goods and people was expected to save about a third of the farm products currently consumed in their support. In this last justification, the Committee cited a Doctor Lardner as their authority.[51]

Satisfied with its assessment of the developmental implications of the program, the Committee turned to financial problems. To complete the program, a loan was needed if the state was to have enough money to proceed without embarrassment and be able to hire competent engineers. Such spending was not to be considered an expenditure, but an *investment*. "It is an investment which will afford an ample profit, and that profit, instead of swelling the wealth of individuals and companies, will be equally divided among the whole mass of our population, by creating and maintaining public revenue, which, in the process of time, will materially lessen the public burden." The Committee reasoned that if five million dollars could be borrowed at five percent and invested in Michigan to bring returns of ten percent, the state would realize a profit of five percent, or two hundred and fifty thousand dollars a year. If the money could be borrowed for twenty-five years and taken at the rate expended over the five years necessary to complete the program, twenty years would remain to repay the debt. The income of the sixth year, invested at seven percent, would be $582,500 at the end of twenty years. Total income of the works, assuming an annual income of $250,000 invested progressively at seven percent, would be $8,325,000 at the end of twenty years. After paying back the principal of five million dollars, and a small sum of arbitrarily estimated costs, $2,925,000 would remain in the possession of the state, along with public works valued at five million dollars. With the principal repaid, income from the works would double, and either the rates would be reduced or the public coffers filled. The Committee concluded that "the investment of such a sum cannot therefore be considered great, when compared with the importance of the work and the advantages to be realized." The mathemetics of the Committee's financial model are unimpeachable, but the basic assumptions, particularly those involving the rate of return, were certainly heroic.

Ten percent, however, was considered a conservative estimate of potential earning power. It was estimated that 57,000 tons of merchandise were shipped west from Detroit in 1836, and that there were 11,494 arrivals and departures from the port (and that this was only twenty percent of the traffic between Detroit and Lake Michigan). Using the mid-point distance as an average, it was calculated that freight at six cents per ton mile would return $342,000 plus $85,000 for return freight. Forty thousand passengers, over the same distance at five cents per mile, would return $200,000. Subtracting twenty-five percent for repairs and expenses, estimated net income would be $470,000, or thirty percent on the estimated cost of the Detroit and St. Joseph. Even these estimates were conservative, the Committee felt, because they did not allow for revenue from the mails or potential growth of traffic. The freight rates must have been considered low, for it was stated that if the cost of transportation could be reduced to $40/100 ton-miles on freight, it would save $32/100 ton-miles over current costs.

Realizing five million dollars would never be sufficient to build all the projects it was sponsoring, the Committee stressed the need for federal aid to make up the deficit. "This aid," it reported, "will justify an extended system and liberal expenditure without which the whole must fail." Urging application to the federal government for aid, they suggested that the Legislature focus its appeals on the military importance of the projects in case of another war with England. Until these extra funds could be realized, it was suggested that the state's efforts be confined to a five-point program. The Detroit and St. Joseph Railroad should be purchased, and a St. Clair-Grand River Railroad surveyed. A railroad should be constructed from Monroe to the navigable waters of the Kalamazoo (probably at Marshall), and from there to the terminus of the St. Clair-Grand River route. A ship canal should be constructed at the Soo, and a canal built through Oakland County from Detroit to the Grand River. Although it placed major emphasis on railroads, however, the Committee refused to pass judgement on the superiority of either canals or railroads until a survey had shown the suitability of the terrain.[52]

On January 27, three days after the report was delivered, the Chairman of the House Committee on Internal Improvements reported three bills into the House: a bill authorizing the five-million-dollar loan, a bill for the purchase of the Detroit and St. Joseph Railroad, and a bill establishing a board of internal improvements.[53] The ensuing debate consumed almost two months, and brought to a head the sectional rivalry that had been temporarily quieted by the truce of 1835. In this intense struggle of sectional ambitions, party politics played only a minor role.[54]

The bills submitted bore little resemblance to the slate of projects recommended by the Committee in its report. The program presented for legislative consideration consisted of an authorization to borrow money, creation of a supervisory board, and the construction of a single railroad across the peninsula. Legislative struggle focused on the bill for purchasing the Detroit and St. Joseph, with the lines of battle drawn between representatives of the southern and central tiers of counties. To include their project in the internal improvements bill, southern forces resorted to delaying tactics, postponing debate and gaining passage of a resolution instructing the Committee on Internal Improvements to investigate the propriety of a second road west through the line of county centers in the first tier.[55] Although the central counties had the largest group of votes, neither tier controlled a majority in either the House or Senate. Southern interests used the second tier's advocacy of a single project to their advantage by supporting a multiple project proposal designed to swing the balance of power held by the sparse population in the north to their side. Alpheus Felch, a leader of the Monroe Democrats, later recalled:

> I remember very distinctly when the proposition was made to amend the bill by substituting three roads in the place of one. It created great alarm among the special friends of the bill. They looked upon it as indicating a design to defeat the entire project, and they knew well that a combination of the votes north and south of the line would seal its fate. But in this they were mistaken. The proposition was made in all sincerity. The proposed loan was large and they reasoned that as near as possible the benefit of it should be given to all who, as members of the State, were to bear the burden of paying it.[56]

Supporters of the single central railroad based their arguments on expediency and profitability; advocates of the multiple route proposal rested their case on the more abstract grounds of equality.

House debate on the internal improvements program continued until after the middle of February. Because most of the discussion was conducted in the Committee of the Whole, nothing appears in the records. But newspaper battles reflected the major arguments being advanced by sectional opponents. Central interests argued that the southern section lacked sufficient population to justify more than ten or twenty miles of road, and offered to construct branch lines connecting points in the south with the central railroad. Southern interests countered with the argument that more than one railroad could be supported by the state, and would produce benefits in which all the public was entitled to share. The major difference between opponents was not over the desirability of roads, but their number location.[57] On February 11, the bill creating a Board of Internal Improvements passed the House, followed shortly by loan authorization.[58] Debate continued on the purchase bill, however, often consuming the attention of the House for the entire day. On February 16, a resolution instructing the

Judiciary Committee to inquire into the propriety of granting one thousand dollars to each of the railroads in the state was unanimously adopted, but no report was made during the balance of the session.[59] Finally, a bill authorizing multiple routes was passed by a vote of thirty-four to eight, and its title changed from "A Bill to purchase the Detroit and St. Joseph Railroad" to "A Bill to provide for the construction of certain works of Internal Improvement and for other purposes."[60]

On February 25, the bill was received by the Senate and submitted to committee, where it remained until March 6, when it was reported out and sent to the Committee of the Whole. There it was debated until March 14, when it was reported with an amendment.[61] On the afternoon of March 14, the full force of sectional antagonism broke loose.

The exact provisions of the Senate amendment, which was really a substitute bill, are not clear. The amendment was not printed, and no record of it seems to exist. Its general outlines, however, are apparent from the context of Senate debates. The Senate substitute seems to have embodied the recommendations of the House Committee on Internal Improvements, authorizing a railroad through the central tier, with a branch from Monroe to the Central through Tecumseh, which would eventually be continued to the rapids of the Grand River. No mention was made of any provision for the northern tiers.

Before the Civil War, the party membership of legislators was not recorded, but available evidence indicates that the sixteen-member Senate was composed of fourteen Democrats and two members with no recorded affiliation.[62] The Senate substitute was supported by nine members and opposed by seven. Amendments offered in the course of debate made it clear that the opposition was willing to make any concession, including continuation of the Detroit and Pontiac west to the mouth of the Kalamazoo, to secure a direct route from Monroe to New Buffalo through the southern tier. Supporters of the bill rejected every concession, and were determined to build no more than one route across the state. In ten roll-call votes, the opposition was unable to gain a single supporter, regardless of the inducements offered. The substitute was finally adopted by a vote of nine to seven, and the following day, the whole bill was adopted by a vote of eight to seven.[63]

Streeter, in his analysis of political parties in Michigan, has stressed the support given by Whigs to the center route, and by Democrats to a multiple program. His conclusions, however, rest on sample votes taken from the House in 1838 and subsequent years, votes in gubernatorial contests, and the editorial positions of the Detroit *Advertiser*. Had he ascertained the political affiliation of legislators instead of assuming that the gubernatorial votes of counties reflected the political loyalty of their representatives and included the Senate in his calculations, his results would have been substantially different. Instead, he assumed that elections in the fall of 1837 reflected the Legislature of the previous spring, and that sectional struggle in the Legislature was the result of political affiliation.[64]

Analysis of the Senate vote cannot utilize the conventional assignment of votes to districts because under the system of apportionment Senatorial districts were composed of several counties and cut across sectional lines. Each district was entitled to three or more members who might or might not reside in different sections.[65] Striking results can be obtained, however, if the Senators are separated by their residence. Of seven Senators in opposition, all reported residences in the first or third tier of counties. The one exception to the rule of local self-interest among the Senate opposition was Calvin Britain, who reported his residence as St. Joseph, the proposed terminus of the central railroad. All of the supporting Senators except two lived either in towns on the proposed route or in counties through which the road passed. The two exceptions, who held the balance of power, were Raynale of Oakland County, whose voting is unexplainable, and Hough, who lived in Tecumseh, through which the proposed branch to Monroe would pass. In the Senate, proponents of the central route had apparently found the key to obtaining a majority for their bill without resorting to multiple trans-peninsular routes.[66]

All this was clear to John Barry, who led the opposition, when he rose on the floor of the Senate to deliver a thunderous protest against the substitute bill. Barry warned the Senate that they were putting the interests of the southern tier in jeopardy, as well as the interests of the state, and violating the golden rule, the essense of all religion and morality. "Now Sir," he stormed, "if this Grand River Rail Road charter is to be forced upon the South, as part of the great southern thoroughfare, by whom is it to be done? I answer, Sir, by those living in the second tier of counties. You impose upon the south what they would almost unanimously reject." He claimed that the south was not selfish, but only wanted a share in proportion to population and taxes. It wanted a railroad from Monroe to New Buffalo with no specified mid-points. The proposition before the Senate gave the south nothing more than it was getting from the Erie and Kalamazoo, except that the road would run through Tecumseh instead of Adrian. "We think it is asking too much, when you say construct for us the middle route, and also a Branch of that route to Monroe before any other great thoroughfare shall be provided for or authorized." If the best policy dictated building only one road at a time, he said, he would accept it. But if the branch to Monroe was built and called the Southern, it would mean the south would never get its road. "In the Middle Tier of counties, you are asking everything: you ask for the seat of government, the University, and the penitentiary." The south would allow that, but it wanted its own railroad. He charged central interests with attempting to make the whole state tributary to them. The people would not stand for it, despite the five or six local routes thrown in as sops to gain a majority for its passage. The bill, he repeated, was a local bill: "It does not provide for internal improvements on that great, broad, and liberal policy, which the people have a right to expect at your hands."[67] Barry's speech, so full of anger and insult that it brought down a rebuke from the President of the Senate, illustrates the high level of antagonism between Democrats when local or sectional interests were threatened.

By the time the bill was adopted in the Senate, feeling was running high in the state. Newspapers along the southern route had joined those in Monroe in advocating multiple routes across the state.[68] Meanwhile, the *Democratic Free Press* was exciting readers with reports of the progress of Canadian railroads that would link Michigan with New York. On February 1, it reported that the Detroit and Niagara Railroad had done everything necessary to begin work but survey the route. It estimated the cost of the road at $6000 per mile, or a total of $1,320,000, and reported that the wooden superstructure of the road, buried in dirt, would last forty or fifty years. A week later, it carried a letter from E. A. Brush, a major stockholder in the Detroit and St. Joseph, encouraging investment in the Detroit and Niagara. Brush, the financial agent of Lewis Cass, cited the flat land of Ontario, and the railroads chartered and under construction from Boston to Buffalo, to support his arguments. As soon as the state assumed the burden of the Detroit and St. Joseph, he said, the stockholders intended to transfer their funds to the project. As he phrased it: "Buffalo and Detroit can never suffer such a project to sleep." Finally, on March 17, the *Free Press* announced the chartering of the Great Western Railroad by the Canadian Parliament, by amending the charter of the London and Gore Railroad to authorize westward continuation to either Port Sarnia or Port Edwardsburg, and an accompanying loan of £200,000 from the government.[69] Such reports only added to the urgency with which supporters of the single central route pushed for passage of their bill. It also substantiated arguments in support of the Northern route, which was to continue the Great Western. Purchase of the Detroit and St. Joseph would not only ensure the completion of the road, but would allow the stockholders to participate in building the connecting link that would tie Detroit to the Coast, perhaps making it the merchandising center of the West.

The Senate substitute was reported back to the House on the afternoon of March 15, and instantly became the subject of discussion. Several amendments giving priority to local projects were proposed and defeated, and it is apparent from the amendments that the short local projects the Senate attached to their single route plan included the St. Clair and Romeo, and perhaps a northern road. These concessions to local demands, however, failed to sway the House, and when the question was taken, the Senate version was rejected thirty-eight to six.[70] The opposition consisted of three Democrats and three men of unknown affiliation, while the whole House consisted of twenty-two Democrats, four Whigs, an independent, and twenty members with no recorded political affiliation. Since opposition votes in February and March fail to correlate with either party or section, it can be assumed that party politics played little role in voting on either the compromise bill passed by the House in February, or the Senate version rejected in March. Indeed, the sections within the House appear to have been contented with the bill they had worked out, since they rejected the Senate substitute with surprising unanimity.

On March 17, the Senate appointed members to a joint conference committee consisting of Davis, Barry, and Moore. The House appointed Felch, Monfore, and Ward. The following day, the conference committee reported favorably on the House version, and both houses unanimously concurred. [71] On March 20, 1837, the Governor signed the Internal Improvements Act into law. Official records are not clear on the course of action taken by the conference committee, but an explanation is given by Robert E. Ward in a letter to his constituents in New Buffalo:

> The internal improvement bill became a law this day.
>
> $100,000 are appropriated for a Rail Road from Monroe to New Buffalo—The Vote was almost unanimous—The House Bill was lost in the Senate, but the House refused to adopt the Senate amendment. A committee of Conference was appointed and the original bill restored. I was on the conference committee & insisted on your road—If they would not allow it, I had it in my power to defeat the whole bill—
>
> Your property is now doubled in value—You must have a hearty rejoicing—
>
> The General Bank Law has also passed—You also can now have a Bank. [72]

With the Internal Improvements Act passed, the other acts of the program were signed into law on the twenty-first. A Board of Internal Improvements was created, and negotiation of a five-million-dollar bond issue was authorized. The loan bill passed with little difficulty. The only amendment in the Senate was offered by John Barry and struck provisions for repayment in Europe. [73] A ship canal was authorized around the falls of the St. Mary's River. [74] Approval of a geological survey had passed a month earlier. [75] Commissioners were appointed to the Board of Internal Improvements and the following day the Legislature adjourned. [76]

The program created by the Legislature had moved well beyond the recommendations of Governor Mason in his annual message. The Internal Improvements Act authorized the construction of three railroads and two canals across the state. One road was to be constructed from Detroit to the mouth of the St. Joseph River and to be called the Central. A second, the Southern, was authorized from the navigable waters of the River Raisin, through Monroe, by the most direct route to New Buffalo. A third, the Northern, was to be surveyed and constructed through the fourth tier of counties, from Palmer, on the mouth of the Black River in St. Clair County, to the head of navigation of the Grand River in Kent County, or the mouth of the Grand in Ottawa County. The Board of Internal Improvements was instructed to undertake surveys of the railroads and hold open hearings on the selected routes, provided the state purchased what had been completed of the Detroit and St. Joseph. In addition, $550,000 was appropriated for the three roads: $100,000 for the Southern; $400,000 for the Central; and $50,000 for the Northern. Twenty thousand dollars was appropriated for

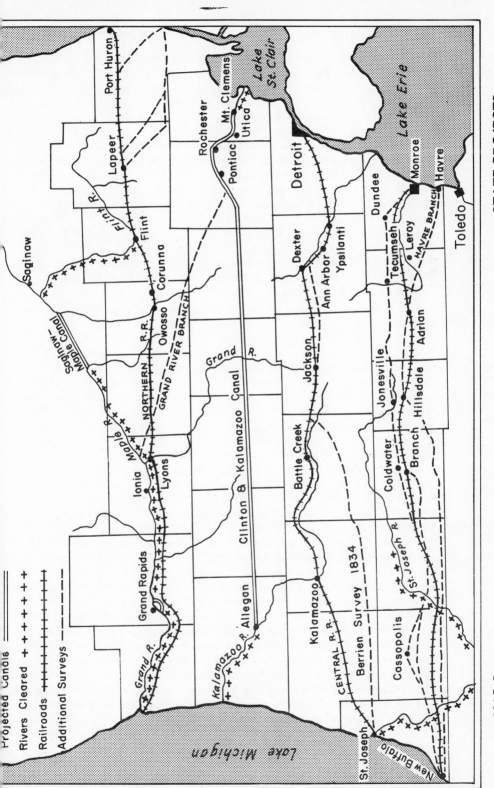

Projected Canals

Rivers Cleared + + + + +

Railroads

Additional Surveys

STATE PROJECTS

MAP 3

surveying a canal or canal-railroad combination from Mount Clemens on the Clinton River to the mouth of the Kalamazoo River, as well as a canal connecting the Saginaw River with the Maple or Grand Rivers. The St. Joseph, Kalamazoo, and Grand Rivers were to be surveyed with a view to constructing slackwater navigation. An additional $40,000 was appropriated for construction on the Clinton and Kalamazoo route, along with $15,000 for the Saginaw-Grand or Maple route. Finally, the commissioners were authorized to purchase the Havre branch railroad charter.[77] By separate acts, the Board of Internal Improvements was authorized to purchase the Detroit and Pontiac Railroad at cost plus seven percent, and the Governor was authorized to survey a ship canal around the falls of the St. Mary's River.[78]

Powers of construction and regulation were vested in the Board of Internal Improvements, a seven-member body appointed by the Governor with consent of the Legislature. The Board, appointed in 1837, was to continue in existence until January 1838. The commissioners were given direct control of construction and operation. A permanent secretary was to be appointed and an annual report filed.[79]

To finance the state's public works, an internal improvements fund was created. Money received from the federal government through the surplus revenue distribution, and the five percent funds, was assigned to the fund as a loan until the authorized loan could be negotiated, and the Board was allowed to loan the funds to specie-paying banks that would post security and pay at least five percent interest.[80] Long-term finance was provided by what became popularly known as the five million loan. The Governor was authorized to negotiate a bond issue of $5,000,000, redeemable at the pleasure of the state any time after twenty-five years following the first of January 1838. The loan was to be negotiated at the best and most favorable terms available, not more than five and one-half percent, and the proceeds were to be credited to the internal improvements fund and appropriated by the Legislature. Bonds were to be payable in New York or elsewhere in the United States, and could not be sold at less than par. In return for the funds from the loan, the state pledged the proceeds of all railroads and canals, the interest on all loans made from state funds, and the interest on all bank stock held by the state. The pledged funds would also act as a sinking fund for payment of both principal and interest.[81]

During the same session, other laws were passed that affected the internal improvements program. On March 15, the Legislature passed the first free banking law in the nation, allowing banks to be organized on application to the Treasury with a minimum of $50,000 capital, thirty percent of which had to be paid in.[82] According to Felch, the act was passed to relieve financial pressure by increasing the supply of money. The Legislature was practically unanimous in its passage.[83] A few days later, a general charter act was passed for manufacturing corporations.[84] Finally, in chartering the City of Monroe, the Legislature empowered the city to finish the canal and piers started by the federal government, and to raise $200,000 either by borrowing or direct taxation.

The program adopted in the spring of 1837 was vastly more complex and inclusive than that projected in the truce of 1835. Even when the Governor suggested a multiple slate of improvements in January 1837, there was little sense of immediacy for any of the projects except the Central. The projection of a trans-peninsular route through the center of each of the lower five tiers of counties was due to log-rolling by politicians from the southern section who harnessed Jacksonian rhetoric to justify their demands on the basis of equality. The inability of sectional interests to harness a working majority for their own projects forced the adoption of improvements that satisfied the demands of politicians who represented large and sparsely populated districts.

The term "sectional rivalry" has been used to describe the forces in the state's political life, but in the largest sense, it is a misnomer. Sectional rivalry, as it appeared in Michigan, was really rampant local interest expressed in approval of projects that temporarily linked local interests together in a general locus. Sectional loyalty could prove as transient as state loyalty when local interests were at stake. People who were incapable of uniting to choose the most economically feasible route across the state were as incapable of uniting when it came to choosing a route through their own section. Neither political ideology nor party struggle played an important role in the decision to undertake the program. The plan for a single road was passed by a Democratic Senate and rejected by a Democratic House. The following year, struggle was just as bitter within the solidly Democratic sections along the Southern and Northern Railroads when the question of route location arose. The battle was fought, and issues settled, by Democrats fighting among themselves, and the projects were the Democracy's railroads.

Analysis of the political forces pressing for adoption of the state's multiple program of public works gives strong support to Carter Goodrich's conclusion:

> In state politics, the suggestion that Whigs favored and the Democrats opposed internal improvements should be viewed with equal caution....In most cases, programs of state action had at their inception wide popular support more often traceable to conflicts of local and sectional interests than to differences in party doctrine.[85]

As Goodrich suggests, the pattern was reversed in Michigan. But although the Democracy was the political force behind the program, it would be incautious to conclude that the Whigs were in opposition. The complete reversal of party patterns suggested by Goodrich cannot be substantiated. Although the Whigs were swept into power in the fall of 1839 on a program of opposition to internal improvement, it was a sectional and not a political desire. Michigan's Democratic Governor endorsed policies similar to those pursued by his Whig successors, and once in power, faced with the reality of limited alternatives, the Whigs proved much less antagonistic to internal improvements than their campaign promises suggested.

Notes, Chapter 5

1. George H. White, "Townsend E. Gridley," *Michigan Pioneer and Historical Collections*, XIV (1894), 407.
2. My italics.
3. Dunbar, pp. 301-303.
4. Floyd Benjamin Streeter, *Political Parties in Michigan, 1837-1860* (Lansing: Michigan Historical Commission, 1918).
5. Richard P. McCormick, *The Second American Party System: Party Formation in the Jacksonian Era* (Chapel Hill, N. C.: University of North Carolina Press, 1961), pp. 13ff.
6. Letter from Stevens T. Mason to John T. Mason, March 1, 1833, in Stevens T. Mason Papers (Burton Historical Collections, Detroit, Mich.). Cited hereafter as S. T. Mason Papers (BHC).
7. Letter from S. T. Mason to John T. Mason, April 16, 1833, *ibid.*
8. Letter from George Corselius to William Woodbridge, January 5, 1835, William Woodbridge Papers (Burton Historical Collections, Detroit, Mich.). Cited hereafter as Woodbridge Papers (BHC).
9. Harold M. Dorr (ed.), *The Michigan Constitutional Conventions of 1835-36: Debates and Proceedings*, "University of Michigan Publications: History and Political Science," Vol. XIII (Ann Arbor: University of Michigan Press, 1940), p. 9. Cited hereafter as *Michigan Constitutional Conventions (Dorr).* Draft letter from William Woodbridge to "Dear Sir," 1836, Woodbridge Papers (BHC). Burton Historical Collection uses "Dear Sir," to indicate that the correspondent is unknown.
10. *Ibid.*
11. Draft of a letter from William Woodbridge to Daniel Webster, ca. 1835, William Woodbridge Papers (BHC).
12. *Messages of the Governors of Michigan*, I, 136; Michigan, *Territorial Laws*, III, 1423.
13. *Messages of the Governors of Michigan*, I, 136.
14. Michigan, *Territorial Laws*, III, 1356-59.
15. Letter from Henry Cole to William Woodbridge, November 28, 1835; letter from R. Sprague to William Woodbridge, Woodbridge Papers (BHC).
16. Draft letter from William Woodbridge to "Dear Sir," ca. 1835, Woodbridge Papers (BHC).
17. *Ibid.*
18. *Proceedings of the Democratic Territorial Convention, Held at Ann Arbor on the 29th and 30th January 1835* (Detroit: Free Press, 1835), bound in a volume of *Misc. Docs. of House and Senate, 1838-1840* [sic] in the possession of the Michigan Division, Michigan State Library, Lansing, Michigan.
19. Draft Letter from William Woodbridge to "Dear Sir," ca. 1835, Woodbridge Papers (BHC).
20. Letter from Lucius Lyon to Col. Geo. Wm. Boyd, December 29, 1835, Lyon Papers, *MP&HC*, XXVII (1896), 468-469.
21. Dorr (ed.) *Michigan Constitutional Conventions* p. 15.
22. White, *Michigan Pioneer and Historical Collections*, XIV (1894), 407.
23. *(Dorr), Michigan Constitutional Conventions,* pp. 394, 479, 462; Michigan, Constitution (1835), Art. XII, sec. 3. Dorr, p. 606, inserts "roads" which was adopted by the convention, but dropped in the formal copy through a clerical error.
24. Ordinance adopted by the Constitutional Convention and submitted to Congress with the Constitution, *Territorial Papers of the United States Senate, 1789-1873*, File Microcopies of Records in the National Archives: No. 200, roll 6 (Washington, D. C.: National Archives and Records Service, General Services Administration, 1951).
25. Hemans, pp. 178-183; Dunbar, p. 305.

26. *Michigan Whig* (Ann Arbor), July 2, 1835.
27. Dunbar p. 333, errs when he says that Mason preferred investment in corporate stock. Mason offered several courses of action, of which this was only one, and was willing to adopt any method which would allow the state to control main trunk lines.
28. *Messages of the Governors of Michigan,* I, 169-171.
29. Michigan, *House Journal,* 1835, p. 91.
30. *Ibid.,* p. 123.
31. *Ibid.,* pp. 164-166; Michigan, *Senate Journal,* 1835, p. 70.
32. Michigan, *House Journal,* 1835, pp. 170, 179, 197, 227, 228.
33. *Ibid.,* pp. 333, 335, 366, 408; Michigan, *Senate Journal,* pp. 388-389.
34. Alpheus Felch, "Early Legislation," *Semi-Centennial Addresses,* p. 515.
35. *Messages of the Governors of Michigan,* I, 185-188.
36. Michigan, *Senate Journal,* 1836, pp. 88, 362, 380, 386.
37. Michigan, *Legislative Acts,* 1836, pp. 61, 62.
38. Gordon, *Michigan History,* XLIII (1959), 262. Although there seem to be no records of a projected state canal, Gordon speaks of one as a certainty.
39. *National Intelligencer,* September 17, 1834, as quoted in the *Michigan Emigrant* (Ann Arbor), October 16, 1834.
40. *Messages of the Governors of Michigan,* I, 136, 140.
41. *Detroit Daily Advertiser,* December 28, 1836; March 9, 1837, as cited in Reagan, pp. 18, 21.
42. Letter from Lucius Lyon to H. H. Comstock, March 29, 1836, Lyon Papers, *MP&HC,* XXVII (1896), p. 291-292.
43. U. S., *Statutes at Large,* V, 59.
44. Dunbar, p. 315; Hermans, pp. 241-247.
45. Letter from Stevens T. Mason to Emily [Mason], January 13, 1837, S. T. Mason Papers (BHC).
46. *Messages of the Governors of Michigan,* I, 192-200.
47. *Ibid.,* 200-220.
48. Michigan, *House Journal,* 1837, pp. 45, 49.
49. *Ibid.,* pp. 112-131. I believe this to be the committee appointed in 1836.
50. *Ibid.,* p. 113.
51. This may be Dionysius Lardner, F. R. S., LL. D., Trinity College, Dublin, Author of *Popular Lectures on the Steam Engine* and a noted railroad advocate.
52. Michigan, *House Journal,* 1837, p. 131.
53. *Ibid.,* p. 144.
54. An opposite point of view is taken by Streeter, pp. 6-9.
55. Michigan, *House Journal,* 1837, p. 157.
56. Felch, *Semi-Centennial Addresses,* p. 519.
57. *Detroit Daily Advertiser,* February 4, 1837, as cited in Reagan, p. 22.
58. Michigan, *House Journal,* 1837, pp. 188. 206.
59. *Ibid.,* p. 226.
60. *Ibid.,* pp. 180, 222, 223, 225, 227, 237, 238, 247-248.
61. Michigan, *Senate Journal,* pp. 191, 227, 240-241, 285.
62. Michigan Historical Commission, *Michigan Biographies* (East Lansing: Michigan Historical Commission, 1924), was used to determine the political party of state officials when such information was given. Unfortunately, the Commission interested itself in antiquarian details more than political affiliation when it compiled these short biographies of state officials. In other cases, membership in party central committees or signature of party campaign literature was used as a basis for determining membership. Lists for the Senate are almost complete, but it proved impossible to determine the party affiliation of a majority of the members of the House. Control of the Legislature was determined by contemporary statements, and the party or factional affiliation of the state printer.
63. *Semi-Weekly Free Press* (Detroit), March 17, 1837, p. 4. Just before the crucial

debates, the *Democratic Free Press* burned to the ground. The *Semi-Weekly Free Press*, its political propaganda column, was published separately for about three months as a bi-weekly, and presents a different version of debates from those found in the legislative journals or the *Free Press*.

64. Streeter, pp. 6-9.
65. Four districts with three Senators, and one with four.
66. Michigan, *Legislative Manual,* 1837, p. 88; Michigan, *Senate Journal,* 1837, pp. 297-299.
67. *Semi-Weekly Free Press* (Detroit), April 25, 1837, p. 1.
68. Reagan, p. 28.
69. *Democratic Free Press* (Detroit), February 1, and February 8, 1837; *Semi-Weekly Free Press* (Detroit), March 17, and April 4, 1837.
70. Michigan, *House Journal,* 1837, pp. 352-356.
71. *Ibid.,* p. 377; Michigan, *Senate Journal,* 1839, p. 325.
72. Letter from R. Ward to the Citizens of New Buffalo, March 18, 1837, in the Wessell Whittaker Manuscripts, Michigan State University Historical Collections.
73. Michigan, *Senate Journal,* 1837, pp. 147, 250, 348, 366, 385.
74. Michigan, *Legislative Acts,* 1837, No. LXXV.
75. *Ibid.,* No. XX.
76. Michigan, *House Journal,* 1837, p. 405.
77. Michigan, *Legislative Acts,* 1837, No. LXXVII.
78. *Ibid.,* No. XX, CXX.
79. *Ibid.,* No. XCVII.
80. *Ibid.,* No. CXVII.
81. *Ibid.,* No. LXXVII.
82. *Ibid.,* No. XLVII.
83. Felch, *Semi-Centennial Addresses,* pp. 521-522.
84. Michigan, *Legislative Acts,* 1837, No. CXXI.
85. Goodrich, *Government Promotion,* p. 266.

6

CONSTRUCTING THE PUBLIC WORKS: THE CENTRAL

When the Legislature adjourned on March 22, 1837, it had approved a comprehensive program of internal improvements and delegated authority for construction. Commissioners for the Board of Internal Improvements had been appointed, and, while the Governor was negotiating a bond issue, temporary funds were provided by earmarking money from the federal surplus revenue distribution and the five percent grant.

When the Board met on May 1, it acted quickly. Money belonging to the internal improvements fund was loaned to the Michigan State Bank at six percent and bond was accepted for the deposits. Levi S. Humphrey was assigned to survey the Southern, the Havre Branch, and the St. Joseph River. D. C. McKinstry was appointed to construct the Central from Detroit to Ypsilanti, while James B. Hunt was given the job of surveying a rail or canal route from Mount Clemens to the mouth of the Kalamazoo River, the Northern Railroad, and the Saginaw-Maple Canal. Chief engineers were employed at a salary of two thousand dollars per year: Joseph Dutton on the Southern; Jarvis Hurd on the Central, and the Clinton and Kalamazoo; and Tracy McCracken on the Northern.[1]

With its formal organization complete, the Board began construction. While other transportation projects were being surveyed and located, the Board purchased the Detroit and St. Joseph from its private owners. At the time of its purchase, $116,902 had been expended in clearing and grubbing a hundred-foot right-of-way to Ypsilanti, as well as partial grading and construction of the superstructure.[2] By paying for materials and machines being shipped to Detroit, the state was able to acquire the road for $139,802.[3]

When the Board reported in January 1838, the first thirty miles, from Detroit to Ypsilanti, were nearing completion and bids were being taken on sections between Ypsilanti and Ann Arbor. To satisfy demands for rapid construction, new methods to shorten the time necessary for embankments to settle were adopted. Wooden blocks, two feet in diameter, were cut to length and placed upright in parallel lines five feet apart at eight-foot intervals. With their bases footed on solid ground the tops were cut parallel to the established

91

grade of the road. Wooden mud sills at least twelve inches square and from sixteen to forty feet long were then spiked to the blocks' upper surface forming a raised road bed of parallel beams. At this stage, ties were spiked to the top of the mud sills at intervals of three feet, and five-by-seven-inch wooden rails keyed into them at a standard gauge of four feet, eight and one-half inches. On top of the rails, on the inside edge, a bar of half-inch strap iron two and one-half inches wide formed the iron surface. The platform raised by this method was used to haul fill for embankments, which were then raised and allowed to settle around the piling and sills. Although original estimates set the cost of this method of construction between six and eight thousand dollars per mile, these figures proved conservative. In later portions of the road and in deep cuts, supporting blocks were abandoned and the mud sills laid directly on the ground or embankments.

The Board reported the road would be ready by February 1838 if the bridge over the River Rouge could be completed. The bridge, which was to plague the state throughout the program, was a particularly difficult engineering problem. Since the road crossed the river at a flood plain it was necessary to raise the bed several feet on piling to avoid the river's vicious flash floods. The resulting structure was frequently undermined by freshets and by flood wood collecting around its supports. Often weakened and in need of expensive repairs, the bridge became the weak link in the Central's carrying capacity.

Although Jarvis Hurd had originally been employed as the Central's Chief Engineer, the Board found it necessary to retain John M. Berrien, Jr., already under contract by the Detroit and St. Joseph. Berrien, who had been persuaded to join the company after his supervision of the federal survey in 1834, remained as Chief Engineer throughout the state's ownership. Under Berrien, the entire route between Ypsilanti and St. Joseph was again surveyed, with two major departures from the original route. West of Ann Arbor, at Honey Creek, the road was rerouted north through Dexter to Jackson, ostensibly because of difficulties in obtaining right-of-way, timber, and saw mills on the route plotted in 1834. As an inducement, the village of Dexter offered twenty town lots to compensate the state for the additional expense. West of Jackson, the road followed the Kalamazoo Valley to Kalamazoo before swinging south to St. Joseph, instead of leaving the valley at Albion, as previously planned. The result of these changes was to confine the road to river valleys, thereby reducing the cost of construction and tapping natural commercial and agricultural centers.

The new route was three or four miles longer, but the Board felt the addition justified because the river route avoided deep cuts and embankments, reducing costs sufficiently to compensate for the additional length. Estimates placed the cost of the remaining one hundred and fifty-three miles at

$1,381,040.90, an average of $9,025.41 per mile. The increased estimates reflected experience in construction to Ypsilanti, and compensated for earlier underestimation of the cost of embankments. The Board's decision to adopt the new route was reportedly unanimous.[4]

The first section was completed by the target date, and on Saturday, February 3, the inaugural train ran between Detroit and Ypsilanti. After suitable ceremonies, the first train, carrying the Governor, state officials, and appropriate dignitaries, departed for Ypsilanti, thus beginning a career that has continued for nearly a century and a half.

When the state purchased the Detroit and St. Joseph, the road was partially completed; the state took over construction under direct management to finish work already in progress. New sections, however, were placed under contract to private builders to avoid the expensive system of direct control. Early in 1838, the Board let the eight-mile segment between Ypsilanti and Ann Arbor in a single contract to Col. David C. McKinstry, who had resigned as commissioner for the Central. Apparently, McKinstry took the contract as a speculative venture, submitting the low bid in hope of being able to subcontract at even lower rates. Unable to relet the contract, McKinstry allowed it to expire. When the Board reported in the winter of 1838, McKinstry's section, due to be completed the previous October, was still unfinished. Meanwhile, the Board had signed contracts for completing the road from Ann Arbor to Jackson. In April 1839, the Legislature authorized the Board to charge damages to McKinstry and sue for his security. Shortly thereafter, William Thompson, the new commissioner in charge of the Central, resumed construction under direct state management. Thompson hired workmen and animals, and was able to open the road in October 1839, although it was not completely finished.

Thompson was handicapped by the failure of the Michigan State Bank in February 1839. Loss of over half a million dollars in state deposits, including payments from the five million loan, brought the state to the edge of bankruptcy. Faced with the alternatives of paying in depreciated notes or suspending operations, the state chose to accept the loss and continue building. Through the Board, Thompson succeeded in drawing warrants from the Bank of Michigan against the July and October installments of the state's loan, until the bank refused to extend further credit against it. At Thompson's request, the bank then arranged to pay for construction in current state money and post notes payable in twelve months. Failure of the state deposit bank, which halted construction on several other state projects, was the first financial difficulty encountered by the state, and the most costly. The Board, feeling certain that they could continue to Dexter during 1840 if the Legislature appropriated funds, located the road between Jackson and Kalamazoo.

The Central suffered a second heavy loss when it was discovered that the bridge over the River Rouge could not carry heavy freight. Teams had to be maintained at the bridge to haul passengers and freight around it, and traffic on the road was slowed to the pace of its weakest link. The Board estimated the loss of revenues between five and ten thousand dollars per year.[5] Late in 1839, the bridge was destroyed by an arsonist, and a temporary structure had to be erected. However, currents caused by flood wood around the pilings undercut the foundations of the temporary bridge. The wood was removed and the supports repaired, but the superintendent reported that any freshet would sweep it away, and recommended a permanent structure. Through 1841, however, traffic on the Central was limited by the bridge's carrying capacity.[6]

Late in 1838 or early in 1839, the road between Ann Arbor and Jackson was placed under contract. By December 1839, grubbing and grading had been completed almost to Dexter, and progress was being made between Dexter and Jackson. West of Dexter, where the road crossed the peninsular watershed between the Huron and Grand Rivers, the heaviest grading and cutting were encountered.

Despite Whig promises in the 1839 campaign to suspend construction, pressure for continuation mounted in Whig counties along the Central's route. Henry B. Lathrop wrote Governor-elect Woodbridge, urging the Governor to press for the road's completion into Jackson because the road would then serve not only Jackson, but two counties to the west. Lathrop complained:

> Our flour from this country this year will not fall much if any short of 80,000 barrels of which not over 6 or 7,000 will be sent by the way of Detroit for the reason that the road from Toledo is now extended to Clinton within 28 miles of this place and add to this the fact that South of the center of the county there are four out of five of our flouring mills which makes it quite easy to go with a load and back every two days which will make a difference to the miller of about 18 cts per bbl. from what it would to take it to Ann Arbor and Detroit.

Lathrop, a powerful Jackson County Whig, urged the Governor to lease the road if other sections objected to its construction while their roads were suspended.[7]

Woodbridge's inaugural address recommended suspending all spending on public works until a federal grant could be obtained or private enterprise could be persuaded to purchase the state's projects.[8] The Whig Legislature, however, unwilling to suspend all efforts, responded with a suspension of all *new* public works contracts.[9]

The new Whig Board found its hands tied. Contracts had been awarded for grading, bridging, and timber for superstructure, and there was a verbal agreement to lay iron from Ann Arbor to Dexter. Contracts for grading and timber from Dexter to Jackson had also been signed. Cancellation of these contracts would have subjected the state to heavy damage suits, and failure to renew contracts abandoned by contractors would have resulted in the deterioration of completed sections. Although the Legislature failed to appropriate funds and the Central exceeded its appropriations on May 15, work continued.[10] With the exception of its iron superstructure, the road to Dexter was completed in July. The combination of an iron shortage and sectional rivalry, however, delayed completion for a year.

In August, the Board attempted to obtain rails being held at Buffalo. The Board owned the iron, but shippers refused to release it until the state honored a protested draft for transportation charges drawn by former commissioner on the Southern, Levi S. Humphrey, on the Bank of the River Raisin. The Board protested that it had already paid once, but a draft was finally drawn on the Bank of Michigan, and the iron was delivered in October. For reasons unknown to the Board, except that Humphrey had negotiated the contract for Governor Mason, forty miles of iron was delivered at Monroe and only sixteen miles at Detroit. Because only thirty-six miles were needed to complete the Southern to Adrian, and an additional two and one-half miles to complete the Central to Dexter, the Board decided to ship the necessary iron from Monroe to Detroit.

When orders were issued to suspend further use of the iron at Monroe, the idea spread that the Whig-dominated Board intended to strip the Southern of its iron. R. Morrison, in charge of the Southern at Monroe, reported to the Board:

> Our folks are *up in arms* at the idea of your taking the iron of[f] from this road to the Centre: They insist upon my laying it down immediately to prevent your taking it: Some of the *biggest folks* say that they will help to mob any one who comes for it, that they will throw it in the dock to keep it of[f] C[entral].
>
> Really, you can have no idea of the excitement about it.[11]

When ordered to ship the iron, Morrison refused. The Board then sent a Mr. B. Briscoe to Monroe to obtain two or three miles of iron. Briscoe reported that when he informed Morrison of his mission, he was told that the local citizens were highly excited and would resist any such attempt. About an hour after his arrival, Morrison confronted Briscoe again, telling him that the citizens knew his intentions and would throw him in the river, or tar and feather him, if he attempted to remove the iron. Briscoe blamed Morrison for the uproar because the iron could have been removed quietly if Morrison had not spread the word of his coming. When no one in town would rent him a team or help load the iron, Briscoe was forced to retreat.

The Board then sent David French to Monroe with four men and a team. When French arrived, a large crowd gathered, "encouraged and incited by the mayor and the principal citizens of that place." A citizen's meeting, presided over by the mayor and Austin Wing, drafted a proclamation restating the principles of sectional equality and declaring that:

The interests of no one section of the state, should be sacrificed to the interests of a great Central Monopoly, or any other. And under which understanding alone, the loan aforesaid have been tolerated.[12]

The declaration made it clear that they would resort to any means to prevent removal of the iron. In the face of such united opposition, French's determination weakened. While he was attending the meeting, other residents of Monroe secretly took the iron out of town. Unable to recover it and afraid that attempts to remove it would result in violence, French was forced to return to Detroit. The matter was then turned over to Governor Woodbridge, but no record of his decision exists.[13]

As late as the winter of 1840, sectional rivalry was so strong that the southern counties thought of themselves as a distinct entity, rather than as part of the state, and of the state government as an object for their exploitation. The people of Monroe were determined to keep every advantage that could be gained, even if it meant denying extension of the state's only profitable public work. In the heart of one of the most severe depressions of the nineteenth century, they proved incapable of cooperating to produce the solvency essential for completion of their own projects.

During 1840, the depression made further inroads into the Central's operations. Faced with declining revenues, the Board reduced fares twenty-five percent in the hope of adding to producers' profits and building long-term traffic. The reduction held traffic volume at previous levels, but revenues fell off by nearly a quarter. The Board hoped that increasing the road's length would allow proportional expenses to fall, eventually restoring absolute losses. On August 1, 1840, service was cut in half by removing one train from each run, and the road operated with only one train daily each way.

In July 1841, the Central was opened to Dexter, fifty-four miles west of Detroit. The Board reported in December that due to stage line competition, the road was no more than paying costs. Despite delays resulting from the shortage of funds, the Board promised completion to Jackson by the first of the year. During 1841, the road had been resurveyed west of Jackson by way of the "Rice Creek route," and contracts let for clearing, grubbing, grading, and timber. Most of the contracts were at low-bid rates, which the Board cited as evidence of the "extreme anxiety of the people of that section of the state, for successful prosecution of the work...."

As the road lengthened, new problems developed. The four locomotives in use on the Central proved inadequate in the fall of 1841. As winter and the close of navigation approached, the back-log of freight was so great that shippers were forced to use teams to haul produce to Detroit. In desperation, the Board authorized night operations, even though the practice was considered unsafe. Believing that four more locomotives, at a total cost of twenty-eight thousand dollars, would be necessary when the road to Jackson was completed, the Board requested the engines be ordered immediately.

In the meantime, having crossed the peninsular watershed, the Board entered negotiations to arrange daily steamboat sailings from St. Joseph to Chicago. When construction to Jackson was completed, travelers would be able to ride from Detroit to Jackson in five and one-half hours, then travel by stage from Jackson to St. Joseph in twenty-four hours, and complete the trip across the lake to Chicago in another five hours. Total travel time from Detroit to Chicago, a distance of over two hundred and fifty miles, would be reduced from between three and five days to between thirty-six and forty hours. The Board hoped the reduction would enable the state to capture more of the passenger trade on the Great Lakes between Buffalo and Chicago.[14] Under legislative pressure, the bridge over the River Rouge was rebuilt during the year.[15]

In the fall of 1841, the Board's financial difficulties increased. After the Michigan State Bank failed in 1839, the state's programs were financed by issuing anticipations through the Bank of Michigan, secured by future installments from the five million loan. When the Bank of the United States failed to pay its October installment in 1841, and the Bank of Michigan, the state's last solvent financial institution, closed its doors, the program was in serious trouble. Not only was the state unable to meet payments on contracts, but it found itself heavily indebted for notes issued against the installments to pay contractors and companies supplying iron. Fortunately, partial relief was in sight. In September 1841, the long-awaited federal grant of five hundred thousand acres was awarded under the Preemption Act. Time was required, however, before the land could be converted into funds.[16]

On January 1, 1842, the Central was opened to Jackson, eighty miles west of Detroit. During the year, gross revenues nearly doubled, and profits rose to almost three times the previous annual total. The Board estimated that the following year profits would rise to one hundred thousand dollars. During the fall, pressure on the road was so heavy that trains were again forced to run at night. Eleven thousand dollars of the net profits were received in specie or bills of specie-paying banks, allowing the Board to purchase two new locomotives from Baldwin and Whitney at the end of October. The balance of the revenues was received in scrip. The Board was also able to add thirty new freight cars and a passenger car; by the end of the year, ten more freight cars were under construction.

The Central's success in 1842 led the Board to recommend that the state concentrate its resources to complete the road. The Board asked that the lands granted by the federal government be used to redeem warrants in circulation and to complete the Central. It was hoped that completion to Kalamazoo would allow the Central to compete successfully for traffic to Chicago then being channeled through the upper lakes. "The present and future interest of the state, depending so largely upon the revenue to be derived from this road," said the Board, "must be considered the apology of the commissioners for urging upon the Legislature the great importance of an early completion of this work." Until the Central was completed, the Board would not recommend the continuation of other projects.

Some reports from the Central during 1842 were not so encouraging. Chief Engineer John Berrien informed the Board that the half-inch iron used on the road was not heavy enough for future construction. Estimating that almost a third of the money spent for repairs on track, cars and machinery was due to the light iron, he said that a half-inch bar "does not possess sufficient weight or strength to prevent its being settled into the rails, crushing, splitting, or breaking them, and rendering renewal of them twice as frequent as would be necessary from the ordinary decay of the timber...." The resulting rough surface magnified the destructive effect of trains on the timber, while the bouncing and jarring tore cars and engines apart, and reduced the power of locomotives.

Many of the expenses charged to repairs, Berrien reported, should have been charged to construction. After the road was built, draining and ditching frequently had to be charged to repairs because construction funds were unavailable. To an extent, the capital creation charged to repairs probably offset depreciation because with the exception of iron, depreciation was not a long-term problem on the bed of a strap iron road. Berrien testified that depreciation was low, because repairs on a road built of such light and perishable materials had to be made when and where demanded. They could not be allowed to accumulate. A strap iron road could never be "as good as new," but was constantly being restored to running order, the highest state of efficiency it could achieve.[17]

During 1842, construction was concentrated on the segment between Jackson and Marshall which the Board hoped would be ready for superstructure by the spring of 1843.[18] At the end of the year, the Governor announced that most of the internal improvements land had been located, promising additional funds for completion of the road's next segment.[19]

Through most of 1843, however, the rate of construction was disappointing. The Board reported in December that work had been slowed by the depreciation of internal improvements warrants and that only when they appreciated, because of the opening of public lands, had the work pace increased. In December, they announced that the road would be completed to Marshall in the spring, and would be ready for superstructure as far as Kalamazoo by June. To complete the road to Kalamazoo, they asked the Legislature for seventy-five thousand dollars for iron and spike.

Procurement of iron, which had been a problem since the exhaustion of initial purchases, became critical after 1842. Before 1842, the difficulties were primarily administrative and legal. Iron purchased by Levi Humphrey through Governor Mason in 1838 was tied up in Buffalo and New York because of disputed drafts and the Board's inability to tell from its completely disorganized records what had and had not been paid. As long as funds from the five million loan could be counted on to provide exchange in the East, it was possible to buy iron by sacrificing domestic construction. When the Bank of the United States failed in 1841 and refused drafts on its October installment, the problem became critical. Domestic construction could be financed by issuing anticipations, treasury notes, warrants, and land scrip, but purchasing iron required ready cash. In this case, cash meant specie or notes of specie-paying banks. As the depression had destroyed the majority of Michigan's specie-paying banks, most of the state's tax revenues and receipts from the public works consisted of anticipations, treasury notes, and warrants issued for railroad construction. The tariff of 1842 further injured the state by increasing the cash outlay required for iron. Under an act of 1843, the Board was authorized to pledge the receipts of the Central and Southern Railroads to pay for iron, and was thus able to buy iron on extended credit. But the tariff required an immediate payment of twenty-five dollars a ton. The price differential was substantial; the Board reported being able to purchase iron imported before the tariff at forty-eight dollars a ton, but was forced to pay sixty dollars a ton for iron imported later. At least part of the tariff differential, however, had fallen upon the supplier because the price paid by the state did not reflect the full duty, and prices quoted for the post-tariff iron were in long tons, while earlier prices quoted were for short tons. The major problem was the necessity for immediate cash outlay; the loss of lower British iron prices was clearly secondary. The Board asked the Legislature to act to have the tariff modified by suspending duties on iron used by railroads authorized before the tariff. The Legislature responded by passing resolutions instructing Michigan's Congressmen to fight for tariff reductions during every legislative session after 1842.[20]

In August 1844, the Central was opened to Marshall, one hundred and ten miles west of Detroit. For the first time, gross revenues exceeded two hundred thousand dollars, and profits were over a hundred thousand. Grading from Marshall to Kalamazoo was reported nearly finished in December 1844, and the Board believed the road could be completed to Kalamazoo by August 1845. The bed was reported good, and the soil beneath it solid. Materials were easy to obtain. The Board advised against further extensions unless new resources could be accumulated. Previous appropriations, it reported, were already sufficient to consume the entire federal grant when interest bonds were counted against the lands. Unless another grant could be obtained, the Board saw no use in authorizing further construction.

The Board was enthusiastic over a new locomotive it had purchased, which had thirty percent greater capacity and could draw heavy trains. By hauling longer trains, speeds could be reduced to ten miles per hour with much less damage to the superstructure. Small engines were forced to haul small trains at high speeds to make the number of trips necessary to fill demands, and the concussion of heavy cars at high speeds broke the strap iron and crushed the rails. The Board hoped that using heavier engines would result in reduced repair bills.[21]

Procurement of iron remained a major problem. Profits during 1844 enabled the Board to reduce its iron debts, contracted under the authorization of 1843, by fifty-seven thousand dollars, but sixty-nine thousand dollars remained due. Nonetheless, the Board believed it could obtain iron without further appropriations. Since revenues soared during 1844, a year of crop failure, the Board believed that 1845 revenues would exceed two hundred and seventy-five thousand dollars. [22] The Board's optimism, however, soon proved unfounded.

The roadbed had been reported nearly complete to Kalamazoo, but iron shortages prevented its completion past Battle Creek, thirteen miles west of Marshall. In April 1845, Governor Barry instructed the Auditor General to call on Charles Butler in New York to collect on a promise to intercede with New York bondholders and persuade them to postpone demanding interest payments falling due January 1, 1846. To get iron to finish the Central, Barry was apparently willing to raise the interest on the bonds from six to seven percent.[23] When this offer was refused, the Governor obtained more iron by making himself personally responsible for the state's iron debt.[24] By the end of January 1846, the road was completed to Kalamazoo.

Unfortunately, iron was not the Central's only problem. On August 23, 1845, the West Lowell bridge collapsed, causing over a thousand-dollar loss in flour and cars. For twenty-six days, only passenger trains could run, while freight piled up or was shipped by wagon. Although the Board worked feverishly to restore the bridge, its collapse cast doubt on the soundness of the rest of the route's bridging, and substantial rebuilding seemed to be called for. As a temporary measure, bridges at the Rouge and Huron Rivers were reinforced. To complicate matters, the Ann Arbor car house burned down.[25] Compared with other problems confronting the Board, however, these were minor aggravations.

Instead of the two hundred and seventy-five thousand dollars predicted by the Board as gross revenue, receipts declined by six thousand dollars and profits by over twenty thousand dollars. The bridge collapse was not the major cause of reduced revenues, however. Until 1845, flour and wheat shipments, the road's heaviest bulk freight commodity, had been a major source of revenue. In examining its accounts, the Board discovered that in the first nine months of fiscal 1845, before the collapse of the Lowell bridge, income from wheat and flour shipments had declined from forty-seven thousand dollars in the same nine months of the previous year, to eleven thousand and five hundred dollars. Since 1844 had been a year of light harvests, the decrease was not surprising.[26] The fiscal year's failure to coincide with the agricultural year, however, produced the apparent inconsistency of declining revenues in a prosperous period. Wheat was harvested in June and July, while the fiscal year began the first of December. Shipments of flour ground from summer wheat harvests did not begin until November, so the major impact of harvests fell on the following fiscal year's performance. But the apparent enigma of receipts falling in a good year led the Board and some legislators to believe that the road was rapidly becoming a losing venture.

As the new crop poured in during the fall of 1845, the Board again found the road inadequate for transportation demand. In part, this was the result of a shortage of rolling stock, but more striking was the road's basic inadequacy to handle the increased need for low-cost heavy freighting capacity. The Board of Internal Improvements reported:

> In a vain attempt to bring forward all the produce which has been brought to the Central Railroad, since the late abundant harvest, 7 locomotive engines and 96 cars and racks have been running night and day, for 3 months. The disaster at Lowell, no doubt occasioned some accumulation of flour and grain at the western stations early in Sept. Nevertheless, the character of the road, and the limited number of our engines and cars must have prevented the prompt removal of freight, had there been no such impediment. The board are fully convinced, that a Railroad through the central tier of counties to be used for freight, and the stock of which should be good to its owners, and achieve the object of its construction must be built in the most substantial manner, and laid with a heavy T or H rail. The best of flat bar roads are of too slight a structure for a heavy freighting business, (such as must ever be done upon the Central road,) as they soon get out of repair and become so uneven, that trains passing rapidly over them, are liable to be, and often are, thrown off the track. The repairs of machinery and cars consequent upon a rough road, even where they are so fortunate as to keep the track, is at least four times greater than the like repairs of machinery and cars running upon the smooth and solid surface of a T rail.[27]

The Board cited the results of using T rails on the Lancaster and Harrisburg Railroad, where repairs were four hundred and twenty-five dollars per mile on the plate portion of the road, and seventy-five dollars per mile on the T rail segments. The Reading, which cost ten million dollars to build, could carry coal at a cost of less than forty cents per long ton over ninety-four miles, even though hauling trains of over three hundred and eighty tons and returning empty. Average cost to the company of car repairs was reported at 5.9 cents per ton hauled, while repair of the Central engines and cars averaged over 92 cents per ton. The Board compared the Fitchburgh Railroad's reports of 28.8 cents in repair cost per mile run by locomotive to the Central's cost of 61.8

cents. Even with allowances for age, the Board found the Central's perfor-mance markedly inefficient when compared to the new roads employing solid T or H rails. A fully loaded engine, it said, could run at twice the speed with three times the load at two-thirds of the cost of a similar train on a plate road, exclusive of repairs.

Critics of Michigan's public works have often pointed to the Board's recognition of the need for rebuilding the road to support charges of inef-ficiency and incompetence. Indeed, the sentiment was reflected in some legis-lators' statements when they learned that the road for which they had sacri-ficed the state's resources for nine years would have to be rebuilt. The Board's recommendations were not an admission of defeat, however, but a recognition of the road's success and potential. They were simply asking that recent tech-nological advances be adopted to bring the road to its highest state of effi-ciency. The new technology, said the Board, would provide cheap and rapid transportation for freight shipments, and almost completely overcome the handicap of living in the interior:

> Whether rail-roads are fit only for the purpose of pleasant or rapid
> travel, or are indeed valuable for the transportation of all articles of
> commerce, is a question no longer doubtful or unsettled; even the history
> of our own imperfect roads is a development of the wealth and resources
> of our country, which, but for their existence, would at this moment be
> unfelt and unknown. It has afforded the settler far distant in the interior,
> the means of rapid intercommunication with his remote fellow citi-
> zens....It has largely increased the value of property, by diminishing the
> cost of transportation of the productions of the mill, the farm and the
> manufactory; it has made valuable the otherwise nearly valueless water-
> power of the interior; it has given a healthy stimulus to trade in crude and
> ponderous mineral and agricultural productions, and has led to the pur-
> chase and settlement of our public lands, and the increase of our popula-
> tion and taxable property. To the central counties of this state, blest as
> they are with a highly productive soil, and extensive water power, great
> mineral wealth, and a salubrious climate, a first class rail-road is of vital
> importance.

Far from considering the road a failure, the Board was concerned with bringing the Central to its full potential. It argued that flour would always be one of the great commercial staples of the central counties and that a road with solid rails would cut the cost of its transportation in half. Unable to determine exactly the quantity of surplus wheat produced within the central counties, the Board arbitrarily estimated that the increment to producers' incomes from a new road would be one hundred and twenty-five thousand dollars annually. Transportation costs on a strap iron road, they argued, often ate up all of the producer's income.

To bring the Central to full capacity, the Board asked that the road between Detroit and Dexter be repaired immediately, and the balance rebuilt in thirty-mile segments annually. Any new construction should utilize heavy rails. Although the road's income was mortgaged to pay interest on the acknowledged public debt, the Board did not hesitate to make its recommendation because:

> The Central railroad of this state may not be inaptly compared to the Erie Canal of the state of New York. It is and must forever be the great channel of business for the central tier of counties, and one of the indispensable and most important links in the great chain of communication between the Atlantic cities and the Valley of the Mississippi.

Completion of projected roads on the northern and southern shores of Lake Erie was expected to bring the road profitable freighting business within two years, adding urgency to the Board's recommendations.

Because the constitution had been amended to forbid the Legislature to borrow money without popular consent, and the Board considered it doubtful that a majority could be persuaded to increase the debt to rebuild either the Central or the Southern, it recommended selling the road to a private corporation capable of renewing the superstructure. Not only could the Central be rebuilt, but over three million dollars of the public debt could be extinguished.[28]

Governor Alpheus Felch's inaugural message echoed the Board's recommendations. Although Felch stressed the removal of government from enterprise and the liquidation of internal improvements debts, rebuilding the road to carry freight at lower rates was basic to his arguments. At the very least, he pointed out, the road would have to be rebuilt between Detroit and Dexter, and this would cost two hundred thousand dollars. If the state made the repairs, no funds would be available to pay the interest on the public debt. If the interest were paid, there would be no money for repairs. The annual interest on the public debt amounted to two hundred and twenty thousand dollars. But repairing the road with strap iron would only restore it to do ordinary business: "We have been accustomed to look to these roads as the means of transporting the rich productions of the wheat growing country in the interior, to the waters upon which they are to be floated to a distant market. Experience has proven, however, that the transportation has been at charges, little, if any less than the cost of carriage by teams." State policies should focus on reducing freight rates, and strap iron roads had proven incapable of hauling freight at reasonable prices. Felch thought it would cost half a million dollars to reconstruct the road with heavy rails from Detroit to Dexter, and the state lacked such resources. Not enough of the land grant remained to finance it, a new loan would be impractical, the road's revenues would be inadequate, and taxation could not even be attempted. Felch recommended selling the road to an interested private group and incorporating safeguards and restrictions into the charter to protect the people from the natural monopoly of a private railroad. These consisted of maximum tolls, completion dates and standards, and the right of the state to repurchase after a stipulated period of time.[29]

When the Select Committee appointed by the House to draft a bill for the road's sale reported early in 1846, it stressed rebuilding to provide transportation for heavy freight. Sale was expected not only to give relief from taxation and reduce the public debt, but to open channels of communication with markets and create outlets for the state's products:

> The failure of the road to meet the expectations of its sanguine friends, arises not from the lack of business to be done, but from the utter incapacity of a road of the light superstructure and rail found upon this road, to transact the business offering upon the line of it. A heavy rail is indispensable, and the state has not the ability to provide such a rail. Doubtless, when the road shall be opened to Lake Michigan, with a proper rail thereon, it will be proven that the great natural advantages of this route, and the vast amount of business to be done upon it, have not been overrated. In preparing a bill for the sale of the road, the price to be obtained, the ability of those to whom it is offered to pay the same, and to complete and rebuild the road with a heavy rail, the time when the road shall be so completed and relaid, the protection to be provided for the people, and especially the agricultural interests, against exhorbitant tolls, and the manner in which the state, at a future day, in case the transfer of this road to private hands, would be attended with serious or unforeseen evils, could re-possess herself of the road without injustice to those individuals who shall invest their fortunes therein, have claimed particular attention.

Although the reports of other committees stressed various aspects of the sale, the Select Committee was primarily concerned with having the road constructed with heavy iron rails and protecting the rights of domestic shippers. To ensure this construction, the company was required to lay rails weighing sixty pounds to the yard, heavier than any then installed in the United States.[30]

The act, which was passed and signed into law on March 28, 1846, was designed to protect the people and provide low-cost transportation. The company was required to pay six percent interest on installments after large down payments. Differences in long-haul and short-haul rates were regulated, and upper limits were set on charges for hauling basic agricultural products and necessities. Grain and flour rates were limited to three-quarters of the fare charged by the state, and all rates were tied to those of three Massachusetts roads in the fall of 1845, subject to revision every ten years. Rate discrimination was prohibited under penalty of a hundred-dollar fine for each occurrence. The company was required to complete the road to Lake Michigan within three years with a penalty of twenty-five thousand dollars for each year that it failed to meet the deadline. Replacement of rails on the first fifty miles within two years was required at a penalty of fifty thousand dollars per year, with the rest of the rails to be replaced as required. Deadlines could be suspended only in case of war with a European power. Three hundred thousand dollars of the company's stock were required to be sold in Michigan, with no person taking more than a thousand dollars. A half percent tax was placed on the company's capital until 1851, when it was to be increased to three-quarters percent, and the state was allowed to purchase the road after January 1867 at market value plus ten percent.

To balance these safeguards, the company was given rights designed to attract private capital. In addition to the usual corporate privileges, a monopoly was granted excluding parallel routes for five miles on either side of the road. The route west of Kalamazoo could be altered to the state line instead of Lake Michigan, which allowed the new company to tap the St. Joseph Valley trade and eventually build to Chicago. The company could own or hire vessels for lake navigation, to compete with the shippers' combinations that had plagued the state and the railroad for a decade. Finally, it was allowed to purchase the road with bonds and warrants issued by the state.[31] The terms were advantageous to both the state and the corporation because the state was able to realize all but a few thousand dollars of its investment in the Central including expenditures in land and reinvested profits, while the company was able to use state bonds and warrants circulating at a twenty-five percent discount to purchase the road.[32]

At the end of January 1846, the Central was completed as far as Kalamazoo, where state construction ended. On September 23, the state treasurer received the half million dollars required for the first installment, and the following day the road passed to the Michigan Central Railroad Corporation. During the year, revenues and profits reached new heights. In the first ten months of the fiscal year, under state management, the road drew in gross revenues of over $239,000, while profits exceeded $104,000. For the total year, gross revenues exceed $339,000, and profits were over $175,000. Under state management, the rate of profit was 7.7 percent for the year, while profits for the total year rose to 10.8 percent as a bumper harvest swelled the volume of business. As the Board observed:

> It will be thus perceived that this road has earned an amount equal to the expectations and predictions of its warmest supporters and friends.
> The Central Rail Road has passed into the hands of the corporators, and although the state has disposed of one of the most important thoroughfares in our country, still, we are induced to believe that in the hands of the company, known for their high respectability and enterprise, Michigan will receive lasting benefits by the continuation and completion of the

Central Rail Road to Lake Michigan, thereby securing the travel and business of the Great West, which hitherto has gone by and around our Peninsula.[33]

Rebuilding the Central with heavier rails was not the only motive prompting the state to sell, but it was at least as important as liquidating the public debt. And to this extent, the desire for low-cost transportation and the economic development it would bring was as strong a motive as it had been in 1837. Accounts of the internal improvements program have focused on the debt as the motive for the road's sale, and assumed that the road was ruined by mismanagement and state incompetence. Too many writers have followed Henry G. Pearson, John Murray Forbes' biographer, who, forgetting the energy with which private interests sought to wrest control of the Central from the state, spoke of the road as a "shabby piece of property," and of the state "placing its dilapidated property on the bargain-counter."[34] At the price set by the state in 1846, the Central was a bargain, but it was neither a shabby piece of property nor dilapidated. It was a profitable economic unit demanding further investment to increase its usefulness to the community.

J. W. Brooks, the engineer appointed by eastern financiers to inspect the Central, substantiates this view. Pearson, who cited Brooks' report as evidence of the road's dilapidated condition, focused on Brooks' criticisms rather than on the fact that he was writing a *Report upon the Merits of the Michigan Central Railroad, As an Investment for Eastern Capitalists*. According to Brooks, the first thirty miles of the road, built under pressure for immediate opening in 1838, were badly deteriorated. In part, the engineers' failure to select decay-resistant timber was responsible for the road's condition, and in part the weakness of the half-inch iron used between Detroit and Jackson. Brooks thought the road from Ypsilanti to Jackson would last two or three more years without extensive repairs. The remainder was constructed with three-quarter inch iron, and "The track between Jackson and Kalamazoo (sixty-seven miles) being for a plate railroad, a very superior track." Brooks criticized the use of bridging in many places where embankments and culverts would have been more expensive but more permanent, and he thought that many more depots would be necessary. More warehouses were needed, and a connection was lacking between the eastern terminal and the Detroit River. But, in general, he was not highly critical. He estimated the total length of bad road bed between Detroit and Kalamazoo at twenty-one miles. With the exception of the embankments in the Huron Valley, he felt the width of cuts and embankments were comparable to those of any well-constructed road. "Excepting in the valley of the Huron River, the line of the road is unusually straight, having a large amount of straight line, with most of the curves quite gentle."[35]

Brooks had no doubts that with new rails and more rolling stock the road would be highly profitable:

This view of the matter is presented to show that a large amount of wheat is grown upon the western as well as upon the eastern portion of that line, and also to show what is quite plain to the most cursory observer of the operations of that road, which is that it does not draw produce in but a very small degree from the country west of its western terminus. The evident reason for this is, that more surplus is grown upon the line, than the motive power, cars or track of the road are equal to the task of bringing to market.

Large amounts of flour are brought by teams 40 miles to Detroit, from mills within sight of the railroad, so unequal is the road and its present equipment to the business upon its line.

He estimated the current domestic business potential of the Central, if completed to Lake Michigan and furnished with adequate rails and rolling stock, at a minimum of half a million dollars.[36]

Of course, Brooks was trying to persuade stockholders to invest in the Central. Nevertheless, he was a competent railroad engineer, and his judgment was essentially sound. Indeed, there was no reason to doubt the road's basic profitability, for it had never failed to show a profit under state management. During the last four years of state ownership, the Central's profits had been the state's primary source of funds for purchasing iron and locomotives to extend both the Central and the Southern.

Table II summarizes the receipts, expenditures, net income, and profits of the Central under state ownership. Because of the system of accounting adopted by the Board in its reports to the Legislature, the data prohibits exact statements of the Central's profit and loss, but they do give an approximate picture of the road's earnings and indicate the order of magnitude of returns. The original books and vouchers, few of which are extant, are necessary for a more precise statement of earnings. However, the few still available indicate that statements would still be tentative, even with this data, because itemization of expenditures in vouchers was vague enough to leave many doubts about their final classification.

The account of receipts reported annually is the most accurate. The only difficulty presented by them lies in the quality of money accepted by the road. During 1838, the Board accepted large amounts of "wild cat" which became valueless unless expended immediately. During later years, warrants and scrip issued by the state to finance construction were also accepted, but since they represent units expended in the creation of the road, accepted at par by their issuer, they present no problems when charged against capitalization to determine the rate of return.

Expenditures present more difficult problems. Disaggregation is not consistent from report to report, and the headings under which expenditures are reported are too inclusive to allow exact accounting. A major difficulty is presented by the charging of capital-creating expenditures to operating costs.

TABLE II
Profits of the Central Railroad, 1838-1846[a]
(Thousands of Dollars)

	Receipts	Expenditures	Net Income	Reported annual investment	Total	Rate of profit (%)[f]	Miles in use	Capital in use[g]	Profit on capital in use (%)
1837				367	367				
1838	83	46	37	210	577	10.2	30	420	8.9
1839	61	44	17	179	757	2.9	38	532	3.1
1840	62	41	21	111	868	2.7	38	532	3.9
1841	71	46	26	195	1,063	2.9	49	686	3.7
1842	137	74	63	111	1,174	6.2	77	1,078	5.9
1843	150	75	75	130[e]	1,303	6.4	77	1,078	7.0
1844	211	89	122	241[e]	1,544	9.3	109	1,526	8.0
1845	206	105	101	99[e]	1,643	6.5	122	1,708	5.9
1846[b]	240	– [d]	105			7.6	145	2,050	6.2
1846[c]	399	– [d]	176			10.7	145	2,050	8.7

[a]Michigan, Legislature, *Annual Reports of the Board of Internal Improvements (Joint Documents,* J. D. No. 4), pp. (1844) 11-12; (1845) 12-15; (1846) 4-7. Sums presented will not balance because all numbers are rounded to the nearest thousand, or tenth of one percent.
[b]Ten months, profit adjusted to twelve-month basis.
[c]Twelve months, last two months under private management.
[d]Not stated in the *Annual Report* of 1846.
[e]Not including iron or locomotives after 1842.
[f]Calculated from reported capital investment at the beginning of the fiscal year.
[g]Estimated from value stated by Auditor General, Michigan, Legislature, *Annual Report of the Auditor General,* 1845 (*Joint Documents,* 1846, J. D. No. 2), p. 2. Includes profits invested in iron and rolling stock.

Unlike private roads, which frequently tapped their capital accounts to pay dividends to stockholders, thus maintaining their capital markets, the state often tapped its income to add to its capital in the absence of funds for such expenditures. Frequently, the repair and building of new cars was entered as a single expense, without stating whether the new cars were replacements or additions to rolling stock. When challenged by the Legislature to produce an accounting of expenditures on rolling stock in 1846, the Commissioner of Internal Improvement was unable to answer because both construction and repair of cars, racks, engines, and tender frames had been charged to "repairs of machinery and cars" until fiscal 1846.[37] Similarly, expenditures charged to "repair of road" fail to separate maintenance expenditures from money spent for improvement. Widening of embankments and easing the slope of cuts after segments of the road were completed was frequently charged to repair accounts, as well as additional ditching to provide adequate drainage. Over a decade, substantial sums charged to repairs were actually expended in improving the road.

At the same time, no account was kept to balance depreciation. In one sense, long-term depreciation on a strap iron road was slight because the nature of the light superstructure demanded constant maintenance and replacement. Rolling stock also demanded constant maintenance, but its depreciation was continuously financed by replacement and repair paid out of current revenues. Long-term depreciation items consisted principally of locomotives and strap iron. During the ten years of state ownership, none of the locomotives was worn out through use, although units purchased at the program's beginning became inadequate for the heavy hauling required in later years and were superseded by technologically superior engines. Obsolescence was a greater factor in depreciation than wear. At an original cost of seven thousand dollars, a price which apparently was fairly constant throughout the period, unit depreciation on locomotives could not have been more than seven hundred dollars per year. Maximum depreciation for the Central's seven locomotives would have been only forty-nine hundred dollars annually.

Iron presents a more serious problem. The maximum life of half-inch strap iron appears to have been nine or ten years under the volume of traffic handled by the Central. As Brooks testified, the segment from Detroit to Ypsilanti was in need of immediate replacement in 1846. The road, in use since 1838, received the heaviest traffic as it was the first section. The segment from Ypsilanti to Jackson, Brooks thought, would last two or three more years. The Board's estimate of two hundred thousand dollars for immediate rebuilding from Detroit to Jackson called for replacing the iron with three-quarter inch strap, which was supposed to have greater strength and durability. At this rate, assuming replacement between Ypsilanti and Jackson could have been postponed for the time estimated by Brooks, depreciation was two hundred and sixty dollars per mile per year over a ten-year period, or approximately two percent per year of the value of the road. Depreciation of locomotives was undoubtedly offset by expenditures for new construction, along with part of the depreciation on the road, leaving two per cent as an adequate figure for depreciation.

The account of net income is, of course, residual, and suffers from the same limitations in inverse proportions to expenditures. Heavy investment, disguised as expenses, will lower net income and the apparent rate of profit as a percent of total investment, while failure to cover depreciation will give net income an upward bias and distort the same rate of profit in the opposite direction.

Data listed under "reported annual investment" are adequate for determining capitalization through 1842, when the Legislature began authorizing purchases of iron and locomotives for the Central and Southern from the net proceeds of the roads. After 1842, reported expenditures, in terms of appropriations, fall short of the road's cost. For this reason, a second column was derived from the Auditor General's report of the Central's cost in 1846, which was given as cost plus ten percent. This figure was deflated to derive cost and divided by total mileage, resulting in an average cost of fourteen thousand dollars per mile. Multiplied by the number of miles of road in use, it provides an appropriate figure for capital in use. This figure has the advantage of including expenditures for iron and rolling stock, which is particularly important in the last four years of state ownership. In deriving the rate of profit on reported investment, capitalization for the previous year is used as a base, on the assumption that a period of gestation of at least one year exists, and that rates so derived reflect profit on capital in use.

During the ten years of state ownership, the Central never achieved the optimistic predictions made by the House Internal Improvements Committee in 1837, but its performance was well above average for investments undertaken by states during the second canal cycle. Indeed, few of these projects showed a profit during their existence. Even when profit estimates are discounted two percent for depreciation, they were sufficient to pay interest on the cost of construction in 1844 and 1846, at the rate the money was borrowed. Failure to meet this rate in 1845 grew out of crop failure, always a hazard in an agricultural economy. Returns prior to 1842 fail to give full credit to the road's potential. When the road was extended to Jackson, west of the peninsular watershed, the Central's income grew rapidly, and each extension into the wheat-producing counties of the west produced further increases in the rate of return. During these four years, income was limited by the inadequacy of rolling stock and motive power. Had the state been able to provide these, the rate of profit might have doubled.

The Central's income was sufficient to attract private enterprise. After the high profits of 1838, the Legislature, in the closing minutes of the 1839 session, passed a resolution authorizing the leasing of the road, only to have it vetoed by Governor Mason. The following year, Mason's veto was supported by the Whig Legislature.[38] Another offer was made during 1842, but the House defeated the bill by a large majority.[39] Three separate offers were submitted by prominent local business groups during 1843.[40] Finally, the state was approached by two separate groups in 1846, both of which attempted to meet the Legislature's objections to the 1842 propositions. One of the proposals, made by local businessmen, promised to complete the road, refurnish it with heavy rails, reduce freight rates fifty percent, and pay six percent interest, if the state would relinquish the remainder of the lands granted by the federal government. Both offers were rejected.[41] Current and potential profits, however, attracted the interest of private enterprise, and the decision of the eastern capitalists to purchase the Central's charter was far from a pioneering venture.

Table III, based on data taken from the company's annual reports, summarizes the Central's income in its first decade under private management.

The profit rate is derived from the ratio of net income to capitalization reported at the beginning of the fiscal year, making it roughly comparable to similar rates derived for the Central under state ownership. It has frequently been asserted that private ownership transformed the Central from an inefficient, dilapidated structure into an efficient, highly profitable road, but the company's reports do not bear this out. The quantities of receipts, expenditures, net income, and capitalization rose dramatically as the road was pushed west to the state border and into Chicago. But rates of return on investment failed to grow accordingly. After an initial high rate during the bumper wheat crop of 1846, returns did not rise dramatically above 1846 and 1847 levels. Like the state, the corporation apparently failed to keep a depreciation account, and the same deflation of returns is applicable. This is particularly significant in light of the higher cost of investment paid by the corporation. While the state had been able to borrow at six percent in 1838, the corporation was forced to pay seven, eight, and even nine percent for construction funds, according to its annual statements. The company maintained a consistent dividend of eight percent on stocks and bonds throughout the period. Dividends were apparently paid out of current income, without impairing or watering the company's capital. The difference between the dividend rate and the actual profit rate is accounted for by the large amount of capital created on credit; in the company's accounting, construction and cash on hand were balanced by the stock and bond accounts, income account, bills payable, and unpaid dividends. Substantial amounts of construction appear, therefore, to have been financed through loans by suppliers, balanced later by increased stock issues in a market maintained by a constant rate of return. The data indicate that the superiority of private enterprise lay not in its ability to employ capital profitably, but in its ability to mobilize capital for construction after state credit had been destroyed.

Table IV illustrates the problem facing the state in 1846. Originally designed to carry passengers and merchandise, the Central was being forced

TABLE III
Profits of the Michigan Central Railroad Company,
1847-1855[a] (Thousands of Dollars)

	1847[b]	1848[c]	1849	1850	1851	1852	1853	1854	1855
Receipts	209	401	427	698	967	1,075	1,149	1,588	2,215
Expenditures	86	288	239	301	400	470	566	903	1,335
Net income	123	113	188	397	566	604	582	674	879
Capitalization[d]	2,000	3,857	5,584	5,968	6,709	8,156	8,859	9,951	12,163
Profit rate (%)	10.6	5.2	4.9	7.1	9.5	9.1	7.2	7.6	8.8
Dividend paid (%)	–	8	8	8	9	14	8	8	6

[a]Michigan Central Railroad Company, *Annual Reports,* 1-19, 1847-1865. (Bound volume in the possession of the University of Michigan Transportation Library.)

[b]Through April 1847. Seven months converted to a twelve-month rate.

[c]Thirteen months, May through May inclusive, converted to a twelve-month rate.

[d]Figures for capitalization are taken from data given by the company for its net worth, including stocks, bonds, income accounts, bills payable, and unpaid dividends. In the company's accounting, these items are balanced by construction expenditures and cash on hand. The rate of profit is derived as a percentage of capitalization at the beginning of the fiscal year in which the income was earned, on the assumption that increases in capitalization during the fiscal year would require a year or more to become incorporated into the physical capital of the road. The procedure has the added advantage of making the rates of return comparable to those derived for the period of state ownership.

to carry great quantities of heavy freight. In nine years, passenger traffic, a major source of revenue, fell short of doubling, while receipts slightly more than doubled. Shipments of merchandise remained fairly constant. During the same period, however, shipments of flour increased twelve hundred per-cent. Most of the wheat appears to have been shipped to milling centers along the route, to be reshipped as flour. [42] Proportionally, passenger rev-enues declined from approximately two-thirds to less than half of gross receipts. Growth of wheat and flour shipments accounted for its relative decline.

The new traffic required facilities capable of handling high-bulk, low-value freight at low rates. Between 1839 and 1842, wheat producers had been able to compete with less efficient lands in the east, but when wheat prices fell even further in 1843 and 1844, most of their profit margins began to be consumed by transportation costs. Partial recovery in 1845 and 1846 only slightly relieved the squeeze of transportation costs. Blaming their problems on the railroad rather than the market, Michigan's millers and farmers expected the road to respond to declining prices by lowering the cost of transportation.[43] Having driven rates for team hauling to competitive levels, the roads appeared inefficient and inadequate when they could not haul at lower rates. Only the adoption of cost-reducing techniques would satisfy the demands of farmers and millers in the central tier.

After ten years of state ownership, the Central was returned to private control. Every effort and every resource the state possessed short of taxation had been mobilized for its completion. Although the depression eliminated increases in the rate of track construction, an average rate of fifteen miles of new road bed per year was added with remarkable regularity. In at least two years when the state did not meet this average, failure resulted from speculation and sectional rivalry, rather than financial difficulty. For a strap iron road, the Central was well engineered and well constructed. The state's most obvious failure was not providing sufficient motive power and rolling stock to handle the press of business, a failure directly traceable to the depression and exhaustion of resources on multiple projects created by sectional rivalry. The road's deterioration grew out of conscious decisions to sacrifice the superstructure to offset shortages of motive power and rolling stock. During the last four years, the pounding and tearing of freight trains operated at double speed to compensate for inadequate carrying capacity took a serious toll on the road bed and rolling stock, and increased running costs out of proportion with receipts. But, the course of action was dictated by economic and political necessity, rather than technological incompetence. In the end, the Central's success proved a powerful attraction to eastern capital.

Had the state been timid and conservative in 1837, the main lines of continental transportation might well have bypassed the peninsula, with trade channeled through northern Ohio and Indiana into Chicago. By aggres-sive action, the Democracy had forced a major route of east-west com-munication through the state's borders. Unlike the canals of Ohio, Indiana,

TABLE IV

Shipments on the Central Railroad, 1838-1846[a]

Receipts by Commodity (Thousands of Dollars)	1838	1839	1840	1841	1842	1843	1844	1845	1846[b]
Passengers	39	36	32	33	59	52	83	89	89
Merchandise	20	15	11	14	19	26	33	32	31
Wheat					5	6	15	11	6
Flour	3	6	10	14	37	46	57	47	77
Quantity (thousands of units)									
Passengers	29	26	25	25	30	30	52	51	46
Merchandise (tons)	9	8	5	8	6	8	10	9	9
Wheat (bu.)					45	61	127	91	59
Flour (bbls.)	15	25	43	63	107	137	144	124	180

[a]Michigan, Legislature, *Annual Reports of the Board of Internal Improvements* (*Joint Documents*, J. D. No. 4), pp. (1844) 11-12; (1845) 12; (1846) 10, 11, 12.
[b]Ten months, from December 1 to September 23.

Illinois, and Pennsylvania, the Central was never abandoned, but has continued for over a century to service local transportation requirements, as well as becoming a major national traffic artery.

Notes, Chapter 6

1. Michigan, *Senate Document No. 11*, 1838, pp. 155, 156.
2. *Ibid.*, p. 161.
3. *Ibid.*, p. 204; *Messages of the Governors of Michigan*, I, 222.
4. Michigan, *Senate Document No. 11*, 1838, pp. 165, 166.
5. Michigan, *Legislative Acts*, 1839, Joint Resolution No. 30. Michigan, Legislature, *Annual Report of the Board of Internal Improvement of the State of Michigan, January 15, 1839, (House Documents*, 1839, H. D. No. 17), pp. 276, 285-286. Cited hereafter as *House Document No. 17*, 1839; Michigan, Legislature, *Annual Report of the Board of Internal Improvements, December 20, 1839 (House Documents*, 1840, H. D. No. 3), pp. 14, 24. Cited hereafter as *House Document No. 3*, 1840. Michigan, Legislature, *Report of the Special Committee Appointed by the House of Representatives, to Investigate the Proceedings, & c., of the Several Boards of Internal Improvement* (Detroit: Dawson and Bates, 1840), p. 391.
6. *Messages of the Governors of Michigan*, I, 305; Michigan, Legislature, *Annual Report of the Board of Internal Improvements, December 4, 1840 (House Documents*, 1841, I, H. D. No. 3), p. 63. Cited hereafter as *House Document No. 3*, 1841.
7. Letter from Henry B. Lathrop to William Woodbridge, December 12, 1839, in Woodbridge Papers (BHC).
8. *Messages of the Governors of Michigan*, I, 314-315.
9. Michigan, *Legislative Acts*, 1849, Joint Resolution No. 5.
10. Michigan, *House Document No. 3*, 1841, pp. 5, 6.
11. Letter from R. M. Morrison to Gen. Van Fossen, October 28, 1840, in Records of the Executive Office, 1810-1910: Reports; Board of Internal Improvements (Michigan, Department of State, Historical Commission Archives).
12. "[Minutes and Resolutions of] the Meeting of Citizens of the City of Monroe, Saturday, December 12, 1840," *Ibid.*
13. Letters from John Van Fossen and Thomas Rowland, Commissioners of Internal Improvement, to His Excellency William Woodbridge, December 24, 1840; John Van Fossen, Thomas Rowland, and Robert Stuart, Acting Commissioners of Internal Improvement, to His Excellency William Woodbridge, January 12, 1841; Robert Stuart to His Excellency, William Woodbridge, August 11, 1840, *Ibid.* Letter from William Woodbridge to the Board of Internal Improvements, ca. 1840, in the Woodbridge Papers (BHC). *House Document No. 3*, 1841, pp. 7, 8. Talcott E. Wing, *History of Monroe County* (New York: Munsell & Co., 1890), p. 222.
14. Michigan, *House Document No. 3*, 1841, pp. 3, 12-13.
15. Michigan, Legislature, *Annual Report of the Board of Internal Improvements, December 15, 1841 (House Documents*, 1842, H. D. No. 3), pp. 17-20. Cited hereafter as *House Document No. 3*, 1842. Michigan, *House Journal*, 1841, p. 659.
16. *Messages of the Governors of Michigan*, I, 385; *House Document No. 3*, 1842.
17. Such accounting practices appear to have been common among nineteenth century railroads. Albert Fishlow reports that: "Until the ICC regulations of 1907 instituted depreciation accounting, the practice of replacement accounting is almost universal. With the latter, equipment replacements—that is, retirements—were charged to current operating expenses at the time the expenditures were made, and

no entry ever appeared in the capital account. Albert Fishlow, "Productivity and Technological Change in the Railroad Sector, 1840-1910," *Output, Employment, and Productivity in the United States after 1800* "Conference on Research in Income and Wealth: Studies in Income and Wealth," Vol. 30 (New York: National Bureau of Economic Research, 1966), p. 591.

18. *Messages of the Governors of Michigan*, I, 471; Michigan, Legislature, *Annual Report of the Board of Internal Improvements, December 16, 1842 (Senate Documents*, 1843, S.D. No. 4), pp. 1-2, 5-6, 9-10. Cited hereafter as *Senate Document No. 4*, 1843.

19. *Messages of the Governors of Michigan*, I, 465.

20. *Ibid.*, 494; Michigan, Legislature, *Annual Report of the Board of Internal Improvements, December 2, 1843 (Joint Documents*, 1844, J.D. No. 5), pp. 1-4. Cited hereafter as *Joint Document No. 5*, 1844.

21. Michigan, Legislature, *Annual Report of the Board of Internal Improvements, December 2, 1844 (Joint Documents*, 1845, J. D. No. 4), pp. 1-4. Cited hereafter as *Joint Document No. 5*, 1845. Concussion or impact is the product of mass times velocity. Heavier engines at half speed reduce concussion by half, while the increased weight is multiplied only by the reduced speed.

22. *Ibid.*, pp. 7-8; *Messages of the Governors of Michigan*, I, 509.

23. Draft of a letter from John Barry to Ch. G. Hammond, April 28, 1845, in Records of the Executive Office, 1810-1910: Reports; Board of Internal Improvements (Michigan, Department of State, Historical Commission Archives).

24. Felch, *Semi-Centennial Addresses*, p. 181.

25. Michigan, Legislature, *Annual Report of the Board of Internal Improvements, December 2, 1845 (Joint Documents*, 1846, J. D. No. 4), pp. 2-3. Cited hereafter as *Joint Document No. 4*, 1846.

26. *Ibid.*, pp. 12-13.

27. *Ibid.*, p. 6.

28. *Ibid.*, pp. 6-11.

29. *Messages of the Governors of Michigan*, II, 44-47.

30. Michigan, *House Document No. 2*, 1846, pp. 1-6.

31. Michigan, *Legislative Acts*, 1846, No. 42.

32. Irene D. Neu, *Erastus Corning: Merchant and Financier, 1794-1872* (Ithaca, N. Y.; Cornell University Press, 1960), p. 76.

33. Michigan, Legislature, *Annual Report of the Commissioners of Internal Improvements, December 7, 1846 (Joint Documents*, 1847, J. D. No. 4) pp. 4-5. Cited hereafter as *Joint Document No. 4*, 1847.

34. Henry G. Pearson, *An American Railroad Builder: John Murray Forbes* (Boston: Houghton Mifflin, 1911), pp. 24, 30.

35. (Detroit: Charles Willcox, 1847), pp. 1-6.

36. *Ibid.*, pp. 16-19

37. Michigan, Legislature, "Communication from the Acting Commissioner of Internal Improvement" (*House Documents*, 1846, H. D. No. 3).

38. *Messages of the Governors of the State of Michigan*, I, 273-274; Michigan, *House Journal*, 1840, pp. 31, 87, 629; Michigan, *Senate Journal*, 1839, pp. 511–513. Michigan, Legislature, "Report of the Committee of Internal Improvements on the Propriety of Leasing the Central Railroad" (*House Documents*, 1840, II, H. D. No. 17), p. 124.

39. Michigan, *House Journal*, 1841, pp. 508, 586, 627, 644, 659.

40. Michigan, Legislature, "Report of the Committee on Internal Improvements, in Regard to Leasing the Central Railroad" (*Senate Documents*, 1842, S. D. No. 6), pp. 30-35; Michigan, *Senate Journal*, 1842, pp. 179, 251, 253, 264, 275; Michigan, *House Journal*, 1842, pp. 366-367.

41. Michigan, Legislature, "Report of Committee on Internal Improvements" *(Senate Documents*, 1846, S. D. No. 20); Michigan, Legislature, "Proposition of J. H. Titus to Lease from the State the Central Railroad" (*Senate Documents*, 1846, S. D. No.

1); Michigan, Legislature, "To the Honorable, the Legislature of the State of Michigan" (*Senate Documents,* 1846, S. D. No. 21).
42. Michigan, *Joint Document No. 4,* 1847, pp. 2, 4, 14.
43. *Historical Statistics of the United States,* p. 124.

7

CONSTRUCTING THE PUBLIC WORKS: THE SOUTHERN, NORTHERN, AND OTHER PROJECTS

Although construction on the Central began quickly, efforts to start work on the Southern moved slowly. Crews were hired to survey projects in the southern tier, but in June 1837, an epidemic, probably malaria, delayed work for the balance of the summer. Surveying was not completed until the end of September, and after the Board gave public hearings to route petitions at Jonesville on October 9, three more surveys were ordered west of Lenawee County. When these were completed, the Board held additional hearings at the end of November, and finally adopted a route running through Adrian, Hillsdale, Coldwater, Mason, Branch, Centerville, and several smaller villages, to New Buffalo. As far as Centerville, the route followed the line of county centers closely, but to the west it curved south to the St. Joseph River and continued a short distance from the Indiana border.

Compelled by law to select "the most direct and eligible route," the Board employed several justifications for its decision. To have run the road on a more northern route in the east, through Tecumseh and Jonesville, would have violated the charter rights of the River Raisin and Grand River Railroad, which had spent four thousand dollars on surveys. The Board preferred to attack the Erie and Kalamazoo Railroad. By cutting across its route at Adrian, they hoped to divert trade then being channeled into Toledo to Monroe, and to destroy the road's inducement to extend to Marshall, where it could tap the central as well as the southern tier. At the same time, they hoped that the Palmyra and Jacksonburg, then in " rapid progress" between Tecumseh and Palmyra, could be persuaded to connect with the Southern instead of the Erie and Kalamazoo. The Board argued that water power for manufacturing was more abundant there than along other locations, and that the route was three miles shorter. The smaller number of farms along the right-of-way would supposedly reduce the cost between twenty and forty thousand dollars, and alternate routes would require heavy grading and curving. By swinging the road south along the border west of Centerville, the Board hoped to destroy the threat of a rail-road from Toledo to Michigan City and to tap grain and merchandise shipments bound for South Bend and the interior of Illinois by way of the Kankakee River and a planned canal at South Bend. As the Board put it: "The inhabitants of our state will not complain of a measure which enables them to become the merchants and millers and factors of the people of Indiana, as well as their common carriers." It was considered unwise to base the system of internal improvements on "the doctrine of non-intercourse with our neighbors," *if* the state could benefit by it. In short, the Board was planning to do to Indiana and Illinois what it objected to in Ohio's channeling of trade over the Erie and Kalamazoo into Toledo. Finally, the availability of water power in the St. Joseph Valley allegedly would allow cheaper shipping of flour and wheat.

At the end of the year, the Board reported that the Havre branch railroad had deeded its charter to the state, and that contracts had been let for construction of the Southern thirty miles west of Monroe.[1] Construction was postponed, however, by prolonged struggles over alternative routes.

The Board's decision was not popular with residents of by-passed towns who deluged the Legislature with petitions. The pressure was so heavy and the implications so serious that on January 29, construction was suspended for thirty days by joint resolution in order to allow the Legislature to review intermediate points on the Southern's route.[2]

Most of the Senate Internal Improvements Committee bitterly opposed Legislative interference. In a report submitted prior to passage of the suspension resolution, the Committee formally protested the Legislature's intentions, arguing that it set a precedent in making the works subject to suspension every time a special interest group sought to gain advantage by petitioning. A minority of the Committee, however, argued that more than five thousand people had petitioned the Legislature and complained of serious abuses. If the works were not suspended, construction would begin and the abuses could not be corrected.[3] Apparently, a majority of the Legislature supported the minority position because a suspension resolution was passed a few days after formal hearings by a joint legislative committee were begun on January 24. The hearings lasted over a month.

Members of the joint committee were split almost from the beginning. House members were appointed from representatives of the central tier and Allegan County, areas not directly interested in the questions confronting the Legislature. With Senator Bradford of Niles, they formed a majority of two Democrats, one Whig, and three of unknown political affiliation. The minority of three Democratic senators represented southern and northern districts directly interested in route locations.

Neither faction of the committee sought to censure the Board. The majority, however, maintained that existing contracts were not binding because the Board had not satisfied legal requirements to publish notice in state newspapers that bids were being accepted thirty days before they were awarded. The minority contended that because contracts were published in three papers, although not state papers, they were legal and binding. Since the contracts were let at bids thirty percent below engineering estimates, they argued against cancellation, and supported Commissioner Humphrey's refusal to suspend construction on legislative orders.[4]

Two routes for the Southern were under consideration, a northern and a southern. The northern route ran above that established by the Board, through the more developed townships of the tier. In the eastern half of the tier, it ran north through Dundee and Tecumseh; west of Hillsdale, it was to be moved north of the established line through Lockport, Cassopolis, and Niles to New Buffalo. The majority of the joint committee favored the northern route, while the minority supported the line established by the Board.

The majority's arguments were chiefly exploitative, while the minority's were developmental. The majority argued that the northern route had the greatest population and would provide the most business. The northern route supposedly had the greatest applied water power and the most fertile land, and would permit the most active exploitation of resources. Further, the majority thought it unwise to compete with projects from other states. Toledo had formed important connections with Buffalo, and as the terminus of the Wabash and Erie Canal, would offer superior commercial services, drawing off the business of the southern tiers of townships on the principle "that the nearest largest market is generally the best market." It doubted the wisdom of construction through Adrian, because on this principle, trade from the west would be drawn over the Erie and Kalamazoo at Adrian, even though transported there from the west on the Southern. Avoiding competition with Ohio and Indiana was considered desirable. In sum, the majority argued that the northern route would be safer from external competition and more likely to produce the greater revenue. In opposing the Board's justifications for selecting the route, they presented arguments to prove that the cost of construction would be no greater on the northern route, and that right-of-way costs could be reduced by crossing the backs instead of the fronts of the numerous farms the Board found it desirable to avoid. Similar reasoning was used to support building the road closer to the center of the tier in its western half.[5]

The minority responded with a series of statements designed to refute the majority opinion. Using a "straight negative, shotgun attack," they sought to counter the majority arguments point by point in a random order. Making it clear that they considered not running the road through the line of county seats "extraordinary" (at least in the east), they asserted that the southern route would be shorter, cheaper, and was already under contract. They attempted to prove that a southern location would serve a greater number of people than the northern route, and that these areas produced more wheat. Finally, and most important, they argued that the road should not be built according to the current best chances of profit, but to serve future needs and develop potential resources in the area.[6]

The Legislature did little to change the Southern's route east of Hillsdale. A joint resolution passed in April directed the Board to curve the road between Petersburg and Monroe to run through Dundee, or to construct a branch if the latter should prove less expensive, but the final decision was left to the Board.[7] West of Hillsdale, important changes were made. In March, the Board was directed to alter the route between Edwardsburg and Bertrand to pass through Niles, and finally, a year later, the main route was altered to run though Lockport, or Three Rivers, and Cassopolis.[8]

Within the southern tier, sectional rivalry proved as powerful a force in route location as it had been earlier in determining routes across the peninsula. Even though rivalry was now expressed in terms of tiers of townships, rather than counties, the motivation was the same. In a new and developing state, towns and farmers were determined to have immediate access to the main routes of east-west transportation. Had the southern tier been an individual state, it would have witnessed a struggle similar to that in Detroit in 1837, and in an area that was solidly Democratic. Unlike the Central, which was built through the second tier's most developed portions, the Southern was designed to open new lands, exploit potential resources, and compete with an operating road connecting the southern tier to Toledo.

In April, with the hearings over, a second series of contracts was awarded for construction between Monroe and Adrian, with the stipulation that they be finished by the first of the following year. The Havre branch was surveyed, located, and advertised, but contracts had not been awarded by December. In addition, the Southern was located between Adrian and Hillsdale. Following the Legislature's directives, surveys were conducted along the new western route from Centerville to Lockport, Geneva, Cassopolis and Niles, and a second on the route to Dundee. At Dundee, when right-of-way land was donated by area residents, the Board decided it would be cheaper to construct a branch than to curve the entire road through the village.[9]

During 1838, Humphrey's high-handed, independent, and often questionable management of construction on the Southern resulted in growing hostility to the Board of Internal Improvements. Although required by the Internal Improvements Act to advertise all contracts in at least three state newspapers, Humphrey had deprived local firms of bidding opportunities by advertising only in papers well outside the construction area. The initial contracts, awarded in December 1837, were given almost exclusively to a single company. When the Legislature ordered operations suspended for thirty days in January 1838, Humphrey refused to comply. When contracts were advertised again in the spring of 1838, public announcements offered to take bids for grubbing and grading, but not for superstructure, and contractors offered bids on those terms. Most of the road was subsequently awarded to the partnership of Cole and Clark, which submitted bids for grubbing, grading, *and* superstructure. Other bids were rejected because they did not include construction necessary for the road's completion. That Cole and Clark, and other firms awarded contracts, were owned by Humphrey's business partners, contributed to the bitterness of local contractors.

A Whig committee's investigation in 1840 uncovered further involvement by Humphrey and his associates. Materials supplied by his friends commanded three and four times the established local prices paid to contractors and suppliers not within the select circle. Vouchers were padded and contractors were forced to sign to receive payment, with Humphrey receiving the difference. Finally, contractors were forced to accept payment in wildcat currency, while state funds advanced to Humphrey from payments on the five million loan were deposited in favored banks in Monroe to provide them with exchange on the East. To quiet complaints during the investigation, the partnership offered contracts and financial rewards to witnesses whose testimony might prove damaging.[10] As long as the Democrats were in power, however, Humphrey's political popularity and his affiliation with the powerful Monroe faction of the Democracy made his removal impossible.

Although contracts awarded in the spring of 1838 stipulated completion by the first of the year, the Board was unable to report completion in December. In his annual message in January 1839, Governor Mason reported that the road would be ready for iron in the spring, and that contracts had been awarded between Adrian and Hillsdale. Final locations on the third division, between Hillsdale and Branch, were also announced.[11] At the end of 1839, however, the road was still incomplete between Monroe and Adrian.

Several factors accounted for the Southern's failure to reach Adrian in 1839. The state's shortage of funds following the failure of the Michigan State Bank delayed construction and prevented the state from paying monthly estimates to contractors. At the same time, another epidemic swept the state, felling workmen and incapacitating whole segments of the population. By the end of the year, only eighteen miles were reported complete, and the balance to Adrian was only half finished. Even in the face of delayed payments, however, contractors continued to push work slowly forward. As Humphrey stated:

> The principal reason...why the southern railroad has progressed, and is still progressing, notwithstanding the embarrassments of the times, is to be found in the strong desire entertained not only by the contractors, but by the public generally that the work should proceed, and their disposition to render every aid in their power to have a road in which the whole southern portion of the state is so vitally interested, completed in order that its immense surplus of produce may find an avenue to market.[12]

In Humphrey's opinion, however, it would not be profitable to place cars on the Southern until it had reached Hillsdale and the wheat land of Hillsdale County.

Failure of the state deposit bank also curtailed other activities connected with the Southern. The Board reported that it had been unable to change the location of western sections between Centerville and Niles because of the lack of funds in the treasury and a shortage of trained engineers. Contracts on the Havre branch, to have been awarded in 1839, were similarly suspended and never revived. The latter was particularly important because it deprived the Southern of the port which was to carry freight from the first tier of countries to Lake Erie for shipment to Buffalo.[13]

During 1840, the new Whig Legislature and Board of Internal Improvements redoubled efforts to complete the Southern to Adrian and put it in operation. In the new state government's desperate search for revenues, the previous Board's decision was reversed and the Southern opened before it reached Hillsdale. Expenditures on the Southern were nearly fifty percent greater than those on the Central during the same period.[14] To provide access to Lake Erie, the Board purchased the River Raisin and Lake Erie Railroad between Monroe and the Lake, and attempted to put it into operation. On November 23, trains began running on the Southern between Monroe and Adrian, but problems of trans-shipment at the eastern terminus kept receipts low for the few days of operation before the end of the fiscal year.[15]

The state's purchase of the River Raisin and Lake Erie, sometimes called the La Plaisance bay road, was a dramatic departure from previous policies. In 1837, at the Governor's request, a select committee of the Legislature had investigated the company to determine whether it was seriously involved in railroad construction, or chartered to cover the issue of bank notes. According to the company's charter, it was allowed to "grant such evidence of debt which may be incurred by said company"; the managers construed the article as granting them unrestricted banking privileges. By an oversight, the Legislature had neglected to insert the usual clause prohibiting banking. After its organization, in which eighteen hundred dollars of its capital was collected from stockholders, the company spent two hundred and fifty dollars for a route survey from Lake Erie to the River Raisin, and purchased from its president two city lots in Monroe on credit for thirty thousand dollars. Against this mortgaged asset, they issued twenty-eight thousand dollars in notes as "evidence of debt." At the time of the investigation, the legislative committee could see no harm in these activities, because, "If the real estate of said corporation is always held subject to the payments of its debts, it is evidently solvent." But the committee, finding that the charter itself was fraudulently conceived, and fearing the precedent, recommended that it be revoked. The Legislature then instructed the Attorney General to initiate proceedings against the company.[16] The company retaliated by beginning construction, and petitioning the state for damages done to its charter rights by competition from the Southern.

Democratic Legislatures and Boards had not responded to the company's claims. During the Southern route battles in 1838, the subject had come up, but both sides took the position that the Southern had not infringed on the company's charter privileges. When the Whigs came to power in 1840, however, there was renewed interest in the claims of the River Raisin and Lake Erie. After examining a petition from over a hundred Monroe residents recommending that the road be purchased as a terminus for the Southern, as well as the company's damage claims, a House committee accepted the advice of Joseph Dutton, the Southern's Chief Engineer, and endorsed its purchase. Following a glowing account of the company's efforts, the committee concluded that the Southern violated the company's charter rights, and, citing the Dartmouth College Case, submitted a bill allowing the state to purchase the River Raisin and Lake Erie. In due course, the bill was passed, empowering the Commissioners of Internal Improvements to pay the company from the 1843 installments on the five million loan.[17]

Following the legislative session, the Auditor General, Secretary of the Treasury, and Secretary of State went to Monroe to settle claims and inspect the railroad. Authorized by the Legislature to spend up to $32,500 for the charter, they were confronted with books and vouchers accounting for expenditures of over $52,000 by the company, which took the position that the Legislature had authorized the Commissioners to allow full costs in awarding damages. When the Commission refused to pay more than the value of the road at current prices, the company accepted an offer of $32,500 with the right to claim interest until paid from the 1843 installments. The Commission, in turn, accepted the road subject to legislative approval.

The Commission also took action to obtain use of wharf and storage facilities at its eastern terminus. "At the eastern termination of said road, there is a ware-house (approached by a long bridge) the property of a distinct incorporate company, called 'La Plaisance bay harbor company,' intercepting the road from the water...." Although the act did not authorize them to treat with this company, the Commission assumed that the terms of the act stemmed from a lack of familiarity with the location, and attempted to secure free access to the water. Terms were negotiated without further cost, to gain use of the bridge:

> for the purpose of running cars thereon, and through said store-house, and also the right to lay down and construct as many railroad tracks, through the land and premises of the last mentioned company, as might be for the interest and convenience of the state, reserving, however, to the company the right to demand and receive the customary rates for storage and wharfage of all property brought on the said railroad track, such charges of wharfage and storage, not to exceed the charge for similar services in the cities of Detroit and Buffalo.[18]

The following year, the Legislature endorsed the Commision's purchase by incorporating the River Raisin and Lake Erie into the Southern Railroad. It refused, however, to approve the contracts with the La Plaisance bay harbor company, on the grounds that the negotiations were "highly exceptionable" and that even if the Legislature were in error the Commission had no authority beyond recommending the matter to the Legislature for consideration.[19] By refusing to accept the terms negotiated by the Commission, the state lost access to Lake Erie, and in effect destroyed the opportunity created by purchasing the road.

The company submitted further claims to gain the balance of sums expended on the road, as well as interest accruing since their investment. In October of 1840, the company was sold to new owners, who, after their charter had been relinquished, attempted to revive the corporation as a bank. In retaliation, the state pressed suit in the Michigan Supreme Court to stop its activities, and no further claims were pressed by the company.[20]

During 1841, construction continued on the Southern. By the end of the year, the road was in operation only as far as Adrian, but the thirty-two miles of road between Adrian and Hillsdale were reported nearly ready for iron. Difficulties in pushing the road bed through a tamarack swamp near Hillsdale were reported as the principal reason for the failure to complete construction during the year. According to engineering estimates, only fifteen thousand dollars would be necessary to complete the road to Hillsdale, exclusive of iron.[21]

By the end of 1841, iron was becoming a serious problem on the Southern. Arrangements had been made with the Corning works to provide three-quarter inch iron and spike to be paid for from the October installment of the Bank of the United States. But when the Bank failed, the Board was unable to provide funds. Iron furnished under contracts from Hicks and Company of New York, over which Monroe had fought the Board the previous year, was half-inch stock considered too hard, coarse and brittle to use. The Board, thinking it bad policy to place such iron on the superstructure, decided to wait for shipments of heavier stock.

Other reports from the Southern were equally discouraging. Although the road to Adrian had been opened the previous year and was reported in excellent condition, it had not been fully spiked. According to the Board, spikes purchased had been of poor quality, and only enough good stock was available to put spikes in alternate holes. As a result, iron on the western half of the second division was expected to deteriorate rapidly. Subsequently, it proved impossible to respike the road for several years. Although the Board blamed the quality of the spike, there is evidence that pilfering of iron and spike by contractors caused most of the shortage.[22]

Reports from the River Raisin and Lake Erie were even more discouraging. No more than nominal repairs had been undertaken because the Board had doubts about the location of the road's eastern terminus. Advantages were offered by the pier at the end of the River Raisin and Lake Erie, the dock at Brest, and the mouth of the Monroe ship canal, but the shallow water in La Plaisance Bay led the Commissioners to conclude that a better terminus than that provided by the newly purchased road should be sought. At the end of 1841, the Board was considering extending the piers at the mouth of the ship canal three hundred feet, which would open the road to navigable water of a constant depth of eleven feet. The cost of completing the ship canal at Monroe was estimated at ninety thousand dollars. In order to use the pier at the end of the River Raisin and Lake Erie, the Board would be forced to engage in extensive dredging for the benefit of a private company. Meanwhile, the road itself had proven almost worthless. The bed was unstable, the curve too sharp for use of locomotives, and the superstructure too rotten to bear the weight of heavy cars or engines. The road was so bad that freight had to be hauled over the tracks by teams.

As a result, the Southern's receipts during 1841 were disappointing. As of April, there were no locomotives in use because Humphrey, who had been issued warrants for their purchase in 1839, refused to return the warrants when the Whig Board replaced him. The Legislature was finally forced to order the warrants' return by joint resolution, and the locomotives were purchased.[23] The Board, however, blamed competition from the Erie and Kalamazoo for the low rate of earning, and expressed hope that the construction of lines from Monroe to Ohio would draw traffic from the E & K to the Southern.[24]

Hope of increasing revenues on the Southern led to efforts to extend the road three miles to Jonesville, which had been on the northern route during the 1838 route battles, instead of Hillsdale. In 1840, a charter had been granted to a group of local residents to build a branch road from the Southern, but the company was apparently unable to raise funds. Early in 1841, a railroad convention was held at Jonesville to encourage the state to continue the road through the village. Restating the principles of sectional equality, the convention produced statistics to prove that carriage of local produce would pay interest on the cost of construction. The convention's position was supported in the Legislature by the Senate Internal Improvements Committee, which recommended continuing the road to Jonesville. During the 1841 session, the Legislature authorized extension on condition that it proved the most economical route and could be constructed out of existing funds.[25]

The same Senate Committee expressed satisfaction at the Palmyra and Jacksonburg's failure to meet interest due on loans from the state. Angered by the competition from the Erie and Kalamazoo, with which the Palmyra and Jacksonburg was to connect, the Committee was hopeful that failure would enable the state to take control of the road and divert it to use by the Southern. Several years were to elapse, however, before the Palmyra and Jacksonburg would be acquired.

During 1842 and 1843, a lack of iron to surface the superstructure slowed construction. The road bed and superstructure had been completed to Hillsdale late in 1841, but iron merchants' refusal to accept pledges of the Southern's net receipts in payment forced the road to confine its operations between Monroe and Adrian. When ten miles of iron were discovered in the Board's possession during 1842, the road was completed between Adrian and Hudson, fifty miles west of Monroe. But until iron was purchased under a joint resolution pledging the Central's and Southern's net receipts in 1843, the road could not be completed. Finally, in October 1843, iron was laid to Hillsdale, and the road opened to its western terminus. Forced to concentrate resources on its only producing road, the state was unable to continue efforts on the Southern.[26]

During the same two years, receipts were discouragingly low. Problems at the eastern terminus forced shippers to seek alternate routes, while competition from the Erie and Kalamazoo drained away business. Attempts by both public and private interests in Monroe failed to lead to completion of the ship canal, and the Lake Erie and River Raisin proved both inefficient and expensive to maintain. Freight had to be hauled to the bay by horses; in 1842, this four miles of road consumed nearly a third of the money charged to operating expenses. Receipts were held down during 1843 by Lake Erie shippers who boycotted the road and delivered goods consigned to Monroe to other ports in violation of contracts, in an attempt to undermine the state's railroads. Inadequate rolling stock also added to the road's inability to achieve a desirable level of profits.[27]

During the last three years of state ownership, little further construction was attempted. With appropriations exhausted, it was forced to stop short of the fertile St. Joseph Valley. In June 1844, the state purchased the Palmyra and Jacksonburg for twenty-two thousand dollars, and annexed it to the Southern as a feeder line. The road, "gratuitously fitted for the iron" by citizens of Tecumseh under an agreement with the Erie and Kalamazoo to iron and stock it, had fallen into the hands of the state as collateral to a loan granted in 1838. The road was reported to be badly deteriorated, but estimates of potential business ran as high as forty thousand dollars, over half of which had been carried by the Erie and Kalamazoo. During 1845, the road was rebuilt between Tecumseh and the Southern by local citizens, whose voluntary labor made it possible to complete the road a year sooner than appropriations would have allowed, and much of the road was put under iron. At the end of the year, the Board asked the Legislature to appropriate funds to repair the road as far north as Clinton. The request was accompanied by estimates of flour output at Clinton and probable revenues over the seven percent required to pay interest on the cost of construction. After a decade, the Board, for the first time in its history, began to use estimated revenues based on area output as a justification for construction. The appropriation was never made, however, because in 1846, the Southern was sold to private interests.[28]

The Southern's last three years were no more encouraging than its first three. Low receipts and high costs, accompanied by seemingly insurmountable problems, added to the state's discouragement with internal improvements. At the end of 1844, the problem of the eastern terminus remained as pressing as it had been in 1840. Public and private attempts to complete the ship canal at Monroe had failed, and the bay proved too shallow for efficient navigation. At the end of 1844, the Board recommended that the Lake Erie and River Raisin be abandoned because it afforded no facilities to shipment, and that its iron be transferred to the Palmyra and Jacksonburg. The solution to the terminus problem adopted by the later private owners, that is, purchase of the Erie and Kalamazoo and shipment to the port of Toledo, was anathema to the Board and politically impracticable. Moreover, the road itself was in poor condition. Part of it was only half spiked, and the portion between Monroe and Adrian, badly decayed. West of Adrian, sections of the road which had lain for as long as four years without iron were in little better shape, and the heavy rains of 1844 added to its deterioration.[29]

The road's gross revenues fell far short of the hundred thousand dollars predicted upon completion to Hillsdale, and were consumed year after year by repairs and purchase of rolling stock and engines. Unlike the Central, which was at least retiring scrip from circulation, the Southern had produced nothing for the state in six years of operation.

Table V presents a statement of revenue, expenditure, and investment for the Southern under ten years of state ownership. The figures are subject to the same limitations as those presented for the Central, with a few additional problems of their own. Receipts, of course, are an exact statement of moneys received by the road during the fiscal year, but expenditures do not reflect costs of operation. As with the Central, substantial sums expended on rolling stock, locomotives, and new construction were reported as operating expenses. The three figures available for net income indicate that actual operating expenses ranged between two-thirds and three-quarters of reported receipts. At no time during the period, however, was income sufficient to pay interest on the cost of construction, or even depreciation. Financially, the Southern was a complete failure through 1846.

There are significant problems in accurately determining reported investment because of conflicting statements by the Board. The major difficulty is encountered in 1840, when the Board presented two different statements of expenditure in its annual report, neither of which included the purchase price of the River Raisin and Lake Erie. Apparently, the Board had spent funds in excess of appropriations and covered it by false reporting; the excess over appropriations was reported in 1841 when new appropriations were passed by the Legislature. The Board's shifting of these sums from 1840 to 1841 does not affect total investment, however, and serves only to give a false sense of timing to the data. During the last four years, reported investment does not include iron and rolling stock because expenditures for these items were financed from net income of both the Central and Southern. However, the sum of reported investment in 1845 falls between values set by the Auditor General for the road with and without locomotives and rolling stock at the end of that year, and therefore seems a reasonable approximation.

Sale of the Southern was an afterthought to sale of the Central, rather than independent policy. Unlike the Central, there was no substantial support for its sale before 1845, and the decision to sell appears to have been a composite one based on several factors. In part, it came from a desire to liquidate as much as possible of the public debt and, because of mounting debts, the need for repairs, and difficulties in borrowing, from a desire to jettison the internal improvements program. Equally as important was the realization that the system was being discarded in any case and that continuation of the road as a state enterprise was therefore unlikely. Residents of the southern section were determined that their road have the same advantages as the Central: corporate charter, heavy rails, and continued

TABLE V

Receipts, Expenditures, and Investment on the
Southern Railroad, 1837-1846[a]
(Thousands of Dollars)

	1837	1838	1839	1840	1841	1842	1843	1844	1845	1846
Receipts					7	16	24	60	68	88
Expenditures					5	16	24[b]	60	68	67
Net Income					2					22
Reported Investment	12	236	227	155[c]	148	53	20	22[d]	14[d]	
Cumulative Total[e]			576	731	879	932	954	976	990	

[a]Michigan, Legislature, *Annual Reports of the Board of Internal Improvements* (*Joint Documents*, J. D. No. 4), pp. (1839) 9-12; (1840) 30-32; (1841) 15, 27; (1842) 12, 14; (1843) 7-8, 11; (1844) 9, 19; (1845) 16, 18-19.
[b]$8,000 of this sum reported expended on rolling stock.
[c]This sum includes purchase of the River Raisin and Lake Erie, but understates expenditure. See note c, VIII, Chapter 9.
[d]Expended on the Tecumseh Branch.
[e]Data presented in this line is totaled from reported investment of the Board of Internal Improvements in the line immediately above. Sums will not agree because figures are rounded to the nearest thousand. The figures represent gross approximations, rather than exact statements because of reinvestment of net income which is disguised as an operating expense, and deliberate disguising of investment by the Board in 1840 and 1841 to remain within limits created by appropriations. Reports of the Board are used because they are the only body consistently reporting investment. Annual figures presented by various investigating committees often present striking contrasts. However, the total in 1846 is close enough to the Auditor General's estimate presented in 1846 of $961,973, or $1,016,973 including locomotives and rolling stock, to justify its use. The loose accounting procedures of the Board, particularly in relation to the Southern, preclude a more exact statement. Michigan, Legislature, *Annual Report of the Auditor General, 1845* (*Joint Documents*, 1846, J.D. No. 2), p. 2.

construction. Once the Central was sold, the Southern had to follow suit to maintain its advantages and competitive position. To that degree, the same sectional rivalry that had led to the construction of multiple roads at the program's inception was still operative.

Two bids were offered to the state for the Southern, in addition to the bid of the purchasing corporation. The first, apparently submitted by a group connected with the Erie and Kalamazoo, offered to purchase the Southern for five hundred and fifty thousand dollars payable in five equal annual installments at interest. In return, the group asked for the privilege of connecting the Southern with the Erie and Kalamazoo, and the right to complete the Palmyra and Jacksonburg to Clinton and renew its connection with the Erie and Kalamazoo. They promised to complete the road to Coldwater, if the company could select the route, and asked for all the privileges granted to the Central.[30] The second group, composed of New York residents, offered to purchase the road for six hundred thousand dollars if the state would grant a charter similar to the Central's, not subject to further legislation. In return, they asked for the right to extend the road to the Indiana line, and the privilege of connecting the Erie and Kalamazoo with the Tecumseh Branch at Palmyra.[31]

There is no record of legislative response to the first proposition, but the second was criticized in detail by the House Select Committee on the Sale of the Public Works. The Committee made it abundantly clear that price was not the most important objective. It believed that railroads were important to economic development in the southern tier and that development was more important than the absolute sale price. It objected to the company's apparent intention of incorporating the road into a system of roads projected from Toledo to Adrian and Chicago because such a system would deprive all the citizens of the southern tier except the residents of Lenawee and Hillsdale Counties of the benefits of a railroad through the tier. "Even the gilded bait of $100,000 would scarcely be sufficient to induce our people to forget their self-respect, their interest and their true policy." The Committee placed priority on keeping the road within the state and as close to its original line as possible. The road's profits were supposed to build villages in Michigan, not in other states.[32] Had debt reduction been the primary motivation, price would have been the major consideration, but the Legislature was determined to retain the road's original route under local ownership regardless of cost.

The bill authorizing sale of the Southern was signed into law in May 1846. Most of the individuals named in the corporate charter were residents of Michigan, particularly the southern tier. Sale price was set at half a million dollars, one hundred thousand less than the best offer. The charter granted privileges and restrictions essentially identical to those granted the Central, with exceptions to suit local circumstance. Nine years were granted to pay the balance of the purchase price, with interest on the unpaid balance, and the company was required to purchase twenty thousand dollars worth of locomotive and rolling stock within six months of the initial purchase. The charter stipulated that construction be completed to Cold-water, through Jonesville, in four years, and to the St. Joseph River and Niles in another four. Three years were allotted to complete the Tecumseh branch to Jackson. If the deadlines were not met, other companies would be allowed to undertake construction and take a share of the road's profits. Maximum tolls were limited by rates set for the Central, and the company was required to furnish the road with heavy T rails. As with the Central, the state retained the right of purchase after January 1, 1867.[33]

When it sold the Southern, the state gave up its last important internal improvement work. Undertaken in a conflict of local interests, poorly constructed and poorly managed, often without competent engineering supervision, the road seemed destined to fail. Yet, other factors were equally important in determining its ultimate failure. The Southern suffered greatly from competition by the Erie and Kalamazoo, which offered superior mercantile and financial facilities at its terminus. The problem of the eastern terminus, never solved under state management, limited the growth of traffic. Unlike the Central, the Southern was not pushed far enough west of the peninsular watershed to develop substantial traffic either in freight or passengers. Its performance compares more favorably with that of the Central when its sister road was completed as far as Jackson. Finally, the Southern, like the Central, lacked sufficient motive power and rolling stock. The Southern's failure was more than a simple failure of state enterprise to develop and manage the road efficiently. The Southern paid the price of second priority when the state found it necessary to concentrate resources in its most productive enterprise. Had it received the same resources and been extended as far, it might well have proven profitable, if not as profitable as the Central. After it was sold to private interests, the Southern's performance improved markedly. Whether the Southern was built "ahead of demand" remains a moot point, because its abstract potential was never fairly tested under state ownership.

Construction on other state projects was much less involved, and even less successful. The Northern Railroad, authorized to run through the fourth tier of counties from the St. Clair River to Lake Michigan, was surveyed in the summer and fall of 1837. Several routes were projected, and surveys encompassed the equivalent of three separate routes lengthwise across the state. In October, the Board met at Flint to determine its location. The only controversy was on the point of commencement, and the Commissioners finally decided on the mouth of the Black River because at that point the rapids of the St. Clair kept the river ice-free year round and the route would intersect the Fort Gratiot road. From the mouth of the Black, the road ran west through Lapeer, Flint, and Corunna or Owosso, to the mouth of the Maple River. At this point it crossed the Grand River, continued west to Grand Rapids on the south side, and finally followed the Grand to its mouth. After determining the route the Board directed the Commissioner in charge to award contracts.[34]

Unlike the Southern and Central, the Northern was a true frontier

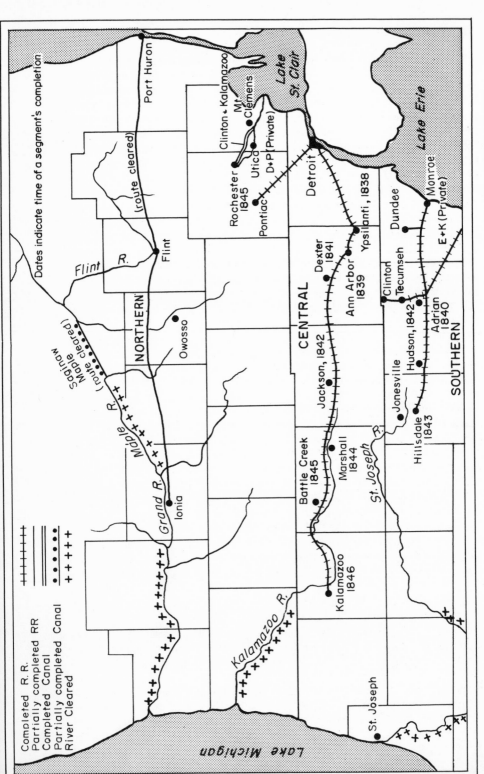

PROJECTS COMPLETED

MAP 4

Legend:
- ++++++ Completed R.R.
- ———— Partially completed RR
- •••••• Completed Canal
- ++++ Partially completed Canal
- River Cleared

Dates indicate time of a segment's completion

Lake Michigan

Lake St. Clair

Lake Erie

Port Huron

Clinton & Kalamazoo
Mt. Clemens
Rochester 1845
Utica
Pontiac D&P (Private)
Detroit

Flint R.
Flint

NORTHERN
Owosso

Saginaw
(route cleared)
Maple R.
Grand R.
Ionia

CENTRAL
Dexter 1841
Ann Arbor 1839
Ypsilanti, 1838
Jackson, 1842

Clinton
Tecumseh
Hudson, 1842
Adrian 1840
Dundee
Monroe
E&K (Private)

SOUTHERN
Jonesville
Hillsdale 1843

Battle Creek 1845
Marshall 1844

St. Joseph R.

Kalamazoo R.
Kalamazoo 1846

St. Joseph

railroad constructed ahead of demand. Population along the route was minimal west of the eastern terminus. The Board and the engineer who made the survey emphasized its developmental nature in reports submitted in 1837, and construction was undertaken with no hope of immediate revenues. Success depended on the completion of main lines of communication west through New York and Ontario, and an influx of population drawn by the construction of a railroad through unpopulated territory. Advantages cited for construction of the Northern were that it was one hundred and twenty-seven miles shorter than the Lake Erie route, and that it would be open year round. The region's mineral resources—coal, salt, iron, gypsum, and lime-stone—were expected to attract both capital and population.[35]

Construction on the Northern was delayed by battles similar to those which delayed the Southern, and hearings were conducted by the same committee. In March 1838, the Joint Committee of Investigation cleared the Commissioners of charges of guilt or personal interest which had been brought by petitioners. In supporting the Board, the majority of the Committee stated that the road must be constructed to serve long-term interests rather than short-term profits, and that every county should share in the proceeds of internal improvement. A minority report signed by Stephen Vickery summarized the opposition view. Vickery apparently spoke for the St. Clair and Romeo Railroad, "whose avowed object and intention, it appears, was to extend their road across the state to the navigable waters of the Grand river or Lake Michigan." The company had spent several thousand dollars before it appeared that the state would become a competitor, and wanted the Northern constructed from Palmer to Flint and west, with the St. Clair and Romeo having the right to connect with the Northern at Flint and carry traffic from Flint to Detroit. Vickery argued that "The state has no right to construct works which will interfere with or injure the vested right and interest of a previously incorporated company, without an adequate compensation in damages; and not even then without consent of the incorporators." The most interesting point in Vickery's dissent, however, was the inconsistency he discovered in the Committee's arguments for the Southern and the Northern. On the Southern, the majority of the Committee had argued in favor of an exploitative road, while on the Northern, it argued the advantages of constructing the road through the least developed sections of the region to utilize its developmental impact. Citing sixteen different factors, Vickery argued in favor of locating the road through the most developed and populous sections of the tier. The Committee gave no reason for its change in criteria, and the evidence is too sparse to allow speculation. It seems likely, however, that population in the fourth tier was so scattered that any argument that was not developmental would have been ludicrous.[36]

The Legislature made only one minor change in route location, directing that the road run through both Owosso and Corunna, instead of only one of the villages, and the road was relocated on the south side of the Black River. During 1838, the acting commissioner was instructed to award contracts for clearing and grubbing between the mouth of the Black River in St. Clair

County and Lyons in Ionia County. Contracts were authorized for fourteen miles of grading between Flint and Ionia. Unlike the Central and Southern, which were built in segments, the Northern was undertaken one step at a time for the entire length, which accounts for its failure to have completed a single section when operations were suspended. At the end of 1838, the Commissioner on the Northern reported that contracts had been awarded for clearing and grading from Port Huron to Lyons, a distance of one hundred and thirty miles, and that grading had been undertaken on a ten-mile segment at Lyons, and on a four-mile segment west of Flint. No explanation was ever offered for the widely separated grading, or for undertaking grading at the western end of the route.[37]

During 1839, one hundred and ten miles of the road were cleared and grubbed, with only twenty miles uncompleted. When the state proved unable to meet its monthly estimates after the Michigan State Bank failed, contractors abandoned the works. By November 1839, sixty thousand dollars had been expended, and another ten thousand dollars was spent in 1840, but for all practical purposes the road was abandoned when new contracts were forbidden by the Whig Legislature in 1840.[38]

Attempts were made to salvage work undertaken before the financial collapse. Through 1839, appropriations for the Northern had reached a total of one hundred and fifty thousand dollars, and in April 1841, thirty thousand dollars of the balance was earmarked for converting the cleared route into a wagon road. Five thousand dollars was diverted to the Grand River road, to be expended under the direction of the Board of Internal Improvements. The Bank of the United States' failure to meet its October installment, however, choked off the state's source of funds, and the Board was unable to place the road under contract. In 1843, the Legislature placed the road under the jurisdiction of township road commissioners, and appropriated resident highway taxes on lands for three miles on each side of the road for its construction and maintenance. Little was done, however, and subsequent attempts to appropriate money for the road failed. Finally, in 1846, the act of 1843 was repealed, and the road abandoned.[39]

The Clinton and Kalamazoo, the third tier's project, was begun under authorization to construct a canal or canal and railroad combination from Mount Clemens, on the Clinton River, to the mouth of the Kalamazoo River. Under the terms of the Internal Improvements Act, after completing surveys, the Board of Internal Improvements would determine whether such a route was practicable and the most desirable form of construction.

There was apparently never any doubt that residents of the third tier wanted a canal rather than a railroad. On April 13, 1837, less than a month after passage of the act, a large meeting was held at Auburn to discuss popular feeling on the third tier's project; sentiment was overwhelmingly in favor of a canal. Preference for canals was based on the fact that they had been proven a safe and profitable method of moving goods, and that they provided water power for mills along the route.[40]

No decision was made on either the mode of construction or the route during 1837. At the end of the year the Board stated that the engineer had not submitted his full report, but that preliminary indications favored the construction of a canal across the peninsula. The engineer reported that such a canal would be two hundred and sixteen miles long, requiring three hundred and forty-nine feet of lockage on the eastern side, and three hundred and forty-one feet on the western slopes. Available summit water was estimated at twice the quantity necessary to compensate for evaporation and one hundred lockages per day. Should traffic exceed these requirements, the engineer thought the Cedar and Shiawassee Rivers could be diverted to supply the needed water. The most serious obstacles to construction were believed to be the summit ridge and the Grand River. Allegan was chosen as the western terminus.[41]

After the engineer submitted his complete report, the Board met in Mount Clemens for public hearings on the proposed project in February 1838. When the route and deviations from the line of county centers had been thoroughly discussed, the Board decided to build a canal. Although this decision satisfied public opinion, the Board had other reasons for deciding against a railroad through the third tier. Three railroads had already been authorized, and railroads were subject to limitations for which a canal would compensate. Light strap iron railroads, although suitable for fast hauling of passengers and merchandise, were not considered practical for hauling bulk freight. In the Board's words: "At this day there is no doubt in the public mind as to the superior advantages of canals over railroads to the country on the immediate line, or when heavy and bulky articles are to be transported." In the overall plan of internal improvement, the Clinton and Kalamazoo was to provide complementary services of heavy hauling, rather than competitive transportation of passengers and merchandise.[42] Prior to the meeting, exact location of the canal had not been made.

During 1838, locations were made between Mount Clemens and Crooked Lake in Livingston County, and work began on eastern sections. Cost estimates on the eastern watershed indicated that the canal would be far more expensive than a railroad, especially in the initial sections. Alternate routes surveyed in the first division could be built at a cost of from thirteen to fifteen thousand dollars per mile, but costs rose to between twenty-eight and thirty-three thousand dollars per mile in the second division. In both cases, the Board chose the low-cost route. By the end of the year, clearing and grubbing were nearly completed, and contracts were awarded for excavation. The Board was forced to report, however, that the sections under contract would be the most expensive and the least useful. The eastern terminus of the canal was twenty miles from Detroit, at a point where only small vessels could navigate the crooked, shallow, and narrow Clinton River. When the canal was completed to Pontiac, twenty-seven miles west of Mount Clemens, it would be only twenty-five miles from Detroit, the state's major market, on the Detroit and Pontiac Railroad. As the Board pointed out, it was hardly reasonable that anyone would choose the circuitous water route to Detroit when they could ship or travel by rail from

Pontiac. The Board suggested that the Legislature either allow improvement of the whole Clinton River, or work on less expensive sections west of Pontiac which would channel goods into the Detroit and Pontiac for transshipment. Even though the eastern counties were more populous, with both the Detroit and Pontiac, and the Detroit and Shelby Railroads extending into the region, they had more direct routes to Detroit than the Clinton and St. Clair Rivers. The Board's recommendations were essentially sound, but politically impractical, and the Legislature failed to act to develop the canal to its fullest potential.[43]

Early in 1839, under the Board's direction, the Chief Engineer reported on a survey of a Clinton and Kalamazoo branch. As surveyed, the branch constituted a second canal across the state. Beginning two miles west of Howell, the route surveyed by Hurd ran through the Cedar River Valley to the Looking Glass River, down the Looking Glass to Waterloo, then to the head of steamboat navigation on the Grand River at Lyons. Crossing the Grand at Lyons, it continued west to Ionia. Based on a canal fifty feet wide and five feet deep, Hurd estimated the cost of the branch at $1,300,000, or $16,750 per mile, and reported favorably on its potential. He believed it would pay for itself in a very few years.[44] Shortly after the survey was submitted, the Michigan State Bank failure stopped the addition of new projects. As late as 1844, however, efforts in Congress to obtain a federal land grant for the Clinton and Kalamazoo included provisions for the Grand River branch.[45]

During 1839, work was slowed by failure of the state deposit bank. Grubbing was nearly completed between Frederick and Rochester, and most of the lock materials furnished. At the suggestion of the Chief Engineer, the engineers of the several projects inspected the route and recommended eliminating the section between Mount Clemens and Frederick. Between these two points, they decided to use the bed of the Clinton River, thus saving nearly forty thousand dollars on the two miles by eliminating two long aqueducts and by-passing quicksand. In March, the river was surveyed for construction of a towpath from Mount Clemens to its mouth, and estimates for construction of the path were placed at thirty-eight thousand dollars. The Board recommended to the Legislature that the river be made into a barge, rather than a ship, canal.[46] The Legislature, however, permanently tabled a resolution authorizing construction.[47]

Although the state reduced its internal improvements program sharply in 1840 by prohibiting new contracts, work on the Clinton and Kalamazoo was not substantially affected until the end of 1841, when existing contracts were completed, appropriations exceeded, and the failure of the Bank of the United States cut off funds. Through early 1840, payments were sustained by drafts on John Ward & Co., and Auditor General's warrants. Payments were a month or two late, but funds were usually found. The Board reported expenditures during 1840 as the heaviest to date. At the end of the year, the Board reported it could complete the canal from Rochester to

Frederick with an additional appropriation of twenty thousand dollars. During the year, the Board reversed its decision to eliminate the section between Frederick and Mount Clemens, and decided to build the expensive section with its aqueducts. No construction was undertaken, however, because the Board lacked the necessary funds.[48]

During 1841, lack of funds curtailed operations, although the Board exceeded appropriations by two thousand dollars. Between Frederick and Rochester, the canal lacked only a feeder at the western end, and a lock at Frederick, to open it for operation. Since filling the canal to keep the banks and lock walls from caving in was essential for its preservation, the Board recommended completion. The estimated cost was seventeen thousand dollars.[49] Although twenty-five thousand dollars had been appropriated, most of it was apparently consumed by existing contracts.

No further construction was undertaken in 1842. The Legislature attempted to solve its financial difficulties by authorizing the Board to lease the canal for twenty years, under the stipulation that persons taking over the canal would construct a feeder at Paint Creek, the western terminus, and an apron and water weirs at the eastern end to allow water to escape. No offers were received, however, and at the end of the year, the Board again asked for funds to complete the canal.[50]

Early in 1843, John M. Berrien inspected the canal bed and made a detailed report. Damage and decay caused by leaving the canal empty were relatively light, although extensive repairs would be necessary. Most of the locks were in good condition, except for warping in their plank lining, and one bank had caved in. One lock was ruptured because a contractor had let in water with the lower level empty, springing the gates. Berrien estimated that repairs would cost a maximum of three thousand dollars. Following Berrien's assessment, the House Internal Improvements Committee recommended appropriating sufficient funds to complete the canal. The problem faced by the Committee, and the state, was that the value of the Clinton and Kalamazoo was unknown. The state had invested heavily to complete the eastern section, but had no idea whether the canal would be profitable. To justify further expenditure, at least six percent, or twelve hundred dollars, would have to be realized on the additional investment. Since filling the canal would provide water power, as well as shipping facilities, the Committee recommended appropriation as an experiment so that the canal might be finished and its value determined. Sixteen thousand acres of land were appropriated for completion, but when bids submitted exceeded the engineer's estimates, the Board was forced to reject them.[51]

In 1844, the Legislature repealed provisions making warrants appropriated the previous year payable in land, and contracts were awarded. In the meantime, it was discovered that additional damage and decay were so heavy that the canal could not be completed with existing appropriations. At its next session, the Legislature appropriated sufficient funds, and in August 1845, most of the levels were filled. The same year, the lock connecting Frederick to the Clinton River was completed, and in November, a small boat began running from Frederick to Utica. Total receipts for the year were $46.90. The following year, the canal earned $43.42, and the Legislature authorized only those repairs which were " absolutely necessary."[52] No bids had been received for leasing the canal, however, and no one had responded by leasing water power.

After 1846, the Clinton and Kalamazoo faded into oblivion, leaving no traces in official records. The Board of Internal Improvements failed to mention it in subsequent reports, and the Board itself was discontinued in 1849. No further laws were passed affecting it, and it was apparently allowed to decay; parts of the bed are still in the state's possession. Involving expenditures of over three hundred and fifty thousand dollars, the canal was the state's greatest financial loss resulting from abandonment or discontinuation. Its failure deprived the state of facilities for heavy freight transportation, and contributed to the need for converting the railroads from light strap iron to solid iron rails to handle loads they were not initially designed to haul.

The Act of 1837 also authorized the Board to construct a canal linking the Saginaw River with the Grand River or its tributary, the Maple. Although the area was undeveloped and sparsely populated, in terms of utilizing natural terrain features to facilitate transportation across the peninsula, the project was probably the most intelligent choice for developing the region north of the central tier. The Saginaw and Grand Rivers, two of the state's largest, form a natural canal route. Maximum elevation above lake level in the depression stretching across the peninsula from Saginaw Bay, up the valley of the Saginaw and Bad Rivers, and down the valley of the Maple and Grand Rivers to Lake Michigan does not exceed seventy-two feet.[53] When surveys were completed in 1837, the engineer assigned to the Northern Canal reported that the two rivers could be linked by only fourteen miles of canal. The rest of the route could be put into operation by inexpensive river improvement.

The route was so promising that the engineer submitted plans for both barge and ship canals. The former was a typical barge canal, forty-five feet wide and five feet deep, but the ship canal was a novel innovation. Sixty feet wide and six feet deep, it was designed without a towpath, for use by steamboats. The canal itself was to be below water level to avoid embankments. The engineer hoped placing the banks below water level would allow boat wakes to dissipate themselves harmlessly in flooded land adjacent to the canal, and overcome the problem of bank erosion that usually prohibited the construction of ship canals in ante-bellum America. In recommending construction of a ship canal, the engineer hoped to provide an alternative to the long and often dangerous Mackinac passage.[54]

Extant records do not indicate which proposal was finally adopted by the Board. During 1838, construction was delayed when the contractor refused to fulfill his obligation. The following year, five miles were placed under contract and one mile completed before contractors abandoned construction after the Michigan State Bank failure. Materials purchased for locks and construction were left in the open to rot. When accounts were finally settled at the end of 1841, a total of forty-seven thousand dollars had been expended for construction, clearing, and grubbing along the route. Another five thousand dollars was diverted from appropriations for construction on the Saginaw Turnpike. Materials either rotted or were expropriated by local residents.[55]

Not completing the Northern or Saginaw Canal was one of the most significant failures in the internal improvements program. Although the financial loss was minor compared to that suffered on the Clinton and Kalamazoo, the canal would have provided a transpeninsular route serving the northern counties at a reasonably low cost. The canal would not only have served the growing needs of a developing region, but might have quieted the demands for sectional equality that forced the state to abandon its projects in the mid-1840s.

An all-water connection between Lake Superior and Lake Huron had been a vision in the Old Northwest for half a century before the state authorized construction. During the eighteenth century, while Britain controlled both banks of the St. Mary's River, possession of solid ground on the south bank had allowed easy portage of the great birchbarks carrying freight from the St. Lawrence Valley to the lands beyond Lake Superior. When Jay's Treaty evicted Britain from the south bank, Canadian companies were forced to portage through low marshy ground. In 1797 or 1798, the Northwest Fur Company completed a canal designed to carry freight canoes around the rapids. Although no monumental feat of engineering, the canal could carry the dominant form of lake shipping around the rapids, and was one of the first functioning canals in North America. This canal was destroyed by American troops in 1814.[56]

Spurred by a desire to exploit the copper and fisheries of the Superior country, as well as the Indian trade of the Canadian Northwest, the Legislature had authorized a ship canal around the falls of the St. Mary's River during the 1837 session. The act instructed the Governor to appoint surveyors responsible to his office to examine the route, and construct maps and profiles. Construction plans were to be submitted to the Board, which was to determine practicability, and twenty-five thousand dollars was appropriated for construction. Surveys were made during the summer and fall, and in December 1837, reports were submitted. Plans called for a canal slightly less than one mile long, with a minimum width of seventy-five feet and a depth of ten feet. Three locks were to be constructed, thirty-two feet wide, each lifting vessels for six feet. According to John Almy, the surveyor, the rock ledge under the rapids would not require blasting, "owing to its peculiar quality and position." Almy estimated the cost of construction at one hundred and twelve thousand dollars. Errors in the estimate, he insisted, would result only from miscalculation of labor costs, not because of the terrain.[57]

The following spring, the Legislature approved construction plans. An additional twenty-five thousand dollars was appropriated so that the canal might be built in one season, thus avoiding the expense of shipping men and materials to the Soo more than once. In September, contracts were awarded to the firm of Smith and Driggs of Buffalo; the following spring five thousand dollars was advanced to finance shipment of men and tools. Crews were recruited, and a third partner, Aaron Weeks, and his men left for the Upper Peninsula.[58]

Meanwhile, the state was headed toward a collision with the federal government. During 1822 and 1823, the federal government had constructed Fort Brady to guard the river frontier with Canada. During construction, a saw mill had been erected which drew water from a race connected to the river. In the summer of 1826, the mill burned to the ground, leaving only the race. In 1838, the race was cleared and deepened in anticipation of rebuilding the mill.[59]

In January 1839, Lieutenant Root, the quartermaster at Fort Brady, informed Quartermaster General Henry Stanton of the state's plans for a canal around the rapids, warning him that:

> According to the engineer's plans, the said canal would cross the public mill race or feeder belonging to the United States' saw-mill, in charge of the Quartermaster's department at this post, which of course would make the mill useless until some other work should be executed in place of the present feeder. As the latter would necessarily subject the United States to expense, I very respectfully request your orders in the case, and whether the contractors shall be allowed to proceed with the work agreeably to their present plan.

Stanton replied in March that the Michigan Legislature could not possibly be thinking of interfering with the improvement made by the United States at Fort Brady, and that "You will, therefore, apprize the contractor that he cannot be allowed, in the execution of his contract, to interfere in any way with that work." He also instructed Root to allow the canal to be constructed through the military reservation, as long as it did not seriously injure the interests of the United States.

On May 12, after Weeks landed men and provisions, Root presented him with copies of the correspondence, and notification that he would not be allowed to cut the mill race. Weeks replied that he was bound by the state of Michigan to excavate the canal on lines laid out by the Chief Engineer, and that it would be impossible to proceed without having exclusive control of the race:

> Therefore, we shall proceed to work on said line of canal, and cannot allow water to flow through said race, where the line of the canal crosses the same, as it will entirely frustrate the object that the State of Michigan has in constructing a ship canal around the rapids of the Sault de Ste. Marie; and the contractors will be obliged to abandon said work at a very great loss to themselves, and we believe to the State of Michigan.

Weeks demanded an immediate answer to his letter. Root took the letter to his superior, Captain Johnson, who replied the same day that Root had his orders: the work could not be carried out peacefully if Weeks insisted on cutting the race, and he would carry out the instructions to their full extent.

Weeks then decided to begin construction and continue until stopped by the Army. After felling a few trees, ostensibly to provide timber for the canal, he took his crew to the mill race and began digging drainage ditches. At that point, he was confronted by Captain Johnson and a company of armed regulars. When Weeks refused to obey, Johnson drew his sabre and wrestled the foreman's shovel away from him. Advancing with fixed bayonets, troops drove the crew from the reservation.[60] Weeks and his men continued to stay at the Soo through the summer, apparently fishing in the rapids. At the end of May, the Quartermaster Department issued orders authorizing construction across the mill race if the race was restored to its original condition when the canal was completed. In July, the Board of Internal Improvements promised to restore the race. Formal agreements were signed by the Board in August 1839, but Weeks refused to resume construction and instead submitted claims to the state for damages.[61]

The state was primarily responsible for the incident at the Soo. Its failure to coordinate its plans with the federal government demonstrated poor planning and bad judgment. Federal authorities were eager to cooperate, even when confronted with unauthorized construction of the canal across a military reservation. With proper preparation, the agreement signed in August 1839 might have been worked out earlier.

Officers at Fort Brady were carrying out their military responsibility, but the contractor's belligerence is surprising. Although supported only by folklore, stories persist that Weeks and Captain Johnson arranged the whole affair when Weeks became disillusioned with the possibility of making profits on his contract, but this version is contradicted by the correspondence between the Fort and the War Department.[62] It seems more probable that Weeks, like contractors who were abandoning jobs along the Northern Railroad and the Saginaw-Maple Canal, doubting the state's ability to pay its obligations after the Michigan State Bank failed, provoked the incident in order to submit damage claims instead of being charged damages for failing to fulfill his contracts. Evidence, however, does not permit anything more than speculation.

The state, however, maintained that the federal government was responsible for the failure of construction. After being notified that construction had been halted, Mason sent an energetic protest to the President, charging that the sovereignty of the state had been violated. The following January, he repeated his charges in his annual message to the Legislature. Arguing that jurisdiction resided with the state regardless of who owned the soil, Mason made it clear that he considered the federal government no more than another property owner:

> Under the federal constitution, the exclusive jurisdiction of the general government within the limits of the states, is confined to places purchased by the consent of the Legislatures of the states in which the

same shall be, for erection of forts, magazines, arsenals, dock-yards and other needful buildings. In the present case, there has been neither consent given or purchase made; and if the "mill race" of the United States had been affected by the construction of this great public improvement, a work so important to the commerce of the country, the federal government could only have had an equitable claim to indemnity by the State of Michigan to be adjusted under her own constitution and laws. The reservation of the lands by the United States, for military or other purposes, vests in the federal government no authority to interfere with an important and needful exercise of jurisdiction by our own Legislature.[63]

Mason's excessive concern with legal right illuminates the state's refusal to establish a working understanding with the federal government before crossing the military reservation. Had water power been the basic issue, a pragmatic solution might have been achieved, for at the only outlet to the world's largest body of fresh water, the raw material was practically inexhaustible. The question was one of jurisdiction and constitutional right, and insistence on the state's rights postponed construction of the canal for almost two decades.

Whigs, as well as Democrats, agreed with Mason's position. In his inaugural message to the Legislature, Woodbridge stated that Mason had been entirely correct in his relations with the federal government.[64] During the 1840 session, the Whig Legislature declared by joint resolution that the federal government's actions were unconstitutional, and the United States was liable for damages suffered by the state. Since the federal government had chosen to stop construction, legislators became convinced that national authorities would have to be responsible for future internal improvements, and instructions were issued annually to Michigan's Congressmen to work for federal appropriations.

In some respects it was fortunate the state was forced to abandon the canal before it became heavily committed to construction. The state was relieved of the necessity of supporting another project on the meager funds available after the state deposit bank and the Bank of the United States failed. Provided with a convenient excuse for abandonment, the political humiliation of having to admit defeat was avoided. If the canal could have been constructed within the engineer's estimates, scarce funds would not have presented serious problems. Subsequent examinations of the route, however, revealed that Almy had been guilty of serious errors, underestimating the necessary amount of rock excavation and omitting a guard lock at the upper end of the canal.[65] When the canal was finally constructed, cost fell just short of a million dollars.[66]

In addition to the six major projects undertaken by the state, a host of minor projects were sponsored. River improvement was an important part of the state's program. Under the Act of 1837, crews were authorized to survey the Kalamazoo, Grand, and St. Joseph Rivers to determine their suitability for slack water navigation.[67] Appropriations for rivers in 1838 included thirty thousand dollars for the Grand and Maple, and eight thousand for the Kalamazoo. The following year, twenty-five thousand dollars was appropriated for the St. Joseph River.[68]

Between 1838 and 1849, work continued when funds and water conditions permitted. In 1838 and 1839, efforts centered on improving rivers forming a part of the state's projected canal system. Large amounts of money were spent on the Grand and Maple Rivers and the Kalamazoo River below Allegan. Because contracts for river work were awarded annually, the Legislature's suspension of new contracts in 1840 slowed work that year and stopped it altogether in 1841. Late in the 1841 legislative session, when the Democrats regained control, suspension of river improvement was lifted.[69] Efforts between 1842 and 1849 centered on developing the St. Joseph as a navigable waterway to compensate for the legislative decision to suspend construction on the Southern, west of Hillsdale. By 1849, the St. Joseph was navigable below Three Rivers, the Kalamazoo below Allegan, and the Grand and the Maple as far west as Grand Rapids. Total cost of the program, which concentrated on removing snags and constructing wing dams, was over fifty-five thousand dollars.[70]

The effect of river improvement on economic development is difficult to evaluate. Since travel was free, receipts cannot be compared to investment to derive a rate of return, and economic benefits fall entirely into the category of non-taxable social gain. No record was kept of quantities of merchandise shipped over the rivers. The Board's survey of exports and imports at the port of St. Joseph, at the mouth of the St. Joseph River, however, provides a fair indication of the volume of trade. Even if only half of the volume shipped represented goods traveling down the river, results were substantial. Between September 1, 1845, and September 1, 1846, 263,645 bushels of wheat and 129,338 barrels of flour were exported, while 3,489,604 pounds of merchandise were imported. Shipments over the Central Railroad from November 30, 1845 to September 23, 1846, totaled 59,914 bushels of wheat and 180,423 barrels of flour. Merchandise shipments to the west totaled 8,241,867 pounds. At that point, only ten thousand dollars had been expended in improving the St. Joseph River.[71] If only ten percent of the St. Joseph trade resulted from river improvement, the money was well spent.

Full use of the Grand River was frustrated by the state's failure to build a canal around the rapids. A canal begun by Lucius Lyon in 1835, and engineered by John Almy who designed the canal at the Soo, was not completed because of the depression. In 1839, the Legislature included twenty-five thousand dollars in the internal improvements appropriation for construction of a canal. The Board submitted estimates in 1839 and 1841 that purchasing the Kent Company's rights and construction, and completing the canal would require at least forty-six thousand dollars. Negotiations to purchase the work deadlocked in 1841, when the state refused to meet the company's price unless rights to the water power from the canal were included. The Board subsequently recommended construction on the far side

TABLE VI
Expenditures Reported by the Board of Internal Improvements, 1837-1845[a]

	1837	1838	1839[b]	1840[b]	1841	1842	1843	1844	1845
Kalamazoo River		3,023	2,063		1,154				811[c]
Grand and Maple Rivers		13,996	7,007	1,474	104	870	737		
St. Joseph River				2,268	1,706			1,041	5,733
Clinton Canal[b]		16,429	93,221	167,512	56,794	538	8,234		17,320
Saginaw Canal[b]		6,271	15,985	14,387	5,172				
Soo Canal	1,152	794	1,006	88					
Grand Rapids Canal		130			88		6		
Havre Branch	61	235	613	211					
Salt Springs		3,000	15,000		5,000[d]	15,000[d]			
River Raisin and Lake Erie RR					32,500				
Northern RR[b]	8,226	12,772	39,122	10,773	7,022	2,013			300
Grand River Road					487	2,714	575		28
Saginaw Turnpike					3,876				
Surveying	31,639	5,832							
Total	41,078	62,352	174,141	234,213	76,403	21,135	9,522	1,041	24,192

[a]Michigan, Legislature, *Annual Reports of the Board of Internal Improvements (Joint Documents,* J. D. No. 4), pp. (1839) 9-12; (1840) 21-27; (1841) 26-27; (1842) 167; (1843) 11; (1844) 39; (1845) 16-17.

[b]Reported expenditures on the Clinton Canal, Saginaw Canal, and Northern Railroad do not balance with total investment reported by the Board at the end of 1840, when added to totals reported at the end of 1839. The conflict of data is the result of the Board's false reporting in order to keep reported expenditures within limits set by specific appropriations. Without original vouchers, adjustment is impossible. Statements of total expenditure on these three projects in the text of the chapter will not balance with the annual expenditures reported above. In these cases, statements published by the Democratic Board in 1842 have been used because they seem to adjust for the Board's previous faulty accounting.

[c]Expended on the Kalamazoo, Grand and Maple Rivers.

[d]Appropriations are used because there is no data available on the rate of expenditure. The salt works were usually able to exhaust their appropriations in a single year.

of the river, on state-owned land. Lyon charged that the state had no intention of purchasing or prosecuting the canal, because it lacked the funds to pay even if the company met the price. According to Lyon, the Board's insistence on inclusion of water-power rights was designed to place the blame for the project's failure on the company.[72] In either case, no further attempts were made to facilitate transportation around the rapids of the Grand, and full realization of benefits from large expenditures on the Grand and Maple Rivers was frustrated.

Large sums of money were also spent in attempts to manufacture salt. Between 1838, when drilling began on lands awarded by the federal government on admission to the Union, and 1846, when the program was discontinued, thirty-eight thousand dollars were appropriated from the internal improvements fund to pay for shafts and equipment.[73] Presumably, all appropriations were spent. Drilling took place near Midland and Grand Rapids; the state hoped to lease both the saline waters raised and the lands around the wells. After six years of drilling without raising water suitable for processing, the state began to consider selling. Restrictions in the federal grant, however, forced them to seek permission from Congress. When the drilling machinery was offered for sale in 1846, permission had not yet been granted.[74]

In addition to projects administered by the Board of Internal Improvements, the state sought to improve transportation by extending credit to private railroads supplementing major routes across the peninsula. During the special session of 1837 and the legislative session of 1838, three hundred and twenty thousand dollars credit was extended to four private railroad companies. Bills were brought forward for aid to several other companies, but since only the titles of the bills were recorded, it is impossible to determine whether aid meant extension of construction deadlines, or loans of the state's credit.

The Allegan and Marshall Railroad was chartered in 1836 to serve the Kalamazoo Valley by extending the Detroit and St. Joseph from Marshall after the road turned south of the river toward St. Joseph. Although construction had not been attempted, in 1838 Andrew G. Hammond petitioned the Legislature for an appropriation. The House Committee on Internal Improvements reported favorably on Hammond's petition, expressing the hope that it would increase pine lumber shipments from Allegan and add to the Central's revenues. Citing grants of credit in other states, the Committee concluded, "It will not be doubted but that individual or corporate companies when able to command the necessary means, possess a great advantage over a state in the construction of public works...." The bill passed the Senate by a one-vote margin, with ballots cast on sectional lines. Under the terms of the act, one hundred thousand dollars was to be loaned to the company, when the company provided matching funds. Each five-thousand-dollar payment was to be matched by the road's stockholders. In case of default, the state was authorized to sell the road at auction, or purchase it at cost plus seven percent.[75] Sixty thousand dollars in funds nominally advanced were deposited in the Michigan State Bank at the time of its failure, and the state's claim had to be satisfied by assets received in settlement of the Bank's debts.[76]

The Ypsilanti and Tecumseh was chartered in April 1838, to connect the Central with the Palmyra and Jacksonburg. The stockholders listed in the act of incorporation were residents of the area served by the road. Three days later, one hundred thousand dollars was granted to finance construction. The act instructed the Governor to negotiate the sale of securities and turn the funds over to the company. In case of default, the state had the right to sell the road at auction. The House voting revealed a pattern of local support, while the same Senators from the first and third tiers opposed the loan who had opposed a loan to the Allegan and Marshall.[77]

When the company applied to the Governor for its funds, it was assured that they would be received in separate installments in August, September, and October. Impatient for the funds, they asked for a warrant for sixty thousand dollars and received a check drawn on the Michigan State Bank. When the check was presented, however, the company was forced to take drafts on the Albany Canal Bank at one hundred and eighteen days, instead of the Morris Canal Bank notes promised when their securities were sold as part of the five million loan. The funds were accepted reluctantly and deposited in the Bank of Tecumseh. Construction began, but when monthly estimates fell due in February 1839, the company was unable to pay its contractors because the Albany Canal Bank, like the Michigan State Bank, had failed. A petition to the Legislature resulted in an additional fifteen thousand dollars which the company used to pay its contractors, but in the process the company was disrupted and discredited, and many of its contractors ruined. Of $75,000 received by the company, $42,761 was expended in construction, and the balance lost through bank failure. Right-of-way had been purchased, and grubbing and grading nearly completed. Timber for piles, ribs, caps, and sills were on the ground. A contract with the Baldwin works for two locomotives, pile-driving machines, and men to run them had been negotiated, but lapsed when the company ran out of negotiable funds. Failure of the Michigan State Bank and loss of the funds it had provided in lieu of drafts on the Morris Canal and Banking Company were responsible for the loss.[78]

Two efforts were made to settle the state's account with the Ypsilanti and Tecumseh. In 1840, the Legislature appointed a commission to secure the money due the state under the loan, but their negotiations were limited by the provision that the road could not be accepted in settlement of claims. The commission's report sided strongly with the company's claims, arguing that the road was due damages from the state for non-fulfillment of contract, and recommending that the state take over the road. In 1841, the same commissioners were authorized to reach a final settlement.[79] No settlement was reported, however, and subsequent attempts to induce the companies granted aid to pay their debts by allowing them to purchase and return state stock produced no results. Apparently, no settlement was ever reached.

The Detroit and Pontiac Railroad Bank, discussed in Chapter 3, had been completed to Royal Oak before 1837. Under instructions from the Legislature, Governor Mason had approached the company in 1836 for the purpose of purchasing their charter.[80] The company replied that it would be willing to sell on the condition that the state complete the road on the located route within two years, and compensate the company by paying cost plus seven percent interest; the bank must be allowed to continue. The company made it clear, however, that they would prefer a fifty-thousand-dollar loan to finance immediate completion.[81]

The Legislature authorized purchase of the Detroit and Pontiac in the spring of 1837, at cost plus seven percent. Under the terms of the act, construction was to be completed within two years, and seventy-five thousand dollars was appropriated for the purchase. A tax of one-half percent was levied on the bank's stock, and the consent of stockholders in both the company and the bank was required before the road could be purchased.[82] Apparently the company rejected the terms, because in 1838, the question of aiding the Detroit and Pontiac arose again.

In March 1838, the Legislature granted one hundred thousand dollars in state bonds to the Detroit and Pontiac. In return for securities carrying the seal of the state and a pledge of its faith, the road was required to post a bond consisting of personal obligations secured by unencumbered real estate for twice the value of the securities. The bond would be forfeited if the road failed to meet payments of interest and principal on the securities. In addition, the road was mortgaged to the state, to be sold at auction in case of failure; the road would automatically revert to the state if the company failed to complete it by May 1839.[83]

The aid offered by the Legislature was quickly accepted by the company, which posted bond for $200,000 secured by mortgages on real estate valued at $242,540. The bond consisted of personal notes of area residents, secured by real estate in their possession, mostly town lots in Pontiac and Royal Oak. Thus the state substituted more negotiable public credit for that of a private company and individuals. In return, $100,000 in state bonds due in 1858 were turned over to the corporation.[84] During 1839, another attempt was made to purchase the railroad, but the bill failed in the House. In December 1839, the Legislature was notified that the Detroit and Pontiac had failed to pay interest on the loan.[85]

Although the Legislature considered foreclosure several times in the next six years, it was never able to bring itself to take over the road or collect the defaulters' bonds. In 1840, the House Committee on Internal Improvements reported favorably on petitions from the managers, Stevens and Williams, asking the state to foreclose and lease the road to the company for ten or fifteen years. The Committee reported that the road had been pulled into bankruptcy by the failure of its bank, not by failure of the road's earning power. The road was liable for the redemption of approximately ninety thousand dollars in outstanding bank notes. Revenues from the road had been used to pay laborers instead of interest. When the Auditor and Treasurer advertised the road and its security for sale, Williams and Stevens petitioned the Legislature for state purchase to avoid ruining local citizens who had posted bond.[86] Efforts to pass a bill allowing settlement, however, failed in both houses.[87]

In 1841, the Legislature again turned to the Detroit and Pontiac. In response to legislative inquiry, the Attorney General reported that under the terms of the mortgage, the road had already become state property and could be absorbed into the internal improvements system by a simple legislative act. He recommended this rather than public sale, if the Legislature was determined to regain its funds. Refusing to comment directly on policy, he recommended that the Legislature take the course which would do minimum injury to those who had posted security for the road. The Legislature restored full corporate rights to the Detroit and Pontiac, regardless of forfeiture provisions in previous charters, but retained all rights given the state.[88]

After 1841, the Detroit and Pontiac continued to operate with the state mortgage hanging over its head. At least part of the state's refusal to assume control was reluctance to become involved in the road's complicated corporate structure and obligations, which included notes outstanding and a hundred-thousand-dollar debt to the State of Indiana. Foreclosing on securities posted for the road would have ruined half the important citizens of Royal Oak and Pontiac, and was politically impractical. In 1842, the company was granted four years to overcome its financial difficulties. In May 1846, the Senate passed a bill which attempted to force payment of debts by August, under penalty of state seizure and absorption into the system of internal improvements, but it was rejected by the House, forty-three to one.[89] At the close of the internal improvements era in 1846, the problem of the Detroit and Pontiac's mortgage was still unsolved.

Aid was granted to the Palmyra and Jacksonburg during the June 1837 session of the Legislature. The road had been chartered the previous year to run from Palmyra to Tecumseh, Clinton, and Jackson as a branch of the Erie and Kalamazoo. Encountering difficulties, it appealed to the Legislature. The House Committee on Internal Improvements, in recommending the bill which had originated in the Senate, declared: "It ought not to operate as a precedent; but from the peculiar situation in which the company is now placed, it is proper to extend the desired relief." House voting on the issue revealed no apparent sectional or political alignment.[90] As passed, the grant provided for a twenty-thousand-dollar loan at seven percent, to be covered by double security. In October, the company accepted the provisions of the loan, and gave the state the desired security in tracts of land held by local residents, in addition to a mortgage for fifteen thousand dollars against the road.[91] Construction pushed forward, and the road was opened to horse-drawn traffic on wooden rails. Between August 1838 and November 1839, the company reported a net income of $7,485 against an investment of

$70,000, or approximately ten percent.[92]

After two years of operation, the road ran into difficulties because of increasing business. The road bed was solid, but the weight of freight cars transporting flour from the Tecumseh mills was crushing its rails beyond repair. By the end of 1840, new rails were required for the entire distance between Palmyra and Tecumseh; the rails from Clinton to Tecumseh only required dressing. Reporting a need for iron and locomotives, the engineer stated that horse locomotion was the road's greatest handicap. Without iron, it took four horses to do the work of one on an ironed road; horse power was reported twice as expensive as steam. Although the road transported twenty thousand barrels of flour in 1840, more than half that carried by either the Central or the Erie and Kalamazoo, profits fell to about two thousand dollars.[93] In 1840, the Legislature authorized the Board of Internal Improvements to lend iron to the road, provided it was not currently needed and the track was widened to standard gauge.[94]

The following year, the House Committee on Internal Improvements reported that the road could be purchased for twenty-four thousand dollars by deducting sums due on loans, depreciation, iron, and two miles which would be worthless to the state, from the original cost of eighty-seven thousand dollars. Even when the cost of placing iron on the road was included, it would be the least expensive route under state control, and would divert important traffic to the Southern.[95] The Legislature responded by repealing the iron loan, and offering to return the securities posted by the company if it would place iron on the road between the Southern and Clinton, and abandon the section between the Southern and the road's terminal at Palmyra. The offer expired in September 1842.[96] The state purchased the road in 1844 and incorporated it into the Southern.

Unlike the Central Railroad, other projects undertaken by the state resulted in heavy financial losses. After eight years of construction and repair, the Southern was sold for half a million dollars less than its original cost. The Northern consumed seventy thousand dollars before it was abandoned. Losses on the Clinton and Kalamazoo amounted to over three hundred and fifty thousand dollars, and forty-seven thousand was lost on the Saginaw-Maple Canal. Loss on the canal at the Soo was nominal. Large sums were expended on rivers, but their usefulness and impact cannot be determined. Seventy-five thousand dollars disappeared into the Ypsilanti and Tecumseh Railroad. In sum, at least a million dollars was lost on these projects, money which would have completed the Central to St. Joseph and provided it with a heavy superstructure. Without the multiple projects forced on it by sectional rivalry, the state would have had one complete transpeninsular route in operation. Multiple projects, along with bank failures, were responsible for most of the state's losses on its internal improvements program.

Notes, Chapter 7

1. Michigan, *Senate Document No. 11,* 1838, pp. 156-170, 175-189, 204-212.
2. Michigan, *Legislative Acts,* 1838, Joint Resolution No. 2.
3. Michigan, Legislature, *Report of the Committee on Internal Improvements Relative to the Suspension of Operations on the Southern Railroad (Senate Documents,* 1838, S. D. No. 9); Michigan, Legislature, *Reports of the Majority and Minority Committees on Internal Improvements, in Relation to the Suspension of Proceedings on the Northern and Southern Railroads (Senate Documents,* 1838, S. D. No. 13), pp. 294ff.
4. Michigan, Legislature, *Report of the Majority of the Joint Committee Appointed to Review the Location of the Northern and Southern Railroad Routes, (Senate Documents,* 1838, S. D. No. 30), pp. 401-416.
5. Michigan, Legislature, *Report of the Majority of the Joint Committee on the Northern and Southern Railroad Routes (Senate Documents,* 1838, S. D. No. 42), pp. 473-487.
6. Michigan, Legislature, *Report of the Majority of the Committee of the Senate, Appointed to Consider the Propriety of the Location of the Northern and Southern Railroad Routes (Senate Documents,* 1838, S. D. No. 31), pp. 416-430.
7. Michigan, *Legislative Acts,* 1838, Joint Resolution No. 20.
8. *Ibid.,* No. 54, and Joint Resolution No. 20; Michigan, *Legislative Acts,* 1839, Nos. 81, 161.
9. Michigan, *Senate Document No. 17,* 1839.
10. Michigan, Legislature, *Report of the Special Committee Appointed by the House of Representatives, to Investigate the Proceedings, & c., of the Several Boards of Interal Improvement* (Detroit, Dawson and Bates, 1840), pp. 400, 421, 423ff.
11. *Messages of the Governors of Michigan,* I, 245.
12. Michigan, Legislature, *House Document No. 3,* 1840.
13. *Ibid.,* pp. 5, 51-60.
14. Michigan, Legislature, *House Document* No. 3, 1841, pp. 21-27. The Board of Internal Improvements reported expending $120,793 from December, 1839 to March, 1841, and $56,981 from April 1 to November 30, 1840. Yet in the same report it stated expenditures at $122,735. The Governor, in his annual message, stated that expenditures were $210,274, including purchase of the River Raisin and Lake Erie. The difference, some $60,000 was paid for in warrants and floating estimates, apparently to escape limits set by appropriations. Since warrants and estimates were absorbed in subsequent years, I have used the figure of $155,000 to avoid double counting. Falsification of accounts by the Whigs makes accuracy difficult.
15. *Ibid.,* pp. 4-6.
16. Michigan, *Legislative Acts,* 1837, Joint Resolution No. LXXIII; Michigan, *House Journal,* 1837, pp. 42, 18-85.
17. Michigan, Legislature, *Report of the Committee to Whom was [sic] Referred the Petition of the River Raisin and Lake Erie Railroad Company (House Documents,* 1840, II, H. D. No. 24, 118ff; Michigan, Legislature, *Report of the Committee on Internal Improvements, Relative to the Purchase of the River Raisin and Lake Erie Railroad (Senate Documents,* 1840, II, S. D. No. 53), p. 490; Michigan, *Legislative Acts,* 1840, No. 100.
18. Michigan, Legislature, *Report of the Commissioners appointed to settle with the River Raisin and Lake Erie Railroad Company (House Documents,* 1841, II, H. D. No. 56), pp. 196-198.
19. Michigan, *Legislative Acts,* 1841, No. 24; Michigan, Legislature, *Report of the Committee on Claims....(House Documents,* 1841, II, H. D. No. 70), p. 218.
20. Michigan, Legislature, *Report of the Committee on Banks and Incorporations (House Documents,* 1841, II, H. D. No. 59) pp. 205-208; Michigan, Legislature,

Report of the Committee on Banks and Incorporations (House Documents, 1841, II, No. 44), pp. 155-160.

21. Michigan, *House Document No. 3,* pp. 11-16; *Messages of the Governors of Michigan,* I, 442.
22. Letter from J. B. Bloren to Gen. Van Fossen, February 20, 1841, in Records of the Executive Office, 1810-1910: Reports: Board of Internal Improvements, 1838-1841 (Correspondence in the Michigan Department of State, Historical Commission Archives).
23. Michigan, *Legislative Acts,* 1841, Joint Resolution No. 15.
24. *Ibid.,* Joint Resolution No. 13; Michigan, *House Document No. 3,* 1842.
25. Michigan, *Legislative Acts,* 1840, No. 103; *Ibid.,* 1841, Joint Resolution No. 17; Michigan, Legislature, *Report of the Committee on Internal Improvements (Senate Documents,* 1841, II, S. D. No. 22). *Extra of the Hillsdale County Gazette,* Feb. 15, 1841, in the Henry Waldron Papers (Michigan State University Historical Collections).
26. Michigan, *Senate Document No. 4,* 1843, p. 2; Michigan, *Joint Document No. 5,* 1844, pp. 1, 9.
27. Michigan, *Senate Document No. 4,* 1843, pp. 2-4, 32; Michigan, *Joint Document No. 5,* 1844, pp. 9, 19.
28. Michigan, *Joint Document No. 4,*1846, pp. 3-5; Michigan, *Joint Document No. 4,* 1845.
29. *Ibid.,* pp. 5, 29, 31.
30. Michigan, Legislature, *Proposition for the Purchase of the Southern Railroad (House Documents,* 1846, H. D. No. 10).
31. Michigan, Legislature, [No Title] *(House Documents,* 1846, H. D. No. 11).
32. Michigan, *House Journal,* 1846, p. 436.
33. Michigan, *Legislative Acts,* 1846, No. 113.
34. Michigan, *Senate Document No. 11,* 1838, pp. 166, 170.
35. *Ibid.,* pp. 217, 226.
36. Michigan, *Senate Document No. 47,* 1838.
37. Michigan, *House Document No. 17,* 1839, pp. 275, 321.
38. Michigan, *House Document No. 3,* 1840, pp. 9-12, 38-40; Michigan, *House Document No. 3,* 1841, pp. 30-32.
39. Michigan, *Legislative Acts,* 1841, No. 42; Michigan, *Legislative Acts,* 1843, No. 83; Michigan, *Legislative Acts,* 1846, No. 55; Michigan, *House Document No. 3,* 1842, pp. 6-7.
40. *Semi-Weekly Free Press* (Detroit), April 25, 1837, p. 3.
41. Michigan, *Senate Documents No. 11,* 1838, pp. 169, 237-238.
42. Michigan, Legislature, *Report of the Commissioners of Internal Improvements on the Survey of a Canal from Mt. Clemens to Lake Michigan (Senate Documents,* 1838, S. D. No. 23) pp. 323-327.
43. Michigan, Legislature, *Report of the Commissioners of Internal Improvements (House Documents,* 1838, H. D. No. 57), pp. 515-516; Michigan, Legislature, *House Document No. 17,* 1839, pp. 275, 291-296.
44. Michigan, Legislature, *Report on the Cedar and Grand River Branch of the Clinton and Kalamazoo Canal (House Documents,* 1839, H. D. No. 50) pp. 834-867.
45. Letter from Lucius Lyon to William Woodbridge, January 20, 1844, in Lyon Papers, *MP&HC,* XXVII, 566.
46. Michigan, *House Document No. 3,* 1839, pp. 6, 13-30, 71-83, Michigan Legislature *Report of the Commissioners of Internal Improvements in Relation to the Improvement of the Clinton River (House Documents,* 1839, No. 40), pp. 664-667; Michigan, *Legislative Acts,* 1839, Joint Resolution No. 3.
47. Michigan, *House Journal,* 1840, p. 522; Michigan, *Senate Journal,* 1840, pp. 516, 598.
48. Michigan, *House Document No. 3,* 1840, pp. 9-10; Michigan, Legislature, *Report of the Committee on Internal Improvements (House Documents,* 1840, II, No. 56) p. 513.

49. Michigan, *House Document No. 3*, 1842, pp. 1, 4, 5, 25; Michigan, *House Journal*, 1841, pp. 294, 394, 434, 451, 557; Michigan, *Legislative Acts*, 1841, No. 50.
50. Michigan, *Senate Document No. 4*, 1843, pp. 1, 4, 5, 25; Michigan, *Legislative Acts*, 1842, Joint Resolution No. 36; Michigan, *House Journal*, 1842, p. 347.
51. Michigan, *Joint Document No. 5*, 1844, pp. 1-2; Michigan, Legislature, *Report*, *(House Documents*, 1843, H. D. No. 9), pp. 42-47.
52. *Messages of the Governors of Michigan*, I, 511; Michigan, *Joint Document No. 4*, 1846, p. 37; *Ibid.*, 1847, pp. 20-22; Michigan, *Legislative Acts*, 1844, No. 27; Michigan, *Legislative Acts*, 1845, No. 27; Michigan, *Legislative Acts*, 1846, No. 139.
53. Alexander Winchell, *Tackabury's Atlas of the State of Michigan* (Detroit: George N. Tackabury, 1884), p. 10.
54. Michigan, *Senate Document No. 11*, 1838, pp. 240ff.
55. *Messages of the Governors of Michigan*, I, 281; Michigan, *House Document No. 17*, 1839, pp. 321-322; Michigan, *Joint Document No. 4*, 1845, pp. 9-10; Michigan, *Legislative Acts*, 1841, No. 37; Michigan, Legislature, *Report of the Committee on Finance, Relative to the Saginaw Canal (Senate Documents*, 1840, II, No. 52) p. 52.
56. Otto Fowle, *Sault Ste. Marie and its Great Waterway* (New York: Putnam's, 1925), pp. 31, 237-252; Roger Pilkington, "Canals: Inland Waterways Outside Great Britain," *History of Technology*, IV, 552.
57. Michigan, *Senate Document No. 11*, 1838, pp. 257-258.
58. *Ibid.*, pp. 315-320; Michigan, *Legislative Acts*, 1838, No. 91; Michigan, Legislature, *Report of the Select Committee, Relative to the Construction of a Ship Canal around the Falls of Ste. Marie (House Documents*, 1838, H. D. No. 64); Michigan, *Legislative Acts*, 1839, Joint Resolution No. 31; Michigan, Legislature, *Communication from the Office of Internal Improvements, Feb. 4, 1840 (Senate Documents*, 1840, H, S. D. No. 33), pp. 295-296.
59. Fowle, p. 375.
60. Letters from Lt. Wm. Root to the Hon. J. R. Poinsett, Jan. 14, 1839; Henry Stanton to Lt. W. Root, March 6, 1839; Smith, Driggs, & Weeks to Lt. Wm. Root, May 13, 1839 in Michigan, *House Document No. 3*, 1840, pp. 83-97. In addition to these and other letters in H. D. No. 3, see "Affidavit of J. B. Van Rensselaar," *Senate Documents*, 1840, II, p. 553. Originals or certified copies of this correspondence are in the William Woodbridge Papers (BHC) filed under June, 1839.
61. Michigan, *House Document No. 3*, 1840, pp. 6, 31-32, 48, 83-97.
62. Fowle, p. 379.
63. *Messages of the Governors of Michigan*, I, 282-316. Mason's Message was never accepted by the Legislature.
64. Michigan, *Legislative Acts*, 1840, Joint Resolution No. 13.
65. Letter from J. J. Abert, Bureau of Topographical Engineers, to the Hon. A. S. Porter, U. S. Senate, Jan. 11, 1841, in the Alpheus Felch Papers (Burton Historical Collections, Detroit). Cited hereafter as Felch Papers (BHC).
66. Dunbar, p. 373.
67. Michigan, *Legislative Acts*, 1838, No. 56; Michigan, *Legislative Acts*, 1839, No. 116.
68. Michigan, *Legislative Acts*, 1838, No. 56.
69. Michigan, *Legislative Acts*, 1841, No. 150.
70. See Table VI.
71. Michigan, *Joint Document No. 4*, 1847, pp. 10-12, 25.
72. Michigan, *Legislative Acts*, 1839, No. 234. Letters from Lucius Lyon to C. H. Taylor, Sept. 8, 1841; Lucius Lyon to Arthur Bronson, Oct. 12, 1835, in Lyon Papers, *MP&HC*, XXVII (1896), 459-460. Michigan, *House Document No. 3*, 1840, p. 42; Michigan, *House Document No. 3*, 1842, pp. 2-5, 33.
73. Michigan, *Legislative Acts*, 1838, No. 55; Michigan, *Legislative Acts*, 1837, No. 1; Michigan, *Legislative Acts*, 1840, No. 92; Michigan, *Legislative Acts*, 1842, No. 10.

74. Michigan, *Legislative Acts,* 1842, No. 47; Michigan, *Legislative Acts,* 1845, No. 90, Joint Resolution No. 3; Michigan, *Legislative Acts,* No. 97.

75. Michigan, Legislature, *Report of the Committee on Internal Improvements, Relative to the Construction of the Kalamazoo and Allegan Railroad (House Documents,* 1838, H. D. No. 66), pp. 571-573; Michigan, *Legislative Acts,* 1838, No. 21; Michigan, *Senate Journal,* 1838, pp. 349, 350, 388, 397, 403, 421.

76. Michigan, Legislature, *Report of the Committee on Finance (Senate Documents,* 1843, S. D. No. 4), p. 31.

77. Michigan, *Legislative Acts,* 1838, No. 84, 174; Michigan, *Senate Journal,* 1838, pp. 376, 389, 404; Michigan, *House Journal,* 1838, p. 430.

78. Michigan, Legislature, *Report of the Committee on Internal Improvements, Relative to the Ypsilanti and Tecumseh Railroad Company (Senate Documents,* 1840, II, S. D. No. 42), pp. 412-414; Michigan, Legislature, *Report of the Ypsilanti and Tecumseh Railroad Company (Senate Documents,* 1839, S. D. No. 14), pp. 393-395; Michigan, *Legislative Acts,* 1839, Joint Resolution No. 12.

79. Michigan, Legislature, *Report of the Commissioners appointed...to provide for a settlement with the Ypsilanti and Tecumseh Railroad Company (Senate Documents,* 1841, I, S. D. No. 12), pp. 607-609; Michigan, *Legislative Acts,* 1840, No. 113; Michigan, *Legislative Acts,* No. 27.

80. Michigan, *House Journal,* 1837, p. 276.

81. Michigan, Legislature, *Proposition of the Detroit and Pontiac (Senate Documents,* 1837, S. D. No. 27), p. 176.

82. Michigan, *Legislative Acts,* 1837, No. CXX.

83. Michigan, *Legislative Acts.* 1838, No. 20.

84. Michigan, Legislature, *Robert Abbott, AJ, SM, to the President of the Senate, 14 Jan., 1839 (Senate Documents,* 1839, S. D. No. 4), pp. 86-87; Michigan, Legislature, *Report of the Auditor General... (Senate Documents,* 1840, II, S. D. No. 56).

85. Michigan, *House Document* No. 14, 1840, II, 2.

86. Michigan, Legislature, *Report of the Committee on Internal Improvements, Concerning Petitions of the Pontiac and Detroit Railroad Company (House Documents,* 1840, II, H. D. No. 39), pp. 316 ff.

87. Michigan, *House Journal,* 1840, pp. 124, 128, 137, 169, 222, 715, 726, 732.

88. Michigan, Legislature, *Report of the Attorney General in relation to the Detroit and Pontiac Railroad Company (Senate Documents,* 1841, II, S. D. No. 19), p. 19; Michigan, *Legislative Acts,* 1841, No. 88.

89. Michigan, Legislature, *Report of the Committee on Finance (Senate Documents,* 1843, S. D. No. 4); Michigan, *House Journal,* 1846, pp. 721, 727.

90. Michigan, *House Journal,* 1837, Extra Session, pp. 463, 466; Michigan, *Legislative Acts,* 1837, Special Session, No. XVI.

91. Michigan, Legislature, *Documents relative to the loan to the Palmyra and Jacksonburg Railroad Company (Senate Documents,* 1838, S. D. No. 27), p. 38.

92. Michigan, Legislature, *Report of the Palmyra and Jacksonburg Railroad Company (House Documents,* 1840, II, H. D. No. 32), p. 300.

93. Michigan Legislature, *A Petition from the Stockholders of the Palmyra and Jacksonburg Railroad Company (House Documents,* 1841, II, H. D. No. 26), pp. 58-64.

94. Michigan, *Legislative Acts,* 1840, No. 115.

95. Michigan, Legislature, *Report of the Committee on Internal Improvements, Relative to the Palmyra and Jacksonburg Railroad (House Documents,* 1841, II, H. D. No. 62), pp. 236-238.

96. Michigan, *Legislative Acts,* 1841, No. 81.

8

PARTY AND SECTION

The Legislature's adoption of a package program of internal improvements in the spring of 1837 failed to heal the sectional struggles that had dogged the state for a decade. If anything, the program aggravated sectional jealousy. From 1837 until 1846, the state was split by a series of battles over appropriations and priorities. For a short period early in the depression, sectional rivalry was manifested in the form of party alignment, but geography dominated ideology in the determination of party strength and internal improvement platforms. When the Democrats regained control in 1842—and each passing election added to their strength—sectional struggle continued unabated. At times, sectional alignments shifted with the locus of self-interest; in place of center against south, west would be pitted against east when continuation of the works across the peninsular watershed was the issue. Then, when the needs of the southern and central sections were satisfied, the third and northern tiers began to demand sectional equality. Sectional rivalry pervaded all aspects of legislative behavior, particularly those involving money or services provided by the state government. For this reason, sectional alignments are most clearly illustrated by the annual struggle over appropriations.

Dust from the internal improvements battle of the spring of 1837 had scarcely settled when sectional forces again clashed. In the summer and fall, gubernatorial elections kept the state in turmoil, while bank suspension and the Panic of 1837 occupied the Legislature. The 1837 campaign was spirited, but based on personal politics. Internal improvement was not an issue, except for Whig charges that Mason would be unable to negotiate the pending loan. Supported by Whig money, Monroe Democrat Edward D. Ellis attempted to split the Democracy by running against Mason, but Mason won by seven hundred and sixty-eight votes, the smallest margin of any nineteenth-century candidate. Apparently, the young Governor's popular support had cooled since 1835 when he symbolized Michigan's defiance of the federal government. Whig support in the gubernatorial contest was strongest in the second tier, the western counties of the first and third tier, and the Saginaw Bay-Thumb area. Democratic strength centered in the southern tier, two counties in the second tier, three counties in the third, and the politically insignificant northern two-thirds of the state.[1] William Woodbridge was the only Whig returned to the Senate, with the possible exception of Vincent L. Bradford, whose political affiliation is not identified.[2] House returns, al-

154

though not completely identifiable, deviated markedly from gubernatorial votes. Washtenaw County, which had supported the Whig candidate, returned four Democrats; the affiliations of its other three representatives are not known. Hillsdale County, which had supported Mason, returned a Whig representative, while politically powerful Wayne County returned three Democrats and five Whigs, proving the fallacy of basing an analysis of legislative voting patterns on county returns in gubernatorial contests. In the intensely personal world of local politics, split tickets were apparently common.

In spite of Governor Mason's warnings, sectional scrambling for appropriations continued through 1838. When the Governor addressed the new Legislature in January, he urged caution in appropriating money for the coming year. Delay or neglect by county officers in collecting taxes had put the state in debt, expenditures for internal improvements had been heavy, and Mason, who had seen the condition of the New York money market on his two trips east to negotiate the five million loan, warned against undertaking any new projects. The loan itself would require the strictest government economy, and revenues from the projects would be meager for "some time to come." Since he considered direct taxation out of the question, Mason suggested that the Legislature create a sinking fund based on the projects' revenues and any other available funds. As an alternative, he proposed state investment in bank stock, or the chartering of a state bank to gain revenues for the sinking fund. Finally, the Governor urged the Legislature to petition Congress for a grant of half a million acres of land for internal improvements, and one section for each mile of roads begun by the federal government.[3]

The Legislature, however, had other plans. Even before the 1838 session officially opened, there were rumors of a second-tier conspiracy to concentrate on the Central at the expense of the state's other projects. In December, Alpheus Felch wrote his new wife that he would be detained in Detroit, perhaps through Christmas, to head off a plot to scuttle the Southern, because he could not leave while "our Southern interests" were in danger.[4] During a March 21 speech in the House, Gantt, of Oakland County, hurled charges of conspiracy at the central tier. In the preamble to his resolution, Gantt insisted that the internal improvements system was a Democratic program, and a compromise between "the north, south, & Center interests of the people," supported by the Governor and his party. That program was in danger from a few *professed* democrats" and most of the Whig members, who were accused of meeting in secret caucus in Detroit and resolving to "defeat the proper and rightful interests of the people of the northern, southern and western divisions of Michigan." According to Gantt, the conspiracy was attempting to choke off appropriations for all projects except the Central in order to enrich the second tier and expand Whig party fortunes in Michigan. Gantt, characterizing the conspiracy as "a dark and injurious stab at the principals [sic] of the executive, the democracy of Michigan," offered a resolution pledging to support only a bill appropriating money according to the ratio of population in counties benefited by the expenditure.[5] Although Gantt's resolution was tabled, it was allowed to remain in the public record despite attempts to have it removed.

Debate on the House appropriations bill opened in earnest a week later. During the first day of debate, repeated attempts to gain appropriations for the Northern Railroad stalled the bill's progress, and a Senate version was rejected. The original House bill was later rejected in favor of a substitute drafted by Robert McClelland, a powerful Monroe Democrat. Finally, after fighting out appropriations for several projects on the floor of the House, the bill was adopted on March 29, by a vote of thirty-one to nineteen. The following day, the Senate accepted the House bill by a vote of ten to five.[6] The bill provided three hundred and fifty thousand dollars for the Central, an equal amount for the Southern, two hundred and five thousand dollars for the Clinton and Kalamazoo, and substantial appropriations for the Northern, canals, and rivers.[7]

Voting on the appropriations bill in both houses followed sectional lines. The strongest opposition came from the central tier, with only one county's representative voting in favor. The western end of the third tier joined the central in opposition, while delegates from two counties in the southern tier divided their votes. The bill's strongest support came from the southern tier and the eastern portion of the third tier. Although voting roughly followed the pattern exhibited in the 1837 gubernatorial election, section rather than party was the dominant factor. Two out of three of Wayne County's Democratic members voted with their Whig colleagues, while three of the four identified Democrats from Washtenaw County voted with the central section. In the south, Hillsdale's lone Whig delegate voted with the southern section. Although a few representatives in each tier voted against their section and supported the dominant elements in their party, it is apparent that sectional considerations exerted the decisive influence. In the upper house, while all four votes against both the Senate and House appropriations bills came from representatives of the second tier, three of the four votes were cast by Democrats.[8]

Attempts were made in both houses to place financial responsibility for public works on the sections benefited by their construction. In the House, central-tier delegates attempted to amend the bill to read:

> And in case the revenue arising from either of said railroads or canals, should prove insufficient to pay the interest on appropriations expended on the same, the tier of counties through which such railroads or canals shall be located, shall alone be liable for the payment of the interest on all appropriations heretofore, now, or hereafter to be made on such railroads or canals.[9]

The amendment, rejected nineteen to twenty-nine, was supported by the same delegates who later voted against the appropriations bill. A similar amendment was successfully attached to a Senate bill appropriating money for river improvement, but the bill failed to pass the House. Senate voting on the amendment revealed no clear-cut sectional alignment.[10]

During the same session, efforts were made to gain a federal land grant for state projects. After examining the question in detail, the Senate Committee on State Affairs, chaired by William Woodbridge, concluded that Michigan was entitled to grants at least equal to those granted to other states, and that in reality all the public domain within its boundaries belonged to Michigan. Recognizing that application should never be based on claims to right alone, however, the Committee offered economic justification for federal appropriation.[11] About the same time, Woodbridge, Michigan's leading Whig, pressured Senator Norvell to work for appropriations, expressing fears that the state would have to suspend its program unless federal lands were granted:

> By casting your eye over the map you will discover this material fact—that almost all the appropriations this state has made, are principally confined to the *Southern* part of our state—and such is, & doubtless will be the relative strength of local interests here for some time to come, that they will probably be confined to that portion of our State—*very greatly* to the injury of Detroit."

Woodbridge suggested that Norvell work for a grant to finance a canal from Detroit to the mouth of the Grand River.[12] By itself, Woodbridge's appeal is simply another letter from a local politician to his federal Senator, but in the context of the internal improvements struggle it illustrates the ease with which the powerful Wayne County Whig could cross political lines and appeal to Detroit's leading Democrat for aid in projects that would mutually benefit their constituencies.

Although the state was reapportioned at the end of the session, sectional balance was not disturbed. Representation in the House shifted slightly in favor of western counties, but neither the southern nor the central tier suffered losses in the number of ballots cast by their sections.[13]

The fall 1838 elections weakened the Democrats' hold on the Legislature. Whig campaign efforts focused on national issues, the Governor's negotiation of the five million loan, and money discovered missing from a parcel carried by the Governor from New York when loan negotiations had been completed. Whig candidates demanded a full investigation; Democratic candidates concentrated on the sub-treasury and a proposed state bank. When elections were over, the Whigs had increased their foothold in the Senate to six of its seventeen members, and captured twenty-one of the fifty House seats.[14]

The Governor's annual message, delivered in January 1839, was full of optimism for the program. Both the Central and Southern were reported progressing satisfactorily, and the canals were either being built, or contracts being awarded. Receipts on the Central, opened the previous February, were so encouraging that Mason predicted the road would yield an income "beyond our most sanguine expectations." He warned the Legislature, however, to use caution in appropriating funds. The system already encompassed 1,109 miles of public works at an estimated cost of $7,794,430, exclusive of cars, locomotives, and machinery, but the estimates showed signs of being low. Finally, after presenting documents explaining his negotiation of the five million loan, he asked for a full investigation.[15]

The 1839 appropriations bill passed without serious incident. Equal appropriations of one hundred thousand dollars were provided for the Central and Southern, and money was provided for improving the Grand River and the canal at Grand Rapids. Although Floyd Streeter's *Political Parties in Michigan, 1837-1860* leaves the impression that sectional struggles similar to those of 1838 dogged attempts to appropriate funds, such struggles are not apparent in the House and Senate records.[16] Considerations of neither party nor section raised serious obstacles to the bill, which passed both houses by comfortable margins: twelve to four in the Senate, and thirty-one to twelve in the House. Less than half the House Whigs voted against the bill; opposition was almost equally distributed between the eastern ends of the second, third, and fourth tiers. Senate opposition centered in Whigs from Wayne and Washtenaw Counties.[17]

During the 1839 session, the Legislature shifted its attention from appropriations and sectional struggles to the Democracy's internal battles. Investigations into the conduct of Mason and the Board of Internal Improvements cleared Mason of charges leveled by the Whigs in the 1838 elections, but attacks on the Board struck at the heart of the controlling faction of the Democratic party.[18] Early in 1838, thirty "Friends of the State Administration" had petitioned the Governor to appoint an entirely new board whose "purity" had not been contested, but Mason refused. A year later, an investigating committee, reporting on the Board's accounts, revealed misconduct prejudicial to the state administration. After a "very arduous and somewhat exciting investigation," the committee reported that accounts of commissioners constructing the Central failed to coincide with reported expenditures. David McKinstry, former commissioner on the Central, was accused of falsely reporting thirty-five thousand dollars expended for construction, and giving three thousand dollars in merchandise purchased with state funds to a store in which he was a partner. Then, in what the committee called "another very objectionable feature in the transactions," he purchased the same goods from the store and charged them to the state. McKinstry was also accused of purchasing large numbers of horses, cattle, and swine with state funds. As the committee phrased it, "A more outrageous transaction than this, if evidence can be relied upon, can scarcely be contemplated, and one which would draw down a severe rebuke upon a more humble individual." McKinstry's successor, James B. Hunt, was also found guilty of dishonest practices. Hunt was accused of paying for bridges over the Clinton and Kalamazoo before the canal was excavated, purchasing blankets he knew to be smuggled from Canada, and paying laborers in depreciated notes. Levi Humphrey, commissioner on the Southern, was accused of a twenty-three thousand dollar error in his vouchers. Although Humphrey was cleared by a special committee, and Hunt presented a case in his defense, the damage was done.[19] McKinstry, former Chairman of the State Democratic Committee, and Hunt, President of the State Democratic

Convention in 1837 and a strong candidate for Democratic Congressional nominee, were thoroughly discredited.[20] Hunt indignantly accused the committee of attacking him for political reasons, but, as he said, "Already the report has spread to other states, that another loco-foco sub-treasurer has taken his departure for Texas, that Judge Hunt . . . has gone to the land of promise."[21] The attacks, clearly motivated by the desire of out-state Democrats to unseat Mason and his Detroit administration, did their work. By the end of the session, Kinsley S. Bingham, Democratic Speaker of the House, reported to Alpheus Felch that the investigations had turned in their favor.[22]

During the 1839 session, the party was split into a third faction by Warner Wing's attempts to be appointed to the United States Senate. Wing's failure to be nominated for Congress at the state convention in the fall of 1838 had threatened an open break the previous year, but the difficulties had been smoothed over. In 1839, however, Wing's faction, determined to make him Lucius Lyon's successor in the United States Senate, refused to compromise until the party was so at odds that no successor was elected. Another Monroe resident was put forward as a candidate, but the party was unable to agree and entered the fall elections badly divided.[23]

Secret opposition developed in the central tier toward the Democratic gubernatorial candidate, and influential party members worked against his election. The politically powerful Edwards family of Kalamazoo County, for example, was accused of working for Farnsworth's defeat. Opposition within the party was thought to extend through the entire central tier from Washtenaw to Kalamazoo County.[24] After a spiritless campaign, the Democracy was swept from control of the state for the first time since 1828. The Whigs carried the central tier except for Wayne and Van Buren Counties, the third tier except for Livingston County, the Thumb, and three counties in the southern tier. In addition to the governor's office, they captured control of both branches of the Legislature.[25]

Unlike the Democracy, the Whigs had entered the campaign of 1839 at a peak of organizational efficiency. Shouting slogans of "Woodbridge, Gordon, and Reform," the Whigs demonstrated their mastery of the political techniques that were to topple Van Buren and the national administration a year later. Ruthlessly exploiting the Democrats' financial difficulties, the Whigs proclaimed the state bankrupt and called loudly for reform. Charging the Democrats with plundering the treasury, they claimed that over half a million dollars, five times the state's current revenues, would have to be raised to regain solvency. Criticizing the Democrats' eighty-thousand-dollar appropriation from the internal improvements fund, they pledged to shift that debt to the general fund, leaving the former unimpaired. Democratic management of internal improvements was pictured as wasteful and ruinous. Criticizing the negotiation of the five million loan, particularly the payment of interest on unpaid installments, the Whigs claimed that only one-fourth of the funds had been expended in ways that would bring returns for payment of interest. The situation was so bad that only a Whig administration could pull the state through the crisis.[26]

With elections over, however, Whig leaders began to alter their position, even before succeeding to power. Party moderates advised Woodbridge that complete reform was unacceptable to most of the electorate, and they would have to be content with partial changes. Although the Whigs had focused their attack on salaries and offices, they felt that abolishing a few offices and slightly reducing government salaries would satisfy most of the people. Franklin Sawyer, one of Woodbridge's lieutenants, advised the Governor-elect that although Whigs stood for a judicious and economical system of internal improvements—and it was questionable if *any* system could be judicious and economical under current conditions—public opinion would not tolerate a complete halt in the program. Sawyer favored stopping the Clinton and Kalamazoo, but urged continuing the Southern to Hillsdale to make funds already expended productive. The Central should be completed as rapidly as possible. Sawyer also advised Woodbridge not to cancel the five million loan. The Democrats, he felt, would try to force the Whigs to increase taxation, undermining their popular support. Since the Democrats had already avoided taxation by drawing on the internal improvements fund, the Whigs would be forced into the contradictory position of cutting expenditures and increasing taxes unless they held on to at least another year's installments to finance state spending. "It is easier to pay interest on the state expenses than the whole amount of these expenses." [27]

By mid-December, Woodbridge had begun to adopt Sawyer's position. It was advisable, he wrote one correspondent, to take the middle ground between the profligate office seeker and the oppressed taxpayer. While reckless spending was to be avoided, so was heavy taxation and "blighting & unprofitable parsimony!" [28] Although of two minds, Woodbridge was privately opposed to suspension of the public works:

> There seems to me to be no subject connected with the administration of our state govt more perplexing than that which relates to our Internal Improvement system—Every view which can be taken of it seems obscured by difficulties.—One thing however seems certain,—and that is that "ways & means" cannot, and probably for many years, be obtained to consummate the plan undertaken.—On the other hand, principles of just economy & prudence, would seem to condemn utterly the idea of a total loss of all the labour and materials hitherto at so immense expense applied to & obtained for the purpose of compleating these great works![sic]

A moderate course—completing the work most likely to produce, meaning the Central between Ann Arbor and Jackson—would be defeated by local interests in the north and south:

> What charges of gross injustice will be urged against those who for the exclusive benefit of the central region, would subject the people of the north and south to the consequences of so heavy Disbursements!—This world must be taken as it is—and it is not wise to contend for that which we know is beyond our reach.

Instead, Woodbridge favored appropriations for completing the Central to Jackson, the Southern to Adrian, and turning the Northern into a good wagon road. Although the present system would have to be abandoned, he hoped a new, less expensive one could be salvaged.[29]

Woodbridge's annual message to the Legislature was less moderate than his private correspondence. The new Governor cast serious doubts on the wisdom of constructing any public works when goods could be shipped by the Great Lakes, and made it clear that he thought the federal government, not the state, should be responsible for the program's completion. In time, works promising to bring a good return should be completed, but in the interim, the Governor advised ceasing all disbursements and suspending further construction. All laws relating to internal improvements should be repealed, except those relating to railroads already in operation. Installments on the five million loan, however, should continue to be received.

Woodbridge estimated that the state had three million bushels of rotting surplus wheat because there was not enough money in circulation to buy and transport it. The new State Bank, chartered in 1839, was unable to open because of specie shortages, and when the United States Bank of Pennsylvania suspended, most Michigan banks followed suit. The Governor proposed that installments on the five million loan be mortgaged to sound banks to expand currency in the state and move its wheat to market.

Taxation to pay for the works and to stabilize finances was to be avoided at all costs. In addition to the fact that Woodbridge regarded direct taxation as a national resource, taxes were already regarded as extreme. The burden resulted, however, not from state taxation, but from township and county taxes. While state and county taxes on a section of land were only $6.40, township taxes might be as high as $40.00. Woodbridge emphasized that before the state could resort heavily to direct taxation, local tax structures would have to be reformed.[30]

If Woodbridge's public pronouncements in January 1840 more strongly favored retrenchment and reform than his private views, they were not substantially different from those put forward by Mason at the same time. In a farewell address, which the Legislature refused to allow him to deliver, the former Governor admitted the state had overextended itself and, in common with other states, would be forced to undertake corrective measures. He deplored that party politics had been focused on internal improvements, and asked the Legislature to seek a nonpartisan solution to the state's difficulties. Like Woodbridge, however, he doubted the wisdom of direct taxation, called for reform in local taxes, and asserted the state's right to a federal grant. His only major divergence from Woodbridge's announced policy was to recommend that if works were suspended or abandoned, a proportionate part of the installments due on the five million loan should also be cancelled.[31] Even this proposal agreed with Woodbridge's campaign policy, and Mason's attempts to cancel the loan in the fall and winter of 1839, for which he was pilloried by a Whig investigating committee, were in line with announced Whig policy before their assumption of power.[32]

The new Whig Legislature immediately began pursuing the question of suspension. Although House and Senate records are badly scrambled, apparently because of the new Whig clerks' lack of an adequate system of keeping minutes, they do reveal that Floyd Streeter's version of events leading to suspension is seriously in error. According to Streeter, voting on the act to suspend followed voter patterns in the 1839 gubernatorial election. His citation, however, is to the wrong bill, for neither house recorded voting on the joint resolution suspending internal improvements. Moreover, Streeter refers to the bill as a "Resolution to discontinue work on internal improvements," but the bill he analyzed was designed to forbid *new* contracts, as was the bill actually passed.[33]

Neither Woodbridge nor the Whig Legislature had any intention of discontinuing the program. On January 15, a week after his address, Woodbridge sent a special message to the Legislature, asking them to launch a full investigation, and suspend the Board's authority to enter into new contracts until ways and means could be provided. The Legislature responded with a joint resolution suspending proceedings by the Board, and authority to enter new contracts or reaward expired contracts.[34] Under the Federal Constitution, the state could not pass laws impairing contracts and, as a party to the contracts, was liable for damages if they were broken. What Woodbridge and the Legislature were attempting to discontinue was the awarding of further contracts by the *Democratic* Board of Internal Improvements. Under an 1839 revision, Board members were appointed for three-year periods; faced with Whig control and possible suspension, the Board had committed the state as far as possible to contractual obligations. In April, regulations controlling the structure and functioning of the Board were again altered, and a *Whig* Board appointed. Following a skirmish with the former commissioners, who contested the legality of their removal, the new Board continued construction in much the same manner as the former body, even reawarding expired contracts in order to complete unfinished sections. When appropriations were expended and the Board decided to continue construction, leaving the Legislature the problem of providing funds, its authority was never seriously questioned.[35] Attempts to repeal the Internal Improvements Act were tabled in the Senate and never given serious consideration.[36] When funds were exhausted in July, Woodbridge chose to suspend final judgment on damage claims stemming from construction rather than stop the works, and promised iron suppliers to intercede with the Legislature for iron appropriations in order to get shipments ahead of payment.[37]

The Legislature's attempt to pass an appropriations bill in 1840 was blocked by sectional claims. According to reports delivered in the Senate and House, the legislators were eager to contract the program and push forward a single work to completion, but could not agree whose projects were to be discontinued for the sake of public economy; each area's representatives submitted bids for the completion of their constituents' special project.[38] Attempts in the Senate to attach provisions for every project undertaken or discussed since 1834 were all defeated by large margins, and the bill finally passed, ten to six. With the exception of one vote, all opposition came from the first and third tiers of counties.[39] Although the bill's contents were never fully revealed, committee reports and house debates indicate that it allocated funds primarily to the Central.[40] Repeated attempts were made in the House to add to and change appropriations in the bill. Roll call votes followed one after another as the House searched for a formula to satisfy local demands. Alignments changed continuously as local interest groups tried to muster support for their projects. An agreement of sorts was finally reached on the last day of the session when one hundred thousand dollars was appropriated for the Southern, and three hundred thousand for the Central. The bill was killed, however, when the House voted twenty-seven to eighteen against suspending its rules to allow both third reading and final passage. Rather than voting along party lines, House members voted according to the sections they represented. Support for the bill came from the central tier and western counties of the first and second tiers, while opposition was concentrated in the eastern half of the northern and southern counties.[41] Even in a Whig-dominated Legislature, the purportedly Whig Central Railroad was unable to muster enough votes to continue construction because local interest proved stronger than party affiliation.

The bill's failure was followed by petition drives and public meetings to encourage the Governor to recall the Legislature to make appropriations for internal improvements. Most leading Whigs, however, counseled Woodbridge against the move. Townsend Gidley, Whig Senator from Jackson County, the next point on the Central's route, was strongly against recalling the Legislature. Warning the Governor that once the road was completed as far as Jackson, most of his supporters there would desert him, Gidley thought it best to wait a year. Groups supporting the Central's extension were seeking their own advancement, not the good of the party.[42]

Despite attempts to reform the state's tax structure, the Whigs were unable to construct a workable system through 1840. At Woodbridge's request, a tabular statement of state, county, and township taxes was drawn up, and the Senate conducted a full investigation.[43] The committee stated that local taxes had reached a limit, and a bill was passed limiting road assessments to one day at $.625 per hundred dollars assessed valuation. The act, however, failed to deal with basic tax allocation problems.[44]

In the fall of 1840, Whig forces swept the state for Harrison in a victory so decisive that leading Democrats feared Michigan had permanently gone Whig.[45] Elections to the Legislature were not so decisive, however; Whig control depended on a narrow margin easily upset by factional differences within the party. Even before the national standard bearer was inaugurated, Whigs had lost control of the state.

The question of electing a United States Senator came before the Legislature early in 1841. Woodbridge had been actively campaigning within the party since the fall elections, and his supporters, convinced that the Detroit faction of the Whig party would not elect him, began turning to the Democrats. Richard Butler, Woodbridge's chief lieutenant in Oakland County, advised him in December that he could bring about a coalition with Oakland Country Loco-focos if the Governor refused to act decisively on the public works and let the Legislature take the blame for whatever developed.[46] In February, Woodbridge was elected by Democrats and a few conservative Whigs.[47] His election, how-ever, angered other Whig factions and destroyed party unity.[48] By a brilliant stroke of policy, the Democrats had split the majority party and exiled their chief opponent to Washington.

The Governor's annual message to the Legislature took a stronger line toward internal improvements than Butler had advised. Woodbridge stated his private convictions that under the terms of purchase from the Detroit and St. Joseph, the state was obligated to finish the Central, and that the Central would be the most profitable of the state's projects. Expressing the belief that the road, when completed, could pay interest on the entire internal improvements debt, he recommended concentrating the state's resources on extending the road to its western terminus. In addition, he asked the Legislature to consider completing improvements on the St. Joseph River and constructing a canal across the loop cast by the river where it ran briefly through Indiana if Indiana refused to cooperate.[49]

Appropriations were passed in 1841 with little difficulty. Early in the session, the Senate Internal Improvements Committee submitted a report recommending that resources be concentrated on the Central. Emphasizing the crisis faced by the state and increasing the estimated cost of the whole system to twenty million dollars, the Committee argued that the "idly cherished hope of carrying a railroad to every man's door..." would have to be abandoned forever, "or the last hope of Michigan will have been taken from her: our farmers will be driven from their farms, and our lands sold for taxes." If all resources were spent on the Central, the Committee argued, the road could be brought to a condition capable of paying the entire interest on the five million loan. Although the Committee, chaired by Townsend Gidley, repeated Woodbridge's sentiments exactly, their bill died quietly in the Senate.[50]

The House Committee on Internal Improvements submitted an appro-priations bill that passed by thirty-two to twelve after the usual attempts to add appropriations for local interests; these were not serious threats, how-ever, to the bill's passage. Opposition centered in the four eastern counties of the third tier, plus three votes from Monroe and Branch Counties in the southern tier. Democrats cast at least eleven of the twelve opposing votes. Oak-land County, normally a Whig stronghold, had returned a solid block of Demo-crats in the fall elections, and they voted against a bill failing to appropriate funds for the Clinton and Kalamazoo Canal. In the upper house, a small group of Whig and Democratic Senators attempted to block the bill's passage and add appropriations for several local projects. They failed, however, and the bill was approved by a margin of twelve to five.[51] The bill provided four hundred and fifty thousand dollars for extending the Central to Jackson and

TABLE VII
Internal Improvements Appropriations,
1837-1845[a] (Thousands of Units)

	1837[b]	1838[b]	1839[b]	1840[b]	1841[b]	1842[b]	1843[c]	1844[c]	1845[c]
Central RR	400	350	100		450		150	64	20
Southern RR	100	350	100		200				
Northern RR	50	60	40						
Soo Canal	25	25							
Clinton Canal	40	205	60			25	16	16	5
Saginaw Canal	15	47							
Grand & Maple Rivers		30							
Kalamazoo River		8							
St. Joseph River				25			5	10	
Grand Rapids Bridge								6	
Tecumseh Branch RR									10
River Raisin & Lake Erie RR					32.5				
Havre Branch RR	20								
Surveys	20								
Salt Springs			3	15	5		15		
Detroit & Pontiac RR	75		100						
Allegan & Marshall RR			100						
Ypsilanti & Tecumseh RR			100						
Palmyra & Jacksonburg RR	20								
Total	765	1,378	340	37.5	675	15	171	96	35

[a]Michigan, Legislature, *Acts,* Nos. (1837) LXVII, LXXV, CXX; (1837, Special Session), XVI; (1838) 20, 55, 56, 91, 121, 174; (1839) 116; (1840) 92, 100; (1841) 13; (1842) 10; (1843) 24; (1844) 50; (1845) 15.
[b]Dollar appropriations.
[c]Appropriations in acres of land.

Kalamazoo, and two hundred thousand for completing the Southern to Hillsdale.[52]

Passage of the 1841 appropriations bill marked a major turning point in legislative policy toward public works. For the first time since 1837, a bill awarding unequal appropriations to the Central and Southern had passed the House, and the opposition had been able to summon only three votes from the southern section. Moreover, the bill's language specifically awarded funds to the Central for continuation and to the Southern for completion to Hillsdale. As written, the bill implied the Board's authority to award contracts for continuing the Central west of Jackson. It is apparent that, for the present at least, the south had accepted the fact that only one road could be completed, and that it would be the Central, not the Southern.

The Legislature also rejected an attempt to link the Central and Southern to railroads projected west along Lake Erie's southern shore. In March, the Board of Internal Improvements forwarded a request from Ohio and Maumee Branch Railroad agents for a twenty-five-thousand-dollar loan to purchase iron, accompanied by the Board's strong recommendation for its passage. Promising to by-pass Toledo and draw business over the Southern and Central to Ohio, the company asked the Legislature to risk its funds for iron only after the superstructure was completed, and promised to secure the loan by a mortgage on the entire road bed. The Board was enthusiastic because the line would connect Michigan's roads with major east-west routes and give the state an advantage over its powerful rivals.[53] The House Committee on Internal Improvements, equally enthusiastic, reported the request favorably. When a bill was submitted, however, the Ways and Means Committee reported that it was firmly opposed to the request which it characterized as an attempt by private enterprise to participate in the spoils of the state. The bill was tabled and allowed to die, but its failure marks a second significant turning point in the state's public policy.[54] Unlike petitions for aid presented the state in 1837 and 1838, passage of the grant would have involved little risk. The company was asking for aid only after the road was ready for operation. State risk was minimized by a mortgage on an investment ten times as great as funds requested, and the road would have by-passed the Erie and Kalamazoo, a major competitor of the Southern. Its summary rejection by the Committee on Ways and Means marked the end of state participation in joint enterprise.

The act of suspension passed by the Legislature in 1840 continued in effect through 1841. Late in April, a bill passed the Senate authorizing the Board of Internal Improvements to award new contracts for construction, but was narrowly defeated in the House.[55] After Woodbridge's election to the U. S. Senate, there were significant political changes. The last shreds of Mason's influence outside Detroit were destroyed by a legislative report examining "the question of corruption in governor Mason," which found him guilty of blatant misconduct in the negotiation of the five million loan.[56] Leadership of the liberal wing of the Democratic party passed from its Detroit leaders, Norvell and Mason, to out-state forces led by Kinsley S. Bingham.[57] At the same time, Whig forces were wasting themselves with factional infighting. After the close of the legislative session, Detroit Whigs, known as the "Canandaigua Clique," joined forces with Democrats led by the Monroe faction of Humphrey, Miller, and Smith to control federal patronage. John Van Fossen, Woodbridge's Commissioner of Internal Improvements, complained to his chief:

> The Canandaigua clique as it is termed, is but a branch of the Monro faction & with professions of oposition [sic] in politicks, is at all times ready to serve their Monro Allies—They are all powerful in the P. Office dept—But it sickens me to look at the condition in which we are placed: A Whig administration & a Whig board of Internal Improvement, actually and absolutely ruled & directed by Levi S. Humphrey, without a whimper of insubordination or even a show of dissatisfaction—

Nothing, he complained, was being done to prepare the party for the fall elections, and he would not lift a finger to help them in any case.[58] Both groups were punished severely by their parties, and, with the exception of Humphrey, who continued to lead the Monroe faction, none of them was returned to the Legislature.

When the Democrats met in Marshall in September, the scent of victory was in the air. Concentrating on healing party rifts, they nominated John Barry, the leader of the conservative out-state Democrats, for Governor. Mason summarized the situation within the party:

> Had it not been for the folly of our party, in nominating a conservative of 1838, we should have had no difficulty in carrying the state....Barry was nominated on the simple ground, that the western part of the state was entitled to the candidate *this year.* Thus far, my name has been left out of the question, and I think the policy of the Whigs will be to let me alone. If we can elect Barry, I shall leave the state contented. I am here long enough, to see the Whigs cutting each others throats, and to feel that every personal enemy I have is politically as dead as a "door nail." De Garmo Jones, and all the Legislative clique who assailed me last winter, have been dropt by their own friends, and in their stead men have been nominated of as decent a character as the Whig ranks could afford.[59]

The most serious bone of contention between the two parties was the national issue of the Bank and sub-treasury. Although convinced that a Bank of the United States was the only answer to the state's problems, Democrats were too deeply committed to the sub-treasury plan to risk party schism by revising their stand. Tyler's veto of the charter of the Bank of the United States in the summer of 1841 sealed the fate of Michigan's Whig party by simultaneously destroying their credibility and removing a major issue dividing Democratic factions.[60] In the fall elections, the Democrats captured both houses of the Legislature and the Governor's office; for the next twelve years, they retained control of the state government.

Michigan's new Governor, John Barry, owed his popularity to his financial conservatism, his supposed independence from faction, and his out-state residence. Apparently devoted to the precept that the state was governed best which spent the least, Barry was a strict advocate of government economy. According to one story, he went so far as to sell the clippings from grass on the capitol lawn, depositing the funds in the state treasury. His inaugural message to the Legislature, however, contained few departures from the policies of his Whig predecessor. The man who had campaigned so furiously for sectional equality in 1837 and led Senate opposition to limited appropriations in 1841, now took the position that:

> The conception of the plan on a scale so magnificent, is to be attributed to the erroneous opinions of wealth, produced by the influence of a too redundant paper currency. The system was altogether too extended for our wants, and required expenditures beyond our means. It was projected at a time when things were too often viewed through a distorted vision.

As had the Whigs, Barry recommended that expenditures be concentrated in making finished portions of the works productive and finishing portions likely to be productive.[61] Failure of the Bank of the United States in October 1841, had cut off the major source of funds for construction, and made the state prematurely liable for the interest on its bonds. Barry suggested attempting to exchange the half-million acres of land granted the state under the Preemption Act for bonds outstanding on the state's internal improvements loan.

His only major deviation from Whig policy lay in methods of financing the program. Instead of scrip or treasury notes, Barry preferred Auditor's Warrants because legally they were not forms of currency. He considered using treasury notes unconstitutional, because they were forms of coining money, while Auditor's Warrants were promissory notes. This distinction was so narrow, however, that for practical purposes, methods of finance remained the same. He recommended, in addition, that only internal improvements funds, and not the general fund, be liable for the redemption of notes.[62] Finally, he recommended that the state constitution be amended to require popular consent for loans contracted for internal improvements.

The Legislature quickly implemented Barry's recommendations. Early in the session, further issue of scrip was prohibited, and the internal improvements fund made liable for its redemption.[63] The Board of Internal Improvements was forbidden to enter new contracts for construction, except for necessary repairs.[64] Although a Senate committee reported favorably on extending the Central and Southern, and engaging in extensive river improvement programs, appropriations bills were killed in both houses before reaching final votes.[65]

The Democracy concentrated on gaining factional supremacy. The Monroe faction, now led by Humphrey, Felch, William Hale, and C. A. Jackson, was attempting to gain control of party patronage and access to the Governor's ear. Factional struggle centered around attempts to take the public printing contracts from John Bagg and give them to printers favorable to the Monroe faction. Within the Executive Office efforts focused on winning over Andrew Hammond, Barry's chief advisor, one of the few with access to the secluded Governor. By the end of the year, Jackson could inform Felch that Hammond was contributing money to the faction's paper, that he was on good terms with Barry, and that transfer of the printing contracts could be handled quietly. In 1843, for the first time under a Democratic administration, the Legislature's journals and official papers were printed by someone other than John Bagg.[66]

Barry's annual message in 1843 added nothing to his previous internal improvement policies. He announced that most of the federal internal improvements grant had been located and was available for appropriation, and urged concentrating the state's resources on those projects bringing the most revenue to the treasury and service to the state's citizens. At the first opportunity, the Southern should be completed to Hillsdale and the Central to the west of Marshall. Although half of the scrip outstanding had been returned, Barry warned that he would veto any bill authorizing its issue. Most of the Governor's 1843 message involved problems connected with the five million loan.[67]

Despite the serious financial problems posed by providing for interest on the public debt and settlement with foreign bondholders of claims stemming from part-paid securities, the Legislature was optimistic. Locating lands from the federal grant had made new resources available, the Central had shown large profits the previous year, and state finances were nearly liquid. The Senate Committee on Finance reported that had it not been for liabilities to the general fund from internal improvements, the state would have been solvent for the first time. Although this committee's recommendations included a proposal for selling the Central to foreign bondholders in exchange for their securities, they made it clear that they preferred alternate courses that would allow the state to continue the road to its western terminus. The House Committee on Internal Improvements, even more enthusiastic, recommended extending the road west of Marshall as a means of paying the interest on the entire state debt, perhaps providing enough revenue to build a sinking fund to reclaim the principal. Goodwin of Calhoun County summarized the Legislature's feelings when he stated that a year before the state was exhausted, faced with a foreign debt, a broken treasury, half a million in outstanding scrip, and a whole series of domestic debts. "One short year since, darkness hung over us like the pall of the grave....[Now,] our railroad shows the whole world what it can accomplish."[68]

At the same time, there were disturbing changes in the doctrine of equality. Until 1841, when the state had been a source of foreign credit through its ability to market bonds, and interest had been paid from installments of principal, areas outside the central tier had used equality to justify their right to a share in the spoils of state enterprise. The central tier had tried to fix responsibility for interest on sums expended on tiers of counties receiving aid for their projects. Failure of the Bank of the United States, however, by prematurely thrusting the burden of interest payments on the state, had led to the realization that the whole state was liable for interest on non-productive investments in all sections. A movement beginning in 1841 resulted in an 1843 constitutional amendment, by joint resolution, limiting bond issue proposals to a single project and forbidding the borrowing of money for internal improvements without a general referendum.[69] During 1843, the doctrine of equality was used to justify the state's continued refusal to finance unproductive projects and concentrate resources in works returning a profit. The House Committee on Internal Improvements summed up the changing application of the equality doctrine:

> The expenditure of money in one part of the state for the immediate benefit of the people of that section, when no corresponding return can be made to the people of the whole state, and especially when it would become necessary to levy a tax on the people at large to meet such an expenditure would be unjust and directly tend to create sectional jealousies, which of all things is mostly to be deplored in a commonwealth.[70]

Gradually, however, the realization developed that all internal improvement works were by their nature local in benefits. Thus, the state found itself saddled with the same problem as the federal government: any grant of aid gave special privilege and was therefore a violation of equality. Limiting investment proposals to a single project effectively prohibited compromise and made it impossible for the state to borrow further funds for public works.

Sectional rivalry blazed up again when the appropriations bill was introduced in the House. Northern interests attempted to annex appropriations for completing the Clinton and Kalamazoo and turning the Northern into a wagon road by delaying, amending, and threatening to block the bill's passage. For a time, an apparent coalition developed between the central tier and western counties of the southern and third tiers, but after extensive debates, efforts broke down as counties and sections attempted log-rolling to incorporate their local projects into the bill. After a week of intensive debate, the bill was passed by a vote of thirty to twenty-two. A few favorable votes came from the eastern counties of the southern tier, but most originated in the central tier and the western counties of the southern and third. Eastern interests outside the central tier were almost solidly opposed to the bill. The bill passed the Senate by a vote of fifteen to three. The dissenting Senators, representing eastern counties of the first, third, and fourth tiers, filed a formal protest charging that the bill violated constitutional provisions for equal application of internal improvements funds.[71]

The final bill provided for extending the Central and purchasing iron for both the Central and Southern. Pledging the net proceeds of both roads, the Legislature appropriated one hundred and nineteen thousand dollars for iron and spike to complete the Central to Marshall and the Southern to Hillsdale. One hundred and fifty thousand acres of internal improvement land were granted for the Central under provisions that payment be made in warrants redeemable when cash from land sales had accrued to the internal improvements fund. Suspension of new contracts on the Central was repealed, but all contracts awarded were required to be at a minimum of twelve percent less than 1841 estimates. Finally, $5,770 was appropriated to pay floating debts on the Clinton and Kalamazoo Canal. Earlier in the session, ten thousand dollars had been appropriated for bridging the Central between Marshall and Jackson.[72]

Barry's annual message in 1844 made few new policy recommendations; it was confined largely to describing changes in the roads and progress during the previous year. Prospects of manufacturing salt in the immediate future were described as "by no means flattering," and the Governor suggested that the state abandon the wells.[73]

Revival of the state's basic financial stability strengthened demands for a multiple program of public works. Although both the House Committee on Internal Improvements and the Committee on Ways and Means reported strongly in favor of construction on the Central, representatives outside areas served by that railroad insisted on aid to their local projects.[74] Appropriation bills for both the Central and the Clinton and Kalamazoo were introduced simultaneously in the House in January of 1844, but the two were separated during debates in the Committee of the Whole. When the Committee reported, only the enacting clause of the original bill remained, as southern interests attempted to gain additional appropriations for their railroad. After a month of running battles and delaying tactics, the bill passed by a margin of thirty to twenty-one, although southern forces had demonstrated their ability to defeat it during debate. On several occasions, southern interests had mustered enough votes to defeat portions of the bill, or the bill itself, but not enough to attach their own appropriations. Whenever the bill was defeated, they allowed it or a substitute to be re-introduced, and finally permitted passage. Opposition to the bill was centered in the southern tier and Oakland County, while support was concentrated in the central and northern tiers. The bill, which passed the Senate by a vote of twelve to five, was opposed by two southern, two northern, and one Wayne County senator. As passed, the bill provided appropriations of sixty-four thousand acres and pledged seventy-five thousand dollars for iron to complete the Central to Kalamazoo.[75]

Local forces, having failed to annex appropriations, then introduced separate bills for improvement of the Shiawassee River, the Grand River, the Paw Paw River, and the Grand River Road, but all were defeated. Appropriations for the Clinton and Kalamazoo Canal passed with the support of the same group that had passed on the Central.[76] In lieu of appropriations, the Legislature attempted to satisfy local demands by appealing to the federal government for aid. Joint resolutions were passed requesting grants to complete the Grand River Road, the Detroit-Saginaw-Straits-Sault Ste. Marie Road, and for one hundred thousand acres to improve the Grand River. A bill granting alternate sections along the Central and the Clinton and Kalamazoo, passed the United States Senate, but failed in the House.[77]

The Legislature first seriously considered selling its public works during the 1844 session. Details of the public debt had been worked out at the previous session; now that the total amount of recognized debt was known, attention turned to liquidating it. During 1843, sale had been suggested as a possible solution to the debt problem, but the committee reporting had favored other measures. In 1844, however, the Committee on Ways and Means reported favorably on the sale of the railroads, and brought forth an implementing bill.

After assessing the worth of the roads and the size of the debt, the committee reported that all but $355,607 of the state's debt would be liquidated if the roads could be sold at cost. The value of the roads was estimated at $2,776,296, and the value of the debt less ten percent damages on the unpaid balance at $3,131,903. If such a sale could be made, the committee believed the natural increase in property values over time would allow the state to liquidate the balance of the debt with the existing two-mill tax.

In justifying the proposed sale, the committee put forth the Legislature's first strong statement favoring private enterprise. Earlier statements of the superiority of private enterprise do exist, but they are usually contained in statements issued during the depths of the depression. The committee, however, submitted its statement as part of a concrete proposition in the midst of growing prosperity.

Expressing the belief that a private corporation could complete the Central to Lake Michigan and add twenty miles to the Southern before the state would be able to begin construction, the committee argued:

> One other important consideration, which suggested itself to your committee, is the fact that the management and control of railroads, by a state, by thus converting the state government into a great competitor in the business of a common carrier, is at war with the grand fundamental principle that governments ought never to come into conflict or competition with the legitimate pursuits of individual or private enterprise.

The only legitimate reasons for departing from that policy were protection of citizens from foreign aggression and enforcement of property laws. The single serious objection the committee could see was the possibility that the works would be able to pay more than they could be sold for, and this they viewed as problematical, while sale was certain. Moreover, if the state could make six percent, the committee regarded it as axiomatic that a private company could make much more, even at reduced rates:

> ... and even granting the certainty of our public works being always managed with such economy and good judgement as to secure a sufficient revenue to meet the interest on their cost, or even upon the entire internal improvement debt, it may be questioned whether the time always occupied by legislation in regard to them, and the adverse local and sectional feeling thereby aroused,—the constant liability of

attempts being made to divert the resources of the state to the construction of works which would yield little or no revenue, and which would be increased in proportion to the profitableness of those previously constructed, as well as the great danger of such works becoming, eventually, in some hands, the engines of political corruption and favoritism, and many other considerations, could not more than counterbalance all the possible or supposable chances of an excess of revenue.[78]

The committee's last statement gave one of the most powerful and least often voiced reasons for removing the state from enterprise: the disillusionment resulting when public works failed to bring non-economic progress. In the beginning, internal improvement advocates had cited the political unity created by better means of communications as a justification. After eight years, the public was convinced that the works were a powerful force dividing the people into rival camps. The public was discouraged by the annual legislative battles over conflicting special interests and angered by having to pay seventy legislators a per diem to solve conflicting claims. In a period when biennial sessions were being advocated to reduce legislative expenses, the largest single cost of state government, the cost reduction of removing the state's most vexing problem from legislative consideration was a strong argument in favor of sale. Finally, the continuous scandals uncovered in the administration of public works, and their powerful patronage potential had convinced the public that high standards of political behavior were impossible as long as the state was involved in business. In sum, the public had discovered that public enterprise had non-economic costs they were unwilling to pay.

With this report, the committee submitted a bill encompassing its recommendations. As drafted, the bill provided for chartering corporations and allowed purchase in stipulated amounts of state securities. The State Treasurer was authorized to deed the road in fee simple to any company meeting the Legislature's terms within eighteen months of January 1, 1844, for a price of $2,588,796 plus any sums expended after that date. The bill included both roads, which apparently were tied together in a package purchase.[79]

Debate on the bill was not vigorous. The first section, usually reserved for major stockholders, was filled with the names of nine state Democratic businessmen and politicians. The final vote was twenty-six to twenty-three, short of the necessary two-thirds for passage of a corporate charter. Voting in the solidly Democratic House followed the usual sectional, rather than party, lines. Only three votes in favor of sale originated in the central tier; the balance were concentrated in the southern and the eastern half of the third and fourth tiers, which voted almost as a solid block. Seventeen of those voting in favor of sale opposed appropriations to extend the Central to Kalamazoo. Members favoring both bills were concentrated in Macomb, Saginaw, and Lapeer Counties.[80] In sum, it is evident that a majority of the House favored selling the railroads, a majority favored continuation, and the two groups were not identical. Statements that continuation and sale were Whig measures supported by the central tier are grossly in error. Instead, Democrats in counties with unsuccessful projects favored sale to avoid taxation, while those in the central tier favored a continuation of state enterprise. A similar bill was indefinitely postponed in the Senate after the House failed to muster a two-thirds majority.[81]

The balance of power among the Democracy's factions shifted slightly during 1844. John Bagg was again awarded the state's printing contracts, after losing them for a year to the southern tier's Detroit printer, and the central tier succeeded in electing a Speaker of the House from their section. Federal patronage, however, remained in the hands of the Monroe faction.[82] Neither faction seemed able to control a consistent majority in either branch of the Legislature.

Governor Barry's 1845 message to the Legislature cautiously opposed sale of the railroads. After holding out hopes of increased revenues, he asked them to postpone a decision until further consideration, thus avoiding errors due to haste. Several alternatives were open, but each needed to be more thoroughly investigated. If the works were not to be sold, then completion would have to be considered: "True policy requires the completion of the Central Railroad to St. Joseph, and the Southern, at least, to the navigable waters of the St. Joseph River...." While this would require means the state did not possess, bills were reported pending before Congress granting additional aid to Michigan's programs, and it would be unwise for the Legislature to base its actions on the assumption the grants would not be made. If the state were then proven unable to complete its programs, Barry recommended that the Legislature consider allowing private associations to complete the roads to their western termini. If they decided on such a joint enterprise, he cautioned them to "guard the rights of the state and secure its citizens from imposition and oppression."

Growing sectional demands prevented any action on the Governor's recommendations during the 1845 legislative session. Early in the session, the House Committee on Internal Improvements reported that twenty thousand acres of land were needed to complete the Central to Kalamazoo, and appropriations were passed without controversy.[83] When the question of extending the roads came before the Legislature, supporters of previous policies limiting expenditures to productive projects were met with violent protests from delegates representing counties north of the central tier.

The House Committee on Internal Improvements was unable to present a unanimous recommendation. A majority of the committee favored extending the Central to Lake Michigan and the Southern to Coldwater. Arguing that these extensions would allow the Central to produce net revenues sufficient to meet interest payments on the entire state debt, and the Southern to tap traffic being shipped through Fort Wayne, the committee attempted to prove that the state was capable of financing construction. Although the two hundred and forty-five thousand unappropriated acres of internal improvement land were liable for payment of warrants and interest after July 1, 1845, the committee believed most of the warrants and bonds were held by eastern capitalists who generally avoided investing in land. The state, however, could earn at least seven percent if it appropriated the lands to internal improvement instead of allowing them to remain unproductive while interest accumulated on warrants and bonds outstanding. With few public works being constructed in the United States, the committee believed the roads could be extended at prices comparable to those realized during the depression. Finally, they favored completing the Clinton and Kalamazoo to its current terminus, but reported against constructing a wagon road on the Northern route because it would not return an income to the state.

Recognizing the problem of sectional rivalry, the committee admitted the appropriations would be unequal:

> Local interests will, undoubtedly, in some portions of our state, cause some to feel that justice and equality has not been meted out with an impartial hand; for past experience admonishes us, that all parts of the State cannot be satisfied....
>
> Expenditures for one part of the State for the immediate benefit of that portion of it where no corresponding return can be made to the people of the whole state—when it must become necessary to levy a direct tax on the people at large, for the ultimate payment of such an expenditure would seem to be unwise, and tend to the most deplorable consequences.[84]

The minority of the committee, however, in a report signed by Horace Steevens of Oakland County, attempted to prove that the Central was running at a loss of nearly fifty thousand dollars a year. Although Steevens' statement has frequently been cited in studies of the Central, it was created to support his sectional views. His figures were derived by increasing the rate of interest and including construction costs in operational accounts. The most important feature of the minority report, however, was its strong restatement of the doctrine of sectional equality. Taking the position that the Central and Southern were *local* improvements, the minority argued that they were entitled to no more aid than any other project. If resources were to be devoted to these two works, taxes resulting from the expenditures would have to be paid by everyone. The south and the center had already received three million dollars from the state, while the north, now containing one-third of the population paying one-third of the taxes, had received only four hundred thousand dollars. All future appropriations should be spent in the north until sectional equality was restored, or the roads would have to be sold to liquidate the state's indebtedness.[85] A second report submitted by a select committee on improvement of the Grand River reinforced Steevens' statement of the northern section's demands for sectional equality.[86]

Faced with united opposition in the north, which held the balance of power in sectional struggles between the central and southern tiers, the House was forced to resort to multiple projects to gain appropriations for its major works. Passage of these internal improvement bills provides a classic example of log-rolling. On February 7, the House Committee on Internal Improvements introduced three appropriation bills for the Central, the Southern, and the Clinton and Kalamazoo Canal. For over two weeks, the Committee of the whole, intermittently debated the bills, which were always taken up and reported simultaneously. On February 25, previously introduced bills appropriating funds for the Grand Rapids Canal and the Flint River were added to the package. The following day an appropriation for the Northern Railroad was included and all six bills were engrossed for third reading. On February 27, the bills were passed in rapid succession: the Central, forty-six to six; the Southern, thirty-five to seventeen; the Grand Rapids Canal, thirty-four to eighteen; the Northern, thirty-two to twenty; and the Flint River, twenty-six to twenty-four. No vote was recorded on the Clinton and Kalamazoo Canal. The Senate passed the bills without amendment, with one exception: the Flint River appropriation was transferred to the Shiawassee.[87] The precision with which the bills were marshalled through the House suggests that their passage was the result of an understanding between sectional forces, but the records contain no clue as to who led and organized their passage. If voices were raised in dissent, there is no indication in the House records. It is clear, however, from reports cited earlier that multiple appropriations were necessary if either the Southern or the Central were to be extended.

In the same orderly manner in which the Legislature had passed the bills, Governor Barry applied his veto; only the Clinton and Kalamazoo bill was signed into law. As passed, the bills appropriated two hundred and forty-three thousand acres, including forty-five thousand for the Southern and one hundred and forty thousand for the Central—seven thousand more acres than the state possessed. Exhausting the state's resources would, in effect, repudiate warrants issued under the act of February 21, 1843, which were payable in lands or other resources coming into the treasury. Warrants outstanding immobilized at least one hundred and fifty thousand acres of internal improvements lands. In addition, Barry objected to the bills because they made no provisions for engineering salaries and superstructure. Because, in order to avoid depreciation, warrants for lands could only be marketed slowly, it was difficult to use them to pay for iron and salaries. Finally, the first tier's Governor was skeptical of continuing work on the Central. Extending the Southern, while not making it a paying proposition, would at least raise the ratio of revenues to cost. "In regard to the revenue upon the Central Road, I have no hesitation in expressing my belief that finished to Kalamazoo or St. Joseph, it will never yield a net annual profit exceeding six percent upon the cost of its construction." Although barely three months earlier he had favored its westward extension, he now maintained that the Central could never earn enough to pay both interest and depreciation.[88]

Attempts to pass the bills over the Governor's veto failed to muster even a majority, and a Senate bill appropriating funds for the Central and Southern was later postponed indefinitely by the House.[89] Partisans of the railroads, however, managed to gain authorization for survey and location of the Central to St. Joseph, and the Southern to Coldwater, before the end of the session.[90]

Following the Governor's veto, efforts to authorize sale of the railroads were renewed. A bill chartering the Michigan Railroad Company, and authorizing the sale of the Central and Southern Railroads, was introduced on February 25 and reported favorably by the Committee on Banks and Incorporations. Voting was delayed, however, until the appropriations bills had been presented to Barry. On March 28, the bill was defeated twenty-two to nineteen. Support for the bill was concentrated in the northern tier and Wayne County. Convinced that they would be taxed for funds not spent in their districts, representatives of the northern tier began pressing for sale of the railroads.[91]

Meanwhile, private groups became interested in purchasing the Central. During the spring of 1845, Detroit newspapers printed articles favoring sale of the railroads to liquidate the public debt, and defending the position that the roads could be run more profitably under private control. In June, papers outside Detroit began echoing these sentiments, and a group of Boston financiers expressed interest in purchasing the railroad. John Brooks, superintendent of the Syracuse and Rochester Railroad, was sent to inspect the road. James Joy of Detroit was engaged by Brooks to engineer the sale. Joy, who later became one of America's great railroad barons, began a campaign to maneuver public opinion and the Legislature into selling the roads by writing letters to the editor of the Detroit *Free Press* under the pseudonym, "taxpayer." In a series of articles, Joy defended the position that private management was always superior to public, and set forth the proposition that if the roads were not sold, Michigan farmers would have to give up one-fifth of their lands to liquidate the debt. As the year ended, efforts to popularize the sale grew more intense.[92]

In the fall gubernatorial campaign, the Monroe faction managed to nominate its candidate. At the invitation of Robert McClelland, Alpheus Felch, a Monroe lawyer and Associate Justice of the State Supreme Court, accepted the nomination. Although a secret member of the faction, he was chosen because his absence from the Legislature during his term on the bench had freed him from the bitterness associated with recent sectional struggles.[93] Felch assured western sections that he favored completing the railroads to Lake Michigan. As one political leader in the west wrote:

> In this country the only question is whether you are in favor of the immediate extension of the Central Rail Road to St. Joseph and notwithstanding my assertion to the contrary some few even of the Democrats contend that you are strenuously opposed to it—that all your interests are in the South and many other Cock & Bull Stories Connected with this only question of importance to you—I think when I saw you at Kalamazoo you remarked that you were in favor of its extention—will you have the goodness to write me a line stating your views with regard to this measure. Not for the purpose of publishing, unless you desire, but to satisfy a few Sterling Democrats in this respect.[94]

Felch and the Monroe Democrats defeated the Whig candidate by a large margin.

Felch's inaugural message to the Legislature stressed the need for selling the Central. Although the Act of March 8, 1843 had pledged the revenues of the railroads to pay the interest on the state's bonds, when interest fell due no money was available because pledges for iron took priority. Under the law, deficiencies had to be paid by taxation, and the Auditor General had sent a circular to the county boards of supervisors informing them of the necessity of increasing the state's rates. Against the state's assessed valuation, a tax of nearly two mills was necessary, and a similar amount would have to be levied to meet the July installment. Stressing the excited state of public opinion, Felch cited two major reasons for selling the works: removing government from business normally conducted by private enterprise, and liquidating the public debt. Believing the latter the more important problem, Felch suggested selling only if the purchase price was sufficient to retire the debt. Depending heavily on Berrien's report that the road would have to be rebuilt with heavy iron rails, the Governor pointed out that the Central's receipts were inadequate to cover both the interest on the debt and the cost of rebuilding. If the state chose to retain control, interest would have to be paid by taxation until the roads could be brought into full production. It would be impossible, Felch thought, to raise the money for rebuilding by a new loan. Since there was a group waiting to negotiate terms of the purchase, the Governor recommended selling.[95]

Reasons advanced by legislative committees for accepting the Governor's recommendations were as diverse as the committees' members. With one exception, there was general agreement that the debt would have to be reduced and the roads modernized, but within these boundaries, a wide range of opinion was expressed. The three members of the Senate Committee on Finance, unable to submit a united opinion, reported separately. Flavius T. Littlejohn, Whig Senator from Allegan County, filed the sole dissenting opinion. After reviewing the factors leading to popular pressure for sale, Littlejohn argued that legislators were not bound to follow their constituents' instructions when these were in error. Unless advocates of sale could demonstrate *"pressing exigency"* for liquidating the debt, Littlejohn refused to support any action granting exclusive privileges to a group of private individuals.[96]

William Hale, the Monroe faction's Detroit leader, stressed financial criteria. Following a detailed review of the public works' financial history, Hale used the more developed eastern states to prove that Michigan could no longer support her internal improvement program. Arguing that the works were unnecessary in the first place, Hale stressed the state's losses and minimized its gains:

> That they have not as yet yielded a cent of profit, the committee are confident could easily be demonstrated. By referring to the reports of the board of internal improvement, it will be perceived, that of the

profits so called, large sums have annually been expended for the construction of new cars and the purchase of locomotives.

Hale's equation of profits to income free for government expenditure outside internal improvements, although grossly in error, has been the source of numerous statements that the roads never earned a cent of profit while in the state's possession.[97]

Finally, William Fenton of Genesee County stressed the theoretical benefits of removing the state from enterprise. Defending the proposition that operating a business was not within the legitimate scope of republican government, Fenton was forced to acknowledge that the Legislature had acted under a constitutional imperative in undertaking a program, but answered that concentration of resources in the state's productive works violated the stipulation of equal application. "This would not be carrying out the spirit of the constitution," which stipulated that its blessings, "like the dews of heaven, should descend upon all." Fenton was more interested in saving the state than benefiting business; internal improvements concentrated the government's attention on conflicting local and sectional ambitions and elevated the questions of route location and road management above even the state's security.

> Principles will be sacrificed upon the altar of gain—the integrity of the people will be destroyed in an indiscriminate worship at the shrine of mammon. The wheels of government which should roll quietly on in an unimpeded track in their onward course towards civil, social and political improvement—will be clogged by the crash of locomotives, and the strife of aspirants for the loaves and fishes which fall from the tables of those in power.[98]

The statements presented to the Senate by the Committee on Finance were polemics designed to convince colleagues and impress constituents. Reports presented to the House contained a more dispassionate and accurate statement of conditions. The report of the Select Committee on the Sale of Works of Internal Improvement, discussed earlier in connection with the Central, stressed the need for rebuilding the road with heavy rails to bring it to peak efficiency.[99] The Committee on Ways and Means presented a comprehensive statement of state finances and expenditures, justifying sale to liquidate the outstanding internal improvements debt.[100]

Outside the Legislature, pressure mounted for sale of the public works. While the bills were being debated, Joy and Brooks met with select Senate and House committees, helped persuade recalcitrants, and suggested tactics to those favoring sale. In order to increase popular pressure, Joy engaged in massive petition drives, sending sample petitions to groups outside Detroit and encouraging them to gain signatures. The petitions were collected and a few submitted to the Legislature each day to create the impression that public opinion was strongly and continuously in favor of sale. By the time the bill was passed, Joy's public relations efforts had raised popular feeling to a high pitch.[101]

The charter of the Michigan Central Railroad Company was introduced into the House on February 16, debated for two weeks, and passed by a margin of forty-one to nine. Opposition votes were scattered throughout the state.[102] In the Senate, the bill's opponents were primarily concerned with details of the charter, rather than the principle of sale. Attempts to prohibit trains from running on Sunday were voted down by substantial majorities, but amendments to protect the state's economic interest received serious consideration. Several of the more important charter limitations were added during Senate debate. When Senators favoring the charter prematurely attempted to force passage, the bill failed to receive the necessary two-thirds majority. In a letter to his wife, Governor Felch described the disappointment in the capital:

> The bill for the sale of the Central Railroad received a vote to-day in the Senate—The Senate refusing to pass the bill. I think they will have it up again and take another vote on it. There is a good deal of excitement here on account of the loss of the bill—and both the house and senate adjourned very soon after coming in this afternoon. My opinion is, notwithstanding the present very dark prospect, that the bill will yet pass and the road will be sold. There is very great anxiety about it in the public mind.[103]

The following day, the bill was returned to committee and reported back with an amendment limiting charges for flour and wheat shipments to three-fourths of the price charged by the state on January 1, 1846. When the amendment was accepted, the bill passed sixteen to two. After some protest, the House accepted the Senate amendments, and the bill was signed into law before the end of March.[104]

As debate drew to a close on the Michigan Central charter, a bill for sale of the Southern was introduced. Although opposed by Washtenaw County delegates who wanted the Tecumseh Branch completed, the bill passed the House by a vote of twenty-eight to seventeen. The Senate, after four days of debate, passed the bill fourteen to two.[105]

Sale of the Central and Southern ended an era of state entrepreneurial activity. Internal improvements continued on a reduced scale from 1846 until 1850, when they were forbidden by the state's new constitution. During those four years, however, the balance of the internal improvement lands donated by the federal government was expended on widely distributed road and river projects. The 1850 constitution's prohibition of state involvement in internal improvement works was generally construed to include road construction. However, this prohibition was interpreted as applying only to projects involving state funds. Grants were accepted from the federal government for constructing the Soo Canal, which, although built by a private firm in exchange for the land grant, was operated by the state for twenty-six years.[106] In addition, Michigan received 3,133,231 acres of land from the national government for railroads between 1850 and 1923, and 5,655,816 acres of swamp land grants.[107] In the last half of the century, the state administered and awarded resources far in excess of those applied between 1835 and 1850.[108]

Between 1837 and 1846, the terminal dates of the formal internal improvement program, Michigan was subjected to the dual strife of party and section. Sectional rivalry, responsible for the adoption of a program of multiple works in 1837, was the most potent factor in legislative struggles and the allocation of state funds. Between 1839 and 1841, when the central tier turned from the Democracy to the Whig party in hopes of gaining enough legislative strength to enforce its claims, party politics threatened to replace sectional rivalry, but the Whig party proved unable to suppress factional struggles and enforce party discipline. When put to the test of voting for appropriations, Whig legislators acted more frequently with their section than with their party. By the middle of 1841, even before the fall elections, the state government had fallen under Democratic control. Although the Democracy retained firm control of the state government after 1842, there were few significant changes in Michigan's internal improvement policy. Necessity forced concentration of the state's resources on its single profitable project, at the expense of works in areas more strongly held by the Democracy. As the depression waned, state finances recovered and sectional rivalry flared again in the Democratic-controlled Legislature. Sectional claims were so powerful in 1845 that multiple bills—in essence, an omnibus bill—were again necessary to pass appropriations for the railroads.

By 1846, the state had trapped itself. Borrowing was impossible because loans could be obtained only for a single project, subject to popular approval at a general election, and no section was willing to risk possible taxation for a loan's redemption when funds would be spent in another tier or area. Heavy settlement in the third and fourth tiers had created a strong new sectional interest, chafing under the supposed inequality of expenditures for which it was now to be taxed. Even if a compromise between the central and southern sections had been possible, the north would have insisted on the restoration of sectional equality. Faced at the beginning of 1846 with the dual problem of rebuilding the roads and resuming deferred interest payments on its bonds, the state had to choose between repudiating its debts and selling its public works. Repudiation of its "just debts" was not even considered. Michigan's hands were tied; sectional rivalry, which had created the program, now forced the state to sell.

Notes, Chapter 8

1. Hemans, pp. 297-312; Streeter, p. 10; *Michigan Manual*, 1911, p. 464.
2. The method used for determining political affiliation is described in Chapter 5.
3. *Messages of the Governors of Michigan*, I, 219-236.
4. Letter from Alpheus Felch to Lucretia Felch, December 14, 1837, in Felch Papers (MHC).
5. Michigan, *House Journal*, 1838, pp. 200, 320, 328.
6. *Ibid.*, pp. 368-385; Michigan, *Senate Journal*, 1838, pp. 327, 329, 330.

7. Michigan, *Legislative Acts,* 1838, No. 56.
8. Michigan, *Senate Journal,* 1838, pp. 296, 315.
9. Michigan, *House Journal,* 1838, p. 380.
10. Michigan, *Senate Journal,* 1838, p. 344; Michigan, *Legislative Acts,* 1840, Joint Resolution No. 5.
11. Michigan, Legislature, *Report of the Committee on State Affairs (Senate Documents,* 1838, S. D. No. 32), pp. 431-450.
12. Letter from William Woodbridge to Hon. John Norvell, March 9, 1838, Woodbridge Papers (BHC).
13. Michigan, *Legislative Acts,* 1838, No. 82.
14. Hemans, pp. 449-450.
15. *Messages of the Governors of Michigan,* I, 245-247.
16. Streeter, p. 13.
17. Michigan, *House Journal,* 1839, pp. 634-663, 658; Michigan, *Senate Journal,* 1839, pp. 503-511; Michigan, *Legislative Acts,* 1839, No. 116.
18. Michigan, Legislature, *Report of the Joint Select Committee to Investigate the Negotiation of the Five Million Loan (House Documents,* 1839, H. D. No. 44), pp. 705-708. Cited hereafter as *House Document No. 44,* 1839. Petition of "Friends of the State Administration," April 2, 1838, in Records of the Executive Office, 1810-1910: Reports: Board of Internal Improvements, 1838-1841 (Michigan Department of State, Historical Commission Archives).
19. Michigan, Legislature, *Report of the Majority of the Committee of Investigation into the General Accounts and Proceedings of the Board of Internal Improvements, Made April 9, 1839 (House Documents,* 1839, H. D. No. 47), pp. 747-817. Cited hereafter as *House Document No. 17,* 1839.
20. Hemans, pp. 297, 310.
21. Michigan, *House Documents,* 1839, pp. 747-817.
22. Letter from Kingsley S. Bingham to Alpheus Felch, March 20, 1839, in Felch Papers (BHC).
23. *Ibid.;* Letters from Lucius Lyon to M. J. Bacon, Feb. 25, 1839; Lucius Lyon to S. Haight, Sergeant-at-Arms, U. S. Senate, April 3, 1839; and Lucius Lyon to Allen Hutchins, April 16, 1839, in Lucius Lyon Papers, *MP&HC,* XXVII (1896), 519-522.
24. Letters from Lucius Lyon to E. Phaphro, Ransom [*sic.*], July 13, 1839; Lucius Lyon to Elon Farnsworth, November 1, 1839, and November 8, 1839; Lucius Lyon to John P. Richardson, November 29, 1839, *ibid.,* pp. 424-528.
25. Streeter, p. 13.
26. *An Appeal to the People of Michigan* (1839), political pamphlet in the possession of the Michigan Historical Commission, in a miscellaneous bound volume entitled *Documents* which is currently uncatalogued.
27. Letter from F. Sawyer to Wm. Woodbridge, November 28, 1839, Woodbridge Papers (BHC). Actually, the Democrats had raided the internal improvements funds to support the general fund.
28. Letter from William Woodbridge to Oliver Johnson, December 5, 1839, Woodbridge Papers (BHC).
29. Draft of a letter from William Woodbridge to "Dear Sir," December 12, 1839, Woodbridge Papers (BHC).
30. *Messages of the Governors of Michigan,* I, 275-286, 308-316.
31. *Ibid.,* pp. 275-286.
32. See Chapter 9.
33. Streeter, pp. 13-15; Michigan, *House Journal,* 1840, p. 73; Michigan, *Senate Journal,* 1840, p. 96.
34. Michigan, Legislature, *Governor William Woodbridge to the Senate and House of Representatives, January 15, 1840 (House Documents,* 1840, II, H. D. No. 16), pp. 122-123; Michigan, *Legislative Acts,* 1840, Joint Resolution No. 15.
35. Michigan, *Legislative Acts,* 1839, No. 103; Michigan, *Legislative Acts,* 1840, No.

63; Michigan, *House Document No. 3,* 1841, pp. 154-156.
36. Michigan, *Senate Journal,* 1840, pp. 105, 107, 121, 131.
37. Letter from William Woodbridge to Mess. Hicks & Co., August 17, 1840, in Records of the Executive Office, 1810-1910: Correspondence (Michigan Department of State, Historical Commission Archives). Letter from William Woodbridge to Mead, Williams and Hart, July 20, 1840, in Woodbridge Papers (BHC).
38. Michigan, Legislature, *Report of the Select Committee on the Five Million Loan...* (*Senate Documents* 1840, II, S. D. No. 63), p. 553; Michigan, Legislature, *Report of the Select Committee on Public Improvement, & c.* (*Senate Documents,* 1840, II, S. D. No. 61), p. 554; Michigan, Legislature, *Report* (*Senate Documents,* 1840, II, S. D. No. 64), pp. 558-559; Michigan, Legislature, *Report* (*House Documents,* 1840, II, H. D. No. 64), p. 565; Michigan, Legislature, *Report of the Committee on Ways and Means* (*House Documents,* 1840, II, H. D. No. 69). pp. 594-596.
39. Michigan, *Senate Journal,* 1840, pp. 562-567.
40. Michigan, *House Document No. 69,* pp. 594-596.
41. Michigan, *House Journal,* 1840, pp. 693-722.
42. Letters from A. S. Porter to Wm. Woodbridge, May 23, 1840; Townsend Gridley to William Woodbridge, May 15, 1840, in Woodbridge Papers (BHC).
43. Michigan, Legislature, *Report of the Committee on Roads and Bridges* (*Senate Documents,* 1840, II, S. D. No. 30), pp. 292-293; Michigan, *Legislative Acts,* 1839, Appendix 9, p. 262.
44. Michigan, *Legislative Acts,* 1840, No. 59.
45. Letter from Lucius Lyon to T. H. Lyon, Nov. 8, 1840, in Lucius Lyon Papers, *MP&HC,* XXVII (1896), 538.
46. Letter from Richard Butler to Wm Woodbridge, December 26, 1840, in Woodbridge Papers (BHC).
47. Streeter, p. 40.
48. Letter from S. V. R. Trowbridge to Wm. Woodbridge, February 26, 1841, in Woodbridge Papers (BHC).
49. Draft, William Woodbridge to "Dear Sir," December 8, 1840, in Woodbridge Papers (BHC).
50. Michigan, Legislature, *Report of the Committee on Internal Improvements* (*Senate Documents,* 1841, II, S. D. No. 17), pp. 14-16; Michigan, *Senate Journal,* 1841, pp. 115, 166, 168, 172, 180.
51. Michigan, *House Journal,* 1841, pp. 267-276. 315, 332, 335; Michigan, *Senate Journal,* 1841, pp. 206, 215, 216-217, 228, 240-241.
52. Michigan, *Legislative Acts,* 1841, No. 13.
53. Michigan, Legislature, *Communication from the Commissioners of Internal Improvements (Senate Documents,* 1841, II, S. D. No. 33), pp. 65-67.
54. Michigan, *House Journal,* 1841, p. 494. Michigan, Legislature, *Report of the Committee on Internal Improvements* (*House Documents,* 1841, II, H. D. No. 71), pp. 269-270; Michigan, Legislature, *Report of the Committee on Ways and Means (House Documents,* 1841, II, H. D. No. 80), pp. 284-285.
55. Michigan, *House Journal,* 1841, pp. 668, 669, 696.
56. Michigan, Legislature, *Report of the Committee on Finance* (*Senate Documents,* 1841, II, S. D. No. 37), pp. 86-146. Cited hereafter as *Senate Document No. 37,* 1841.
57. Streeter, p. 31.
58. Letter from John Van Fossen to William Woodbridge, August 12, 1841, in Woodbridge Papers (BHC).
59. Letter from Stevens T. Mason to Charles [Anderson], September 28, 1841, in S. T. Mason Papers (BHC).
60. Letter from Stevens T. Mason to Charles [Anderson], August 17, 1841, in S. T. Mason Papers (BHC); Letter from John Van Fossen to William Woodbridge, August 30, 1841, in Woodbridge Papers, (BHC).
61. *Messages of the Governors of Michigan,* I, 443.

62. *Ibid.*, 447-448.
63. Michigan, *Legislative Acts,* 1842, No. 20.
64. *Ibid.,*Joint Resolution No.3.
65. Michigan, *House Journal,* 1842, pp. 32-34; Michigan, *Senate Journal,* 1842, pp. 244, 255-258, 274; Michigan, Legislature, *Report of the Committee on Internal Improvement (Senate Documents,* 1842, S. D. No. 5), pp. 24ff.
66. Letters from William Hale to Alpheus Felch, January 23, 1842; C. A. Jackson to Alpheus [Felch], October 26, 1842, in Felch Papers (MHC).
67. *Messages of the Governors of Michigan,* I, 472. Barry's fiscal policies are discussed in Chapter 9.
68. Michigan, Legislature, *Report of the Committee on Finance (Senate Documents,* 1843, S. D. No. 4), pp. 28, 34; Michigan, Legislature, *Report of the Committee on Internal Improvement (House Documents,* 1843, H. D. No. 6), p. 31; "Speech of William Goodwin," *Democratic Free Press* (Detroit), March 7, 1843, p. 2.
69. Michigan, *House Journal,* 1841, pp. 615, 648, 661; Michigan, *Senate Journal,* 1843, pp. 412, 419; Michigan, *Legislative Acts,* 1842, No. 10; Michigan, Legislature, *Report of the Committee on the Judiciary of the Senate (Senate Documents,* 1845, S. D. No. 10).
70. Michigan, Legislature, *Report of the Committee on Internal Improvements (House Documents,* 1843, H. D. No. 6), p. 26.
71. Michigan, *Senate Journal,* 1843, pp. 217, 223, 226, 238, 278, 349. Michigan *House Journal,* 1843, pp. 26, 266, 269, 277-282, 287-289, 295-301.
72. Michigan, *Legislative Acts,* 1843, No. 24; Michigan, *House Journal,* 1843, pp. 104-105, 119.
73. *Messages of the Governors of Michigan,* I, 488.
74. Michigan, Legislature, *Report of the Committee on Ways and Means (House Documents,* 1844, H. D. No. 11); Michigan, Legislature, *Report of the Committee on Internal Improvements (House Documents,* 1844, H. D. No. 2).
75. Michigan, *Senate Journal,* 1844, pp. 296, 299, 372, 374; Michigan, *House Journal,* 1844, pp. 172-190, 247-257, 302, 373, 381-389, 392-393; Michigan, *Legislative Acts,* 1844, No. 50.
76. Michigan, *Senate Journal,* 1844, pp. 319, 343-345, 391; Michigan, *House Journal,* 1844, pp. 103, 159, 163, 168-169, 204, 205, 299, 402.
77. Michigan, *Legislative Acts,* 1844, Joint Resolutions Nos. 5, 8, 10. Letter from Lucius Lyon to Charles Butler, June 5, 1844, Lyon Papers, *MP&HC,* XXVII (1896), 583.
78. Michigan, Legislature, *Report of the Committee on Ways and Means (House Documents,* 1844, H. D. No. 3).
79. *Ibid.,* pp. 5-6.
80. Michigan, *House Journal,* 1844, pp. 343, 344.
81. Michigan, *Senate Journal,* 1844, pp. 160-161, 189, 203, 267, 285.
82. *Messages of the Governors of Michigan,* I, 505-520; Letter from William Hale to Alpheus Felch, October 14, 1844, in Felch Papers (MHC).
83. Michigan, *House Journal,* 1845, pp. 64. 88, 116, 121, 218; Michigan, *Legislative Acts,* 1845, No. 15.
84. Michigan, Legislature, *Report of the Committee on Internal Improvements (House Documents,* 1845, H. D. No. 9).
85. Michigan, Legislature, *Minority Report of the Committee on Internal Improvement (House Documents,* 1845, H. D. No. 11).
86. Michigan, Legislature, *Report to the Select Committee (House Documents,* 1845, H. D. No. 13).
87. Michigan, *House Journal,* 1845, pp. 162, 172, 180, 182, 195, 200, 251, 268-273, 321, 405, 423-425, 231, 253, 233-235. Note: Titles given the bills by Barry in his veto message, and those reported in the Legislature do not agree.
88. *Messages of the Governors of Michigan,* I, 521-527.
89. Michigan, *House Journal,* 1845, pp. 498, 503.

90. Michigan, *Legislative Acts*, 1845, Joint Resolution No. 20.
91. Michigan, *House Journal*, 1845, pp. 248, 276, 514.
92. Berndt, pp. 95-96; Reagan, p. 67. These theses explore the private negotiations in greater depth than is necessary for this study.
93. Letter from R. McClelland to A. Felch, May 19, 1845, in Felch Papers (BHC).
94. Letter from J. B. Baker to Alpheus Felch, September 16, 1845, in Felch Papers (MHC).
95. *Messages of the Governors of Michigan*, I, 35-48.
96. Michigan, Legislature, *Report from the Finance Committee: Sale of Railroads* (*Senate Documents*, 1846, S. D. No. 9).
97. Michigan, Legislature, *Report of the Committee on Finance* (*Senate Documents*, 1846, S. D. No. 9).
98. Michigan, Legislature, *Report of the Committee on Finance* (*Senate Documents*, 1846, S. D. No. 8), pp. 12-24.
99. Michigan, Legislature, *Report of the Select Committee on the Sale of Works of Internal Improvement (House Documents*, 1846, H. D. No. 2).
100. Michigan, Legislature, *Report of the Committee on Ways and Means* (*House Documents*, 1846, H. D. No. 1).
101. Berndt, pp. 95-106.
102. Michigan, *House Journal*, 1846, pp. 178, 189, 203-222, 240-243, 245, 333, 336;
103. Letter from Alpheus Felch to Lucretia Felch, March 18, 1846, in Felch Papers (MHC).
104. Michigan, *Senate Journal*, 1846, pp. 281-283, 292, 294.
105. Michigan, *House Journal*, 1846, pp. 355, 395, 401-423, 434-442, 446-448, 523-524; Michigan, *Senate Journal*, 1846, pp. 403, 408-414, 420-422, 433, 454-457, 566, 575.
106. Dunbar, p. 373.
107. Benjamin Horace Hibbard, *History of the Public Land Policies* (Madison, Wisconsin: University of Wisconsin Press, 1965), pp. 264, 275.
108. The use of public land grants for purposes of internal improvement in the period after 1850 is an untouched subject demanding scholarly attention. The resources applied suggest that the state did more through use of federal resources after 1846 than before. New patterns and forces must have developed which would give insight into Michigan's subsequent development.

9

FINANCING THE PUBLIC WORKS

Recent literature has lumped the financial problems encountered in public internal improvements programs during the second construction cycle together under the convenient phrase, "poor cyclical timing." The phrase is useful because it incorporates a multitude of problems: sharp deflations in property values, deterioration of tax bases, deranged currencies, contracting financial markets, and a sharp decrease in the quantity of funds available through borrowing. In Michigan, financing the public works became the most serious problem resulting from the decision to adopt a multiple program. "Poor cyclical timing" helps explain the state's difficulties, and the depression suffered by the Atlantic economy between 1839 and 1844 is a convenient backdrop. The phrase is too mechanistic, however, to explain Michigan's problems, which were essentially the result of human failure, growing out of ill-advised attempts at central banking and conflicts of interest. [1]

Michigan's basic plan was simple. Until a loan could be negotiated, construction was to be financed by funds realized from the federal surplus revenue distribution. To provide long-term support, the Legislature authorized the Governor to negotiate the sale of five million dollars worth of bonds. Except for a provision forbidding sale of the stock at less than par value, the Governor's authority was almost unlimited. Minimum face value of the bonds was set at one thousand dollars, payable twenty-five years after January 1, 1838; interest was limited to five and one-half percent, payable semi-annually. Proceeds from the sale were to be deposited in the State Treasury, subject to appropriation for internal improvements by the Legislature. Interest was payable only in the United States, although sale of the bonds could be negotiated abroad. To secure the loan, the state's faith was pledged for payment of principal and interest, and the proceeds of the state's railroads, canals, and bank stock were pledged to a sinking fund. [2] By a single act, the state committed itself to honoring one man's negotiations for a sum equal to twelve percent of its assessed property valuation. In its haste, the Legislature failed to reserve even the powers of review and ratification. From the moment the act was signed into law, the Governor was essentially a free agent, and success or failure depended on his good faith and judgment.

Governor Mason's negotiations and manipulations of what came to be known as the "five million loan" created a tangled web involving not only the sale of bonds, but currency and exchange stabilization, attempts at central banking, and criminal misuse of public funds. The events between March 1837, when the loan was authorized, and November 1838, when the final contracts for the bond sale were signed, are still not entirely clear. The originals of printed documents have been lost or destroyed, along with the private papers of deeply involved individuals; some transactions apparently rested on verbal agreements alone. Mason's reports to the Legislature, never entirely candid, often omitted evidence that would have reflected poorly on his actions. Subsequent investigating committees stretched the truth to justify or condemn the Governor's actions, and witnesses—including Mason— perjured themselves to avoid more serious incrimination. Despite conflicting testimony and documents, however, the weight of evidence is heavily against Mason's conduct of the state's financial negotiations. Those who explain Michigan's financial disaster in terms of the Governor's financial inexperience have seriously underestimated his understanding of banking and his bargaining ability.[3]

Almost from the beginning, Mason's negotiations were dominated by the Panic of 1837 and the resulting financial disruption. Although prospects for marketing the state's bonds were dim in the spring of 1837, the loan act was passed before news of the collapse of American credit reached Detroit. As soon as the Legislature adjourned, Mason boarded a steamer for New York. Arriving in the midst of the Panic, he soon became convinced there was no hope of immediately placing the loan. After interviewing several bankers and stock brokers, Mason left a copy of the loan act at the Phoenix Bank with John Delafield, who had handled a bond issue for the state the year before, and asked him to correspond with American and foreign bankers about placing the bonds.[4] When he returned home, the Governor, finding that the Panic had not yet reached Michigan, called the Legislature into special session and asked for measures to soften its impact. According to Mason, the Panic was the result of over-banking and over-extension of credit; if the economy were allowed to adjust, it would quickly run its course. In the meantime, the state would have to protect its banks and specie reserves, and provide a circulating medium. To save specie and the charters of banks that had already stopped payment, or would be forced to, he asked the Legislature to authorize suspension until New York resumed specie payments. The Legislature responded with an act embodying Mason's suggestions and, in addition, made bank notes receivable at par for state taxes.[5] During the next six months, the Governor began to forge the connection between state banking policies and the loan that would ruin both him and the state.

Mason gradually assumed even more authority over the loan than the Legislature had granted him. During the summer and fall of 1837, it became increasingly apparent that the state's loan could not be placed in Europe unless changes were made in the form of the bonds. Although Mason repeatedly reported that he had not been informed of the need for raising the interest rate to six percent and making the bonds payable in Europe until his trip to New York in the autumn of 1837, he had been aware of the need early in the summer. Writing to John Delafield in July, he expressed regrets that the need for alteration had not been discovered while the Legislature was in session. Clearly exceeding his authority, the Governor authorized Delafield to raise the interest rate to six percent, guaranteeing that the necessary amendment would be adopted without question.[6] When Mason visited New York in the fall of 1837, arrangements were made for advances from Delafield and for marketing the loan. Assured by Delafield that an amended loan act could be placed in the London market by James King of Prime, Ward & King, Mason returned to Detroit to have the amendment passed.[7] By placing the loan in the hands of Prime, Ward & King, New York correspondents of Baring Brothers, the Governor had an important opportunity to market the state's bonds with one of Europe's leading financial houses.

Arriving in Detroit, he immediately dispatched his law partner and Secretary of State, Kintzing Pritchette, to New York with half a million dollars in bonds and promises that the amended law would be forwarded as soon as it had been passed.[8] On November 11, a special message was sent to the Legislature, which had met in adjourned session, calling for changes in the original loan act. In line with Delafield's suggestions, Mason asked that the interest rate be raised to six percent, and the bonds be made payable outside the United States. Apparently on his own initiative, the Governor asked that if the bonds were made payable in Europe, they should be redeemable at the rate of $4.44 per pound sterling, or $.40 per guilder, both on principal and interest. Since the gold par rate of exchange had been increased to $4.87 by Congress in 1834, these terms amounted to a ten percent premium in favor of the state at the time of redemption. The Legislature responded by raising the interest rate and making it payable in Europe, with no explicit provision for repayment of principal abroad. In addition, it required any differences in exchange rates to accrue to the state, while redemption was restricted to the rate suggested by Governor Mason.[9] In essence, the amended bill required that the state receive the benefits of any difference in exchange when selling, and allowed it to redeem principal and interest at the par value of the dollar prior to 1834, a ten percent discount. This provision was a major reason for its rejection in Europe.

When Mason forwarded copies of the amendment to Delafield, he emphasized that the provision was added to avoid having differences in exchange rates cost the state money: "I have assured them you will avoid entering into any contract in Europe by which the interest and difference of exchange could by possibility exceed the six per centum per annum, the limit of the annexed law." If it could be arranged, he would prefer that the loan be marketed in the United States, with the balance financed at the original interest rate. At the same time, however, the Governor made it clear that he did not want to interfere: "The negotiation is in your hands."[10]

Within days after awarding Delafield the state's agency, Governor Mason began to use the bond issue to support Michigan's suspended banks. In a November 21 letter to Delafield reminding him of his pledge to take one hundred and fifty thousand dollars of the bonds if the funds were needed by the state, Mason stated: "I can dispose of a half million of six per cents to our banks here at a *small premium*, taking their own paper. Is it your opinion that I should make such arrangements."[11] Before Delafield's reply arrived, however, the Governor sold the bonds to Oliver Newberry of Detroit, a prominent stockholder in several of the city banks, and reported to the Legislature the existence of arrangements to have other funds advanced from New York.[12] To Mason's surprise, his New York agent was firmly opposed to marketing any part of the loan through a third party. Early in January, writing to Delafield to notify him of drafts on him for one hundred and fifty thousand dollars, he informed his agent that he had assigned the bonds to Newberry, and that they would pass through Delafield's hands so as not to interfere with his negotiations: "This arrangement was made before your last letter was received. No other bonds have or will be issued, as the state is now enabled to await the result of Mr. King's negotiation in Europe."[13]

Mason's sale of securities to Newberry destroyed any possibility of succeeding through his New York agents. Attempts to have the bonds pass through Delafield's hands failed when Newberry deposited them with John Ward & Co., of New York, and refused to turn them over. Prime, Ward, & King reacted angrily to the discredit reflected on their representatives, who were claiming sole agency, and rejected a sale then being negotiated for two million dollars of Michigan's bonds. Under these conditions, the company temporarily refused to honor Mason's drafts.[14]

At first, Mason was apologetic, offering to increase the state's loan to five and one half million, in order to absorb Newberry's securities while giving Delafield full control over five million dollars in bonds.[15] Two weeks later, however, he became more belligerent. Sending John Norton, the Michigan State Bank's cashier, to New York to explain the situation and negotiate with Delafield for payment of the one hundred and fifty thousand dollars in rejected drafts, he wrote that he had originally been afraid he had interfered with the European sale:

> But my apprehensions of interference with Mr. King in Europe, are relieved by the fact disclosed in a copy of the letter of Prime, Ward, & King dated January 27, 1838, which informs me, that my sale of bonds to Newberry defeated the sale *on their part* of two millions of bonds. Of course this sale of two millions, was in the *American Market,* as the information of my transfer to Newberry could not at that date have reached the European Market. I am thus relieved from the apprehension, that Mr. King might by possibility be making arrangements for the whole five million in Europe, and thus involve you in difficulty by obligations in Europe beyond the remaining four and a half....
>
> I have no disposition to take the loan from your hands, but should you desire otherwise, Mr. Norton is authorized to receive the remaining bonds in your possession, to be disposed of according to my instructions.[16]

Although expressing hopes that the contract would not be broken, and asking that their agreement be put in writing when he visited New York in April, Mason's tone had changed noticeably.

Frustrated in his attempts to market bonds for support of the state's banks, Mason was nevertheless not without alternatives. When he transmitted a proposition from a Detroit banking convention requesting that they be allowed to sell state bonds to gain exchange on the East, he recommended aiding the banks by chartering a state bank for the same purpose. The state's banks needed aid, he felt, because losses always fell on the people who were the holders of their paper.[17] For the short term, however, the Governor planned to use Eastern funds to support local notes without authorization. On February 19, as part of a message explaining negotiations on the state's loan, he told the Legislature not to worry about the rejection of drafts on Delafield, because they were not drawn against the loan: "The drafts drawn on him were for a voluntary advance on his part, and drawn to relieve the exchanges between Detroit and New York."[18] To implement his plan, Mason sent the following letter to Delafield with Norton on his mission to New York:

> In a conversation with Mr. Norton, the evening before his departure, he suggested that he would like, in addition to his $90,000 due on my draft, to be enabled to command some additional funds, to purchase and redeem Michigan notes in your market. Mr. Norton is a particular personal friend of mine, and is the fiscal agent of the state, and cashier of the state deposit bank. You may, therefore, if you have received funds on the bonds in your possession, transfer to Mr. Norton, $50,000 or $100,000, taking his certificate of deposit from "John Norton, Jr., cashier of the state bank," which will be cashed at the state deposit bank. This letter is inclosed to Mr. Norton, who will deliver it to you.[19]

Whether the draft was to be used for the benefit of the bank, Mason, or Norton, it is apparent that the Governor approved and authorized the use of state funds gained through the loan for exchange stabilization operations between New York and Detroit. Credits gained in New York would have returned a profit to someone through the purchase of depreciated state notes in the Eastern market for redemption in Michigan. Even if the Governor was not attempting to speculate in notes with state funds for his own profit or the profit of his friends, he had no legal authority to engage in either central banking or exchange stabilization.[20] Through Norton's negotiations with Delafield, he was able to gain the advance of one hundred and fifty thousand dollars from Prime, Ward, & King in the form of drafts on London.

Mason's attempts to support the notes of Michigan's banks ultimately cost the state its chance to market the loan in Europe, along with substantial brokerage fees. Shortly after Prime, Ward, & King reopened their joint exchange account with Barings on December 16, 1837, Michigan's bonds were consigned to them for sale. According to Ralph Hidy: "An attempt to

buy a Michigan loan failed in competition with higher bids from the Bank of
the United States, a result very pleasing to the Barings, who were concerned
about the proximity of that 'backwoods' state to the seat of the Canadian
Rebellion."[21] No word of the bid by the Bank of the United States ever
reached the American negotiators, but when Mason arrived in New York in
the spring of 1838, he found that the bonds had been returned to Prime,
Ward, & King, who were demanding repayment for the advances drawn on
London. Mason then attempted to heal the rift with Prime, Ward, & King by
redeeming the bonds deposited by Oliver Newberry with John Ward & Co.
Ironically, none of the bonds had been sold; although deposits from Newberry were reported by the Treasurer from February through September,
Mason retrieved the whole lot from John Ward & Co. by paying two
hundred thousand dollars into Newberry's account, and depositing the balance of three hundred thousand dollars in bonds with John Delafield.[22]
Shortly thereafter, the Governor attempted to prove to Delafield that the
rates of exchange stipulated by the amended act would not apply to
payment of interest and principal, but it was too late.[23] The next day,
James King, who had just returned from Europe, formally notified Delafield
that Prime, Ward, & King would no longer handle Michigan's account.

In notifying Delafield of his refusal to handle Michigan's securities, King
emphasized that two factors were responsible for his rejection of the contract: the stipulations regulating the rate of exchange, and Mason's violation
of the agency agreement by marketing bonds through Newberry. Although
the exchange rate provisions made it impossible to sell the securities in
Europe, King had planned to market them in America on his return. On
arrival, however, he discovered that Mason's violation had spoiled the American market. King made it clear that Newberry's agency was the primary
reason for his returning the bonds to Delafield.[24] As a result of Mason's
dealings, the state had lost the opportunity to sell three million dollars of its
bonds through solvent brokers in London, together with $11,755 in interest
on Delafield's advances and $916 in commissions and expenses.[25]

Mason was not entirely candid when he reported his negotiations to the
Legislature in the spring of 1839. With one exception, none of the correspondence with Delafield was presented, although the letters given to the
Legislature were supposed to include all the material relating to the loan. In
the one letter presented, that of James King revoking his agency on April
28, 1837, the portion emphasing the role of Mason's agency to Newberry
was deleted before publication. The Governor similarly failed to report the
details of his negotiations with Newberry, and the fees paid to Delafield for
his advances were explained away as charges for purchasing the exchange to
realize drafts on London. His single mistake in covering his tracks was his
refusal to pay Delafield an additional commission on the bonds which would
have been sold if Mason had not interfered. Delafield, angry at Mason's
refusal to adjust the commission, submitted the entire correspondence to the
Legislature in 1841, much to the delight of a Whig investigating committee.[26]

. Rejected by Delafield, and Prime, Ward, & King, and under heavy pressure from his former agents to repay their advances, Mason turned to other financiers.[27] On May 8, 1838, a contract was negotiated with E. R. Biddle, in behalf of himself and friends in Philadelphia, for the entire loan at par. Eighty thousand dollars was accepted as a down payment, but after waiting nearly a month, Mason returned the contract because Biddle was unable to complete arrangements with his friends.[28] Finally, on June 1, 1838, a new contract was signed with E. R. Biddle awarding an agency to the Morris Canal and Banking Company.

The contract signed by Mason and Biddle awarded the Morris Canal and Banking Company an agency to sell five million dollars of Michigan's bonds, for a commission of two and one-half percent. To compensate for the loss of bonds sold in the name of Oliver Newberry, bonds granted by the state to the Allegan and Marshall Railroad and the Ypsilanti and Tecumseh were included in the contract. Funds realized through the sale of securities, along with any exchange benefits from foreign sales, were to be deposited in a New York rather than a Detroit bank. In case the bonds were sold below par, the agents were pledged to make up the difference, after subtracting their commission. If the bonds could be sold above par, benefits up to five percent were to be divided between the state and its agent; proceeds of sales above five percent over par would accrue to the company. In return, the company was pledged to advance two hundred and fifty thousand dollars on signing the contract, and one million and fifty thousand dollars as needed by the state. After July 1, 1839, the balance was due in quarterly installments of two hundred and fifty thousand dollars, even if the company had failed to market the loan. The state was required to supply the company with bonds for one million dollars ahead of installments. In addition, the company reserved the right to call in and sell any part of the unsold balance at any time on thirty days notice, deducting their commission at the time of sale and depositing the proceeds to the account of the State of Michigan. Finally, the agency of the Morris Canal and Banking Company was made irrevocable.[29]

Neither the legality nor the wisdom of this contract was ever seriously challenged by the Legislature. Indeed, all the advantages accrued to the state. Although the bonds were not really sold at par, the granting of a commission was not prohibited by law, and the Legislature seemed to accept Mason's explanation that it had been added to shield the company from loss if the bonds were not sold at their face value. In compensation, the state was guaranteed regular quarterly payments with which to finance their internal improvements program, and payments were to be continued even if the company was unable to sell the bonds. In effect, the company was guaranteeing payment even if the market collapsed. If the entire issue were sold, the proceeds were to be paid over to the state on receipt of the balance of its bonds. Serious opposition developed, however, to Mason's continued and unauthorized alterations in the terms of the contract.

On June 4, three days after the original contract had been signed,

Mason consented to its first alteration. According to the new arrangement, the Governor agreed to receive the first $1,300,000 of the company's obligation in Morris Canal notes, disbursing them at specified periods ninety days later than the original agreement: $250,000 on August 1, and $100,000 on the first of each following month. The same day, Theodore Romeyne who acted as Mason's advisor and partner during the transaction, was sent to Delafield with $150,000 to exchange for the $1,200,000 in bonds held by the state's former agent against his advances.[30] After signing the supplementary agreement, Mason and Romeyne watched as $110,397 was counted, marked, and packed in a trunk provided for its return to Michigan. No objection was raised to the June 4 alteration by the investigating committee in 1839, perhaps because it was never put into operation.

During the Governor's return trip to Michigan with Romeyne and the money, $4,630 mysteriously disappeared from the middle of the trunk in which it was carried. Seizing the opportunity to break the June 4 agreement, Mason suggested another alteration in the contract, substituting ninety-day sight drafts for the notes stipulated. At the end of June, John Norton was sent to New York to negotiate a second alteration. On July 14, a new agreement was signed, authorizing Norton to draw on the company on the due date of installments and making the drafts payable at ninety days sight. No interest was to be charged the company for the additional ninety days it held the state's funds.[31] By Mason's two alterations the company was awarded an average of one hundred and eighty days free use of funds credited to the state, although the original contract had awarded $1,300,000 payable on demand.

The new contract was bitterly protested in Michigan. Even the legislative committee investigating the arrangements in 1839 momentarily turned from the mystery of the missing bills to grumble that it could not discover "the necessity or the authority by which drafts were substituted for the notes of the Morris Canal and Banking Company...."[32] In answer to the committee's questions, Mason offered two reasons for the change:

> This modification was made in consequence of the risk in transporting the bills of the company, and from a sincere desire to relieve our commercial interest at home by throwing exchange into the hands of our banks. These drafts were offered to the banks of the city of Detroit, on the conditions that they would pay out their own paper, or such other paper as they would make equal to cash at their own counters, and the proposition was rejected by all but the *Michigan State Bank*.[33]

Although the Governor explained that the ninety days free use was granted to the company to compensate for its losses of interest on the notes the state had agreed to circulate, no explanation was offered for the contract to disburse notes, or why he had signed such a contract when the original agreement had allowed the state to draw on the bank at sight.

No explanation was found for the Governor's alterations until 1840, when the Whig Treasurer, Robert Stuart, gained access to the books of the

Morris Canal and Banking Company. The documents uncovered supplied the answers to questions raised by the Whigs from the beginning of Mason's involvement with the Morris Bank. On June 4, 1838, a second contract had been signed between the company and Theodore Romeyne acting as a supplemental agreement to the first alteration, which was also signed on that date. In return for the state's agreement to take the bank's notes on a delayed schedule, Romeyne was awarded one-half of the interest charged on the bonds between May 1, 1838, and the date the funds were disbursed, and two and one-half percent interest on the time the bills were in circulation. Ostensibly, the contract was awarded to release the company from Romeyne's claims to title, right and interest in the loan, as well as for agencies, commissions, and professional services.[34]

Faced with the evidence before a formal Senate investigation, Romeyne told the whole story. Before their trip east in April 1838, he and Mason had worked out a plan to buy two of Michigan's wildcat banks to finance the state's internal improvements program. Local bank notes were to be paid to contractors, and the proceeds of the loan used to redeem their issues and speculate on Michigan bank notes in New York. To purchase the banks, the partners consented to the June 4 modification, for which they received advances of ten thousand dollars. The balance was to be paid when the contract was completed on June 1, 1839. The two men expected to realize half of the thirty-five thousand dollars charged the state in interest on deferred payments, and two and one-half percent on the circulation of Morris Bank and Canal notes. To trace the bills of the Morris Bank and identify them on their return to the company, the bills were marked with special stamps which, for the partner's convenience, were imprinted inside the crown of Romeyne's hat.

Even before Mason and Romeyne left New York, the Governor became dissatisfied with the arrangement. Mason used the disappearance of the marked money from a locked trunk in his custody to terminate the contract. Convinced that there would be little profit in circulation of the Morris notes, and afraid that his currency support and speculation programs would be endangered, the Governor proposed to compensate the Morris Bank and Canal Company by offering to substitute ninety-day sight drafts for the circulation of their notes. To avoid the state's loss of the fifteen thousand dollars in interest charged on these drafts, Mason arranged for the Michigan State Bank to advance installments when they were due, compensating the bank with the exchange benefits to be derived from holding funds in the East. F. H. Steevens, President of the Michigan State Bank, testified that the Governor was rewarded for placing the exchange with the bank by being allowed substantial overdrafts that were to be covered by the profits from exchange sales.

Aside from the thirty-five thousand dollars which the state lost through interest on deferred payments, Mason's negotiations with the Morris Bank and Canal Company in June and July 1838 were not of major importance to the state's financial affairs. They do, however, point up that the Governor

was capable of putting state funds to unauthorized uses. Mason denied all
the charges leveled by the 1840 investigating committee, but in the attempt
to refute their accusations he presented evidence substantiating their position.[35] Compared, however, to the damage done the state's program by the
Governor's third modification of the loan contract and his currency specula-
tions, his actions in the early summer of 1838 are relatively unimportant.

Mason's third modification came in November 1838. Late in the summer, the Morris Bank began to pressure Mason to deposit the balance of the
securities in a safe New York bank, subject to transmission on his authorization. Although complaining that the release of bonds by the University of
Michigan and the Detroit and Pontiac Railroad had depressed the price of
Michigan bonds, the bank held out hopes of a sale to Rothschild in
London.[36] During the Governor's visit to New York in November, the bank
offered a new contract which Mason accepted. After a November 7 meeting,
an exchange of letters confirmed the details of the new understanding. On
November 10, E. R. Biddle offered to credit the balance of the loan to
Michigan's account if the state would allow the company to deduct its two
and one-half percent commission and accept the obligations of the Bank of
the United States for three-quarters and the Morris Canal and Banking
Company for one-quarter of the sums due, to be paid at the dates specified
in the original contract. An account was to be kept to credit the state with
interest on unpaid installments, which could be drawn against at thirty days
sight.

The new arrangement suggested by E. R. Biddle added nothing to the
state's advantages under the original contract, except the powerful backing
of the Bank of the United States. The June 1 contract had required the
company to pay the balance of the loan before receiving its commission and
the state's bonds; the new arrangement allowed it to collect its commission
immediately, while retaining control of both the state's bonds and funds. In
spite of this, Mason replied to Biddle's letter that negotiating the loan had
been a thankless task, and he would give the responsibility for determining
the state's best interests to the bank. Assured by E. R. Biddle that the
contract was to the state's advantage, Governor Mason authorized his New
York banker on November 19, 1838, to release the bonds held on deposit to
the Morris Canal and Banking Company.[37] A copy of the new contract was
forwarded from New York to Detroit for Mason's approval; it was then
signed on January 29 by Nicholas Biddle in Philadelphia. The new contract
obligated the Bank of the United States of Pennsylvania to assume three-
quarters of the balance due the state under the original agreement, and the
entire balance if the Morris Bank defaulted. In return for the remaining
$3,700,000 in bonds, the two banks promised to pay $4,194,250, which
included interest on the unpaid installments. The state was required to pay
interest on the entire five million.[38]

The new arrangement caused difficulties for the state almost from the
beginning. Earlier historians have overemphasized the sale as the source of
Michigan's difficulties after the Bank's failure left the state liable for redemp-

tion of negotiable bonds for which it had received no payment. This result was as unforeseeable as it was unfortunate; in the immediate future, more serious difficulties were encountered. In February, the state deposit bank failed, carrying with it almost every penny of the state's resources. Because the new contract had allowed the Morris Bank to collect its commission from the March and April installments, the state had no means with which to carry on its internal improvements for over three months. To continue the program, the state was forced to borrow money in anticipation of the June installment at six percent. But in June, it was discovered that under the terms of the contract, which credited interest on unpaid installments due the state against interest due the bondholders on the entire loan, the interest on unpaid installments was deposited in the state's interest account only when the installment fell due. Instead of receiving interest on the entire unpaid balance each period, the state received interest on each installment for the entire period it had been in the bank's possession when that installment fell due. Thus, instead of receiving three months interest at six percent on the $3,700,000 in bonds held by the banks the first quarter, the state received three months interest at six percent on $250,000, which was the quarterly installment. At the last payment, instead of receiving nothing because the unpaid balance was zero, the state would receive forty-five months interest at six percent on that installment. Because interest due on unpaid installments grew instead of diminished over time, the charges against the state for interest on its entire bond issue were heaviest the first year, instead of the last, and the state was forced to meet almost all of the $150,000 due semi-annually on the loan from its own resources. Believing, however, that it was only liable for interest on the payments it had received, the state had issued anticipations for all but a small portion of the June installment, and was consequently forced to borrow $102,110 to meet its obligations to the bondholders. Finally, the state discovered that it was being charged half a percent interest for using funds from the interest account to pay interest due the bondholders because the state could only draw on the interest account at thirty days sight. As a result, the new contract accepted by the Governor in November cost the state $55,508 more than its financial arrangement under the contract of June 1, 1838. Although the state threatened legal action, it was finally forced to consent to the Bank's terms.[39] The state was plagued by serious financial difficulties throughout 1839, even though it had sold its bonds to the nation's strongest banking institution and gained assurance that installments would be paid promptly. Through Mason's three contract modifications, the state lost $121,881 in negotiation of the five million loan, exclusive of the Governor's expenses.[40]

The state's losses through contract modifications, however, were small when compared with the money lost through currency support and speculation. Governor Mason's willingness to use receipts from the state loan to support notes of Michigan's banks was clearly illustrated in his previously cited letter to Delafield and statements to the Legislature. The Governor was willing to use exchange deposited in the East to redeem the notes of local banks at substantial discounts, or to sell exchange on the East in Detroit. At the same time, the state deposit bank fell under the control of its cashier, John R. Norton, the Governor's staunch political ally. The president of the bank later testified:

> Mr. Norton assumed the exclusive control of the bank as represent-ing the majority of the stock held in the east, and to have the power to turn out of the bank such officers as he pleased. When the board of directors ought, lately, to have met, either they or Mr. Norton did not attend, and no important business could be done, nor control exercised over the operations of the bank. In May 1838, witness told Mr. Webb how matters were going on, and unless proxies from the eastern stock-holders were sent on to some other person than Mr. Norton, matters would result badly; told him of the connection between governor Mason and Mr. Norton, which was of a very intimate and confidential nature....For several months previous to this [the Bank's failure in February, 1839] probably nearly a year, witness had not been in Mr. Norton's confidence. When a certain set of persons was in Mr. Norton's room, and witness came in, they all went out. The set consisted partly of Mr. Pritchette, governor Mason and Henry Howard.[41]

From January 1, 1838, after the Governor had arranged for sale of the securities to Oliver Newberry for exchange speculation, and just before his first draft on John Delafield at the Phoenix Bank for the same purpose, the Michigan State Bank began to receive wildcat notes among its general deposits, a practice that continued until the first week in November. In October, while Norton was absent, the assistant cashier and the president decided to stop receiving the notes, which included most of the funds deposited from the receipts of the Central Railroad. When Norton returned to Detroit, he ordered the bank to continue receiving the notes, explaining that refusing to accept them was causing disturbances in the country. On November 1, 1838 the assistant cashier asked how long the bank would continue to honor wildcat notes, and was told by Norton that the practice would be stopped in two or three days. Immediately after the fall elections, Norton ordered the bank to refuse the notes of free charter banks.[42]

In attempting to back the issues of Michigan's country banks, Norton was acting with the Governor's encouragement. Although for a few days in June, Mason considered setting up his own bank, his support of Norton's currency operations increased after he finally marketed the state's bonds. Early in August 1838, the Governor attempted to include all of Detroit's special charter banks in his efforts. On August 2, in a circular letter sent through John Norton, stating his long standing concern about the condition of the banks, the Governor offered to back the city banks with all the eastern credit at his command to sustain them in a run for specie if they would expand their issues. In addition to furnishing a greater supply of money for marketing crops, the measure was designed to give credit in the city to the paper of all solvent country banks. An attached memorandum offered to give the banks drafts for $25,000 in August and $15,000 on the first of each month if they would be parties to the agreement: "If the city banks can throw into the interior of the State a circulating medium of their own paper, the country banks will be enabled to settle their balances at their own counter satisfactorily to the banks of the city." A note on the back of the memorandum in Mason's distinctive hand recorded the proposition's fate: "Rejected by all but Michigan State Bank, S. T. M."[43] On August 6, the Governor was forced to write to E. R. Biddle, asking him to cancel the authorization to accept drafts from the various city banks. "The banks above named having failed to comply with an arrangement proposed for the relief of the country these drafts have been withdrawn & cancelled, and a draft for the whole amount $75,000 substituted in favor of John Norton Jr. Cashier of the Michigan State Bank."[44]

On February 29, 1839, the Michigan State Bank went to the wall, carrying with it $514,540 in state deposits. Most of the state funds were credited to accounts of the state's internal improvement program. Overdrafts allowed by the bank to members of the Board of Internal Improvements, many of them unauthorized, reduced the state's claims to $349,296. Senate investigating committees blamed the suspension on the bank's practices of enlarging its discount of paper on state funds, allowing unlimited overdrafts to individuals and public contractors, extending illegal advances to public officials to help them evade the law, and receiving the notes of wildcat banks. In addition, it accused the cashier of substituting wildcat notes for good money in bundles of state funds placed in the bank's vault for storage (i.e., not deposited). After several investigations, the state reached a settlement on May 15, 1840. Assets with a nominal value of $797,000 were assigned to the state in satisfaction of its claims, but only a small portion of the settlement was ever realized. Indeed, the state never pressed its claims with vigor; lists of the assets accepted reveal heavy claims against most of the state's prominent citizens.[45] No administration attempting to realize the claims could have survived.[46]

After the bank's failure, the Legislature accepted the Governor's recommendation to create a state bank on the model of the Bank of the United States. Hoping to prevent depreciation by controlling note issues, the Democratic Legislature discovered the principle that: "The common system of banking is unequal, and constitutes a moneyed monopoly when conducted by chartered companies, and is calculated to combine individual wealth into powerful, and too often fraudulent compacts," A state bank, receiving state deposits, would be capable of controlling the issues of any chartered bank. By combining the capital of the people with the capital of the state, the legislature hoped to divert the profits of banking to the state government, and reduce the burden of taxation. The act provided for a system joining public and private credit equally in the capital of the bank, while reserving control to the government. Several branches were chartered to allow the bank to disburse local benefits and harness local capital. The state was forced to drop the plan, however, when it was unable to borrow enough specie to initiate the bank.[47]

In November 1839, Governor Mason attempted a final modification of the loan contract; he sent his law partner, Kintzing Pritchette, to New York to negotiate its cancellation. During the fall election campaign, the Whigs had promised to repeal the Internal Improvements Act and cancel the loan; around January 1, 1840, Governor-elect William Woodbridge had called on Mason to inquire into the possibility of terminating the contract.[48] Between elections and assuming power, however, the Whigs changed their minds. In negotiations between December 20 and February 1, Pritchette gained an agreement from both banks to return the unpaid balance of the state's bonds. During the negotiations, T. Dunlap, new president of the Bank of the United States, informed Pritchette that all Michigan's bonds had been transmitted to Europe, "and either sold or disposed of for a period of time." Finally, however, Pritchette brought the bank to terms through its New York office and returned to Michigan with agreements for the state's ratification.[49] The new Whig Legislature, ostensibly angered by the Governor's assumed authority to act in their stead, refused to have anything to do with the contract, and accused Mason of being involved in a secret plot to defraud the state. The former Governor was charged with attempting to discredit the Whig party by depriving the new administration of its only financial resources, and bankrupting the state for his own political advantage.[50] As a consequence, the agreement negotiated by Pritchette was never put into effect.

The Whig position on Pritchette's negotiations, although presented in the form of a political diatribe, was predicated on the essentially sound assumption that canceling the loan would bankrupt the state. Taxes due from the counties were heavily in arrears, in some cases almost three years, and warrants issued for internal improvements, along with iron contracts, appropriations for state expenses, and outstanding claims threatened to consume all the installments due on the loan through April 1841. To have canceled the loan would have meant bankruptcy with a suspended debt equal to ten times the annual state tax assessment at a time when the counties were almost unanimously refusing to meet current taxes.[51] The Legislature took advantage, however, of E. R. Biddle's offer extended during the negotiations to grant security for the state's future installments from the Morris Bank. At the end of March 1840, the State Treasurer, Robert Stuart, was required to secure the balance due the state.[52]

While Stuart was en route to New York, the Morris Bank and Canal Company failed, rejecting drafts on the April installment. Learning that it would take at least eight weeks to effect a settlement, Stuart turned to the Bank of the United States, only to find that the Bank refused to honor its obligation to meet the Morris Bank's share of the installment. Attempts to reach a settlement with the Morris Bank were extended through December, due primarily to the protracted absences of E. R. Biddle, who had recently discovered the delights of touring isolated areas in the mountains of western Pennsylvania. During one of these absences, Stuart gained access to the company's files and contracts, where he uncovered evidence to support a chancery bill asking for damages and custody of documents outlining the agreements between Mason, Romeyne, and the Morris Bank. E. R. Biddle attempted to convince him that the state's best interests would be served by taking a second mortgage on the Morris Canal and advancing money for its enlargement; the Indiana loan commissioner had been persuaded to make such a settlement. Stuart, however, was not impressed: "They made me the offer, *alone*, or jointly with him: *but as the Clinton Canal may be enough for our purposes*, I declined, greatly to their astonishment, *as they said.*" Failing to reach an adequate settlement, Stuart filed his chancery bill and began attaching the company's property. He reported on November 30: "The Chancery Bill has tamed them like lambs, & I think they have offered us *now*, all the security they can give...." If the bank would supply security for half of the sum outstanding, Stuart stated, he would consider the state fortunate.[53]

Stuart's report was submitted to the Legislature on January 14, 1841. When the Morris Bank failed, it owed the state $737,500 in principal, or $823,000 with interest on unpaid installments from January 1, 1839. In place of the unpaid bonds, the company had offered assets with a nominal value of $621,000, in return for an agreement by the state to postpone collection until January 1, 1844. After that date, its obligations were to be paid with interest in annual installments of $100,000. The property offered as security consisted mainly of farm and coal lands in Pennsylvania and New Jersey, obligations to deliver iron, railroad stock and a judgment against the Long Island Railroad, and title to the Morris Bank's New York office. Stuart had been impressed by the company's plans for widening their canal, and their connection with Pennsylvania's internal improvements, which held promise of allowing them to dominate the New York coal market. He had hopes of the state being paid if it waited patiently. Impressed by Stuart's recommendations, the Legislature granted the Treasurer full authority to effect a settlement.[54] Stuart's hopes that lenient treatment would allow the state to recoup its losses proved to be in vain, however; as time passed the value of the pledged securities dwindled. Only a little over $20,000 was ever collected on the collateral security.

Even before the Legislature authorized Stuart to accept the Morris Bank's offer, the Bank of the United States closed its doors. Although the Bank failed in February, no action could be taken until two months later, when the state's drafts against the April installment were protested. The Bank immediately offered to pay the installment in its own notes, but the state refused to accept them because they were at a fifteen to twenty percent discount. Under pressure from the state, drafts on the April and July installments were finally met by deposits of funds current in New York. In October, however, the state's drafts were again protested, and no further payments were received. With its failure to honor the Treasurer's drafts in October, the Bank defaulted on six remaining payments for a total of $1,306,312, including interest falling due on unpaid installments.[55] When the new Democratic Legislature met in January 1842, it was already in default on interest payments to its bondholders, because interest was to be met from installments through January 1843.

During the two years they controlled the state government, the Whigs continued the Democracy's policy of avoiding unpopular and impracticable tax increases. Faced with an empty treasury and large amounts of delinquent taxes, the Whigs continued the Democratic practice of raiding the internal improvement fund to support expenditures charged to the general fund. In 1838, the Democrats had begun the practice of financing the state government by shifting $80,000 of the federal surplus revenue deposit to the general fund. After 1839, when the Michigan State Bank failure wiped out the entire balance, the state continued to finance its operations by transferring money from the internal improvements fund under the guise of drawing against the federal surplus deposits. Since the only sums accruing to the internal improvements funds were payments on the five million loan, it is clear that both parties were diverting the loan to the use of the state government. In an effort to offset the loss of revenues available to the public works program, the Whigs raided the sinking fund and credited the proceeds to internal improvement, a clear breach of faith with its bondholders.[56]

Throughout 1840 and 1841, the Whigs continued another practice initiated by the Democrats in 1839, financing the public works by anticipating installments of the five million loan. After the Michigan State Bank failure, the Democrats provided funds for construction by selling anticipations to the Bank of Michigan, which in turn issued its notes to the internal improvements commissioners to pay contractors. In March 1840, the Whigs continued the practice by authorizing the Auditor General to sell drafts on the next five installments. By 1841, however, the Bank of Michigan was experiencing serious difficulties, and the state began issuing its own anticipations. An act of April 1841 authorized the Treasurer to engrave and issue notes for one, two, five, and ten dollars against the next four installments of the loan.[57] Only two of the four installments were ever received by the state, and anticipations for remaining installments could not be redeemed. The balance formed a floating debt, usually referred to as Treasury Notes or scrip in contemporary accounts, which the Democrats were forced to redeem after they regained control in 1842.

Partial relief was promised when Congress passed the Preemption Act in the autumn of 1841. This act awarded Michigan ten percent of the proceeds of all public land sales within her borders plus a proportional share of federal land revenues after ten percent had been awarded to other states named in the act. In addition, half a million acres of public land within the state's boundaries were awarded for purposes of internal improvements, with the stipulation that the lands be sold at the minimum government price of $1.25 per acre. The revenue promised by the act proved elusive, however, and in 1842 Congress repealed the award of ten percent. The act's general distribution clause remained in operation a few months longer before it was suspended, and although the legislation was nominally in effect until 1862, Michigan realized very little revenue from the sale of her public lands. Michigan Democrats, who supported the theory that the state already possessed the lands, doubted the propriety of accepting the federal grant. Constitutional scruples were laid aside, however, when Governor Barry assured the Legislature that accepting what was already theirs would not compromise the state's claim to the balance. Although the grant was accepted in January 1842, it could not be put to use for at least a year because the lands had to be located and machinery created for marketing it. Thus the federal land grant was of little help to Michigan through 1842.[58]

When the Democracy returned to power in January 1842, it concentrated on staving off bankruptcy and waiting for the crisis to pass. There were few major changes in the state's system of finance or methods of supporting the internal improvements program. Further appropriation awaited the location of lands granted by the federal government. Funds were provided during the year by the issue of auditor's warrants.

Governor Barry's inaugural message made it clear that he considered the treasury notes issued by the Whigs unconstitutional and preferred the substitution of auditor's warrants: treasury notes constituted an issue of currency, while auditor's warrants were only promissory notes. Barry also warned the Legislature that failure of the Bank of the United States had made the general fund liable for redemption of the treasury notes, which would consume state revenues for more than two years. If the system were allowed to continue, the state would be without funds of any kind until 1844. Since the scrip had been issued to finance the public works, the Governor recommended that the railroads be made to absorb the burden.[59]

The Governor's suggestions were quickly enacted by the Legislature. An act of February 10, 1842 ordered that treasury notes received by the public works be canceled and destroyed, and the internal improvements sinking fund made liable for redemption of treasury notes received by other government agencies. State officers were forbidden to accept anything but gold, silver, Michigan treasury notes, or notes of specie-paying banks in settling debts due the state. In effect, the Legislature again raided the sinking fund to support the general fund and finance further construction of public works.[60]

The most pressing problem confronting the Legislature in 1842 was effecting a settlement for the unpaid balance on its bonds. This problem remained the most perplexing issue before the state for the next four years. It is clear from both the statements and actions of the Legislature between 1842 and 1846 that it never seriously considered repudiation of its debts. It is equally clear, however, that the legislators had no intention of honoring bonds for which payment had not been received. Their efforts during these years were concentrated on reaching an acceptable settlement within these limitations.

Governor Barry's inaugural message urged the Legislature to work out a settlement consistent with maintaining the state's faith and credit; every just debt had to be acknowledged. But he cautioned against submitting to any settlement that would make the people liable for unjust debts. Recommending the organization of a commission to negotiate a settlement with the banks, Barry stated that the commission should keep in mind that the state had suffered damages from the bank suspensions. If no settlement could be reached, the committee should attempt to learn the names of the bonds' current holders, and report their findings to the Legislature.[61]

By taking events out of context and overemphasizing the defeat of resolutions categorically rejecting the doctrine of repudiation in both the House and Senate, earlier writers have created the impression that Michigan hung on the brink of repudiation in 1842. The strength of public support for repudiation is allegedly indicated by the fact that those resolutions were rejected eight to five in the Senate, and forty to six in the House.[62] This evidence creates a distorted impression if the context of the debate in which the resolutions were offered is not considered. The Senate had been debating proposals to adopt statements reserving the right to contest the legality of bonds for which the state had received no payment. A substitute measure, listing the damages suffered by the state through nonpayment by the banks and warning potential investors against accepting the unpaid bonds, had already been accepted and was up for third reading when Senator Fuller proposed that the resolution be amended to read:

> *Resolved.* That the doctrine that might makes right, and that therefore a state or nation may, by virtue of its sovereignty, repudiate an honest debt, is unworthy of the age and of a free people, and wherever else it may have found a response belongs not to the moral and political code of the people of Michigan.[63]

Fuller's resolution was itself out of context with the resolution on the floor of the Senate. Moreover, in terms of the Legislature's consistent use of the term repudiation. Fuller's resolution would not have prevented the state from refusing to honor its unpaid bonds, as it condemned only the repudiation of *just* debts, and the bonds for which Michigan had received no payment were never considered just debts. Neither rejection nor acceptance of Fuller's amendment would have had any real significance.

A resolution entered in the House by Norman Little cited the growing lack of faith in state securities and agitation for repudiation in Michigan's newspapers, and denied that the doctrine of repudiation had any place in Michigan's public policy. But earlier writers have failed to cite the complete resolution. In addition to its anti-repudiation clause, the bill also read:

> *Resolved.* That the committee of ways and means be requested to report to this House, a bill for the payment of interest now due, and to become due the present year and the first of January next, on the bonds of this state.[64]

Little's resolution would have required a state incapable of raising one hundred thousand dollars for domestic expenses to increase taxes to supply four hundred and fifty thousand dollars within ten months for payment of interest not only on bonds for which the state had been paid, but also on those for which it had received no payment. Whether the House rejected the resolution for its anti-repudiation clause or its taxation clause cannot be determined. That it would reject those bonds for which it had received no payment was well understood, and in place of the several bills and resolutions offered during debate, a bill was passed that revealed the state's actual plans for adjustment of the five million loan.[65]

The adjustment proposed by the Act of February 17, 1842, required the Attorney General and State Treasurer to make out a statement of money received by the state from the loan and the two hundred thousand dollars in ʾsecurities issued for the railroads' benefit, plus interest accruing from July 1, 1841. Damages were to be assessed against the contracting parties for failure to pay installments, and expressed as a percentage of the unpaid balance. After damages had been deducted from receipts, the estimate was to be submitted to the Governor, who was required to issue a proclamation in papers in Michigan, New York, and Philadelphia, requiring holders of the state's bonds to deliver them to the Treasurer. After the amount for which the state had received no value had been deducted along with damages and interest, new bonds were to be issued for the balance. When all the bonds had been returned and canceled, the Secretary of State was authorized to enter negotiations with the holders of the new bonds for sale of the railroads and other public works at either cost or present fair valuation, along with any lands received from the federal grant necessary to satisfy the state's obligations.[66]

Apparently fearing that the settlement would not be adequate if left to the Treasurer and Auditor General, the Legislature set the rate of damages due the state at twenty-five percent of the unpaid installments on the day the adjustment act became law. The Governor issued the proclamation required by law on April 7. Holders of the state's bonds were given the option of returning the whole sum and having new bonds issued for a total of $2,342,960, or returning $2,857,039 for simple cancellation. If the bonds were returned, the Governor promised to offer the state's public works for sale.[67]

Previous historians have maintained that the Legislature's dictation of the terms of settlement was a clear-cut case of repudiation under the strict definition that repudiation constitutes refusal to acknowledge or pay a debt. According to this interpretation, when the state put its bonds in the hands of the Bank of the United States, the terms of the agreement constituted a clear sale of negotiable securities payable at face value. The state's legitimate quarrel, then, was with the banks, which held the balance of the proceeds of the sale. Under the existing laws of commerce, third parties (the bondholders) were liable for neither the nonfulfillment of contract nor the damages chargeable to the bank's failure.[68]

The state, however, never accepted the existence of a third party that could be defrauded. Although it had been known from the time of Pritchette's negotiations in the winter of 1839 that the Bank of the United States had hypothecated the bonds abroad, the fate of the securities and the terms under which they had been held by the Bank's foreign creditors were unknown in 1842.[69] Two years earlier, both parties to the contract had offered to return the balance of the unpaid bonds, and in allowing bondholders to return securities equal to the unpaid balance, the Legislature was clearly acting on the assumption that a single holder, or holders in the case of the contracting banks, still had possession of the securities and could return them without damaging their equity. The alternate course proposed, allowing the holders to submit their bonds for partial cancellation of the face value, was similarly based on the assumption that the holders were a single group capable of acting in concert. In subsequent reports, the Legislature claimed that the act had been meant as a warning, to keep the banks from disposing of the bonds before the state could cancel the unpaid balance. Throughout its negotiations with the bondholders, the state consistently took the position that the bonds placed in the hands of the Bank of the United States under the agreements of November 1838 and January 1839 were legally in the Bank's possession when the state made known its refusal to honor the unpaid balance.[70]

Neither interpretation is supported by conclusive evidence. Governor Mason's contract with the Bank of the United States consists of an inconclusive letter and an obligation by the Bank to pay installments at stipulated periods. Mason's statements on whether the transaction was an agency or a sale are typically inconsistent and cannot be cited as evidence for either side. Evidence presented by legislative committees in 1845 and 1847, supposedly taken from annual reports of the Bank's trustees, along with actions of the state's foreign bondholders, tends to support the contention that the Bank still had control over the securities hypothecated abroad. A search of relevant archives has failed to uncover these reports, however, so the committees' assertions constitute only hearsay evidence.[71]

Response to the Governor's proclamation was nominal; by 1843, none of the state's bondholders had submitted their bonds for adjustment. Under pressure from bondholders who had paid full value, the state attempted to work out a new solution. In December 1842, the State Treasurer completed his tabulation of the holders of Michigan's bonds, enabling the Legislature to discriminate between those who had paid a full consideration and those holding bonds as security. In his annual message, the Governor reported that bonds with a face value of $3,855,000 were still the property of the Bank of the United States, hypothecated to foreign banking houses, and added that: "The circumstances of the hypothecation warrant the belief that the equity existing between the states and the Bank has been in no way affected by that transaction." Both the message and the Treasurer's tabulation were submitted to the Legislature for consideration.[72]

Late in January, Charles Butler, who had been hired to protect the interests of Michigan's creditors, arrived in Detroit to lobby for the bondholders who had purchased their securities before November 1838. Butler presented documents to the Legislature in which he claimed to represent $1,362,000 worth of bonds held mainly by New York banks which had acquired them from a lot purchased by the Farmer's Loan and Trust Co., from the Morris Canal and Banking Company under its original agency.

If Butler's account of subsequent proceedings is accepted, he alone was responsible for the act that followed. Butler was prone to exaggerate his accomplishments, however, and his account provides an interesting supplement, rather than a sound basis for description of the Legislature's attitude.[73]

Before Butler's arrival, a bill embodying most of his recommendations had been introduced in the Senate. In a letter to the Senate submitted February 1, Butler stated the bondholders' case. Bonds purchased before the state's contract with the Bank of the United States were purchased in good faith and in no way affected by the subsequent transactions of that company and the state; these purchasers disassociated themselves completely from those who had accepted Michigan's bonds at a later date. By January 1843, the state was a year and a half in arrears in its interest payments, and the parties insisted on their right to payment in specie or its equivalent; if the state could not pay, then it would have to issue bonds for the interest and compensate the holders by a greater determination to pay at the end of the time negotiated. Butler further argued that the state had no right to divert the proceeds of the railroads to finance their continuation, since these funds had been pledged to the bondholders at the time of their sale. In either case, the holders of the bonds would have to be compensated by January 1, 1844. If the state's revenues were inadequate for redemption of interest, the state would have to resort to taxation to redeem its pledge of faith.[74]

In its answer to Butler, a Joint Committee made it clear that the state had no intention of repudiating its just debts. A new formula had been created for determining liability, however, based on the assumption that the state was a party to two separate contracts in marketing its bonds, one with the Morris Bank, and the other with the two banks together: "When the *terms* of that contract were broken and violated by the faithlessness and defaults of that party, the faith of the state was no longer pledged for the fulfillment on her part, under that contract." In short, the state would honor all bonds sold under its first contract, but had no intention of honoring either principal or interest on sums not received from the bonds which it regarded as still in the legal possession of the Bank of the United States. Although the committee took issue with Butler on almost every point, its only serious difference with the representative of the New York bondholders was over their right to demand taxation by the state to support the bonds. The only specific pledge given by the state, the committee argued, was its pledge of faith to apply the proceeds of its public works, loans, and bank stock to the redemption of principal and interest. "The pledge was undoubtedly given in good faith, and intended to mean just what it states." Both the state and the bondholders were the victims of bank failure, and both parties should realize that interest could not be required on their investment until the programs were completed. The committee warned that it would be advisable for the bondholders to exercise restraint in their claims, instead of forcing the state to an act of desperation.[75]

Despite official protests, the Senate passed a bill satisfactory to Butler, including a taxation clause, by a margin of twelve to four.[76] The House Committee on Ways and Means, although reporting the bill favorably, recommended that resumption of interest payments be postponed until at least July 1, 1845: " Notwithstanding the earnestness and urgency with which the agent of a large portion of the bond holders has insisted on earlier payment of interest money, yet the committee are of the unanimous opinion that earlier payment would be bad policy, and alike injurious to the state and to the bona fide bond holders." After appropriate protest, the bill was amended according to the committee's recommendations and passed by a vote of twenty-eight to twenty.[77] Although Butler claimed there were long speeches favoring repudiation—and it is likely that there were—it is apparent from his descriptions that he considered anyone who opposed his own solution as being in favor of repudiation.   The Senate accepted the amended version, which was then sent to the Governor. It was widely feared Barry might exercise his veto power, but, after lengthy consultation, he signed the bill. According to Butler, the Governor's reluctance stemmed from a belief that the taxation would mean his defeat in the fall elections.[78]

The act passed by the Legislature on March 8, 1843, provided an equitable settlement for holders of bonds purchased before November 10, 1838. Specifying the eligible bonds by number, the act reaffirmed the state's intentions of honoring both principal and interest, and authorized the Governor to issue interest bonds covering payments from July 1, 1841 to July 1, 1845, whenever the bondholders surrendered their coupons for interest due between those dates. The interest bonds would be redeemed in 1850, and the state would resume interest payments on both the original and interest bonds on July 1, 1845. The total value of securities honored under this arrangement was $1,387,000, including $1,187,000 reported sold before November 10, 1838, and $200,000 reported sold by Oliver Newberry. The net proceeds of the state's public works were pledged to support its debts, but with certain exceptions: the state reserved the right to appropriate these funds for completion of the Central Railroad to Marshall and the Southern Railroad to Hillsdale, for the purchase of rolling stock and locomotives, and for redemption of scrip. Obviously, the state was reserving the proceeds of the roads to put them in condition to earn money to pay interest on the bonds when it fell due. Under the terms of the act, if these revenues were not sufficient, the Treasurer was authorized to pay out any funds in the Treasury to make up the balance, and to levy taxes if these resources failed. In addition, interest bonds were to be accepted in payment for lands held by the state after July 1, 1845.[79]

Granting full credit to the holders of the fully paid bonds did not increase the state's total liability; losses were recouped by shifting financial responsibility to the holders of the partially paid bonds. Bonds taken by the Morris Canal and Banking Company, and the Bank of the United States after November 10, 1838 which were hypothecated abroad and only partially paid when the Bank failed, were credited with payments received after November

10, after twenty-five percent damages charged against the unpaid balance had been deducted. According to the report of the House Committee on Ways and Means, this amounted to $998,000 against bonds with a face value of $3,813,000. The act required the two banks to deliver these bonds for cancellation of their face values. Once canceled, interest bonds from July 1, 1841, to July 1, 1845 would be issued against the adjusted balance, and the bonds treated in the same manner as the fully paid securities.[80]

The act of March 8, 1843 formulated the state's basic policy toward its bonds and bondholders. From time to time, the rate of damages was adjusted downward, but no change was made in the basic repayment formula. Michigan's actions were severly rebuked in public journals both in the United States and abroad. Michigan was classified as a repudiating state because it had violated the mercantile principle that: "If a purchaser gives a bill of exchange for goods he has a perfect right to sell, the vendor cannot cancel this right, and make the ultimate purchasers the sufferers, because the bill happens to be dishonored."[81] The Legislature, however, was undisturbed by the clamor, and holders of the fully paid bonds were quick to turn in their interest coupons for funding.[82]

Having dealt with its outstanding debts, the state returned to the problem of financing its internal improvements program. New patterns of supplying resources had to be adopted for the program between 1843 and 1846. By order of the Legislature, all scrip then in the Treasury and unissued notes were to be destroyed, along with the plates. At the same time, a land office was opened in Marshall and authorized to accept land warrants in payment. Following federal practice, all lands for sale had to be exposed to auction before being offered for private sale at the minimum price of one dollar and twenty-five cents per acre. Most of the lands offered under the federal grant were located in the western end of the Grand River Valley and the area directly north.[83] With these resources and those realized by the bond settlement, the state adopted a pattern of appropriating public lands to pay local contractors, and pledging the receipts of its public works to purchase iron, locomotives, and rolling stock.

The new system was subject to serious limitations. Endless delays resulted because the purchase of iron was restricted by the railroads' earning power, and their net receipts were often in scrip which had to be destroyed. The progress of grubbing, grading, and bridging was similarly restricted by the market's ability to absorb land warrants. Even though construction was not limited by the land grant's ability to produce cash, warrants depreciated when issued in excess of demand, raising contractors' bids above acceptable limits. When this situation developed, construction had to wait until settlement had absorded enough lands to appreciate warrants and increase the demand for state lands. Although the system enabled the state to finance construction, extension of the roads was slowed by the lack of ready cash.[84]

During his annual message to the Legislature in 1845, Governor Barry again brought up the matter of the part-paid bonds. Although refusing to comment on the justice of certain bondholders' claims, the Governor made it clear that the equity between the state and the Bank had in no way been affected by the Bank's transfer of these securities to their present holders. He asked, however, that the Legislature reconsider the damage assessments set by the 1842 and 1843 acts. Later in the session he sent down three memorials from the state's European bondholders.[85]

The first of these memorials, presented by Morrison, Sons & Co., stated that they had advanced money to the Bank of the United States, for which they had received $262,000 in Michigan bonds as security. The bonds were deposited with them as the Bank's agents, and in this capacity they had loaned more money than could ever be liquidated by sale of the bonds. After settling with the Bank on June 9, 1843, there remained a sum outstanding equal to the amount originally loaned against the securities, "in satisfaction of which we were obliged to take the Michigan State bonds which we still hold."

The second and third memorials, signed respectively by the secretary and members of the Committee of Michigan Bond-holders, argued against the state's legal right to discriminate between holders or pay anything other than the face value of the bonds, with interest. The bondholders maintained that the bonds received in trust by the Bank's foreign creditors were accepted in a deed of trust which conveyed the absolute power of disposing of them without reference to the Bank in case of its default and deprived the Bank of all right to interefer without repaying the loan made by European creditors. The transfer of the stocks, when the Bank was unable to pay their advances, was absolute, and could not be disputed by the state. Moreover, Denison & Co., which had originally received the bonds held by the Committee, claimed to have received no prior notice of the state's intention of disputing their right of possession. The laws of both England and America recognized the rights of the innocent holder of this kind of property, even though the party from whom it had been received had no right of transfer. The state had failed to warn the current holders not to accept before they were transferred, or when the Bank was still able to substitute other securities; consequently the state was liable for payment. Since the Legislature made no objection to the contract at the time of its consumation on the basis of fraud, illegality, or impropriety, and accepted the installments, the Committee argued that the contract was valid. Moreover, the memorialists contended that the Bank of the United States alone had paid the state a total of $1,838,687.50, instead of the $998,000, which the state recognized, after deducting damages.[86] Finally, they accused the state of deducting damages against the entire loan from the bonds sold after November 10, and asserted that the installment received by the state from the Morris Canal and Banking Company in 1843 proved that damages were assessed against the whole loan and not the disputed part. All bondholders would have to be treated equally, without discrimination against Europeans.[87]

A Joint Committee appointed by the Legislature to deal with the claims attempted to refute the bondholders arguments. Much of its effort was directed toward correcting erroneous impressions created by the memorials:

damages were charged only against the unpaid balance, and the entry in the state's books credited to the Morris Canal and Banking Company was the result of liquidating collateral pledged by the company for the bondholders' protection. The Joint Committee concentrated, however, on establishing three basic points. The last annual report of the stockholders of the late United States Bank of Pennsylvania confirmed that the Bank had not yet consented to the sale of any of the Michigan bonds hypothecated in Europe, except the $272,000 pledged to Morrison, Sons & Co.; this left a balance of $3,583,000 on which the Bank had not permitted sale. Moreover, Morrison's petition stated that they had not gained or accepted full control of the bonds until June 9, 1843, thereby admitting that the previous hypothecation did not vest in them the rights of a purchaser. Finally, the Joint Committee argued that the Governor's 1842 proclamation could not be used as evidence that the state admitted the necessity of warning potential purchasers not to accept transfer because the proclamation had never forbidden transfer, but merely stipulated the rate at which transfer would be acceptable.

The committee denied that the bonds were legally subject to the same rules of transfer as commercial paper:

> Stocks and bonds cannot be regarded as commercial paper, giving to the innocent holder before due, the right of recovery, without reference to the equities between the original parties; but that the holder of such stocks at the time of his purchase is bound to ascertain the right to issue the same—the due legal execution, and the equitable terms, conditions and considerations attending the transfer and delivery by the state authority. The rule as to commercial paper, results, in part, from the established and well defined usages in commercial dealings and the necessity of credit in matters of business before paper is dishonored, and also, in part, from the existence of a fixed legal remedy for the enforcement of business engagements of that description.
>
> But the bonds and stocks of a state are based upon an entirely different footing. Ordinary business transactions do not necessarily demand credit for them. Neither is there a legal remedy provided.—The judicial tribunals of a state are but the creatures of its sovereignty, and cannot sit in judgement upon its acts and liabilities in that capacity.[88]

Furthermore, the Constitution did not allow the federal government to interfere with a state's rights in this capacity. The bonds could only be regarded as pledges of faith, and a purchaser accepted them on the basis of that faith, not on the legal remedies devised for commercial paper: "That faith will be kept inviolate when deliberately extended, and rightfully obtained, whilst inceptive fraud in procuring the pledge, will ever vitiate the engagement at maturity."[89]

The Joint Committee also maintained that the legal and equitable rights of the holders of such bonds or stocks by absolute purchase differed greatly from those of pledges of collateral security. Holders of the latter were obligated to exhaust the assets of the principal before resorting to the security. This, the memorialists had not done, since the Bank's stock was still circulating at five and one-half percent, and the assets still had some value. Moreover, in addition to denying discrimination against Europeans, the state claimed the memorialists were guilty of discrimination when they sold the hypothecated Mississippi and Pennsylvania bonds at market value while demanding that Michigan restore full value.

W. L. Jenks, an attorney, comparing the Joint Committee's arguments to a brief presented "by a pettifogging lawyer in behalf of a client with a bad case," stated: "The legal doctrines thus propounded by the Committee find no support in any legal treatise or Court decision."[90] Jenks' interpretation of the law of commercial transactions is unassailable, but he errs in asserting that state securities were absolutely governed by commercial law. The eleventh amendment of the United States Constitution gave the several states immunity from prosecution by citizens of other or foreign states in federal courts. This immunity had been in effect for forty years before the state marketed its bonds and was clearly understood at the time the state negotiated its agreement with the Bank. The state had every *legal* right to adjust its securities by any means it chose; to have done otherwise would have, in effect, violated the eleventh amendment. What the state was attempting to prove, and this Jenks overlooks entirely, was that it had legitimate grievances which commercial law would not recognize, and the state, under the Democratic Party, was by its actions and assertions, writing law and not reading it.

Although the Legislature would probably have refused to honor the unpaid balance if the bonds had simply been sold abroad before October 1842, the state had a legitimate grievance. Several European financial houses were deeply involved with the Bank of the United States in its attempt to control international exchange and frustrate the contractions of the Bank of England. These houses had extended additional credit to the Bank of the United States when the Bank suspended in 1839 to avoid having their own assets destroyed by its failure. Neither the Bank nor its creditors were entirely candid in revealing the terms of the European houses' acceptance of pledges of American state securities, which have never been fully disclosed. In the case of Michigan, its securities had apparently remained under the Bank's control until the act of March 8, 1843 ordered their return for cancellation of unpaid portions. By its own admission, Morrison's accepted these securities from the trustees in full payment of its advances on June 9, 1843, when it could legitimately have asked for the assignment of uncontested assets in their place. The balance of the securities, some $3,583,000, remained under the Bank's control until after January 1, 1846, when foreign creditors accepted them in satisfaction of their advances. The Legislature cited trustees' reports which apparently revealed that although hypothecated abroad, the bonds "were still the property of that institution, and held by the trustees as part of its assets."[91] Although these reports do not seem to be extant, the date of the protests confirms the Legislature's assertions. The Bank had already demonstrated its ability to obtain the return of Michigan's bonds during its negotiations with Kintzing Pritchette in 1840. In failing to return the unpaid securities and substitute undisputed assets to secure its debts, the Bank or its trustees were guilty of bad faith. The European houses were equally guilty when they accepted disputed assets in settlement of their claims in the hope that commercial law would force the state to tax its citizens to recoup the Bank's losses in exchange and cotton support operations. The state could have legally resorted to simple repudiation, following the example of eight other American states; however, it attempted from the beginning to return value for value received. Its resort to its sovereignty and its unwillingness to apply commercial laws to its unpaid bonds were justified by the actions of both its agents and the houses receiving its bonds. By strict definition, its actions constituted partial repudiation, but the repudiation was mitigated.

Michigan's determination to return full value to its creditors and avoid repudiation of what it considered its just debts was nowhere more clearly demonstrated than between July 1, 1845 and December 1846. Under the terms of the act of 1843, the first interest payment fell due in July 1845, but no funds were available. Receipts of the Central and Southern, inadequate to pay interest on the entire loan in any case, were subject first to redemption of scrip, interest on internal improvements warrants, and debts incurred for iron and locomotives. Over two hundred thousand dollars in scrip had been redeemed, but only about twenty thousand dollars of the redemption had been through the internal improvements fund; the balance was a debt of that account to the primary school fund, the university fund, and the general fund, which had received the notes. Furthermore, the Board of Internal Improvements had informed the Legislature that the net proceeds of several years would be required to install the heavy T or H rails that would bring the roads to the performance level necessary to return the interest on the entire loan; to restore the roads to normal operating condition would require at least a year's revenue. About the same time, the bondholders apparently refused to allow the state further extensions on its postponement of interest payments. Without sufficient funds to meet its debts, the state was forced to resort to taxation. Fulfilling the terms of the act of 1843, the Auditor General informed the counties of the assessments required to meet interest payments on the adjusted debt.

When the Legislature met in 1846, its alternatives were severely restricted. Sectional rivalry and the constitutional amendment of 1843 seemingly prohibited further borrowing. Even if the domestic political situation would have permitted further bond issues, the state's refusal to accept potential lenders' interpretation of its responsibility made its credit worthless. The state had alienated the most powerful European bankers and brokers, including Baring's, Hope's, Rothschilds', Morrison's, and Denison's. Taxation was similarly prohibited by sectional rivalry. Three alternatives remained open: defaulting interest payments, repudiating its debts, or selling the public works to meet its obligations. To meet its acknowledged debts and to bring its railroads to the most efficient technological level, the

Legislature decided to sell. Default and repudiation never received serious consideration.[92]

Liquidation of the loan dragged on for half a century following sale of the public works. Under the terms of the sale, the state received $1,125,000 in bonds recognized as fully paid, and $119,000 in part-paid bonds at the rate of $403 per $1000, which was equivalent to $302 per $1000 face value plus interest from July 1, 1841. Although subsequent acts allowed individual redemption at this rate, few of the bonds were returned. By a suit in the Supreme Court of Pennsylvania, Hope & Co. and Rothschilds' won permission to force the trustees of the Bank of the United States to settle their accounts without first resorting to their collateral. In 1850, the accepted rate of redemption was written into the state's new constitution. Finally, an act passed in 1855 required the disputed bonds to be returned for cancellation of the unpaid balance, on penalty of suspending interest after the stipulated time limit. This threat broke the bondholders' resistance, and all but $215,000 were surrendered by the end of the year. Small quantities of the bonds continued to come in for years; in 1899, with only $21,000 outstanding, the Legislature canceled the balance on the presumption that they were either lost or destroyed.[93]

Michigan's experience with its "five million loan" was bitter and ultimately forced the sale of its public works. "Poor cyclical timing" cannot begin to explain what was essentially a human failure. In the end, Michigan's financial failure was the result of the Jacksonian Democracy's assault on central banking, and one man's futile attempt to apply a local corrective to the financial chaos the Democracy had created.

Notes, Chapter 9

1. Within the last half century, at least three studies of Michigan's loan have been published. The oldest of these, Lawton T. Hemans, *Life and Times of Stevens Thompson Mason, the Boy Governor of Michigan* (Lansing: Michigan Historical Commission, 1920), deals extensively with Mason's role as the state's chief financial agent for the loan between 1837 and 1840. Unfortunately, Hemans was not above suppression of evidence and fell prey to the biographer's natural sympathy for his subject. A second study, produced by William L. Jenks, "Michigan's Five Million Dollar Loan," *Michigan History*, XV (1931), pp. 575-634, has been considered a standard source by state and local historians for over thirty years. Although scholarly and exact, the strengths of Jenks' article are also its weakness: excessive preoccupation with legal details submerged the larger story and allowed him to avoid the evidence suppressed by Hemans. Unfortunately for Jenks, his work was published in a journal which prohibited documentation, and consigned it to the rank of folklore. Finally, a better known article, if less scholarly than Jenks', is chapter VIII of Reginald McGrane's *Foreign Bondholders and American State Debts* (New York: MacMillan, 1935).
2. Michigan, *Legislative Acts*, 1837, No. LXXVII.
3. I am aware in adopting this point of view that the evidence can support cases both for and against Mason's guilt. After thoroughly reviewing the evidence, cited in

subsequent notes, I am convinced of the validity of the Whig case. If anything, the Whigs neglected to discover the full story of Mason's illegal use of state funds.

4. Michigan, *House Document No. 44*, 1839, p. 721.
5. *Messages of the Governors of Michigan*, I, pp. 208-213; Michigan, *Legislative Acts*, 1837, Special Session, No. LX.
6. Letter from Stevens T. Mason to John Delafield, July 1837, in Records of the Office of Secretary of State, Great Seal and Archives: Claims submitted to the Legislature, 1837-1839 (Michigan Department of State, Historical Commission Archives); Michigan, *House Document No. 44*, 1839, p. 721.
7. *Ibid.*, p. 722.
8. Letter from Stevens T. Mason to John Delafield, November 6, 1837, in Records of the Office of Secretary of State, Great Seal and Archives: Claims submitted to the Legislature, 1837-1839 (Michigan Department of State, Historical Commission Archives).
9. Michigan, *House Journal*, Adjourned Session, 1837, pp. 5-6; Michigan, *Legislative Acts*, Adjourned Session, 1837, No. 1.
10. Letter from Stevens T. Mason to John Delafield, Nov. 15, 1837, in Records of the Office of Secretary of State, Great Seal and Archives: Claims submitted to the Legislature, 1837-1839 (Michigan Department of State, Historical Commission Archives).
11. Letter from Stevens T. Mason to John Delafield, November 21, 1837, *ibid.*
12. *Messages of the Governors of Michigan*, I, 219-236.
13. Letter from Stevens T. Mason to John Delafield, Jan. 6, 1837, Records of the Office of Secretary of State, Great Seal and Archives: Claims submitted to the Legislature, 1837-1839 (Michigan Department of State, Historical Commission Archives).
14. Letters from John Delafield to Oliver Newberry, Jan 26, 1838; John Delafield to Stevens T. Mason [copy], Jan. 23, 1838; Prime, Ward, & King to John Delafield, Jan. 27, 1838, *ibid.*
15. Letter from Stevens T. Mason to John Delafield, Feb. 6, 1838, *ibid.*
16. Letter from Stevens T. Mason to John Delafield, Feb. 19, 1838, *ibid.*
17. *Messages of the Governors of Michigan*, I, 239.
18. *Ibid.* This statement was completely false.
19. Letter from Stevens T. Mason to John Delafield, Feb. 24, 1838, in *Senate Document No. 37*, 1841, p. 97.
20. Stevens T. Mason, *To the People of Michigan* (Detroit, May 11, 1841), p. 17. Mason admitted the draft and letter, but defended himself by a statement from Norton that the money was for use by the bank, not for himself or personal friends. The fact that the funds were not granted in no way excuses his action.
21. Hidy, p. 261.
22. Letters from Prime, Ward, & King to John Delafield, April 10, 1838; Oliver Newberry to Messrs. John Ward & Co., April 16, 1838, in Records of the Office of Secretary of State, Great Seal and Archives: Claims submitted to the Legislature, 1837-1839 (Michigan Department of State, Historical Commission Archives). See also, Michigan, *House Document No. 44*, 1839, pp. 717-718.
23. Letter from Stevens T. Mason to John Delafield, April 26, 1838, Records of the Office of Secretary of State, Great Seal and Archives: Claims submitted to the Legislature, 1837-1839 (Michigan Department of State, Historical Commission Archives).
24. Letter from J. G. King to John Delafield, April 28, 1838, in Michigan, *Senate Document No. 37*, 1841, pp. 98-99. The incomplete document presented by Mason is in Michigan, *House Document No. 44*, 1839, pp. 720-721. Mason's defense is published in *To the People of Michigan*, p. 17. The certified copy of the original is in Records of the Office of Secretary of State, Great Seal and Archives: Claims submitted to the Legislature, 1837-1839.
25. Letter from J. D. Beers to John Delafield, May 30, 1838, *ibid.*; Michigan, *Senate*

Document No. 37, 1841, p. 99; Michigan, *House Document No. 44,* 1839, p. 718.

26. Letters from Stevens T. Mason to John Delafield, June 4, 1838, and June 5, 1838; Letter and Affidavit of John Delafield, Jan. 28, 1841, in Records of the Office of Secretary of State, Great Seal and Archives: Claims submitted to the Legislature, 1837-1839. Because of Mason's omissions and commissions, the story of the first year's negotiations has never been fully told. Hemans consistently refused to consider evidence unfavorable to Mason, and Jenks rarely ventured from the printed documents. In citing the documents presented by the Whigs from Delafield's folder, I have used only those which Mason later acknowledged, and citations include the construction placed on the evidence by all parties.

27. Letters from Prime, Ward & King to Jno. Delafield, May 11, 1838, and May 31, 1838; S. T. Mason to J. Delafield, May 19, 1838, and May 26, 1838, *ibid.*

28. Michigan, *House Document No. 44,* 1839, p. 722.

29. *Ibid.,* pp. 708-711.

30. *Ibid.,* pp. 711-712. Stevens T. Mason to John Delafield, June 4, 1838, in Records of the Office of Secretary of State, Great Seal and Archives: Claims submitted to the Legislature, 1837-1839.

31. Michigan, *House Document No. 44,* 1839, pp. 712-713.

32. *Ibid.,* p. 707.

33. *Ibid.,* p. 723. Italics mine.

34. Michigan, *Senate Document No. 37,* 1841, pp. 111-114.

35. *Ibid.*; Michigan, *House Document No. 44,* 1839; Mason, *To the People of Michigan*; Theodore Romeyne, *To the People of the State of Michigan* (Detroit, June 7, 1841); Draft of a letter from S. T. Mason to Edw. R. Biddle, July 15, 1838, in Records of the Office of Secretary of State, Great Seal and Archives: Five Million Dollar Loan (Michigan Department of State, Historical Commission Archives). In this letter, Mason acknowledges the second contract of June 4. Michigan, *Senate Journal,* 1841. p. 358, the senate deadlocked 7 to 7 on a resolution to censure Mason. The votes do not follow party lines absolutely.\

36. Letter from James B. Murray to Stevens T. Mason, August 1, 1838, in Records of the Executive Office, 1810-1910: Correspondence (Michigan Department of State, Historical Commission Archives); Letter from George Griswold to Stevens T. Mason, July 31, 1838, in Records of the Office of Secretary of State, Great Seal and Archives: Five Million Dollar Loan, 1835-1853 (Michigan Department of State, Historical Commission Archives).

37. Letters from S. T. Mason to E. R. Biddle, Nov. 3, 1838, Nov. 11, 1838; E. R. Biddle to S. T. Mason, Nov. 10, and Nov. 11, 1838, and in Michigan, *House Document No. 44,* 1839, pp. 712-717. Letter from S. T. Mason to Ruben Withers, Nov. 19, 1838, in Records of the Office of Secretary of State, Great Seal and Archives: Five Million Dollar Loan, 1835-1853 (Michigan Department of State, Historical Commission Archives); Letter from B. Murray to S. T. Mason, Nov. 7, [1838], in the S. T. Mason Papers (BHC).

38. Michigan, Legislature, *Report of the Auditor General* (*Senate Documents,* 1840, II, S. D. No. 3), pp. 274-276.

39. *Ibid.,* pp. 8-9, 272-273; *Messages of the Governors of Michigan,* I, 270; Michigan, Legislature, *Communication from the Auditor General* (*House Documents,* 1840, H. D. No. 49), pp. 831-833: Letter from S. T. Mason to C. C. Trowbridge, May 7, 1839, in Records of the Executive Office, 1810-1910: Correspondence (Michigan Department of State, Historical Commission Archives).

40. Michigan, *Senate Document No. 37,* 1841, pp. 112-114.

41. *Ibid.,* p. 137. It is important to note that the Michigan State Bank was a private institution chartered by the Legislature, in which the state had chosen to deposit its funds. The state did not own stock or appoint directors. The State Bank, chartered later, was a separate institution. In the records, both institutions have the same name, but the private institution can be distinguished by use of a lower case "b" in its corporate title—Michigan State bank.

42. Michigan, Legislature, *Report of the Special Committee appointed by the House of Representatives, to Investigate the Proceedings, & c., of the Several Boards of Internal Improvement* (Detroit: Dawson and Bates, 1840), pp. 388, 396.

43. Copy of a letter sent to John Norton by Stevens T. Mason, August 2, 1838, in Records of the Office of Secretary of State, Great Seal and Archives: Five Million Dollar Loan, 1835-1853 (Michigan Department of State, Historical Commission Archives). Another copy can be found in the John R. Norton Papers, Burton Historical Collections, under the date of August 4, 1838.

44. Draft in Mason's hand to E. R. Biddle, August 6, 1838, in Records of the Office of Secretary of State, Great Seal and Archives: Five Million Dollar Loan, 1835-1853 (Michigan Department of State, Historical Commission Archives). This is still the private bank.

45. Michigan, Legislature, *Report of the Committee appointed to settle the Claims of the State against the Michigan state bank* (*Senate Documents*, 1839, S. D. No. 36); Michigan, Legislature, *Report of the Committee on Incorporations* (*Senate Documents*, 1839, S. D. No. 37); Michigan, Legislature, *Report of the Select Committee appointed to investigate the conduct of the commissioners appointed to settle with the Michigan state bank* (*Senate Documents*, 1841, II, S. D. No. 42); Michigan, Legislature, *Report of the Commissioners Appointed by the Legislature to settle with the Michigan state bank* (*House Documents*, 1841, II, H. D. No. 37); Michigan, Legislature, *Report of the Select Committee Relative to the real value of the assets of the Michigan state bank* (*Senate Documents*, 1842, S. D. No. 17).

46. In addition to his abstract interest in central banking, it appears that Mason held an unspecified amount of stock in the Michigan state bank, and was receiving fees for negotiating the exchange of the bank's notes from outstate banks, and banks outside the state. To support this conclusion, see an undated receipt signed by Hiram Norton to Mason and Pritchette paying $48 for negotiating the receipt of Illinois Canal scrip by the Michigan state bank at par, in Stevens T. Mason Papers (BHC), and the assignment of power of attorney for sale of Mason's Michigan state bank stock to William Hale, Feb. 3, 1842, in the Stevens T. Mason Papers (MHC).

47. *Messages of the Governors of Michigan*, I, 253; Michigan, Legislature, *Report of the Committee on Banks, & c*, (*House Documents*, 1839, H. D. No. 29), pp. 574-578; Michigan, Legislature, *Report of the Board of Fund Commissioners* (*Senate Documents*, 1840, II, S. D. No. 11), pp. 174-178; Michigan, Legislature, *Report of a Select Committee Relative to a State Bank and Branches* (*Senate Documents*, 1840, II, No. 49), pp. 466-474; Michigan, *Legislative Acts*, 1839, Nos. 37, 59, 112.

48. Drafts of letters from William Woodbridge to "Dear Sir", Feb. 1, 1840, and Feb. 3, 1840, in Woodbridge Papers (BHC). The letters were apparently to be sent to Mason. Typed copies of the drafts can be found in the Woodbridge Papers, Jan. 1-Jan. 15,1840.

49. The Whig committees were in error when they accused Pritchette of fraud by carrying out his negotiations with the BUS through "The Bank of the United States in New York." Contrary to the Whig opinion, it was an agency of the BUS of P, although not a legal branch. Hammond, pp. 484, 600.

50. Michigan, Legislature, *Report of the Majority of the Committee on Finance* (*Senate Documents*, 1840, II, S. D. No. 58), pp. 496-525; Michigan, Legislature, *Report of the Committee on Finance* (*Senate Documents*, 1840, II, S. D. No. 67), pp. 571-586; Michigan, Legislature, *Report of the Minority of the Committee on Finance* (*Senate Documents*, 1840, II, S. D. No. 59), pp. 525-536.

51. Michigan, Legislature, *Report of the Majority of the Committee on the Five Million Loan* (*House Documents*, 1840, II, H. D. No. 50), pp. 531-550.

52. Michigan, *Legislative Acts*, 1840, No. 93.

53. A series of unpublished letters from Stuart to Woodbridge adds depth and authenticity to the story of the state's negotiations with the Morris Bank and Canal Company. See: Robert Stuart to William Woodbridge, May 28, September 30, and

November 30, 1840, and Robert Stuart to John C. Calhoun, July 31, 1841, in the Woodbridge Papers (BHC).

54. Michigan, Legislature, *Special Message Concerning the Five Million Loan (Senate Documents*, 1841, I, No. 8), pp. 266-312; Michigan, *Legislative Acts*, 1841, Joint Resolution No. 23.

55. *Messages of the Governors of Michigan*, I, 421; Michigan, Legislature, *Communication from the State Treasurer (House Documents*, 1841, II, H. D. No. 75) pp. 272-273; Michigan, Legislature, *Special Message in Relation to the Protested Drafts Against the April Installment of the 5,000,000 Loan (Senate Documents*, 1841, II, S. D. No. 41), pp. 159-161.

56. Michigan, *Legislative Acts*, 1838, No. 14; Michigan, *Legislative Acts*, 1839, No. 95; Michigan, *Legislative Acts*, 1840, No. 24.

57. Michigan, *Legislative Acts*, 1840, No. 61; Michigan, *Legislative Acts*, 1841, No. 65; Harry N. Scheiber, "George Bancroft and the Bank of Michigan," *Michigan History*, XLIV (1960), pp. 82-89.

58. U. S., *Statutes at Large*, V, c. 65; Hibbard, 174, 187; *Messages of the Governors of Michigan*, I, 438, 448; Michigan, *Legislative Acts*, 1842, No. 6.

59. Michigan, *Legislative Acts*, 1842, No. 20.

60. *Ibid.*

61. *Messages of the Governors of Michigan*, I, 446.

62. Jenks, *Michigan History*, XV (1931), 600-601; McGrane, p. 155.

63. Michigan, *Senate Journal*, 1842, pp. 64, 74, 99.

64. Michigan, *House Journal*, 1842, pp. 73-74, 123, 146, 162-163, 260, 265.

65. *Ibid.*, p. 266.

66. Michigan, *Legislative Acts*, 1842, No. 60.

67. *By His Excellency John S. Barry, Governor In and Over the State of Michigan: A Proclamation*, April 7, 1842, in Records of the Office of Secretary of State, Great Seal and Archives: Executive Acts, 1842-1843; Michigan, *Legislative Acts*, 1842, No. 38.

68. Jenks, *Michigan History*, XV (1931), 602-603.

69. Hidy, p. 277; Walter B. Smith, *Economic Aspects of the Second Bank of the United States* (Cambridge: Harvard University Press, 1953), p. 218.

70. Michigan, Legislature, *Report of the Committee of Ways and Means (House Documents*, 1847, H.D. No. 1), pp. 1ff.

71. Ibid.; Michigan, Legislature, *Report of Joint Committee on the Subject of Certain State Bonds (Joint Documents*, 1845, J. D. No. 15). A search of the Library of Congress, the National Archives, and the Historical Society of Pennsylvania has proven fruitless. The liquidation of the assets of the BUS of P is still one of the untold stories of American history, and apparently no one has done research that would give any guidance in a search for these papers. How reports relating to the liquidation of America's greatest nineteenth century financial institution could disappear without a trace is a source of bewilderment.

72. *Messages of the Governors of Michigan*, I, 473.

73. G. L. Prentice, *The Union Theological Seminary in the City of New York:...with a Sketch of the Life and Public Services of Charles Butler, L. L. D.* (Asbury Park, N. J.: M. W. & C. Pennypacker, 1899), pp. 435-452. Butler seemed to accomplish the most through prayer.

74. Michigan, Legislature, *Report of the Joint Committee (Joint Documents*, 1843, J. D. No. 11), pp. 426-435.

75. *Ibid.*, pp. 415-439.

76. Michigan, *Senate Journal*, pp. 253, 262, 353.

77. Michigan, Legislature, *Report From the Committee of Ways and Means (House Documents*, 1843, H.D. No. 15), pp. 71 ff.

78. Prentice, pp. 447-448.

79. Michigan, Legislature, *Report from the Committee on Ways and Means (House Documents*, 1843, H. D. No. 15), p. 74; Jenks, *Michigan History*, XV (1931), 611.

80. Michigan, *Legislative Acts,* 1843, No. 73.
81. Jenks, *Michigan History,* XV (1931), 613-616; McGrane, 162-163.
82. Letter from John J. Adam to John S. Barry, May 31, 1843, in Records of the Office of Secretary of State, Great Seal and Archives: Five Million Dollar Loan, 1835-1853 (Michigan: Department of State, Historical Commission Archives).
83. Michigan, *Legislative Acts,* 1843, No. 1.
84. *Messages of the Governors of Michigan,* I, 494.
85. *Ibid.,* 517.
86. The difference between the Bank's figures and the state's can be accounted for by the interest paid prior to 1842 against unpaid installments, which the state refused to acknowledge. Michigan, Legislature, *D. V. Bell, Auditor General, to the President of the Senate, March 10, 1846 (Senate Documents,* 1846, S. D. No. 18).
87. Michigan, *Joint Document No. 15,* 1845.
88. *Ibid.,* pp. 1-9.
89. *Ibid.*
90. Jenks, *Michigan History,* XV (1931), 617-618.
91. Michigan, *House Document No. 1,* 1847.
92. Michigan, Legislature, *Annual Report of the Auditor General, Dec. 1, 1845 (Joint Documents,* 1846, J. D. No. 2), pp. 1-7; Michigan, *House Document No. 1,* 1846.
93. The best detailed account of transactions after 1846 is Jenks, *Michigan History,* XV (1931), 625-633. A peculiar feature of Jenks' analysis is that in his bitter condemnation of the state's policy, which was based on a failure to understand that a government has higher obligations than the maintenance of commercial morality, he failed to see the victory scored by the state in forcing two of the major houses holding hypothecated securities to compel the trustees of the BUS of P to settle for the disputed bonds by action in the courts. Nor does he have a harsh word for other holders who failed to resort to the same measures, and he failed to realize that the European financial houses or the trustees still refused to surrender the bonds for cancellation of the unpaid balance after the court decision. Whichever party ended up in final control, they were speculating with the bonds, in hopes of forcing the state to pay the entire balance.

10

THE MICHIGAN EXPERIENCE

The study of a single program of public works in a single state cannot offer sweeping reinterpretations of the history of either transportation or internal improvements. Michigan's experience may be atypical, but without studies of other states and other periods, there is little basis for comparison. Nonetheless, elements of the program and its effects shed light on problems of current interest in the study of internal improvements and American economic development.

Carter Goodrich, the distinguished historian of American internal improvements, has suggested in *Government Promotion of American Canals and Railroads* that doctrinal strictures against government participation in economic activity excluded the sectors of transportation and communication during the 1830s and 1840s. If a project could be accomplished by private means, it was usually assumed that it would be left to that sector; however, government was expected to undertake construction of any necessary project too expensive for private means. Hostility toward government enterprise usually resulted from the fear that government would be corrupted by engaging in business: "On this point, Jacksonian opposition was based on a desire to keep business out of government—if the modern phrase can be applied—rather than a desire to keep government out of business."[1] Statements by Michigan's governors and legislators as late as 1840, as well as those found in newspapers, support Goodrich's interpretation, and between 1840 and 1846, expressions of this attitude were still common. After 1840, however, the idea that the laissez-faire doctrine should be applied to the state's railroads became increasingly common; legislative documents after 1843 frequently stated that government could not run a railroad as efficiently as private enterprise. James Joy, Detroit agent for the Eastern interests, played on this theme for over two years while attempting to convince the Legislature to sell the Central. The decision to sell was based not only on the need for financial stability, but also on the desire to rebuild the roads with T rails and to incorporate the efficiencies of private management into their rate structure. As Goodrich himself suggested in an earlier article, the belief that government management of railroads was less efficient than private enterprise was frequently expressed in the 1840s, particularly by the *American Railroad Journal.*[2] If he had explored this theme more thoroughly in his later work on government promotion, his interpretation would be more precise.

219

The structure of Michigan's finances and the failure of the Michigan State Bank help explain the relationship of state expenditures to the business cycle. H. Jerome Cranmer's recent study of annual investment in canals suggests that expenditures on internal improvements reached a peak in 1840, declined substantially in 1841, and fell off precipitously in 1842. Harvey Segal, commenting on Cranmer's study, has suggested that investment peaked in 1841, and fell off more drastically in 1842 than Cranmer's data suggests. Data presented in Table VIII (facing) seems to suggest that Michigan's experience more nearly fits the curve plotted by Cranmer than that suggested by Segal.[3] Through 1840, the Legislature appropriated substantially more than the Board of Internal Improvements spent, and the timing of expenditures depended heavily on the pace of construction and the availability of funds. When appropriations were exhausted, the Board acted autonomously, forcing the Legislature to honor its commitments. Consequently, appropriations are an inaccurate guide to actual expenditures, and data for 1840 and 1841 have to be adjusted to account for construction financed by floating estimates and paid for out of funds appropriated the following year.

Because of construction on the Detroit and St. Joseph in anticipation of state purchase, Michigan's initial investments were substantially greater than those of states delayed by the necessity of surveys and technical preparations. Investment reached a peak in 1839 as other projects were added to those already under construction. Although the Michigan State Bank failure in 1839 forced the abandonment of three projects in their initial phases, construction on the remaining works continued as long as the state was able to issue anticipations against installments of its bond issues. Expenditures dropped slightly in 1840, but remained above those of 1838. By certifying estimates in excess of appropriations in 1840, and submitting them for payment the following year, the Board was able to continue construction despite the Legislature's ban on new contracts and its failure to authorize needed funds. In 1841, however, actual construction dropped dramatically when the Board was forced to meet previously certified estimates from new appropriations, and anticipations reached their legal limits. After the Bank of the United States failed to meet its installment in October 1841, construction expenditures declined until the autumn of 1843, when funds from the federal land grant began to be realized. In 1844 and 1845, the state experienced the "echo effect," as federal funds were used to complete the more profitable projects. When adjusted to reflect actual construction, Michigan's railroad investment more closely approximates the curve plotted by Cranmer for canal construction in the second internal improvements cycle than that projected by Segal, and to this extent tends to support Cranmer's conclusions.

Although exact estimates are difficult to derive, data presented by the Legislature suggest that federal, local, and private resources played a more important role in the state's program of transportation improvement than earlier treatments have indicated. Local aid and assistance from private

TABLE VIII
Appropriations and Expenditures,
1837-1845[a] (Thousands of Dollars)

	1837	1838	1839	1840	1841	1842	1843	1844	1845
Appropriations	765	1,378	340	37.5	675	15	171[b]	96[b]	35[b]
Reported Total Expenditures	420	508	580	467	418	184	158	264	137
Adjusted Total[c]				523	362				

[a]Summarizes Tables II, V, VI, VII.
[b]Acres of land.
[c]Adjustment includes $56,000 expended in 1840 in excess of appropriations on the Southern and financed by use of floating estimates and warrants not reported in official totals until 1841.

individuals defies quantification because it was usually given in the form of free right-of-way, grants of property and station sites, water privileges, reduced construction bids, and free labor to complete projects, often at critical junctures. For example, very little of the Central's right-of-way west of Wayne County had to be purchased, and residents along the Tecumseh Branch donated their labor to complete the road when state funds were exhausted. Voluntary local aid reduced the cost of construction on both the Central and Southern Railroads. Data for private investment in works of joint state and private enterprise are similarly unavailable because of the state's loose enforcement of charter provisions requiring annual reports. Residents along the route of the Palmyra and Jacksonburg provided at least sixty-three thousand dollars in paid-in capital subscriptions, and although no report of private investment was ever submitted, residents of Pontiac bonded themselves for over two hundred thousand dollars to secure the state's loan to the Detroit and Pontiac.[4] Private investment in the Ypsilanti and Tecumseh was never reported, but the state deposited sixty thousand dollars in the account of the Allegan and Marshall, which was to be provided with funds strictly on a matching basis.[5]

In addition to private and local assistance, data published by the Legislature reveal a surprising level of federal contribution to the state's financial resources.[6] Between 1836 and 1845, the state spent $4,024,633 of its own resources on its internal improvements program. During the territorial period and the first ten years of statehood, federal disbursements for road construction and river improvement, in addition to direct grants to the state's treasury, totaled $1,628,415. Excluding the $337,108 used to construct the Territorial Roads, federal funds constituted twenty-five percent of the resources committed to transportation improvement in Michigan between 1836 and 1845. Although a small part of these funds was diverted to support the expenses of state government, and the balance was lost in the failure of the Michigan State Bank, their misuse and loss does not diminish the size of federal contributions.[7]

In spite of the fact that most of the state's bonds were hypothecated abroad to secure the debts of the Bank of the United States, most of the funds provided by the state government were generated within the domestic economy. Approximately sixty percent of the resources mobilized by the state originated from the sale of its bonds, and a further twenty-five percent was created from the state's own resources. The balance was provided by milking other state accounts, such as the primary school and university funds, and from miscellaneous assets. Approximately half of the resources realized through bond sales was provided through the fully paid bonds sold prior to November 15, 1838, nearly all of which were purchased in the United States. Forty percent of the bonds designated as fully paid, or $570,000, were held by the Farmer's Loan & Trust Company of New York. An additional twenty-four percent, amounting to $334,000, were purchased by New York banks chartered under that state's free banking law and deposited with the Comptroller of Currency as security for their note issues.

Most of the balance of the fully paid bonds, about thirty percent with a par value of $433,000, was purchased by New York banks, private individuals, and estates. The remaining half of the funds realized through bond sales was received from the Bank of the United States and the Morris Bank from their assets, while the securities were hypothecated abroad to guarantee advances made by foreign creditors to the Bank to liquidate obligations created by its cotton speculations.[8]

In addition to resources provided through bond issues, $1,289,000, a sum equal to that realized from its fully paid securities, was raised through the use of short and intermediate term credit. After the Michigan State Bank failure, construction was financed by a variety of interest-bearing paper issues, including anticipations, scrip, and Auditor General's warrants. Iron was similarly purchased by pledging the receipts of the state's railroads. When the Bank of the United States failed, the state was accountable for anticipations issued in excess of installments received, and subsequent Legislatures resorted to issuing Auditor General's warrants to continue construction. Receipts from the Central and Southern Railroads allowed the state to redeem $504,000 of its obligations, and a further $276,000 was redeemed by other funds. The balance, $508,000, remained outstanding at the end of 1845. Since the warrants could be legally redeemed for internal improvements land at par value, it seems fair to infer that financiers who had purchased the state's interest-bearing paper from local contractors preferred it to land and held it willingly.[9] From the structure of state finances during the internal improvements program it seems proper to conclude that most of the capital invested in Michigan's transportation program, perhaps as much as ninety percent, was generated within the United States. In this respect, Michigan's experience proved more nearly typical of the pattern described by Nathan Miller in New York during the opening phases of the first canal cycle (1816-1822), than that of states drawing heavily on foreign capital during the second cycle (1834-1840). It should be apparent, however, that this condition was neither desired by the state nor to its advantage; had foreign funds been available, Michigan's experience might have been more favorable.

The program undertaken by the state in 1837 and acts of subsequent years encompassed a broad range of projects, including three railroads, three major canals, loans to four private railroads, improvement of half a dozen rivers, and two salt works. Until 1839, when the state deposit bank failed, construction continued on a broad front. When the state was unable to meet the monthly estimates of its contractors, however, work stopped permanently on all projects except the Central and Southern Railroads, the Clinton and Kalamazoo Canal, the St. Joseph River, and the salt works. After 1840, further investment was guided by the need to create revenue. With the exception of the St. Joseph River, efforts were concentrated on extending profitable projects, and minimizing losses by putting partially completed works into condition to produce a return. After appropriations were exhausted on the Clinton and Kalamazoo Canal, work was suspended until 1844, when contracts were awarded which allowed it to be completed from Frederick to Rochester in August 1845. In the next eighteen months of operation, the canal produced gross revenues of about ninety dollars; having proven its inadequacy, it was abandoned.

Original plans for the Southern Railroad called for its completion to Hillsdale before being opened to traffic because competition from the Erie and Kalamazoo at Adrian would make operation unprofitable. In its frantic quest for revenues, however, the Whig Board of Internal Improvements rushed to complete the road to Adrian and, under instructions from the Legislature, purchased the River Raisin and Lake Erie to provide the Southern with an eastern terminus. By hurrying construction and using half the necessary number of spikes, the Board was able to open the railroad from Lake Erie to Adrian late in the summer of 1841, and to complete most of the road bed to Hillsdale by the end of the year. Completion of the entire road to Hillsdale was delayed until October 1843 because of the state's inability to purchase iron. After 1843, construction was confined to rebuilding sections built during the rush to completion and opening the Tecumseh Branch.

Although the Southern was hastily completed to create revenues which would minimize losses on its cost of construction, receipts on the road remained disappointing, a result that should have been expected. Original decisions on route location had been based on the desire to make the road developmental, and major concentrations of population and industry between Monroe and Hillsdale had been deliberately avoided. Competition from the Erie and Kalamazoo, failure to provide an adequate eastern terminus with shipping facilities, and inadequate rolling stock and motive power added to the road's inability to produce. Although the Southern produced net revenues, most of them were consumed in constructing new cars and financing new construction. In any case, net revenues were never sufficient to cover interest on its cost of construction, and the road failed to meet the test of profits.

From the beginning, the Central Railroad was the state's most successful project. After the 1834 federal survey, its construction was popularly accepted as a certainty, and settlers poured into its potential route. In anticipation of a state program, construction was begun in 1836 by a private corporation, which willingly sold the road to the state in 1837. The road was opened between Detroit and Ypsilanti in February, 1838, and during the first year of operation the Central earned substantial revenues. Because of its earning capacity, the Board of Internal Improvements and the Legislature favored concentrating the state's resources on the Central in the hope it would earn enough profits to pay the interest on the state's debt. Construction continued steadily through 1844, when most of the road was completed as far as Kalamazoo, one hundred and forty-seven miles west of Detroit. Difficulties in raising money to purchase iron, however, delayed its completion to that village until early 1846. After crossing the peninsular divide in 1842, the Central consistently earned high profits. Even with allowances for depreciation, net income was sufficient to pay interest on the cost of construction in two of the last three years of state ownership. Success in the last five years of state control was not a temporary condition; profits continued high through the next decade and the balance of the century, when the Michigan Central became one of the most successful railroads in the United States.

The Central's success under state management helped create the factors that led to its sale. With every available resource harnessed to extend the railroad's grading and superstructure, the state lacked funds to purchase necessary cars and locomotives. From the time it reached Jackson in 1842, the road's facilities were strained to meet the demand for heavy hauling. Trains were operated at night during seasons of peak demand, although the practice was regarded as dangerous; during the daylight hours, overloaded locomotives were run at twice the recommended safe speed. Under the strain of continuous operation and the jarring impact of high speed on strap iron rails, locomotives and cars were shaken to pieces, and the cost of operation mounted dramatically. Rails were broken and timbers crushed under the heavy loads bouncing over their surface. Assuming that marginal costs would decline with the road's extension, the Board of Internal Improvements enthusiastically endorsed extending the Central between 1842 and 1844, raising hopes that the rate of profits might increase to fifteen percent, enough to pay interest on the state's entire debt. After three years of turning away business and watching increasing costs, caused by operating at the limit of the road's inadequate carrying capacity, eat into profits, the Board concluded that rebuilding the Central to incorporate the latest technological advances was the only way to bring the road to its full potential.

In recommending the transition from strap iron to heavy rails, the Board recognized the state's inability to provide the necessary resources for reconstruction, and asked that the road be sold to waiting private interests to guarantee prompt action. Although liquidation of the state's debts was also a major consideration in Michigan's decision to sell the Central, the need for providing the road with heavy rails played an important role. The committee preparing the bill authorizing its sale concentrated on this necessity, rather than finances, and the charter contained strict provisions requiring the Central's immediate reconstruction. To this extent, providing efficient, low-cost transportation to the interior was as important a motive in the state's decision to sell in 1846 as it had been in 1837.

Of the six major projects undertaken by the state, only the Central Railroad met the classical criterion for allocation of resources: the ability to return profits greater than the cost of investment. Three other public works were abandoned before completion, the fourth, after being placed in operation, failed to show even a net income. The fifth of the state's public works, the Southern, is difficult to evaluate because competition, poor route location, and inadequate terminal facilities combined to undermine any profits which might have accrued to a road through the southern tier. The Central's profits, however, were sufficient to cast doubt on the assumption that Michigan's railroads were constructed ahead of demand.

In a recent study, *American Railroads and the Transformation of the Ante-Bellum Economy,* Albert Fishlow has challenged the traditional Schumpeterian model in which state or private capital played an heroic role by constructing railroads through the virgin wilderness, bringing settlement and profits in their wake. Fishlow argues that railroads in America were rarely built ahead of demand in the Schumpeterian sense because of the commercial nature of American agriculture. He contends that projects in the East, by breaching the Appalachian barrier and continuing west, created an anticipation of transportation improvement that induced settlement along potential routes well before construction, and reversed the sequential role of entrepreneurs described in traditional interpretations. At the same time, however, Fishlow assumes that his pattern was more prevalent in the 1850s than the 1830s, and, conversely, that construction ahead of demand was more common in the earlier period. In examining the rates of return of the Michigan Central and Michigan Southern between 1852 and 1855, when profits ranged from 4.6 to 9.6 percent, Fishlow concludes that these roads were not operating ahead of demand at this date, but that they had been in the late 1830s and early 1840s, and that this is indicated by the substantial degree of state involvement.[10] Listing Michigan among the states constructing railroads before the existence of sufficient demand, he also cites the inefficiency of simultaneous construction of a series of projects, poor cyclical timing, and lack of technical know-how as reasons for failure.[11]

Fishlow's inversion of the traditional roles of settlement and investment in the 1850s is acceptable, but his assumption that the Central and Southern railroads were constructed ahead of demand is based on inadequate data and the preconception that government participation is an automatic indication of underdeveloped markets. The acid test of demand, of course, rests on the measurable relationship of profits to the interest rate, and this test was met by the Central Railroad under state management. The Southern did not meet this criterion, but even Fishlow concedes that an abstractly profitable road can be undermined by such external factors as cyclical downturn, bad management, and wasteful competition. To estimate the abstract profitability of railroads affected by external factors and constructed through areas of intermediate population density (between eighteen and forty-five inhabitants per square mile), Fishlow offers a rule of thumb: "If some railroads in an area of given population density earn satisfactory returns it is evidence that such a region can support railroads even if the recorded profits of other enterprises indicate otherwise."[12] The Central, which ran through a tier immediately north of the Southern, had similar densities and earned satisfactory profits. And the Erie and Kalamazoo, which was in direct competition with the Southern, not only showed a profit, but completed construction and purchased iron with its revenues. The existence of such successful competition is certainly evidence of a demand for railroads in the southern tier, and supports the argument that construction by the public sector is not an automatic indication of premature investment.

Although state enterprise may be necessary for promotion of railroads ahead of demand, state construction is not necessarily evidence of an absence of demand, even when the original justifications for a program were developmental expectations. Michigan's decision to undertake state enterprise involved political and social values—political economics, in the archaic sense—as well as pure economic rationality, and these values continued to be important considerations, even to the moment of sale. Moreover, the state never expected to operate its works at a loss, a consideration that construction ahead of demand in a frontier environment would suggest, even though developmental expectations were expressed. It was expected that the Central would be profitable from the beginning, and the possibility of loss was never seriously considered. Developmental impact was even more important in locating the Southern, but it too was expected to earn profits when extended into the St. Joseph Valley. As Fishlow has pointed out, high expectations accompanied most railroad projects, and the production of profits, combined with adequate population, is the only real test of demand. Between 1837 and 1845, construction in Michigan was concentrated in those areas with populations of from eighteen to forty-five per square mile, which Fishlow admits may well indicate a highly successful agriculture. It seems obvious that, given resources and the state of technology, a wide range exists between a level of development sufficient for profitable demand and optimal economic development. Within this range, a political body may act on expectations of economic development without contemplating short-term loss or being ahead of demand; Michigan was doing that on its two southern projects. The analytical distinction between exploitative and developmental transportation projects obscures the fact that both motives may operate simultaneously. In Michigan's case, a federal survey and the widespread assumption that a road or roads would be built through the central and southern tiers brought in settlement before the actual decision to build and converted a developmental situation into a partially exploitative one. In this intermediate range, the lack of entrepreneurial skills and organization, as well as the absorption of local capital in numerous other local opportunities, precluded local action. At the same time, uncertainty and the postponement of returns acted as a barrier to investment of outside private capital. The narrowness of the range in which purely developmental criteria can operate is illustrated by the ability of residents of Toledo, Adrian, and Pontiac to construct successful local railroads with their own resources. Given these conditions, accompanied by the hostility to corporate enterprise, control by foreign capital, and granting of natural monopolies that characterized Jacksonian democracy, a call for state enterprise can be expected. And logically, therefore, it is clear that public enterprise and the expression of developmental expectations cannot be cited as *prima facie* evidence of construction ahead of demand.

Although Michigan's experience may not have been universal, it points to the need for further evidence before assuming that railroad and canal construction undertaken by states west of the Appalachian barrier was necessarily premature because the private sector failed to respond to demand. Michigan's Democrats were firmly convinced that state control of main trunk lines was necessary as protection against exploitation, and it is clear that political and social values operative in the 1830s obstructed the responsiveness of private capital in a way not true of the 1850s. The basic assumption behind Fishlow's evaluation of railroad construction in the 1830s and 1840s is tautological, and requires substantiation. Lumping public-enterprise projects together and assuming that public participation necessarily indicates prematurity is an invalid analytical procedure.

In addition to evaluating the success or failure of projects by the classical profit criterion, modern studies of transportation projects have attempted to assess their developmental impact and measure the external economies that add value to total community output without being returned to the project in the form of receipts. Attempts to quantify the value added to community output by reduced transportation costs, however, have generally been unable to surmount the obstacles posed by the developmental effects of reduced shipping costs. Harvey Segal's study of the economic impact of American canals, which attempts to harness benefit cost analysis, concludes that the benefits accruing to the community through reduced shipping rates were sufficient to cover the costs of the entire system, including interest on total canal investment. Based on the assumption of zero price elasticity of demand for canal transportation, Segal's results are acceptable only because his conclusions are so cautious and the margins between actual costs and maximum returns are so great that relaxed assumptions would not essentially damage his hypothesis. Faced with the problem of relaxing his assumptions and approaching reality by assessing the effect of an elastic demand curve, however, Segal understandably abandons the problem and concludes that actual savings cannot be accurately estimated because the elasticity of demand along the curve is unknown.[13] Application of this procedure to Michigan would result in similar limitations, in addition to problems imposed by special local conditions. Detroit wheat prices could be derived by deducting average transportation costs from Detroit to the East Coast from New York prices and assuming that interior value was zero as consumption reached local limits. Similar problems are posed by merchandise shipments, which are reported only by gross weight without any indication of the value of the product mix. Even the unknown quantity of wheat and flour exports could be overcome by applying appropriate assumptions for local consumption to gross output data because although only a small portion of total output was shipped by rail, the railroads drove wagon rates to competitive levels, and wheat not consumed locally could be assumed to have been shipped at those rates. The net result of this labor, however, would only set an upper limit for returns that might have accrued had the railroads been completely exploitative, which in Michigan's case does not even remotely approach reality. If used only to prove that the Central really returned benefits equal to its cost, a fact already known, the effort would be to no effect. In the case of the Southern, it would be impossible to disaggregate the effects of competition by the Erie and Kalamazoo, which charged unknown rates and carried an unknown quantity of goods and passengers.

Two recent studies by Robert Fogel and Albert Fishlow have attempted to measure the railroads' impact on American economic growth.[14] Although disagreeing on methodology and conclusions, both writers explore the direct benefits of reduced transportation costs and external economies created by railroads and canals. Both studies contain interesting implications for evaluating the effect of transportation development on the total U. S. economy and for the structure of economic planning, but very little of their methodology is applicable to the development of a single state functioning as a small segment of a region or sector. Backward linkages did develop, but the effects were felt largely by areas outside the state. Locomotives were usually purchased from Baldwin in Philadelphia, while strap iron and spike were purchased from the Corning works or foreign suppliers. No local demand for coal developed because the engines burned wood supplied by local farmers and cutters in the process of clearing their farms. Some impetus was given to the growth of wheel casting and car building facilities in Detroit, which the Michigan Central later developed into a major industry, but the state-wide effects of direct input demand during public ownership appear minimal. A majority of the construction and maintenance funds were earned by local labor, and either invested in farm improvement or consumed immediately. In either case, multiplier effects were probably small because the imbalance of trade between Michigan and the East, draining banks' specie resources and eventually destroying the currency, persisted throughout the period. Had the problem not been serious and persistent, Governor Mason's attempts to support local currency would have been meaningless.

Forward linkages, or the development of industries using transportation outputs as components of production, appear to have been minimal except for agriculture. Allowed to remain undisturbed, Michigan might have developed industries using transportation as an input traceable to facilities constructed at public expense during the two or three decades following the state program. Within three decades, however, railroad investment had risen so dramatically that initial public efforts dwindled to a small portion of the total; attempting to disaggregate the effects of early public and subsequent private investment would be absurd. In any case, Michigan remained basically a primary-products producer throughout the nineteenth century, relying on agricultural products and their processing, lumbering, and mining for the majority of the state's income until the development of the automobile drastically altered its economic structure.

Although the effects of the state's internal improvement program were probably negligible in other industries, the Central and Southern seem to have exerted important influences on Michigan's agriculture. Although unable to agree on analytical procedures, the importance of technical alternatives, and the impact of railroads on the American economy, both Fishlow and Fogel agree on the importance of low-cost transportation to American agricultural development, regardless of the form which hauling facilities assumed.[15] Because of Michigan's proximity to major lake shipping routes, Fogel's assumption that forty miles is a practical limit for hauling agricultural commodities to a point for shipment by water is useful for evaluating the impact of the Central and Southern Railroads on the state's agricultural development.[16] Appendices VIII through X are constructed on the assumption that without some kind of transportation improvement other than roads, feasible commercial agriculture would have been limited to counties bordering on one of the Great Lakes and their connecting waters, approximately thirty miles in most cases. The counties listed are outside this area of feasible commercial agriculture, and represent seventy percent of the land area in Michigan's southern four tiers of counties, and a major part of the land suitable for agriculture.[17] Although a portion of the land within forty miles of lake transportation is included within these counties, the distortion is not severe enough to call for a more detailed breakdown. If the assumed maximum hauling distance is applied in the same manner to railroads, and the state's two railroads are assumed to run reasonably close to the line of county centers within the grid system on which Michigan was surveyed, then the effects of the Central Railroad or the railroad's competition with wagon rates must be extended equally to both the first and third tiers of counties because the distance to the Central Railroad, from the northern border of the third tier and the southern border of the first is approximately forty-five miles. At the same time, the effects of the railroad can be assumed to diminish over distance, with the strongest influence being felt in the center. The fourth tier, outside the area of feasible agriculture created by the railroads, can be seen to act as a control factor. The results of these tables do not represent a quantification of indirect benefits, but do indicate a general tendency.

Wheat production in the interior counties of the four southern tiers appears to have responded in predictable patterns to the improvement of transportation. Output in the central tier grew from 500,000 bushels in 1837 to over 2,200,000 bushels in 1854. The first and third tiers exhibit a remarkable symmetry of response, growing to approximately 1,500,000 bushels in 1854. Heavy output in the eastern counties of the first and third tiers can be explained by their proximity to lake ports and the existence of railroads external to the state's system. Output in the fourth tier, outside the area of feasible commercial agriculture created by the Central, exhibited a typically low response, producing only half the wheat output of the first and third tiers, even though possessing about two-thirds the number of farms in these tiers. Taken from east to west, output in the fourth tier shows a predictable pattern of declining toward the center of the state and then increasing again as the western coast is approached. In other tiers, output declined from east to west, an effect which might be traced to increased freight costs over distance.[18]

Flour production and capital investment in milling produced similar patterns of response. Output of flour in the central tier grew from $303,000 in 1837 to $1,410,000 by 1854, while the output in the southern tier grew from $173,000 to only $517,000, and in the third tier from $124,000 to $601,000. While the central tier exhibited a fairly even distribution of investment and output, counties directly to the north and south tended to decline from east to west, and the fourth tier again demonstrated investment inversely proportional to the distance from the lakes. An interesting feature of the growing milling industry is the relative decline in the ratio of capital investment to gross output over time. Although the southern counties had the largest investment in milling facilities at the beginning of the period, capital expansion grew at a relatively slow pace as increasing production absorbed excess capacity. In the central counties, the expansion of investment more nearly followed increases in output, although it too experienced the savings of a declining ratio of capital to output. By allowing the conversion of units constructed for local milling to full time use, and the introduction of new units at higher levels of demand for milling, important capital savings should have resulted.[19]

The effect of improved transportation was also reflected in patterns of land use and values at the end of the internal improvements era in Michigan. In spite of relative differences in total population, the number of farms in the southern three tiers was remarkably uniform with a range of only 150 units between the highest and lowest. The northern tier lagged considerably, with approximately seventy percent of the number of farms contained in southern counties. Within the tiers, however, the higher level of development in counties having railroads was reflected in land values and utilization. Farms within the central tier uniformly exhibited a higher ratio of improved to unimproved land, exceeding all save the most eastern counties in other tiers. New land in the central counties appears to have been brought into production at a much higher rate than in any other portion of the state. This ratio is reflected by the higher average number of improved acres per farm in the central counties. Moreover, land within the tier appears to have been developed at a much more uniform rate than land within other sections. The value of this development is clearly evident in the average value of farms in 1850. Farms in the central counties were reported as having an average value ranging from $200 to $500 above counties in other sections of the state, reflecting the level of land improvement and proximity to commercial shipping facilities. Had the railroads not been built, it is reasonable to assume that a pattern similar to that exhibited by the fourth tier would have developed.[20]

The pattern of land use and values in the southern four tiers of Michigan in 1850 and 1854 reflects the structure of grain farming in the Old Northwest before the widespread introduction of the reaper and thresher. Heavy percentages of improved land were devoted to wheat production only on those farms with extremely high and low ratios of land improvement, reflecting the tendency of farms in initial stages to plant an immediate crop both for cash and home consumption, followed by diversification until improved transportation made it profitable to open even more land for the purpose of devoting more acreage to commercial agriculture. Investment in tools and machinery was so low and remarkably uniform among the tiers that no significant pattern could be discerned, and the data were not included in the appendices. Specialization in wheat production was regional, and not reflected to a high degree within the units themselves. As long as wheat was harvested largely by farm families and occasional itinerant farm labor, unit specialization which would be reflected in large acreages devoted to a single crop with heavy investment in agricultural machinery was retarded. Although improved transportation appears to have stimulated regional concentration, unit specialization required still greater market expansions than those provided by domestic railroads and widespread adoption of innovations in agricultural technology, conditions which could only be developed in areas outside the state's control. The substantial growth of wheat production in counties outside the area of feasible commercial agriculture, however, appears to give ample evidence to support the conclusion that Michigan's program of internal improvements made significant contributions to the state's agricultural development.

Within the political and philosophic context in which Michigan operated in the late 1830s and early 1840s, few alternatives were presented other than the course of action undertaken. Direct investment in productive facilities other than transportation projects was forbidden by the basic economic philosophy of the American people, which, except in the case of natural monopolies, allowed government intervention in business only when it encompassed problems too complex to be solved by individuals or private groups. Planning had not yet been invented, in the modern sense, and even the feeble attempts within the Legislature to allow the Board of Internal Improvements to assign priorities to investment met with failure in the face of local ambitions. Other than construction of a multiple program of public works, bringing transportation improvements to the doorstep of all of its residents, few alternatives were open to the state.

Even in the primitive state of railroad technology in 1837, canals represented a high-cost alternative bringing minimal rewards. Cost estimates for construction of the Clinton and Kalamazoo were over twice that of either the Central or the Southern, and errors in railroad estimates resulted from faulty assumptions involving the cost of earthmoving. Since earthmoving was a greater part of the cost of canals than railroads, it is reasonable to assume that the expense of canals would have been much greater. For the original cost estimate of the Clinton and Kalamazoo, Michigan could have constructed a trans-peninsular railroad with heavy rails and adequate rolling stock, and the canal would not have solved its special problem; winter and ice would have closed the canal at precisely the time when roads became solid enough to allow the shipment of its major agricultural product. Wheat harvested in the summer and milled in the fall would have had to await the solidification of roads the following summer before being shipped to market. The canal system suggested by Robert Fogel illustrates the limits of absurdity which can be reached by a high level of abstraction and minimal familiarity with the environment being discussed. To bring the area beyond feasible commercial agriculture into production, Fogel proposes a canal system adjacent to the Grand, Maple, Chippewa, Thornapple, and Kalamazoo Rivers, which he estimates would have cost $7,000,000 or nearly twice the expenditure by Michigan during the internal improvements era, including suspended or abandoned projects and the money lost in bank failures. Although Fogel's system could have been built, it would have placed the state's most productive agricultural counties on the fringe of feasible commercial agriculture, and forced the state to ship into Lake Michigan and through the Straits of Mackinac to reach Detroit and points east. As we have seen, the state improved and opened the Grand and Maple Rivers, without substantially stimulating output in the fourth tier. A small sum of additional investment in Fogel's system could have made it into a trans-peninsular trunk line, instead of a local work draining into a lake closed by storms and ice in the Straits of Mackinac six months of the year.[21] Investment in one or more trans-peninsular railroads clearly represents a more productive investment than any system of canals.

The most productive way in which the state could have invested its funds would have been the construction of a single, well-stocked railroad from Detroit to St. Joseph or Chicago, with feeder lines running to selected points in the first and third tiers. Such a system could have been economically constructed, profitably operated, and gradually extended, while the state would have been able to exist well within its means. Such a program would have clearly guaranteed profitable operation, and stimulated a high level of agricultural growth. This fact was understood from the beginning by responsible members of the state government, even by the legislators opposing the construction of a single road. Local ambition, combined with desire to share equally in the results of economic growth, however, took priority over the rational allocation of investment.

A study of this scope, confined to a single state in a single decade, cannot hope to offer conclusions affecting the allocation of investment in currently underdeveloped countries. It suggests, however, that within some environments, various levels of economic growth and regional equality may be viewed as mutually exclusive. The growth effects of social overhead capital, which stem from its lumpiness and economies of scale, can easily be dissipated when the scale is reduced and investment spread to achieve regional equality. Finally, it points to the need for national planning, and the reduction of local influences in decision making. After building and selling the Democracy's railroads, Michigan turned to private enterprise to solve its transportation problems, but in other cultures, the choice may not be as simple.

Notes, Chapter 10

1. Goodrich, *Government Promotion,* p. 42.

2. Carter Goodrich, "Revulsion against Internal Improvement," *Journal of Economic History,* X (1950), 161.
3. Cranmer, *Trends in the American Economy in the Nineteenth Century,* pp. 555-558.
4. Michigan, *Senate Document No. 27,* 1838, p. 38; Michigan, *Senate Document No. 4,* 1839, pp. 86-87.
5. Michigan, *Senate Document No. 4,* 1843, p. 31.
6. See Appendices V, VII.
7. See Appendix VI.
8. See Appendix VII.
9. See Appendix VI.
10. Fishlow, pp. 165-166.
11. *Ibid.,* pp. 196-199, 178, 183, 190.
12. *Ibid.,* p. 170.
13. Segal, *Canals and American Economic Development,* p. 243.
14. Robert William Fogel, *Railroads and American Economic Growth;* Albert Fishlow, *American Railroads and the Transformation of the Ante-Bellum Economy.*
15. Fogel, p. 237; Fishlow, p. 303.
16. Fogel, pp. 77-78.
17. Fogel's map, p. 81, gives a distorted picture of the area of feasible agriculture in Michigan. Much of the area within forty miles of the coastline has no value for agricultural purposes, particularly in the northern half of the lower peninsula, and nearly all of the upper peninsula. With the exception of a narrow belt favorable to fruit growing on the western coast, and a small area extending north to Midland, much of the land north of the fifth tier is suitable to forestry, and little else. Even though Fogel's map is only a visual aid, it gives a false impression, and does not seem to have been carefully constructed. Michigan's upper peninsula, about a third of its total land area, is represented as part of Wisconsin.
18. See Appendix VIII.
19. See Appendix IX.
20. See Appendix X.
21. Fogel, pp. 81-97.

BIBLIOGRAPHIC ESSAY

This study was drawn from a wide variety of sources, including printed and manuscript public records, private papers of public officials, travel accounts, and secondary works. A discussion of the most useful sources follows.

I. Printed Public Records

Printed public documents form the most abundant and accessible source of evidence relating to the internal improvements program. All such documents, however, must be used with care and treated as points of view, rather than absolute statements of fact. During the Territorial Period, the *Journal of the Legislative Council of the Territory of Michigan* (1824-1836) records the proceedings of the Territory's legislative body, although failing to record actual debates. Acts of the Territorial Council have been compiled in *Laws of the Territory of Michigan* (Lansing, 1894) from the original records by the State. Unfortunately, after the passage of half a century, many of the original acts were missing, and although a supplemental volume was published (Vol. IV), the acts are incomplete, chronologically scrambled, and not numbered. Similarly, the last two volumes of the *Journals,* encompassing the Council's chartering of railroad-banks, were deliberately removed from the original records and destroyed by an unknown person. Records of correspondence between the national government and the territory are printed in the *Territorial Papers of the United States,* compiled and edited by Clarence Edwin Carter for the Department of State (Washington, D. C.: Government Printing Office, 1942), volumes X-XII. These records are supplemented by the *Territorial Papers of the United States Senate, 1789-1873,* roll six of *File Microcopies of Records in the National Archives: No. 200* (Washington, D.C.: National Archives and Records Service, General Services Administration, 1951).

The *Michigan Constitution of 1835,* as well as records of the transition from a territorial to a state government, can be most conveniently used in *The Michigan Constitutional Conventions of 1835-1836: Debates and Proceedings,* edited by Harold M. Dorr, "University of Michigan Publications: History and Political Science," Vol. XIII (Ann Arbor: University of Michigan Press, 1940). The debates, committee reports, and proceedings of the conventions were never officially printed, and Dorr's collection is a composite from newspapers, journals, reports, and supporting papers. The debates are fragmentary.

Executive messages are conveniently located in *Messages of the Governors of Michigan,* edited by George N. Fuller, 4 vols. (Lansing: Michigan Historical Commission, 1925). Although the Fuller edition covers the messages of the Governors from 1824, it is in places fragmentary, and often omits important material. Governors frequently attached lengthy documents to their messages, or sent material to the Legislature, and for these, legislative documents must be consulted. The Annual Message of the Governor is usually *Joint Document No. 1.* Annual reports of other Executive Departments were published in the *Joint Documents of the Legislature of the State of Michigan.* Such reports are usually lengthy and informative.

Although the Journals of the House and Senate do not record actual debates, they are useful for determining the composition of forces working to establish various programs. Occasionally, documents were printed in the journals rather than in the published legislative documents collections, for reasons best known to the clerks of the respective houses. The most useful publications, however, are the *House Documents* and *Senate Documents.* Officially published as *Documents accompanying the Journal of the Senate of the State of Michigan at the Annual Session in . . .* or of the House; the documents printed are miscellaneous in nature. Consisting of committee reports, statements of policy, annual reports of corporations, petitions, and in short, anything the Legislature decided to print, these volumes must be searched thoroughly to be of any use.

The most useful of the documents is the *Annual Report of the Board of Internal Improvements,* printed as a House or Senate Document until 1840, when two members of the executive office were appointed to the Board. After that, it was printed among the *Joint Documents.* Reports of the Board encompass every aspect of the internal improvements program, including pricing policies, building techniques, engineering reports, and occasionally, political policy recommendations. Because the Board was forced to explain its actions and techniques to seventy legislators every year, most of whom were recently elected, its reports constitute an important source of material relating to early railroad techniques. Nowhere, to my knowledge, does there exist such a fertile source of basic information. Unfortunately, the *Minutes and Proceedings of the Board of Internal Improvements* could not be located for use in this study. That such a body of information did exist is certain because there are excerpts in the documents of the Legislature. I was unable to uncover them in any of the state archives, however, and there is always the possibility they were destroyed in the Cass Building fire. If they are extant, however, their use should add depth to the story of Michigan's internal improvement era.

Two other sources deserve special mention. Michigan, Department of State, *Manual Containing the Rules of the Senate & House of Representatives of the State of Michigan with the Joint Rules of the Two Houses and*

Other Matters, usually referred to as *Michigan Manual,* is useful because of the "other matters" published, including constitutions, legislative districts, and census data. Finally, the *Report of the Special Committee Appointed by the House of Representatives, to Investigate the Proceedings, & c., of the Several Boards of Internal Improvement* (Detroit: Dawson and Bates, 1840) should be mentioned because it contains a complete account of every penny expended by the Boards of Internal Improvements through April 1840, and because by a fluke, it was printed when the Legislature was not in session and received no document number. Consequently, one must know it exists to use it.

II. Manuscript Public Records

Unpublished government documents are stored in the Michigan Department of State, Historical Commission Archives (Lansing, Michigan). Collections pertaining to the period are sparse, but extant papers fill many gaps. Because the collection is currently being reboxed, citations by box number would have been worthless. Correspondence of the Governors is contained in "Records of the Executive Office, 1810-1910: Correspondence." Documents supporting the standard account of the negotiation of the five million loan consist of one box entitled "Records of the Office of Secretary of State, Great Seal and Archives Section: Five Million Dollar Loan, 1835-1853." Documents relevant to Mason's negotiations with John Delafield consist of one folder in "Records of the Office of Secretary of State, Great Seal and Archives Section: Claims Submitted to the Legislature, 1837-1839."

III. Manuscript Collections

Private papers of public officials examined for this study can be found in two major depositories: the Burton Historical Collections (BHC) of the Detroit Public Library, and the Michigan Historical Collections (MHC), Ann Arbor.

Burton Historical Collections

The most important and useful body of documents in the Burton Collection is the William Woodbridge Papers, a massive collection consisting of some twenty-five boxes for the period between 1835 and 1846. The Stevens T. Mason Papers (one box of letters) consist mainly of letters from Mason to his family. The John R. Norton Papers (five boxes) are really the papers of the Michigan State Bank, of which Norton was cashier. For some reason, almost every paper relating to the bank's transactions with the state has been removed, but the collection would be useful in the study of commercial transactions. Letters in the Alpheus Felch Papers pertaining to the period 1837-1846 are confined to a single box, with few documents of value. Finally, the James Joy Papers, along with the Papers of Joy & Porter, are of little value for the period between 1842 and 1846.

Michigan Historical Collections

Manuscripts in the Michigan Historical Collections, Ann Arbor, are of little value in the study of Michigan's internal improvements. The Alpheus Felch Papers are the most important collection, consisting of two large boxes donated by the Felch family. The Stevens T. Mason Papers give extensive coverage to the Toledo War, but have little else of value. The Jacob A. Barker Papers contain photostats of five important letters relating to the Erie and Kalamazoo Railroad. Originals are currently in the hands of the Ohio Historical Society Library, Columbus, Ohio. Finally, the Papers of the Erie and Kalamazoo Railroad, 1834-1952, are deposited in the Michigan Historical Collections, and consist of about ten feet of papers. The collection is badly disorganized, and all that could be discovered relating to the period from 1834-1847 was confined to three folders that contained few papers of value.   A word of caution should be given in regard to one manuscript deposited in the Michigan Historical Collections: M. C. McConkey, James Joy Biography (5 manuscript volumes, undated and unpublished). The study is grossly inaccurate, and it must be used with such caution that it would be better to do the research without bothering to consult McConkey.

Published Manuscript Collections
     The "Letters of Lucius Lyon," *Michigan Pioneer and Historical Collections*, XXVII (1896), pp. 412-605, are the single scholarly contribution of the Pioneer and Historical Society in the publication of nearly forty volumes of geriatric reminiscences. Lyon's papers are extremely useful in the study of economic conditions, speculation, and politics.

IV. Secondary Sources
     Michigan's history is peculiarly distinguished by a lack of scholarly historical studies. In the century and a half since the Territory was established,   not a single scholarly work covering the entire history of the region has been produced. For the period from 1825 to 1860, studies are even less abundant.

     F. Clever Bald, *Michigan in Four Centuries* (New York: Harper & Brothers, 1954), is the best of the general studies, and the most disciplined. R. Carlyle Buley's prizewinning *The Old Northwest Pioneer Period* (Bloomington: Indiana University Press, 1951), is the best known study of the Old Northwest, but has the unfortunate quality of being based primarily on the *Pioneer and Historical Collections,* which are unreliable at best. Buley suffers also from a lack of discrimination in accepting sources. Willis Dunbar, *Michigan: A History of the Wolverine State* (Grand Rapids, Michigan: Eerdmans, 1965), is currently the most popular general history. James Henry Lanman, *History of Michigan,* (New York: 1839) is the oldest of the general histories, and useful as a primary source for the period of this study. Finally, the work of Henry M. Utley and Byron M. Cutcheon, *Michigan as a Province, Territory and State, the Twenty-sixth Member of the Federal*

Union, 4 vols. (New York: Americana Press, 1906), is perceptive, and useful because of its study of national laws affecting Michigan.

Special studies dealing with Michigan in the period from 1820-1860 are scarce. Floyd B. Streeter, *Political Parties in Michigan, 1837-1860* (Lansing: Michigan Historical Commission, 1918), is useful for determining the membership in parties and factions, but its causal analysis is faulty and based largely on intuitive evidence. A fine old study by Hannah Emily Keith, "An Historical Sketch of Internal Improvements in Michigan, 1836 to 1846" *Publications of the Michigan Political Science Association*, IV (July 1900–July 1902), pp. 1-48, is useful, if somewhat dated. William L. Jenks, "Michigan's Five Million Dollar Loan," *Michigan History*, XV (1931), pp. 575-634, is a fine piece of scholarship, although unfortunately undocumented. Chapter VIII of Reginald McGrane's *Foreign Bondholders and American State Debts* (New York: Macmillan, 1935), is useful for the period, also.

Several volumes of travel accounts are useful. Mrs. C. M. Kirkland, *Forest Life in Michigan*, 2 vols. (New York: C. S. Francis & Co., 1842), or any other of Mrs. Kirkland's many books is useful as a background for settlement in Michigan. Thomas Cather, *Voyage to America, The Journals of Thomas Cather*, edited by Thomas Yoseloff (New York: T. Yoseloff, 1961), gives an interesting picture of conditions in outstate Michigan in 1836. Similarly, the letters of Alexis de Toqueville, in *Toqueville and Beaumont in America*, edited by George Wilson Pierson (New York: Oxford University Press, 1938), give an interesting account of life and travel in Michigan in 1831. The best of these accounts, and one of the classics in frontier travel literature, is John M. Gordon, "Michigan Journal, 1836," edited by Douglas H. Gordon and George S. May, *Michigan History*, XLIII (1959).

Biographies of prominent Michiganians are even less abundant than scholarly studies. Michigan Historical Commission, *Michigan Biographies* (Lansing: Michigan Historical Commission, 1924), is useful for some purposes, although essentially a rehash of an antiquarian study done in the 1880s. Lawton T. Hemans, *Life and Times of Stevens Thomson Mason, the Boy Governor of Michigan* (Lansing: Michigan Historical Commission, 1924), is the most thorough study of Mason's career, but unfortunately blinded by prejudice in favor of the young governor. Although a miserable popular biography filled with inaccuracies, Kent Sagendorph's *Stevens Thomson Mason: Misunderstood Patriot* (New York: Dutton & Co., 1947), is by far the most perceptive study of Mason. Sagendorph's portrait of Mason as a machine politician is remarkably close to the truth.

Studies bearing on the national experience and state internal improvement programs are legion. George Taylor's *The Transportation Revolution, 1815-1860*, Vol. IV: *The Economic History of the United States* (New York: Rinehart & Company, 1957), has served as a standard reference, supplemented by Frank Walker Stevens', *The Beginnings of the New York Central Railroad: A History* (New York: G. P. Putnam's Sons, 1926). Carter Goodrich's classic study of *Government Promotion of American Canals and*

Railroads, 1800-1900 (New York: Columbia University Press, 1960), has supplied much of the analytical framework for this study, along with questions posed by Robert A. Lively in "The American System: A Review Article," *Business History Review,* XXIX (March, 1955), pp. 81-95. A second study, *Canals and American Economic Development,* edited by Carter Goodrich (New York: Columbia University Press, 1961), has raised interesting questions which I have attempted to answer. A recent, brilliant study by Albert Fishlow, *American Railroads and the Transformation of the Ante-bellum Economy,* Vol. CXXVII, *Harvard Economic Studies* (Cambridge: Harvard University Press, 1965), has added depth to the analytical vehicle and raised questions to be answered. Similarly Robert William Fogel's *Railroads and American Economic Growth: Essays in Econometric History* (Baltimore: Johns Hopkins Press, 1964), has raised questions that deserved answering. The political framework for analysis was provided by Richard P. McCormick, *The Second American Party System: Party Formation in the Jacksonian Era* (Chapel Hill: University of North Carolina Press, 1961). Finally, Bray Hammond, *Banks and Politics in America from the Revolution to the Civil War* (Princeton N.J.: Princeton University Press, 1957), has served as a standard reference on banking practices.

APPENDIX I
Land Sales and Population[a]

Year	Public Land Sales (acres)	Population
1818	37,865	
1819	24,910	
1820	6,523	8,896
1821	7,444	
1822	17,359	
1823	34,017	
1824	78,246	
1825	106,752	
1826	59,361	
1827	42,410	
1828	26,895	
1829	67,860	
1830	147,061	31,639
1831	320,476	
1832	252,211	
1833	447,780	
1834	498,423	87,273
1835	1,817,247	
1836	4,189,823	
1837	773,522	175,000
1838	97,533	
1839	134,984	
1840	26,106	212,267
1841	18,167	
1845		302,552
1850		511,720
1854		758,292

[a]U. S., Congress, Senate, *Report of the Secretary of the Treasury,* 27th Congress, 3d Session, 1843, pp. 5-10; *Historical Statistics of the United States,* p. 13; *Abstract of the Whole Number of Persons Residing in that Part of the Territory of Michigan...as Ascertained in Conformity with the Provisions of an act of the Legislative Council of said Territory,* Entitled *"An Act to Provide for taking a census, and for other purposes."* Approved September 6, 1843 (S. M'Knight, 1834). Cited hereafter as Michigan, *Census of 1834.* Michigan, *Legislative Manual,* 1838, pp. 70-75; Michigan, *Legislative Manual,* 1861, pp. 195-240.

APPENDIX II
Population by Tier and County[a]

Tier & County[b]	1834	1837	1840	1845	1850
First or Southern					
Monroe	8,542	10,646	9,922	12,287	14,698
Lenawee	7,911	14,540	17,889	22,923	26,372
Hillsdale	–	4,729	7,240	11,111	16,159
Branch	764	4,016	5,715	9,064	12,472
St. Joseph	3,168	6,337	7,068	10,097	12,725
Cass	3,280	5,296	5,710	8,078	10,907
Berrien	1,787	4,863	5,011	7,865	11,417
	25,452	50,427	58,555	81,425	104,750
Second or Central					
Wayne	16,638	23,400	24,173	31,737	42,756
Washtenaw	14,920	21,817	23,571	26,979	28,567
Jackson	1,865	8,702	13,130	16,825	19,431
Calhoun	1,714	7,960	10,599	15,594	19,162
Kalamazoo	3,124	6,367	7,380	10,163	13,179
Van Buren	–	1,262	1,910	3,743	5,800
	38,261	69,508	80,763	105,041	128,895
Third					
Macomb	6,055	8,892	9,716	13,491	15,530
Oakland	13,844	20,176	23,646	30,241	31,270
Livingston	–	5,029	7,430	10,787	13,485
Ingham	–	822	2,498	5,267	8,631
Eaton	–	913	2,379	4,613	7,058
Barry	–	512	1,078	2,602	5,072
Allegan	–	1,469	1,783	2,941	5,125
	19,899	37,813	48,530	69,492	86,171
Fourth					
St. Clair	2,244	3,673	4,606	6,621	10,420
Lapeer	–	2,602	4,265	5,314	7,029
Genesee	–	2,754	4,268	9,266	12,031
Shiawassee	–	1,184	2,103	7,419	5,230
Clinton	–	529	1,614	3,010	5,102
Ionia	–	1,028	1,923	5,101	5,597
Kent	–	2,022	2,587	6,153	12,016
Ottawa	–	628	208	1,200	4,835
	2,244	14,420	21,574	44,084	62,260

[a]Michigan, Legislative Council, *Census of 1834*; Michigan, *Legislative Manual*, 1838, pp. 71-75; U.S. Census Office, *Sixth Census of the United States*: 1840; Michigan, *Legislative Manual*, 1861, pp. 195-240.

[b]Counties listed from east to west by tier.

APPENDIX III
Population Density by Tier and County[a]

Tier & County	1834	1837	1840	1845	1850	Area in Sq.Mi.[b]
First						
Monroe	15.2	18.9	17.7	21.9	26.6	562
Lenawee	10.5	19.3	23.7	30.4	35.0	754
Hillsdale	–	7.9	12.0	18.5	26.9	601
Branch	1.5	7.9	11.3	17.9	24.6	506
St. Joseph	6.2	12.5	13.9	19.9	25.0	508
Cass	6.7	10.9	11.7	16.6	22.4	488
Berrien	3.1	8.4	8.6	13.6	19.7	580
Second						
Wayne	37.4	38.6	39.8	52.3	70.4	607
Washtenaw	20.8	30.5	32.9	37.7	39.9	716
Jackson	2.6	12.3	18.6	23.9	27.6	705
Calhoun	2.4	11.2	14.9	22.0	27.0	709
Kalamazoo	5.5	11.2	13.0	17.9	23.2	567
Van Buren	–	2.1	3.1	6.2	9.6	607
Third						
Macomb	12.6	18.5	20.2	28.0	32.3	481
Oakland	15.8	24.0	27.0	34.5	35.7	877
Livingston	–	8.8	13.0	18.9	23.6	571
Ingham	–	1.5	4.5	9.4	15.4	559
Eaton	–	1.6	4.2	8.1	12.4	567
Barry	–	0.9	2.0	4.7	9.2	549
Allegan	–	1.8	2.2	3.5	6.2	829
Fourth						
St. Clair	3.0	5.0	6.2	8.9	14.1	740
Lapeer	–	3.9	6.5	8.1	10.7	657
Genesee	–	4.3	6.6	14.4	18.7	643
Shiawassee	–	2.2	3.9	13.7	9.7	540
Clinton	–	0.9	2.8	5.3	8.9	571
Ionia	–	1.8	3.3	8.9	9.7	575
Kent	–	2.3	3.0	7.1	13.9	862
Ottawa	–	1.1	0.4	2.1	8.6	564

[a]Derived from data in Appendix II.
[b]Economic data sheets compiled by the Michigan Economic Development Department, October 1961.

APPENDIX IV
Railroad Charters Granted by the Territory and
State of Michigan, 1830 to 1837[a]

Date	Company	Route	Authorized Capital	Started
1830	Detroit & Pontiac (renewed, 1834; bank, 1835)	Detroit to Pontiac	100,000	X
1832	Detroit & St. Joseph (renewed, 1834; bank, 1835)	Detroit to St. Joseph	1,500,000	X
1833	Romeo & Mt. Clemens	Romeo to Mt. Clemens, within Macomb County	150,000	
1833	Erie & Kalamazoo (bank, 1835)	Toledo through Adrian to the Kalamazoo River	1,000,000	X
1834	Shelby & Detroit	Detroit to Shelby, Macomb County	100,000	X
1835	River Raisin & Grand River (bank & railroad)	Monroe through Tecumseh, Clinton & Marshall to Grand Rapids	1,500,000 for road 100,000 for bank	
1835	Macomb & Saginaw (bank & railroad)	Mt. Clemens to Lapeer to the Saginaw County seat	1,000,000 for road 100,000 for bank	
1835	Detroit & Maumee	Detroit to Monroe to Maumee Bay	500,000	

[a]Michigan, *Territorial Laws,* III, pp. 844ff, 960ff, 1125ff, 1287ff, 1300ff, 1387ff; *Ibid.,* IV, pp. 112ff, 134ff, 142ff, 148ff, 153ff, 155, 156; Michigan, *Legislative Acts,* 1836, pp. 267ff, 277ff, 287ff, 297ff, 307ff, 318ff, 328ff, 338ff, 348ff, 358ff, 369ff; Michigan, *Legislative Acts,* 1837, pp. 217ff, 227ff, 269ff, [Adjourned Session] 16ff.

APPENDIX IV (continued)

Date	Company	Route	Authorized Capital	Started
1835	Maumee Branch (amended charter)	Maumee River to the Erie and Kalamazoo, then west to the mouth of the Galain River at Lake Michigan (New Buffalo)	1,500,000	X
1835	Shelby & Belle River	From the northern terminus of the Shelby & Detroit through Romeo to Belle River	100,000	
1836	Monroe & Ypsilanti	From the River Raisin & Lake Erie at Monroe to the Detroit & St. Joseph at Ypsilanti	400,000	
1836	Allegan & Marshall	Allegan to Bronson, Battle Creek, Verona, & Marshall	400,000	?

APPENDIX IV (continued)

Date	Company	Route	Authorized Capital	Started
1836	Clinton & Adrian	Clinton to Adrian	50,000	
1836	St. Clair & Romeo	Palmer to Romeo	100,000	
1836	Palmyra & Jacksonburg	Palmyra to Clinton to Jackson	300,000	X
1836	Kalamazoo & Lake Michigan	Kalamazoo to the mouth of the Black River	400,000	
1836	Havre Branch	From Havre in Monroe to either the Maumee Branch or the Erie and Kalamazoo	100,000	
1836	Monroe & Ann Arbor	Ann Arbor to the River Raisin & Lake Erie	300,000	

APPENDIX IV (continued)

Date	Company	Route	Authorized Capital	Started
1836	River Raisin & Lake Erie	Lake Erie at or near La Plaisance Bay, through Monroe & Dundee to the Erie & Kalamazoo at Blissfield	300,000	X
1836	Constantine & Niles (railroad and canal)	Railroad or canal from Constantine to Niles	250,000	
1837	Gibralter & Clinton	Gibralter, Wayne County, to Clinton in Lenawee County	400,000	
1837	Detroit & Shiawassee	Detroit to Farmington, Kensington, Byron, to Shiawassee, to Biddle City	500,000	
1837	Saginaw & Genesee	Saginaw River to the Northern Railroad		
1837	Port Sheldon & Grand Rapids	Port Sheldon to Grand Rapids	250,000	X

APPENDIX V
Federal Resources Expended in Michigan for Internal Improvements[a]

Territorial roads	$ 337,108
La Plaisance Harbor	19,603
River Raisin	20,000
U.S. Surplus Deposit, 1837	286,751
Five percent fund	174,224
River Raisin, 1836	15,000
River Raisin, 1837	30,000
River Raisin, 1838	15,000
River Raisin, 1844	20,000
St. Joseph River, 1836	20,000
St. Joseph River, 1837	15,000
St. Joseph River, 1838	21,000
St. Joseph River, 1844	20,000
Five hundred thousand acres of land at $1.25 per acre	625,000
U.S. land revenue distribution of 1841	9,729
Total	$1,628,415

[a]Michigan, Legislature, *Report of the Committee on Federal Relations* (*House Documents,* 1847, H. D. No. 16). Data presented in the committee report is a minimum assessment of federal aid because the committee was attempting to prove that Michigan had not received its fair share of federal funds.

APPENDIX VI

State Expenditures on Internal Improvements by Source[a]

Five million loan	$2,560,630
Five percent fund	174,224
Outstanding internal improvements warrants	508,468
Internal improvements lands sold	258,012
Outstanding land warrants	25,991
Due on Palmyra and Jacksonburg bonds	26,300
Proceeds of Central and Southern railroads, from 1838 through 1845 inclusive	504,951
U.S. Distribution of 1841	9,729
Received from State Bank assets	47,293
Overdrafts from other funds	276,991
Total	$4,392,589
Minus Resources supplied by the federal government	467,956
Total	$3,924,633
Plus Detroit and Pontiac Bonds	100,000
Total state resources applied to internal improvements	$4,024,633

[a]Michigan, Legislature, *Report of the Committee on Ways and Means* (*House Documents,* 1846, H. D. No. 1), pp. 12, 13.

APPENDIX VII
Disposition of State Internal Improvement Bonds[a]

New York Banks, deposited with the Comptroller of Currency	$ 334,000
U.S. Bank, hypothecated with:	
Hope & Co.	1,220,000
Rothschilds & Co.	798,000
Morrison & Sons	262,000
Denison & Co.	1,533,000
Farmer's Loan & Trust Co., N.Y.	570,000
Banks, estates, private individuals, and full paid bonds	
purchased by the B.U.S.	483,000
Total	$5,200,000

[a]Michigan, Legislature, *Communication from the State Treasurer in Relation to the Five Million Loan and Other State Bonds* (*Joint Documents,* 1843, J. D. No. 1), pp. 54-61. Bonds are listed by number and purchaser.

APPENDIX VIII
Michigan Wheat Production by Tier and County[a]
(Thousands of Bushels)

	1837	1840	1850	1854
Lenawee	132[b]	168[b]	314[b]	446[b]
Hillsdale	43	81	220[b]	341[b]
Branch	28	67	156[b]	208[b]
St. Joseph	–	131	257[b]	365[b]
Cass	54	95	160[b]	209[b]
Tier Total	256	542	1,106	1,570
Washtenaw	165	161[b]	523[b]	760[b]
Jackson	163	177	477[b]	654[b]
Calhoun	105	193	391[b]	481[b]
Kalamazoo	104	171	228[b]	354[b]
Tier Total	536	702	1,618	2,248
Oakland	–[b]	265[b]	604[b]	779[b]
Livingston	41	85	304	360
Ingham	3	23	82	146
Eaton	4	16	51	113
Barry	–	13	20	109
Tier Total	47	402	1,060	1,507
Lapeer	15	35	85	142
Genesee	–	36	121	164
Shiawassee	3	20	62	74
Clinton	3	24	54	99
Ionia	4	32	77	171
Kent	3	19	69	170
Tier Total	28	166	468	820

[a]Lanman, *History of Michigan*, 293-294; Michigan, *House Document No. 31*, 1841, pp. 70-86; Michigan, Department of State, *Census and Statistics of the State of Michigan*, 1854, pp. 381, 391. Figures will not necessarily total, because of rounding.
[b]Indicates that the county had been reached by a railroad on or before that date.

APPENDIX IX
Flour Production and Capital Investment in Milling[a]
(Thousands of Dollars)

		1840		1850		1854	
		capital	flour	capital	flour	capital	flour
Lenawee	200		84c	237	335c	132	273c
Hillsdale	33		4	79	120c	83	5c
Branch	60		27	47	103c	15	86c
St. Joseph	31		26	143	206c	95	132c
Cass	49		32	21	26	15	21
Tier Total	373		173	527	790	340	517
C/O[b]		2.2			.7		.7
Washtenaw	53		85c	218	553c	235	540c
Jackson	83		99	146	310c	147	223c
Calhoun	135		81	–	– c	287	561c
Kalamazoo	11		39	78	175c	50	86c
Tier Total	282		303	442	1,038	719	1,410
C/O[b]		.9			.4		.5
Oakland	126		104c	211	225c	218	440c
Livingston	12		18	61	109	71	147
Ingham	–		2	27	21	21	2
Eaton	–		–	14	39	32	11
Barry	–		–	7	16	7	1
Tier Total	138		124	320	410	349	601
C/O[b]		1.1			.8		.6
Lapeer	28		58	–	51	20	69
Genesee	–		7	63	94	63	167
Shiawassee	19		3	31	37	23	30
Clinton	–		–	7	33	7	1
Ionia	–		7	–	–	29	47
Kent	40		8	34	79	27	148
Tier Total	87		83	135	294	169	462
C/O[b]		1.0			.5		.4

[a]Michigan, *House Document No. 31*, 1841, pp. 70-80; Michigan, Dept. of State, *Census and Statistics of the State of Michigan*, 1854, pp. 383, 393, 399.

[b]Ratio of capital investment to gross output. This ratio is not a true c/o ratio, which would require the use of value added, but if marginal costs do not change substantially, a safe assumption with existing technology, the crude measure will give the same directional measurement as the more refined data.

[c]Indicates the county had been reached by a railroad on or before that date.

APPENDIX X

Land Use and Values, 1850-1854[a]

Counties by tier	Number of farms, 1850	Ratio of improved to unimproved land on farms, 1850	Average improved acreage per farm, 1850	Average value of farms, 1850	Percent of improved land in wheat, 1854
Lenawee	2471	1.0	56	1660	23
Hillsdale	1411	.9	56	1460	27
Branch	1463	.7	44	1100	27
St. Joseph	1354	.9	69	1866	26
Cass	952	.7	63	1578	29
Total	7651	.9	57	1542	
Washtenaw	2546	1.1	71	1956	27
Jackson	2282	.9	65	1627	36
Calhoun	1834	.9	65	1637	32
Kalamazoo	1000	.9	73	1997	26
Total	7662	1.0	68	1757	
Oakland	3559	1.1	66	1838	32
Livingston	1653	.9	62	1384	29
Ingham	1084	.5	37	905	31
Eaton	747	.5	36	957	27
Barry	750	.4	32	829	35
Total	7793	.8	55	1430	
Lapeer	628	.9	56	1245	25
Genesee	1476	.6	37	1081	26
Shiawassee	746	.5	42	985	26
Clinton	652	.4	32	844	28
Ionia	613	.7	49	1219	28
Kent	885	.5	41	1134	23
Total	5000	.6	41	1083	
State Total	34,879	.8	55	1488	26

[a]Derived from data presented in Michigan, Department of State, *Census and Statistics of the State of Michigan*, 1854, pp. 380, 390.

INDEX